Interest Rate Risk Modeling

Founded in 1807, John Wiley & Sons is the oldest independent publishing company in the United States. With offices in North America, Europe, Australia, and Asia, Wiley is globally committed to developing and marketing print and electronic products and services for our customers' professional and personal knowledge and understanding.

The Wiley Finance series contains books written specifically for finance and investment professionals as well as sophisticated individual investors and their financial advisors. Book topics range from portfolio management to e-commerce, risk management, financial engineering, valuation and financial instrument analysis, as well as much more.

For a list of available titles, please visit our web site at www.WileyFinance.com.

Interest Rate Risk Modeling

The Fixed Income Valuation Course

SANJAY K. NAWALKHA
GLORIA M. SOTO
NATALIA A. BELIAEVA

John Wiley & Sons, Inc.

Published by John Wiley & Sons, Inc., Hoboken, New Jersey.
Published simultaneously in Canada.

For general information on our other products and services, or technical support, please contact our Customer Care Department within the United States at 800-762-2974, outside the United States at 317-572-3993 or fax 317-572-4002.

Wiley also publishes its books in a variety of electronic formats. Some content that appears in print may not be available in electronic books. For more information about Wiley products, visit our web site at www.wiley.com.

Library of Congress Cataloging-in-Publication Data:

Nawalkha, Sanjay K.
Interest rate risk modeling : the fixed income valuation course / Sanjay K. Nawalkha, Gloria M. Soto, Natalia A. Beliaeva.
p. cm.—(Wiley finance series)
Includes bibliographical references and index.
ISBN-13 978-0-471-42724-7 (cloth / cd-rom)
ISBN-10 0-471-42724-1 (cloth / cd-rom)
1. Interest rate risk—Mathematical models. 2. Bonds—Valuation—Mathematical models. 3. Fixed-income securities—Valuation—Mathematical models. I. Title: Fixed income valuation course. II. Soto, Gloria M. III. Beliaeva, Natalia A. IV. Title. V. Series.
HG6024.5.N39 2005
332.63'23—dc22 2005000048

Printed in the United States of America.

10 9 8 7 6 5 4 3 2 1

To our parents
—Natalia and Sanjay

To J. Alberto
—Gloria

Preface

This is the first book of the trilogy on a fixed-income valuation course by Wiley finance covering the following three areas of fixed-income valuation:

1. Interest rate risk modeling
2. Term structure modeling
3. Credit risk modeling

Unlike other books in fixed-income valuation, which are either too rigorous but mathematically demanding, or easy-to-read but lacking in important details, our goal is to provide readability with sufficient rigor. In the first book, we give a basic introduction to various fixed-income securities and their derivatives. The principal focus of this book is on measuring and managing interest rate risk arising from general nonparallel rate changes in the term structure of interest rates. This book covers five types of interest rate risk models in the fixed-income literature. These models can be applied in a variety of contexts by financial institutions ranging from commercial banks to fixed-income hedge funds. These institutions can design and execute strategies that range from simplest duration-based hedging to the more sophisticated immunization or speculative yield-curve programs, based on multiple risk measures with off-balance sheet positions in swaps, interest rate options, and interest rate futures.

The five interest rate risk models covered in this book are the duration and convexity models in Chapter 2, M-Absolute/M-Square models in Chapter 4, duration vector model in Chapter 5, key rate duration model in Chapter 9, and principal component duration model in Chapter 10. Applications using some of these models are given for regular bonds in Chapters 2,4,5,9, and 10; Treasury futures and Eurodollar futures in Chapter 6; bond options and callable bonds in Chapter 7; forward rate agreements, interest rate options, swaps, and swaptions in Chapter 8; mortgage securities in Chapter 10; and default-prone corporate bonds in Chapter 11.

Chapter 3 also shows how to estimate the term structure of interest rates from a cross-section of bond prices using the Nelson-Siegel exponential model and the McCulloch's cubic spline model. The interest rate options, such as caps, floors, collars, and swaptions in Chapter 8 are priced using the LIBOR market models of Jamshidian and others. The default-prone zero-coupon bonds in Chapter 11 are priced using the models of Merton and Nawalkha-Shimko et al., while default-prone coupon bonds are priced using the first passage probability models of Longstaff and Schwartz, and Collin-Dufresne and Goldstein.

All three books of the trilogy come with software in a user-friendly excel/VBA format that covers a variety of models in the three respective areas. The software is organized to correspond with the models covered in different chapters, so it can be used as a powerful supplement in the learning process. Using the software for the current book, the user could, for example, design a multiple factor hedging strategy using the three key rate durations or using the three principal component durations. The user could solve for the notional amounts corresponding to interest rate swaps of different maturities to protect against the height, slope, and curvature shifts in the yield curve using a three-element duration vector model. The user could pick from a variety of multiple factor hedging and speculative strategies, such as immunization, bond index replication, and speculative yield-curve strategies, using a variety of interest rate contingent claims, such as regular bonds, bond options, Treasury futures (on T-bills, T-notes, and T-bonds), Eurodollar futures, forward rate agreements, interest rate options (e.g., caps, floors, and collars), swaps, swaptions, and default-prone corporate bonds. Finally, based on Craig Holden's excel program, the software for Chapter 3 also demonstrates a pedagogically useful term structure "movie" using monthly zero-coupon rates as well as forward rates over the period from 1946 to 1991.

After reading chapters on given topics from these books, the reader should be able to follow the examples and be ready to apply these models without searching for missing details from other sources (as we often did while writing this book). Though many of our programs require coding in advanced scientific languages, such as C, C++, the final output is always presented in user-friendly excel/VBA spreadsheets. These spreadsheets allow the readers with basic excel skills to instantly play with these models.

This book will be useful to both fixed-income practitioners, as well as graduate and advanced undergraduate students in an introductory course in fixed-income valuation.

Since this book is a part of the trilogy, it is integrated both conceptually and in terms of the mathematical notation, with the next two books to follow. This implies low cost to the user in reading the next two books, especially for practitioners who do not have the luxury of taking fixed-income courses. The second book on term structure modeling covers various term structure models from the basic Vasicek/CIR models to the more advanced quadratic, HJM, and LIBOR market models. The third book covers both the structural and reduced-form models on credit risk as well as valuation of credit derivatives.

Various aspects of this trilogy on the fixed-income valuation course, including the book descriptions, software details, and future updates are available on the web site www.fixedincomerisk.com.

Sanjay K. Nawalkha
Gloria M. Soto
Natalia A. Beliaeva

Acknowledgments

We would like to thank the many individuals who helped with this book project, some in small ways, others in substantial ways, including Christopher Schwarz, Aixin Ma, Hossein Kazemi, Bing Liang, Nelson Lacey, Sanjiv Das, Huston McCulloch, Hyuna Park, Saira Latif, and Ying Li. A special thanks goes to Bill Falloon, the senior editor at John Wiley & Sons, who was supportive, understanding, and patiently gave us extensions on this ever-expanding project.

SANJAY K. NAWALKHA
GLORIA M. SOTO
NATALIA A. BELIAEVA

I would also like to express my gratitude to my wife, Shalini, and my son, Ankrish, who have very patiently loved me through this three-year intense affair with my laptop; the Art of Living teachers who showed me how to beat the stress with the magic of healing breath; and my deeply loving parents for their support.

SANJAY K. NAWALKHA

I would like to express my gratitude to Sanjay Nawalkha. His good judgment and his ability to bring out the best in everyone involved have undoubtedly been the driving force behind this book series. I would also like to thank Philip Thomas for being a real English (he says Welsh) gentleman and for being there when I needed his particular skills. And finally, I would also like to express my profound gratitude to my parents, Justa and Pablo, to my brother, Pablo and, in particular, to my husband, J. Alberto, for the support and love they have always provided.

Gloria M. Soto

I would like to express my gratitude to my family: my husband, Sergei, my daughter, Sasha, and my parents, Nina and Alexander, for their love and continuous support.

Natalia A. Beliaeva

Contributors

Donald R. Chambers, PhD, serves as the Walter E. Hanson KPMG Chair in Finance at Lafayette College in Easton, Pennsylvania. Dr. Chambers has published over 30 articles and frequently serves as a consultant to the alternative investments industry. Dr. Chambers received his PhD in Finance from the University of North Carolina at Chapel Hill.

Cosette Chichirau is the Director of Enterprise Risk Management with MassMutual Financial Group, Springfield, Massachusetts. She is currently a part-time PhD candidate in finance at the University of Massachusetts, Amherst. She also holds an MBA from the University of Massachusetts, Amherst.

Timothy Crack is a finance professor at Otago University in New Zealand. He is the author of two popular books—*Heard on the Street* and *Basic Black-Scholes*. After graduating from MIT, he first worked as an Assistant Professor at Indiana University. He then headed a research team at Barclays Global Investors in London. He has also worked as an independent consultant to the NYSE.

Iuliana Ismailescu is a PhD candidate in finance at the University of Massachusetts, Amherst. She also holds an MBA from Pace University, New York.

Nelson Lacey, CFA, PhD, is an Associate Professor of Finance at the Isenberg School of Management at the University of Massachusetts, Amherst. Dr. Lacey serves currently as Chairman of the Department of Finance and Operations Management and as the Director of Curriculum and Examinations for the Chartered Alternative Investment Analyst Association.

Contents

List of Figures

List of Tables

Interest Rate Risk Modeling

CHAPTER 1

Interest Rate Risk Modeling

An Overview

Financial institutions and other market participants manage many types of risks, including interest rate risk, credit risk, foreign exchange risk, liquidity risk, market risk, and operational risk. This book, the first volume of a trilogy on fixed-income modeling, gives a detailed introduction to various modeling techniques used by practitioners for measuring and managing interest rate risk. The importance of managing interest rate risk cannot be overstated. The total notional amount of outstanding over-the-counter (OTC) single-currency interest rate derivatives was about $165 trillion as of June 2004, of which 85 percent represented swaps and forward contracts (see Table 1.1). This amount is 62 percent higher than what it was just 18 months before in December 2002. The explosive growth of OTC interest rate derivatives over the past quarter century suggests that managing interest rate risk remains a chief concern for many financial institutions and other market participants, even as U.S. interest rates have declined steadily since reaching their peak in 1980 to 1981. With near record low interest rates prevailing in January 2005, a potential change in the interest rate regime is likely and could lead to huge wealth transfers among various counterparties in the OTC interest rate derivatives market. This could be painful if these participants have not used swaps wisely to hedge against the mismatches in the asset-liability cash flow structures.

The use of swaps or any other derivatives to hedge any type of risk can be thought of as similar to the consumption of medicine. In the right dosage, swaps or derivatives are effective but can be quite harmful in an overdose or if used for a purpose not intended. The perceived abuse of derivatives by Warren Buffett and others does not imply that derivatives should be shunned, but that these should be used wisely in the right dosage and at the appropriate time (Buffett, 2002).

TABLE 1.1 Notional Amounts Outstanding of OTC Single-Currency Interest Rate Derivatives by Instrument Maturity and Contract Type (in billions of U.S. dollars)—All Counterparties (net)

	December						June
	1998	1999	2000	2001	2002	2003	2004
Forwards and Swaps							
Maturity of one year or less	16,069	21,787	21,683	25,115	33,213	41,084	49,397
Maturity over 1 year and up to 5 years	17172	18761	21217	25233	33898	49866	56,042
Maturity over 5 years	8,773	10,164	12,291	16,286	20,801	31,028	35,275
Total	42,017	50,711	55,191	66,634	87,912	121,978	140,714
Options							
Maturity of one year or less	2,116	3,087	2,424	2,770	3,725	5,390	7,760
Maturity over 1 year and up to 5 years	4,233	4,418	4,706	5,333	6,239	9,048	10,052
Total	7,997	9,380	9,476	10,933	13,746	20,012	23,912
All Contracts							
Maturity of one year or less	18,185	24,874	24,107	27,886	36,938	46,474	57,157
Maturity over 1 year and up to 5 years	21,405	23,179	25,923	30,566	40,137	58,914	66,093
Maturity over 5 years	10,420	12,038	14,638	19,115	24,583	36,603	41,376
Total of all contracts	50,015	60,091	64,668	77,568	101,658	141,991	164,626

Source: From the web site of Bank for International Settlements, http://www.bis.org/statistics/derstats.htm.

A typical example of a market participant interested in managing interest rate risk is a commercial bank whose assets mostly consist of fixed and floating rate loans (some with embedded options), while its liabilities consist of deposits in checking, savings, money market accounts, and some debt securities. Naturally, for most large banks, the average maturity of the assets is longer than the average maturity of the liabilities, as banks typically lend in the intermediate to long maturity sector and borrow in the short maturity sector. Average maturity, more popularly known as the *duration* of a security, is the most commonly used risk measure for measuring the interest rate risk exposure of the security. Duration has been shown to explain perhaps 70 percent of the returns of default-free securities; however, since bank assets are also exposed to credit risk, bank asset duration explains a lower percentage of the asset returns. Generally, other risk measures, such as default-prone bond duration, slope duration, and others, are needed to explain the asset returns not explained by traditional duration.

Due to a positive gap between the asset duration and the liability duration, bank equity duration is generally positive. Since banks are highly leveraged financial institutions, the bank equity duration tends to be a lot higher than its asset duration. The high-equity duration resulting from an asset-liability duration mismatch has been of major concern not only for the shareholders of the banking firms, but also for the regulating institutions assigned with the responsibility of avoiding major banking crises. An illustrative example of a crisis unleashed by the asset-liability duration mismatch is the savings and loans (S&Ls) bank crisis that unfolded in the late 1970s and 1980s in the United States. The factors causing that crisis are many, including an artificial ceiling on the interest rates that the S&Ls could pay to their depositors, causing an exodus of the bank customers to other more lucrative investments; a sharp increase in interest rates triggered by the high inflation of the early 1980s; controversial responses by the Federal Reserve Bank, which increased the cost of capital for S&Ls (when they offered new products to circumvent the interest rate ceiling); and a reluctance by regulatory authorities to take timely steps to keep this crisis from snowballing. These factors ultimately resulted in a huge mismatch between the cost of funds and the earnings generated from the assets. Many S&Ls made negative net income margins, leading to a general deterioration of capital solvency ratios, and even resulting in negative book values of equity in some instances.

The ultimate bailout efforts of the government cost U.S. taxpayers around $180 billion. Yet, that loss was only 3.2 percent of the U.S. gross domestic product (GDP). Banking crises in other developing countries have caused even higher economic losses. For example, the restructuring costs of the 1980s bank crises in Argentina and Chile were 55.3 percent and 40 percent of their respective GDPs (Caprio and Klingebiel, 1996). The huge costs to many Asian economies, including the Hong Kong economy, during the Asian currency crises of 1997 to 1998 are well known. These events highlight the importance of risk management for the banking industry, especially in the developing world.

The surge in oil prices to almost $50 a barrel in year 2005, the continued rise in commodity prices, pick-up of inflation in China and other parts of Asia, and the strengthening economies of the United States and Europe have made financial institutions concerned about the effects of higher interest rates on their profitability measures and capital solvency ratios. Increases in interest rates can significantly erase the equity values of highly leveraged institutions such as commercial banks, government agencies such as Fannie Mae and Freddie Mac, fixed-income hedge funds, and other investment companies. Many financial institutions also hold some percentage of their assets in mortgage loans, which are likely to experience a lengthening of average maturity or *duration* as interest rates rise. Given that much of the world has recently witnessed record low interest rates, and many nations are still at record high valuations for real estate, significant risks exist for losses in this market. A potentially sharp increase in interest rates may also lead to additional costs tied to provisions for losses in other sectors, as the creditworthiness of corporate customers may deteriorate due to higher borrowing costs. On the positive side, to the extent that many banks now have a bigger percentage of earnings tied to non-interest income, they will be somewhat immune to the increases in the interest rates.

Near term increases in the interest rates are likely to be nonparallel, rising more at the shorter end, as the currently steep shape of the U.S. Treasury yield curve flattens out. It is well known that the traditional duration and convexity risk measures are valid only when the whole yield curve moves in a parallel fashion. If short rates increase more than the long rates, then the slope of the yield curve will experience a negative shift, while the curvature will most likely experience a positive shift (from a high negative curvature to a low negative curvature) as shown in Figure 1.1. Though this is the more likely scenario, other scenarios may lead to other types of shifts in the yield curve.

How do the managers of financial institutions, such as banks, insurance companies, and index bond funds hedge against the effects of nonparallel yield curve shifts? How do hedge funds managers design speculative strategies based upon yield curve movements? This book addresses these issues by giving a detailed introduction to the widely used models in the area of interest rate risk management over the past two decades.[1] We discuss five types of interest rate risk models in the fixed-income literature. These models are given as the duration and convexity models (Chapter 2), M-Absolute/M-Square models (Chapter 4), duration

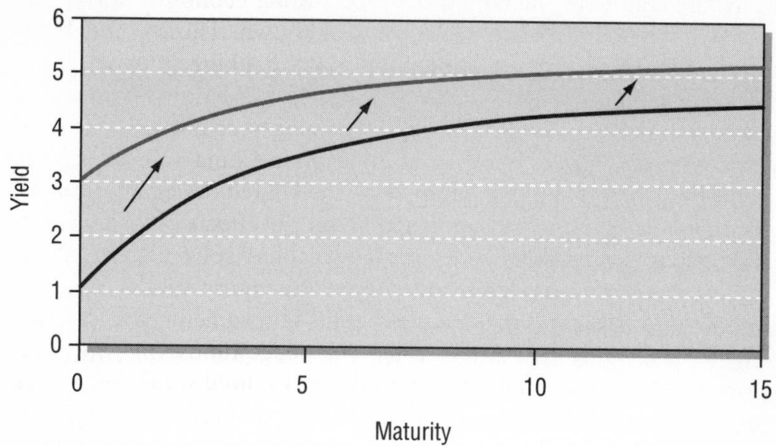

FIGURE 1.1 Nonparallel Yield-Curve Shift

vector models (Chapter 5), key rate duration models (Chapter 9), and principal component duration models (Chapter 10). We consider applications of these models to regular bonds (Chapters 2, 4, 5, 9, and 10); T-Bill futures, T-Note futures, T-Bond futures, and Eurodollar futures (Chapter 6); call and put options on bonds, and interest rate options, such as caps, floors, and collars (Chapters 7 and 8); forward rate agreements, interest rate swaps, and swaptions (Chapter 8); mortgage-backed securities (Chapter 10); and default-prone corporate bonds and stocks (Chapter 11). Virtually all chapters of the book have Excel/VBA spreadsheets that allow the reader to work with these models. In the remaining part of this chapter, we briefly summarize the five types of models covered in this book and discuss how financial institutions can use these models.

DURATION AND CONVEXITY MODELS

Consider a bond with cash flows C_t, payable at time t. The bond sells for a price P, and is priced using a term structure of continuously compounded zero-coupon yields given by $y(t)$. The traditional duration model can be used to approximate percentage change in the bond price as follows:

$$\frac{\Delta P}{P} \cong -D\Delta y \tag{1.1}$$

where

$$D = \text{Duration} = \sum_{t=t_1}^{t=t_N} t w_t$$

and

$$w_t = \left[\frac{C_t}{e^{y(t) \times t}} \right] / P$$

Duration is given as the weighted-average time to maturity of the cash flows, where the weights are defined as the present values of the cash flows divided by the bond price. The duration model given in equation 1.1 assumes that the yield curve experiences infinitesimal and parallel shifts. Hence, the change in the yield Δy, is assumed to be *equal* for all bonds regardless of their coupons and maturities. However, we know that shorter maturity rates are more volatile than the longer maturity rates, so the assumption of parallel yield curve shifts is obviously false.

Convexity is given as the weighted average of maturity-squares of a bond, where weights are the present values of the bond's cash flows, given as proportions of the bond's price. Convexity can be mathematically expressed as follows:

$$CON = \sum_{t=t_1}^{t=t_N} t^2 w_t \tag{1.2}$$

For large changes in the interest rates, the definitions of duration and convexity in equations 1.1 and 1.2, respectively, are used to derive a two-term Taylor series expansion for approximating the percentage change in the bond price as follows:

$$\frac{\Delta P}{P} \cong -D\Delta y + \frac{1}{2} CON(\Delta y)^2 \tag{1.3}$$

Equation 1.3 suggests that for bonds with identical durations, higher convexity is always preferable. This is because if CON is positive, then regardless of whether Δy is positive or negative $(\Delta y)^2$ is always positive, making a higher-convexity bond preferable to a lower-convexity bond.

However, the above result is based on the assumption of a large and parallel shift in the yield curve. Not only are large and parallel shifts in the yield curve inconsistent with arbitrage-free term structure dynamics, such shifts occur rarely in the bond markets. Even under slight violations of the assumption of parallel yield curve shifts, higher convexity may not be desirable.

M-ABSOLUTE AND M-SQUARE MODELS

An alternative view of convexity, which is based on a more realistic economic framework, relates convexity to *slope shifts* in the term structure of interest rates. This view of convexity was proposed by Fong and Vasicek (1983, 1984) and Fong and Fabozzi (1985) through the introduction of the new risk measure, M-square, which is a linear transformation of convexity. The M-square of a bond portfolio is given as the weighted average of the squares of the distance between cash flow maturities and the planning horizon of the portfolio:

$$M^2 = \sum_{t=t_1}^{t=t_N} (t-H)^2 \times w_t \tag{1.4}$$

where the weights are defined in equation 1.1, and H is the planning horizon. A bond portfolio selected with minimum M-square has cash flows clustered around the planning horizon date and, hence, protects the portfolio from immunization risk resulting from nonparallel yield curve shifts. Though both convexity and M-square measures give similar information about the riskiness of a bond or a bond portfolio (since one is a linear function of the other), the developments of these two risk measures follow different paths. Convexity emphasizes the *gain* in the return on a portfolio, against large and parallel shifts in the term structure of interest rates M-square emphasizes the *risk exposure* of a portfolio due to slope shifts in the term structure of interest rates. Hence, the convexity view and the M-square view have exactly opposite implications for bond risk analysis and portfolio management. Lacey and Nawalkha (1993) find that high convexity (which is the same as high M-square) adds risk but not return to a bond portfolio using U.S. Treasury bond price data over the period 1976 to 1987.

Unlike the M-square model, that requires two risk measures for hedging (i.e., both duration and M-square), Nawalkha and Chambers (1996) derive the M-absolute model, which only requires one risk measure for hedging against the nonparallel yield curve shifts. The M-absolute of a bond portfolio is given as the weighted average of the absolute distances between cash flow maturities and the planning horizon of the portfolio.

$$M^A = \sum_{t=t_1}^{t=t_N} |t - H| \times w_t \tag{1.5}$$

where the weights are defined in equation 1.1, and H is the planning horizon.

Though the M-absolute model immunizes only partially against the height shifts, it reduces the immunization risk caused by the shifts in the slope, curvature, and all other term structure shape parameters by selecting a minimum M-absolute bond portfolio with cash flows clustered around its planning horizon date. The relative desirability of the duration model or the M-absolute model depends on the nature of term structure shifts expected. If height shifts completely dominate the slope, curvature, and other higher order term structure shifts, then the duration model will outperform the M-absolute model. If, however, slope, curvature, and other higher order shifts are relatively significant—in comparison with the height shifts—then the M-absolute model may outperform the traditional duration model. Using McCulloch and Kwon's (1993) term structure data over the observation period 1951 through 1986, Nawalkha and Chambers (1996) find the M-absolute model reduces the immunization risk inherent in the duration model by more than half.

DURATION VECTOR MODELS

Though both M-absolute and M-square risk measures provide significant enhancement in the immunization performance over the traditional duration model, perfect immunization is not possible using either of the two measures except for the trivial case in which the portfolio consists of a zero-coupon bond maturing at the horizon date. Further gains in immunization performance have been made possible by the duration vector model, which uses a vector of higher order duration measures to immunize against changes in the shape parameters (i.e., height, slope, curvature) of the yield curve. The immunization constraints of the duration vector model are given by:

$$D(m) = \sum_{t=t_1}^{t=t_N} t^m \times w_t = H^m, \quad \text{for } m = 1, 2, 3, \ldots, Q \tag{1.6}$$

where the weights are defined in equation 1.1, and H is the planning horizon. About three to five duration vector constraints (i.e., Q = 3 to 5) have shown to almost perfectly immunize against the risk of nonparallel yield curve shifts.

Since the shifts in the height, slope, curvature, and other parameters of the term structure of interest rate shifts are generally larger at the shorter end of the maturity spectrum, it is possible that an alternative set of duration measures that are linear in $g(t)$, $g(t)^2$, $g(t)^3$, and so on, and which put relatively more weight at the shorter end of the maturity spectrum due to the specific choice of the function $g(t)$, may provide enhanced immunization performance. Consistent with this intuition, Nawalkha, Soto, and Zhang (2003) and Nawalkha, Chambers, Soto, and Zhang (2004) derive a class of *generalized duration vector models* using a Taylor series expansion of the bond return function with respect to specific functions of the cash flow maturities. These papers find that $g(t) = t^{0.25}$ or $g(t) = t^{0.5}$ perform significantly better than the traditional duration vector for short planning horizons when three to five risk measures are used. Though the duration vector and the generalized duration vector models, significantly outperform the M-absolute and M-square models, the improvement in performance comes at the cost of higher portfolio rebalancing costs required by these models.

KEY RATE DURATION MODELS

The key rate duration model of Ho (1992) describes the shifts in the term structure as a discrete vector representing the changes in the *key* spot rates of various maturities. Interest rate changes at other maturities are derived from these values via linear interpolation. Key rate durations are then defined as the sensitivity of the portfolio value to key rates at different points along the term structure. The key rate duration model can be considered an extension of the traditional duration model given in equation 1.1, as follows:

$$\frac{\Delta P}{P} = -\sum_{i=1}^{m} KRD(i) \times \Delta y(t_i) \tag{1.7}$$

where the yield curve is divided into m different key rates.

Similar to the duration vector models, an appealing feature of the key rate model is that it does not require a *stationary* covariance structure of interest rate changes (unless performing a VaR analysis). Hence, it doesn't matter whether the correlations between the changes in interest rates of different maturities increase or decrease or even whether these changes are positively or negatively correlated. Also, the model allows for any number of key rates, and, therefore, interest rate risk can be modeled and hedged to a high degree of accuracy.

However, unlike the duration vector models, which require at most three to five duration measures, the number of duration measures to be used and the corresponding division of the term structure into different key rates, remain quite arbitrary under the key rate model. For example, Ho (1992) proposes as many as 11 key rate durations to effectively hedge against interest rate risk. Hedging against a large number of key rate durations implies larger long and short positions in the portfolio, which can make this approach somewhat expensive in terms of the transaction costs associated with portfolio construction and rebalancing.

PRINCIPAL COMPONENT DURATION MODELS

The principal component model assumes that the yield curve movements can be summarized by a few composite variables. These new variables are constructed by applying a statistical technique called *principal component analysis* (PCA) to the past interest rate changes. The use of PCA in the Treasury bond markets has revealed that three principal components (related to the height, the slope, and the curvature of the yield curve) are sufficient in explaining almost all of the variation in interest rate changes. An illustration of the impact of these components on the yield curve is shown in Figure 1.2.

The first principal component c_h, basically represents a parallel change in the yield curve, which is why it is usually named the level or the height factor. The second principal component c_s, represents a change in the steepness or the slope, and is named the slope factor. This factor is also called the "twist factor" as it makes the short-term rates and long-term rates move in opposite directions. The third principal component c_c, is called the curvature factor, as it basically affects the curvature of the yield curve by inducing a butterfly shift. This shift consists of short rates and long rates moving in the same direction and medium-term rates moving in the opposite direction.

The yield changes can be given as weighted linear sums of the principal components as follows:

$$\Delta y(t_i) \approx l_{ih}\Delta c_h + l_{is}\Delta c_s + l_{ic}\Delta c_c \quad i = 1, \ldots, m \tag{1.8}$$

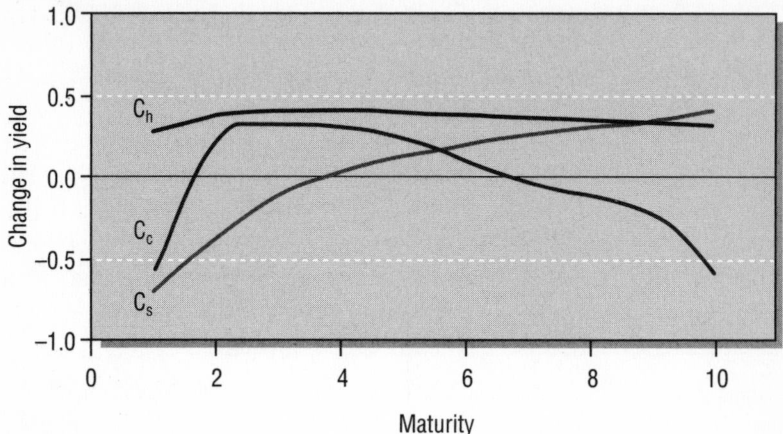

FIGURE 1.2 Shape of the Principal Components

where Δc_h = Change in the first component
Δc_s = Change in the second component
Δc_c = Change in the third component

The variables l_{ih}, l_{is}, and l_{ic}, are the factor sensitivities (or loadings) of the yield change $\Delta y(t_i)$ on the three principal components respectively. They correspond to the three curves shown in Figure 1.2. The sensitivity of the portfolio value to these three risk factors is measured by principal component durations (PCDs) given as follows:

$$\frac{\Delta P}{P} = -\sum_{i=h,s,c} PCD(i) \times \Delta c_i \tag{1.9}$$

The first three principal component durations given in equation 1.1 explain anywhere from 80 percent to 95 percent of the ex-post return differentials on bonds, depending on the time period chosen.

Since the principal component model explicitly selects the factors based on their contributions to the total variance of interest rate changes, it should lead to some gain in hedging efficiency. Further, in situations where explicit or implicit short positions are not allowed, the duration vector or the key rate duration model cannot give a zero immunization risk solution, except for some trivial cases. With short positions disallowed, significant immunization risk is bound to remain in the portfolio, and this risk can be minimized with the knowledge of the factor structure of interest rate changes using a principal component model.

However, the principal component model has a major shortcoming: It assumes that the covariance structure of interest rate changes is stationary. In situations where this assumption is violated, the use of the model might result in poor hedging performance.

APPLICATIONS TO FINANCIAL INSTITUTIONS

The five types of models discussed can be applied in a variety of contexts by financial institutions, from designing and executing simple duration-based hedging strategies to the most sophisticated dynamic immunization programs based on multiple risk measures, with off balance sheet positions in swaps, interest rate options, and interest rate futures. A few examples of these applications are discussed next.

Consider an insurance company that sells guaranteed investment products (GICs) to institutional investors and/or individuals. To guarantee a high yield over a prespecified horizon, the insurance company may use high-quality AAA-rated corporate bonds to design a dynamic immunization strategy, instead of simply investing in a riskless zero-coupon bond (e.g., Treasury STRIPs). The extra yield on high-quality bonds will compensate for the additional risk introduced by the AAA spread changes over the Treasury yield curve changes. Since the largest portion of the yield changes for high-quality corporate bonds are due to changes in the Treasury yield curve, a one- to three-factor duration vector model (see equation 1.6), or one to five risk measure based key rate duration model (see Figure 1.2) can be used. Though using more risk measures will lead to better immunization performance, doing so will require higher transaction costs and may even require explicit or implicit short positions.[2] Hence, the number of risk measures should be carefully selected after running many yield curve scenarios with transactions cost analysis.

As a second example, consider a commercial bank interested in protecting the value of shareholder equity from interest rate risk. The equity duration can be computed using the asset duration and the liability duration. An appropriate model that can be used to protect a bank's equity is the M-square model with a prespecified target equity duration. This model does not require that the M-square of the assets be set equal to the M-square of the liabilities, but that the difference between the M-squares of the assets and the liabilities be minimized. Since by the nature of their business (lend in long maturity sector, borrow in short maturity sector), banks cannot fully adjust the maturity structure of their assets and liabilities, the M-square model is more suited for a bank, instead of the duration vector model or the key rate duration model.

Next, consider a bond fund that attempts to replicate or beat the return on an index such as the Lehman U.S. government bond index. A principal component (PC) model can be used to get the empirical PC durations of the Lehman bond index by first obtaining the PCs using the historical data on changes in the Treasury rates of different maturities, and then running regressions of the returns on the Lehman index on the three important PCs. These regressions give three empirical PC durations, related to the so-called height, slope, and curvature factors (see equation 1.7). The bond fund can then select from a pool of bonds with an objective function that maximizes the yield, while constraining the empirical PC durations of the fund to equal those of the Lehman index. Since both the PCs and empirical PC durations change with time, the bond fund managers can use the most recent data (i.e., past six months) to design these strategies, which can be updated periodically, every two weeks, or every month.

Finally, consider a bond hedge fund manager who wishes to *speculate* on the changes in the shape of the yield curve. The type of yield curve shift depicted in Figure 1.1 is quite likely given the current economic scenario and the U.S. central bank policy. The figure shows a positive height shift, a negative slope shift, and a positive curvature shift, as the steep yield curve moves up, and flattens out. In order to benefit from this type of expected yield curve shift, the hedge fund manager can create a portfolio with cash bonds and Treasury futures, with a negative $D(1)$, a positive $D(2)$, and a negative $D(3)$. The exact magnitudes of $D(1)$, $D(2)$, and $D(3)$ (see equation 1.4) will depend on the confidence the hedge fund manager places in the particular types of shifts, and risk/return trade-off that she desires. For example, if she feels strongly that the slope shift will be negative, but unsure about the curvature shift, then she will take more exposure to slope shifts by increasing the $D(2)$ of the portfolio, but have the $D(3)$ of the portfolio close to zero.

The examples above demonstrate how managers of different financial institutions with varying objectives can use various multifactor models for hedging or speculating against the risk of nonparallel yield curve shifts. Of course, transactions costs and other market frictions require that managers simulate the performance of the trading strategies under realistic market conditions before putting these models to use.

INTERACTION WITH OTHER RISKS

The analysis until now has focused on interest rate risk measures for default-free securities. However, a typical bank balance sheet also includes corporate and individual loans that are exposed to credit risk, call risk, foreign exchange risk, liquidity risk, and other risks. The interaction between interest rate risk and the other risks is of crucial importance in implementing an overall risk protection strategy. Major banks in the United States, including Bank of America, are developing systems to measure different risks in an integrated manner. Since the focus of this book is on interest rate risk, we now consider how some of these other risks interact with interest rate risk. This not only provides insights into the overall effects of interest rate changes on bank assets and liabilities, but also allows for integrating interest rate risk with other types of risks in designing a total risk management system.

The interaction between credit risk and interest rate risk is of crucial importance as most bank loans are subject to the risk of credit downgrade or default. Many studies document the inverse relationship between credit spread changes and interest rate changes. In a rising interest rate environment, credit spreads tend to narrow, and vice-versa, which in general implies that corporate loans are *less* sensitive to interest rate changes (or have lower durations and convexities) than the equivalent default-free bonds. However, this is not always true. Nawalkha (1996) outlines specific conditions under which the credits spreads could either narrow or widen as interest rates increase, implying that the durations of corporate bonds could be either lower or higher than those of default-free counterparts. He finds that relatively short (long) maturity loans issued to corporations with high (low) interest rate sensitive assets, have longer (shorter) durations than those of equivalent default-free bonds.

The interaction between the call risk (due to the prepayment option) and interest rate risk may prove to be the most challenging aspect of risk management for some banks in the current environment in which most homeowners have already refinanced at record low interest rates. The mortgage prepayment options would lose much of their value if interest rates were to rise by a few percent in the next couple of years. This could significantly lengthen the duration of mortgage loans and mortgage-backed securities. Interest rates have been trending downward for most of the past quarter century, and a potential switch in the interest rate regime is likely, given the recent surge in oil prices, the continued rise in commodity prices, and the rising world GDP. The interaction of the lengthening of the mortgage durations with interest rate increases could expose the banks with significant holdings in mortgage assets to a high level of interest rate risk. This risk could get compounded further, if increases in interest rate also deflate the sky-high valuations of real estate in many parts of the world, reducing loan to value ratios, and increasing provisions for loan losses related to the mortgage assets.

The effects of foreign exchange risk can be devastating as many banks and regulators learned during the Asian currency crisis of 1997 to 1998. Like stock market bubbles and crashes, currencies also go through periodic upswings and downswings, which can wreck havoc on the balance sheets of financial institutions exposed to explicit or implicit currency-related risks. Further, economies such as Hong Kong, which have a fixed exchange rate system, must rely on a domestic exchange fund to support the currency peg. The artificially imposed currency peg creates a strong link between currency and interest rate risk. For example, during the Asian currency crisis, the speculative attack on the Hong Kong dollar led to an increase in the overnight rate all the way up to 280 percent on October 23, 1997. Although this quickly subsided, medium term rates remained higher than usual for many weeks, creating a panic in the stock market and wiping out much value from the banking and real estate stocks. The spread between London Interbank Offer Rate (LIBOR) and the Hong Kong Interbank Offer Rate (HIBOR) also increased significantly during this period, making it more costly to borrow dollars from the local banks. In general, currency crises have more severe effects on banks with more extreme duration gaps resulting from severe maturity mismatches between the assets and the liabilities, making the values of assets and liabilities deviate more sharply.

A good risk management system must consider the interactions of all risks in a unified framework. Duration and other interest rate risk measures are sensitive to credit risk, call risk, and foreign exchange risk, among other risks. Only by considering the combined effects of these risks on the interest rate risk profile of a bank can senior bankers get a perspective on the true risk exposure of a bank to interest rate changes.

NOTES

1. See Nawalkha (1999) for a review of this literature.
2. For example, the purchase of put options on Treasury bond futures creates implicit short positions.

CHAPTER 2

Bond Price, Duration, and Convexity

Investigation of a fixed-income security begins by observing its price-yield characteristics in relation to its risk and cash flow profile. Unlike corporate bonds that are subject to both default risk and interest rate risk, default-free securities such as U.S. Treasury bonds are subject to interest rate risk only. The interest rate risk of a default-free bond typically rises with its maturity. However, due to the presence of coupons, a more appropriate measure of risk of a default-free bond is its *duration*[1] which is defined as the weighted-average maturity of the bond. In many ways, duration is to fixed-income what *beta* is to equity. Duration explains perhaps 70 percent of ex-post bond returns differentials—although this number varies based on the length of time used to compute returns, the amount and types of interest rate volatility in the time period analyzed, the level of default risk in the bonds, and the liquidity of the market being analyzed.

Duration captures only the *linear* relationship between bond returns and the changes in interest rates. However, part of the relationship between bond returns and changes in the interest rates is nonlinear. To capture the *nonlinear* relationship between bond returns and the changes in interest rates, Redington (1952) introduced the concept of convexity. This chapter discusses the duration and convexity risk measures and clarifies a number of fallacies about them in the fixed-income literature. However, before introducing these risk measures, we give a brief introduction to compounding and discounting rules.

BOND PRICE UNDER CONTINUOUS COMPOUNDING

Consider the future value of a single sum formula given as:

$$FV_t = PV\left(1+\frac{APR_k}{k}\right)^{t\times k} \tag{2.1}$$

This chapter coauthored with Timothy Crack and Nelson Lacey.

where t is the holding period given in number of years, APR_k is the annual percentage rate with k compounding periods over one year. Federal regulations require that all quotes of interest rates be given by using an APR. Obviously, the APR quote must be given together with the compounding frequency k, as the compounding frequency affects the future value in equation 2.1. To appreciate the importance of compounding frequency, consider a student who in a desperate moment borrows \$1,000 for one year from a pawnbroker at an APR_{12} of 300 percent. Not having read the small print carefully, she goes back to return the sum of \$4,000 (\$1,000 principal plus \$3,000 interest) to the pawnbroker at the end of the year. To her dismay, she finds that she owes \$14,551.92 instead, which is \$10,551.92 more than what she thought. The pawnbroker shows her the following calculation:

$$FV_t = 1000\left(1 + \frac{300\%}{12}\right)^{1\times 12} = 1000(1 + 0.25)^{12} = \$14,551.92 \qquad (2.2)$$

Since interest on interest, and interest on interest on interest, and so on are higher with more frequent compounding, it leads to a higher future value in equation 2.2. Of course, the reason *monthly* compounding frequency makes such a huge difference is because we assumed an unusually high APR_{12} equal to 300 percent. At more reasonable values of APR_{12} like 10 percent, the compounding frequency would not have made such a big difference.

The most common compounding frequencies in the fixed-income markets are annual, semiannual, monthly, and daily. It is always possible to find equivalent APRs under different compounding frequencies, such that the future value remains the same in equation 2.1. To allow mathematical tractability, it is often easier to use an APR with *continuous compounding*, where interest on interest is paid out continuously, or with infinite compounding intervals in a year. Let y represent the APR assuming continuous compounding. Then by using the compounding rule, equation 2.1 can be rewritten as:

$$FV_t = \lim_{k\to\infty} PV\left(1 + \frac{y}{k}\right)^{t\times k} \qquad (2.3)$$

Since k goes to infinity, applying the exponential constant e, equation 2.3 can be rewritten as:

$$FV_t = PV \times e^{yt} \qquad (2.4)$$

If an *APR* is quoted with a compounding frequency *k*, then an equivalent *APR* under continuous compounding can be given as follows:

$$y = \ln\left(1 + \frac{APR_k}{k}\right) \times k \tag{2.5}$$

Equation 2.5 follows by equating the right sides of equations 2.1 and 2.4, and then taking logarithms of both sides of the equation.

As an example, given APR_{12} (i.e., an *APR* with monthly compounding), the continuously compounded *APR* is given as:

$$y = \ln\left(1 + \frac{APR_{12}}{12}\right) \times 12 \tag{2.6}$$

By dividing both sides of equation 2.4 by e^{ty} we get the present value of a single sum as follows:

$$PV = \frac{FV_t}{e^{yt}} \tag{2.7}$$

By applying the present value rule (equation 2.7) to every cash flow of a bond, the price of a bond with a periodic coupon C paid *k* times a year, and face value *F*, is given as follows:

$$P = \frac{C}{e^{yt_1}} + \frac{C}{e^{yt_2}} + \frac{C}{e^{yt_3}} + \ \ldots \ + \frac{C}{e^{yt_N}} + \frac{F}{e^{yt_N}} \tag{2.8}$$

where $t_1, t_2, t_3, \ldots, t_N$ are the *N* cash flow payment dates of the bond. Assuming the bond matures at time $t_N = T$, and the time intervals between all cash flow payments are equal, then $N = Tk$, and $t_1 = 1/k$, $t_2 = 2/k$, $t_3 = 3/k, \ldots, t_N = N/k$. Substituting these in equation 2.8, the bond price can be expressed by the following formula:

$$P = \frac{C}{e^i - 1}\left[1 - \frac{1}{e^{Ni}}\right] + \frac{F}{e^{Ni}} \tag{2.9}$$

where $i = y/k$ is the continuously compounded *APR* divided by *k*.

Unlike bonds, annuities like the mortgage loans do not make a lump-sum payment at the maturity date. Setting $F = 0$ in the above equation, the annuity formula is given as follows:

$$P = \frac{C}{e^i - 1}\left[1 - \frac{1}{e^{Ni}}\right] \tag{2.10}$$

Perpetuities are annuities with infinite life. Setting N = infinity, in equation 2.10, the perpetuity formula is given as:

$$P = \frac{C}{e^i - 1} \tag{2.11}$$

Note that equations 2.9, 2.10, and 2.11 assume that all variables are defined in periodic units. For example, if a fixed-income security, such as a bond, annuity, or a perpetuity, paid out coupons semiannually (the most common scenario for U.S. bonds), then equations 2.9, 2.10, and 2.11 can be used with the variables defined as follows:

where C = Semiannual coupon
$i = y/2$ = Continuously compounded *APR* divided by 2
N = Number of semiannual coupon payments

Similarly, if a fixed-income security paid out coupons monthly (e.g., mortgage loans or MBS), then equations 2.9, 2.10, and 2.11 can be used with the variables defined as follows:

where C = Monthly coupon
$i = y/12$ = Continuously-compounded *APR* divided by 12
N = Number of monthly coupon payments

Example 2.1 Consider a 30-year home-equity loan with 360 monthly payments (i.e., 30 × 12 = 360) of \$100. Suppose that the quoted *APR* with monthly compounding for the loan is 6 percent and we wish to calculate y, the continuously compounded *APR*. Using equation 2.5, this yield is calculated as:

$$y = \ln(1 + APR_k / k) \times k = \ln(1 + 0.06 / 12) \times 12 = 0.0598505$$

The present value of the loan can be computed in two different ways. Using the discrete monthly rate $= APR/12 = 0.06/12 = 0.005$, the loan's present value is given as:

$$P = \frac{100}{(1+0.005)} + \frac{100}{(1+0.005)^2} + \cdots + \frac{100}{(1+0.005)^{360}}$$
$$= \$16{,}679.16$$

Using the continuously compounded yield, $y = 0.0598505$, the loan's present value is given by equation 2.8 as follows:

$$P = \frac{100}{e^{(0.0598505)\times(1/12)}} + \frac{100}{e^{(0.0598505)\times(2/12)}} + \cdots + \frac{100}{e^{(0.0598505)\times(360/12)}}$$

$$= \$16{,}679.16$$

Since both approaches give identical answers, we can use the second approach based upon continuous compounding, which turns out to be more tractable mathematically. Throughout this chapter and for much of this book, we will use continuously compounded yields.

We do not have to do a summation of the 360 terms as shown above. The present value of the mortgage loan can be computed directly by using the formula in equation 2.10, with $C = \$100$, $i = y/12 = 0.0598505/12 = 0.00498754$, and $N = 360$, as follows:

$$P = \frac{\$100}{e^{0.00498754} - 1}\left[1 - \frac{1}{e^{360\times 0.00498754}}\right] = \$16{,}679.16 \quad (2.12)$$

DURATION

Duration is the weighted-average maturity of a bond, where weights are the present values of the bond's cash flows, given as proportions of bond's price:

$$D = \sum_{t=t_1}^{t=t_N} t\, w_t \tag{2.13}$$

and

$$w_t = \left\{ \frac{C_t}{e^{ty}} \right\} / P \tag{2.14}$$

Under continuous compounding, the duration measure gives the negative of the percentage price change of a bond, divided by an infinitesimally small change in the yield of a bond:[2]

$$D = -\lim_{\Delta y \to 0} \frac{\Delta P / P}{\Delta y} = -\frac{\partial P / \partial y}{P} \tag{2.15}$$

The duration measure defined by equations 2.13 and 2.15 increases with maturity, decreases with coupon rate, and decreases with the yield. By using an approximation of equation 2.15, we get the following expression for the percentage change in the bond price:

$$\frac{\Delta P}{P} \cong -D\Delta y \tag{2.16}$$

Hence, the percentage change in bond price is proportional to its duration, for an infinitesimally small change in the yield. Equation 2.16 assumes a parallel and infinitesimal shift in the yield curve. Nonparallel shifts in the yield curve result in unequal changes in the yields for different bonds, which invalidates using the given definition of duration, since Δy on the right side of equation 2.16 becomes different for different bonds.[3]

By definition, the magnitude of duration is always less than or equal to the maturity of the bond. However, this is true only for securities such as bonds that have non-negative cash flows. If one or more of the cash flows are negative, then duration may exceed the maturity of the underlying security, or may even be negative. Negative cash flows are introduced when computing the duration of fixed-income derivatives such as option and futures, which are priced as portfolios of long and short positions in regular bonds. For example, the duration of a call option on a bond is greater than

TABLE 2.1 Computing Duration

Maturity	Cash Flows ($)	Present Value of the Cash Flow ($)	Weight of the Cash Flow	Product of Weight and Maturity	Product of Present Value and Maturity
t	C	$PV = C/e^{t \times y}$	$w = PV/P$	$w \times t$	$PV \times t$
1	100	95.12	0.079	0.079	95.12
2	100	90.48	0.075	0.149	180.97
3	100	86.07	0.071	0.213	258.21
4	100	81.87	0.068	0.271	327.49
5	100	77.88	0.064	0.322	389.40
5	1,000	778.80	0.643	3.218	3,894.00
Total		P = 1,210.23	1.000	D = 4.251	5,145.20

the duration of the underlying bond since this option is a leveraged security. Similarly, the duration of a put option on a bond is generally negative since this option represents a leveraged short position. The following example shows the calculation of the duration of a regular coupon bond.

Example 2.2 Consider a five-year bond with $1,000 face value. The bond makes annual coupon payments at a 10 percent coupon rate. Assume that the continuously compounded annualized yield of this bond equals 5 percent (i.e., $y = \ln(1 + APR) = 5\%$). Table 2.1 shows how to compute the price and duration of this bond.

The first column of Table 2.1 gives the maturity of each cash flow of the bond; the second column the dollar value of each of these cash flows; the third column gives their present values; the fourth column gives the weights defined as the present values of the cash flows as proportions of the bond price; the fifth column gives the product of the weights and the maturities; and the last column gives the value of the product of the present value and the maturity of each cash flow.

The sum of the present values of the cash flows gives the bond price. The duration of the bond is given by equation 2.13 as:

$$D = \sum_{t=1}^{t=N} t\, w_t$$

and shown at the bottom of the fifth column as $D = 4.251$ years.

The last column of Table 2.1 allows us to compute duration in a different way. Substituting equation 2.14 into equation 2.13 gives:

$$D = \frac{1}{P}\sum_{t=1}^{t=N}\frac{tC_t}{e^{ty}}$$

Therefore, duration also can be computed by dividing the sum of the products of the present value and the maturity of each cash flow by the bond price. This gives again:

$$D = \frac{5145.20}{1210.23} = 4.251 \text{ years}$$

The duration of a bond portfolio is a weighted average of the durations of the bonds in the portfolio, where the weights are defined as the proportions of investments in the bonds. To illustrate the computation of portfolio duration, consider another bond B with a maturity of 10 years and a coupon rate of 10 percent. Using the same yield, the price of bond B is \$1,373.96 and its duration is 7.257 years. The duration of bond B is longer since it has a longer maturity.

Now consider a bond portfolio including one bond A and two bonds B. The portfolio value is thus \$1,210.23 + 2(\$1,373.96) = \$3,958.15. The portfolio duration is computed as follows:

$$D_{PORT} = \frac{1210.23}{3958.15}\times 4.251 + \frac{2\times 1373.96}{3958.15}\times 7.257 = 6.338 \text{ years}$$

Finally, consider a third bond C with the same characteristics as bond A but with a higher coupon rate of 12 percent. Using the same yield, the price of bond C is equal to \$1,296.52, which is higher than bond A's price of \$1,210.23 since bond C has a higher coupon rate. Bond C's duration is 4.161 years, which is lower than the duration of bond A (4.251 years). In general, higher coupon rate gives a lower duration, since the weight of the earlier cash flows (i.e., coupons) gives more weight to lower maturities.

Example 2.3 Reconsider the \$1,000 face value, 10 percent coupon rate, five-year bond introduced in the previous example. As shown earlier, this bond has a price of \$1,210.23 and a duration of 4.251 years. Now suppose that interest rates increase (due to unexpected news on inflation) so that the yield of the bond rises up to 6 percent.

The new bond price consistent with the new yield can be computed using equation 2.8 as follows:

$$P_{new} = \frac{100}{e^{0.06}} + \frac{100}{e^{0.06\times2}} + \frac{100}{e^{0.06\times3}} + \frac{100}{e^{0.06\times4}} + \frac{1100}{e^{0.06\times5}} = \$1,159.96$$

The change in the bond price is given as:

$$\Delta P = P_{new} - P_{old} = 1159.96 - 1210.23 = -\$50.27$$

and the percentage bond price change is given as:

$$\frac{\Delta P}{P} = \frac{P_{new} - P_{old}}{P_{old}} = \frac{-50.27}{1210.23} = -0.04154 = -4.154\%$$

Using the duration risk measure, we can approximate the percentage change in the bond price using equation 2.16, as follows:

$$\frac{\Delta P}{P} \cong -D\Delta y = -4.251 \times 0.01 = -0.04251 = -4.251\%$$

The percentage price change approximated by duration is very close to the true percentage price change. The difference between actual and approximated percentage price change is –4.154 percent – (–4.251 percent) = 0.097 percent, or about a dollar on the $1,210.23 initial price. In this example, if the yield decreased to 4 percent, then the bond price would have increased to $1,262.90, giving a percentage bond price change equal to 4.352 percent. In the latter case, the difference between the actual and estimated percentage change would have been 4.352 percent – 4.251 percent = 0.101 percent.

Regardless of whether the yield increases or decreases, the actual minus the estimated percentage price change is *always positive*. This is due to the so-called *convexity* of the bond, which is related to the curvature of the bond price-yield relationship shown in Figure 2.1. However, as indicated in the next section, and demonstrated later in Chapter 4, the convexity gains resulting from the curvature of the bond price-yield relationship are illusory and disappear when the assumption of a parallel shift in the term structure of interest rates is violated *even slightly*.

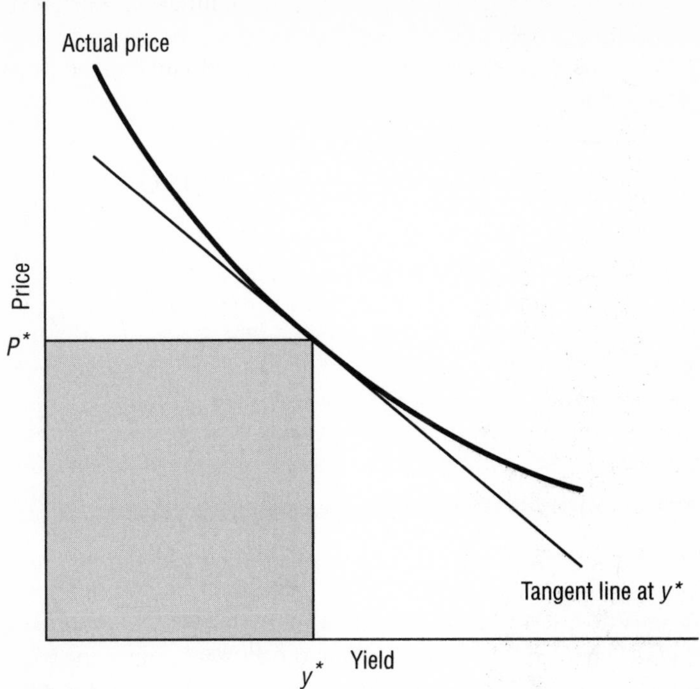

FIGURE 2.1 Bond Price/Yield Relationship with Tangent Line

CONVEXITY

Convexity is given as the weighted average of maturity-squares of a bond, where weights are the present values of the bond's cash flows, given as proportions of bond's price. Convexity can be mathematically expressed as follows:

$$CON = \sum_{t=t_1}^{t=t_N} t^2 w_t \tag{2.17}$$

Under continuous compounding, the convexity measure is obtained as the second derivative of the bond price with respect to the yield of the bond, divided by the bond price:[4]

$$CON = \frac{\partial^2 P / \partial y^2}{P} \tag{2.18}$$

For large changes in the interest rates, the definitions of duration and convexity in equations 2.15 and 2.18, respectively, are used to derive a two-term Taylor series expansion for approximating the percentage change in the bond price as follows:

$$\frac{\Delta P}{P} \cong -D\Delta y + \frac{1}{2}CON(\Delta y)^2 \tag{2.19}$$

Equation 2.19 suggests that for bonds with identical durations, higher convexity is always preferable. This is because if CON is positive, then regardless of whether Δy is positive or negative $(\Delta y)^2$ is always positive, making a higher convexity bond preferable to a lower convexity bond.

However, this result is based on the assumption of a large and parallel shift in the yield curve. Not only are large and parallel shifts in the yield curve inconsistent with arbitrage-free term structure dynamics, such shifts occur rarely in the bond markets. As will be shown in Chapter 4, even under slight violations of the assumption of parallel yield curve shifts, higher convexity may not be desirable.

Bond convexity increases with maturity, decreases with coupon rate, and decreases with yield. By definition, the magnitude of convexity is always less than the square of the maturity of the bond. If the underlying security has one or more negative cash flows then convexity may exceed maturity-square, or may even be negative. For example, the convexity of a call option on a bond is generally greater than the convexity of the underlying bond since this option is a leveraged security. Similarly, the convexity of a put option on a bond is generally negative since this option represents a leveraged short position.

Example 2.4 The convexity of a bond is computed identically to the duration of a bond, except that the longevity of each cash flow is replaced by the longevity squared. Table 2.2 gives the convexities of the three bonds considered in Example 2.2.

As can be seen, convexity increases with maturity and decreases with coupon rate. The convexity of a bond portfolio can be calculated as the weighted average of the convexities of the individual bonds. For the portfolio of bonds A and B, the convexity of the portfolio is given as the weighted average of the individual bond convexities:

$$CON_{PORT} = \frac{1210.23}{3958.15} \times 19.797 + \frac{2 \times 1373.96}{3958.15} \times 63.162 = 49.903$$

TABLE 2.2 Bonds' Characteristics

Bond	Maturity (years)	Annual Coupon Rate (%)	Yield to Maturity (%)	Price ($)	Duration (years)	Convexity (years squared)
A	5	10	5	1,210.23	4.251	19.797
B	10	10	5	1,373.96	7.257	63.162
C	5	12	5	1,296.52	4.161	19.172

COMMON FALLACIES CONCERNING DURATION AND CONVEXITY

If you draw the traditional textbook plot of a bond's price versus its yield as shown in Figure 2.1 and ask finance students what the slope is at any given point, they invariably answer that the slope is the duration of the bond. Ask them if changing slope (as yield changes) illustrates changes in this duration, and they invariably answer yes—wrong again.

Although Figure 2.1 is a common tool for explaining duration and convexity concepts, these explanations generate substantial confusion. The confusion has two main sources. The first source of confusion is that different books use quite different definitions of duration and convexity, sometimes without due care or clarity. Unfortunately, each definition carries different properties. The second source of confusion is that the traditional textbook plot in Figure 2.1 is simply not well suited to explaining the roles of duration and convexity.[5]

Let us try to interpret D and CON in relation to the simple plot of bond price versus bond yield given in Figure 2.1 as is often done in textbooks or in the classroom. In the familiar case of a zero-coupon bond of maturity T, all weights except w_T are zero, and thus $D = T$, and $CON = T^2$.

It is well known that limiting the analysis to duration only (i.e., ignoring convexity) is equivalent to assuming that the bond pricing relationship is linear in yield and thus that the relationship in Figure 2.1 follows the tangent line. Many other statements can be made about Figure 2.1. We find some or all of the following interrelated statements in each of several different sources in the literature and it is our experience that this is how many people think about Figure 2.1 with respect to our definitions of D and CON:

1. Duration measures the sensitivity of a bond's price to changes in its yield, and is thus given by the (negative of the) slope of the plot of bond price versus bond yield.

2. Duration decreases (increases) as bond yield increases (decreases)—this property holds for all option-free bonds.
3. Duration is the steepness of the tangent line in Figure 2.1. The steeper the tangent line, the greater the duration; the flatter the tangent line, the lower the duration.
4. Yield-induced changes in duration accelerate (decelerate) changes in prices as yields decrease (increase). This is why absolute and percentage price changes are greater when yields decline than when they increase by the same number of basis points.
5. Bond convexity is a second-order measure of the sensitivity of a bond's price to changes in its yield, and is thus given by the curvature (i.e., rate of change of slope) of the plot of bond price versus bond yield.
6. Bond convexity is the rate of change of duration as yields change.
7. Bond convexity decreases (increases) as bond yield increases (decreases)—this property holds for all option-free bonds.

Although appealing, each and every one of these statements is false for our definitions of duration and convexity unless accompanied by additional assumptions or restrictions. We give simple counter examples in the next section. We shall also demonstrate that if the (flawed) intuition behind these statements is applied to bonds with embedded options it creates substantial confusion.

Simple Counter Examples

Consider a five-year zero-coupon bond (i.e., a "zero"). The plot of bond price versus yield to maturity for the zero looks like that in Figure 2.1. A zero has duration equal to its maturity, so a five-year zero has D equal to five—regardless of its yield. It follows immediately that in the case of the zero, the changing slope of the plot in Figure 2.1 cannot be equal to the negative of the zero's Macaulay duration because the zero's D is fixed at five regardless of yield. We also conclude that D need not change with changing yield (even though the tangent line in Figure 2.1 flattens out with increasing yield).

The curvature of the plot in Figure 2.1 means that decreases (increases) in yield *are* associated with accelerated (decelerated) changes in price per basis point change in yield. However, in the case of a zero, changes in D cannot be the cause. Also, the convexity of a zero equals its maturity squared regardless of yield. However, the rate of change of the zero's duration with respect to its yield is zero (because the zero's duration does not change with yield). Thus, bond convexity cannot be simply the sensitivity of duration to changes in yield. We also conclude that convexity (fixed at

$CON = 25$ for our five-year zero) need not change with changing yield (even though the curvature of bond price in Figure 2.1 decreases with increasing yield). With a little math, it can also be shown that bond convexity is not the curvature of price with respect to yield. This result appears in the next section along with explanations.

Let us emphasize here that this is not simply a matter of the given statements failing to hold for zeroes or failing to hold when using continuous yields. The problem is deeper than that—it is just that it is easiest to see when looking at zeroes and using continuous yields. The casual statements mentioned in the previous section overlook the following interrelated facts about Figure 2.1:

1. The slope is not (the negative of) duration.
2. The curvature (i.e., rate of change of slope) does not illustrate changing duration.
3. The curvature (i.e., rate of change of slope) is not bond convexity.
4. Changing curvature does not illustrate changing convexity.

Explanation of the Fallacies

To confuse the slope and curvature of Figure 2.1 with (the negative of) duration and with convexity, respectively, leads to a fundamental misunderstanding of these concepts. We need to return to first principles to understand what is going on. We must examine the Taylor series expansion of bond price as a function of yield. By multiplying both sides of the two-term Taylor series expansion of the bond return given in equation 2.19 by P, we get:

$$\Delta P \cong -DP\Delta y + \frac{1}{2} CON \times P(\Delta y)^2 \tag{2.20}$$

It follows from equation 2.19 that duration and convexity are directly related to the first two coefficients in a second order approximation of "instantaneous bond return" (i.e., $\Delta P/P$) with respect to change in the yield. If instead of relating instantaneous bond return to change in the yield, as in equation 2.19, we relate change in the price to change in the yield, as in equation 2.20, we find that the roles of duration and convexity are "contaminated" by price level. This can be shown directly by the definitions of the first and second order derivatives of bond price with respect to the yield, given as:

$$\frac{\partial P}{\partial y} = -DP \tag{2.21}$$

$$\frac{\partial^2 P}{\partial y^2} = CON \times P \tag{2.22}$$

Equation 2.21 says that the slope of the plot in Figure 2.1 is not $-D$, but $-DP$ (i.e., the negative of what is known as "dollar duration"). Equation 2.22 says that the curvature (i.e., rate of change of the slope) of the plot in Figure 2.1 is not *CON*, but $CON \times P$ (i.e., what is known as "dollar convexity"). That is, when you relate price to yield, price contaminates the roles of duration and convexity. We suspect that many of the earlier statements drawn from the literature refer to dollar duration and dollar convexity, respectively.

The definition in equation 2.21 also yields the following:

$$\frac{\partial D}{dy} = D^2 - CON \tag{2.23}$$

Thus, the sensitivity of duration to changes in yield is not convexity, but the difference between duration squared and convexity. This can be calculated directly by a practitioner who has already calculated both duration and convexity. This equality also yields a very nice property for zero-coupon bonds: $CON = D^2$, because the duration of a zero does not change with yield. It follows that convexity is fixed regardless of yield for a zero, and therefore that convexity of a zero also does not change with yield.

It is dollar duration (i.e., DP) that measures the dollar change in the price of a bond for a given change in yields. Thus, changing slope in Figure 2.1 does not illustrate changing duration. Rather, changing slope in Figure 2.1 illustrates changing dollar duration and this does not necessarily tell us anything about duration, D. Similarly, the curvature in Figure 2.1 illustrates dollar convexity (i.e., $CON \times P$) and this differs substantially from convexity, *CON*. The numerical examples in Table 2.3 show just how different the aforementioned concepts can be.

From Table 2.3 Panel A and Panel B, it can be seen that duration does not change with yield for a zero-coupon bond, but duration does decrease slowly with increasing yield for a coupon-bearing bond; dollar duration decreases rapidly with increasing yield regardless of coupon rate; convexity does not change with yield for a zero-coupon bond, but convexity does

TABLE 2.3 Numerical Examples

Panel A: Five-Year Zero-Coupon Bond with Face $100

Yield	y	0.00	0.05	0.10	0.15	0.20	0.25
Price	P	100.00	77.88	60.65	47.24	36.79	28.65
Duration	D	5.00	5.00	5.00	5.00	5.00	5.00
Convexity	CON	25.00	25.00	25.00	25.00	25.00	25.00
Slope	$-DP$	−500.00	−389.40	−303.27	−236.18	−183.94	−143.25
Curvature	$CON \times P$	2,500.00	1,947.00	1,516.33	1,180.92	919.70	716.26

Panel B: Five-Year 15% Annual-Coupon Bond with Face $100

Yield	y	0.00	0.05	0.10	0.15	0.20	0.25
Price	P	175.00	142.59	116.77	96.14	79.61	66.33
Duration	D	4.14	4.05	3.94	3.83	3.71	3.59
Convexity	CON	19.00	18.38	17.70	16.99	16.23	15.44
Slope	$-DP$	−725.00	−577.08	−460.45	−368.37	−295.58	−237.95
Curvature	$CON \times P$	3,325.00	2,620.30	2,067.36	1,633.21	1,292.08	1,023.84

decrease slowly with increasing yield for a coupon-bearing bond; dollar convexity decreases rapidly with increasing yield regardless of coupon rate; and, finally, other things being equal duration and convexity decrease with increasing coupon level, but dollar duration and dollar convexity increase with increasing coupon level.

Applications to Callable Bonds

We have demonstrated that many statements about duration and convexity do not hold in the simple case of a zero-coupon bond. Let us now take the more complicated example of a security with an embedded option—a callable zero-coupon bond—to illustrate how misleading these statements can be if applied more generally.

Consider a $100 face value 10-year zero-coupon bond that is callable (European-style) in one year at 80 percent of its face value. Figure 2.2 plots the bond's price, duration, and dollar duration as a function of yield. The bond price as a function of yield first steepens, and then flattens as yield increases (see Figure 2.2 Panel A). Inferring duration from the slope in Figure 2.1 implies *incorrectly* that duration first increases and then decreases as yield rises—whereas, the duration of the callable bond is monotonically increasing in yield (see Figure 2.2 Panel B).[6] The correct inference is that it is dollar

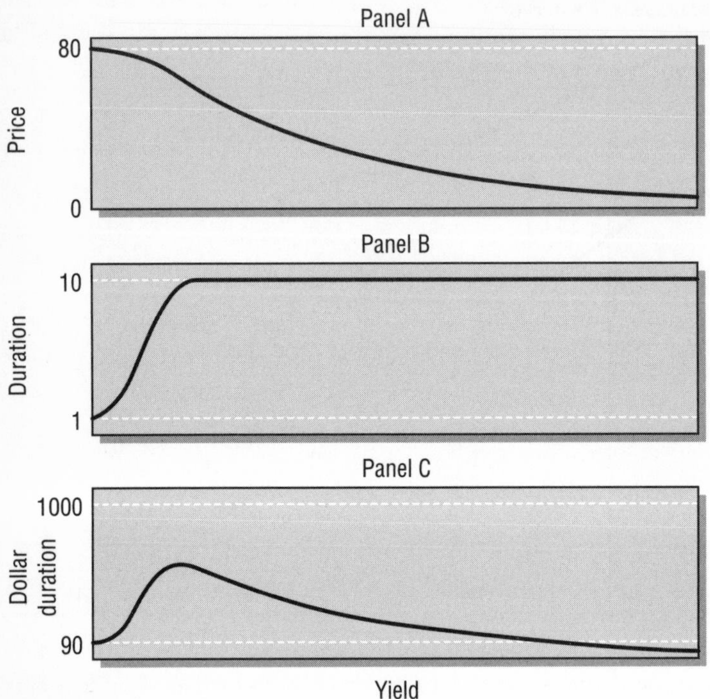

FIGURE 2.2 Callable Zero-Coupon Bond

duration that first increases and then decreases with increasing yield (see Figure 2.2 Panel C). We conclude that inferring duration from the slope of the price-yield relationship causes substantial confusion in the case of a callable bond.

A New Graph

There are two problems with the traditional plot of bond price versus yield given in Figure 2.1. The first problem, as discussed, is that the slope of the tangent line at the initial yield is not duration, and the change in slope with respect to yield is not convexity. The second and related problem is that the traditional plot shows *dollar* changes in bond prices for changing yields. However, a \$2 change in a \$100 bond is not the same as a \$2 change in a \$50 bond—the plot compares apples and oranges. Two ways to reduce these problems come immediately to mind: either plot log price against yield, or plot instantaneous return (i.e., $\Delta P/P$) against yield.

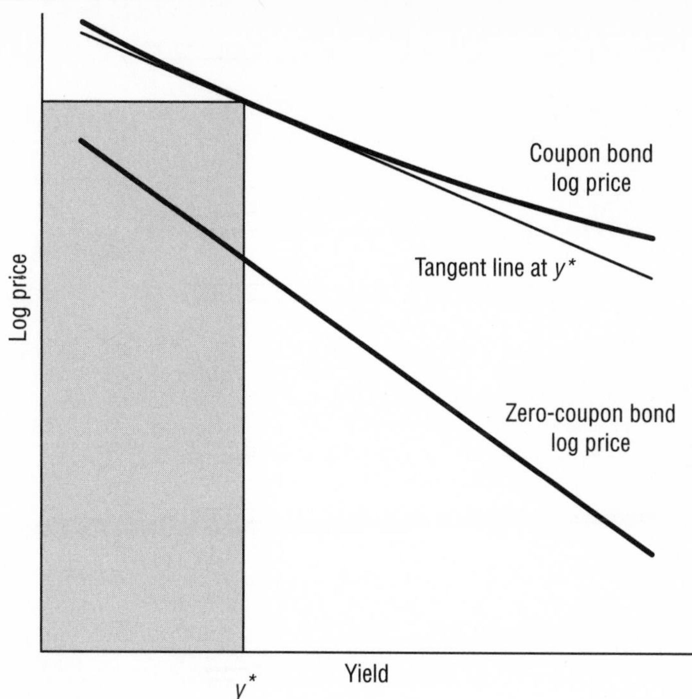

FIGURE 2.3 Log Price versus Yield

Suppose we follow the first approach and plot log price against yield as shown in Figure 2.3. In this case, the slope of the plot is easily shown to be $-D$, where D is the duration of the bond.[7] The change in slope can be shown to be $-(D^2 - CON)$. The vertical change along the plot from the initial point is the log of 1 plus the instantaneous return on the bond.[8] The plot is unbounded below (because log of the price is unbounded below as $P \to 0$). In the special case of a zero-coupon bond (where $CON = D^2$ so the change in slope is zero), the plot of log price versus yield is a straight line (see Figure 2.3).

The plot of log price versus yield (Figure 2.3) has substantially less curvature than the traditional plot of price versus yield—in the case of a zero it has no curvature at all. There is a simple economic reason for this reduced curvature: the absolute value of the slope in Figure 2.3 is duration, and duration does not change very much with changing yield. Contrast this with the traditional plot (Figure 2.1) where the slope is $-DP$, which does vary a lot with changing yield because P varies a lot.

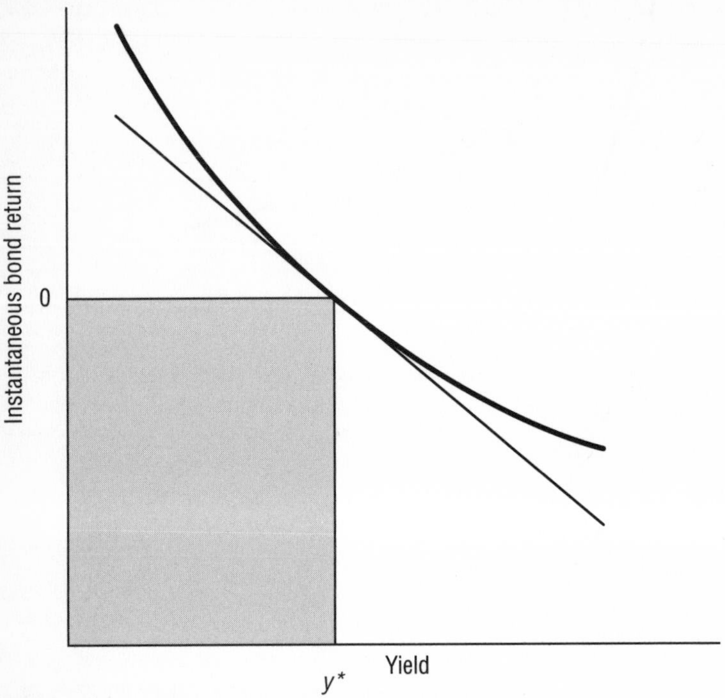

FIGURE 2.4 Instantaneous Return versus Yield

Unfortunately, even though the slope of the log price versus yield graph is equal to $-D$, the curvature (i.e., change in slope) of the graph does not give convexity. To address this shortcoming, we recommend a second approach that plots instantaneous return against yield (see Figure 2.4). The instantaneous bond return is the instantaneous price change divided by initial price $(P - P^*)/P^*$. The slope of the tangent line *at the initial yield* is easily shown to be $-D$, where D is the duration of the bond. The rate of change of slope *at the initial yield* is easily shown to be CON, the convexity.[9] Thus, duration and convexity are first and second order measures of the sensitivity of a bond's instantaneous return to changes in its yield. Given that the value of the slope and its rate of change are $-D$ and CON, respectively, this plot is more appropriate than plotting log price versus yield (it also avoids the potential confusion arising from log price being unbounded later).

For different initial yields, the curve in Figure 2.4 "slides" sideways as shown in Figure 2.5. The change in slope of the tangent line for increasing yield is minor compared to that in the traditional plot of price versus yield (with no change at all for a zero). The reason is the same as that given earlier for the log price plot: the slope here is $-D$ and D does not change much with

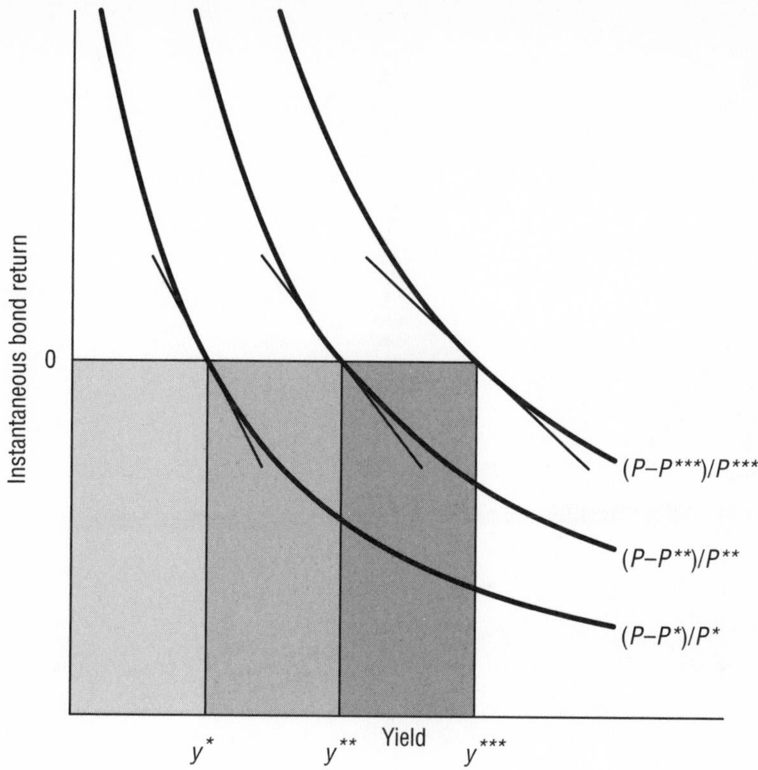

FIGURE 2.5 Instantaneous Return versus Yield for Different Initial Yields

yield, where as for the traditional plot the slope is $-DP$ which changes a lot because P changes so much with changing yield. The curvature (or change in slope) of each curve at its initial yield is the convexity of the bond and decreases as the initial yield increases.[10] Finally, compared to the initial point, the vertical change along the plot in Figure 2.4 is the instantaneous rate of return on the bond.

Figure 2.6 presents the plot of instantaneous return versus yield for the callable zero-coupon bond that we discussed earlier. It can be seen that the duration (absolute value of slope at initial yield) increases for increasing initial yield—as in Figure 2.2 Panel B—and the convexity (change in slope at initial yield) goes from negative to zero to positive as initial yield increases. This is because increasing yield decreases the likelihood that the embedded call will be exercised. This in turn lengthens the expected maturity of the callable zero and increases its duration and convexity. This differs from Figure 2.5 in which duration and convexity decrease with increasing yield (the case of a noncallable coupon bond). The monotonically increasing relationship

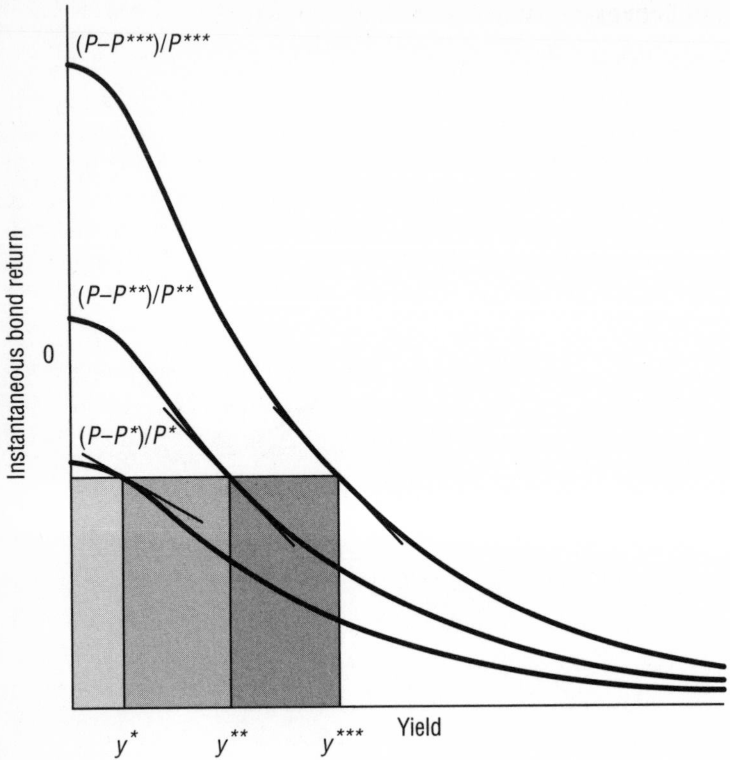

FIGURE 2.6 Instantaneous Return versus Yield for Callable Zero

between the duration of a callable zero-coupon bond and its yield cannot be inferred directly from the traditional price-yield graph such as Figure 2.2 Panel A—thus illustrating the importance of our new plot. Some other fallacies concerning duration and convexity that are outside the scope of this chapter are outlined in Appendix 2.1.

FORMULAS FOR DURATION AND CONVEXITY

Closed-form formulas for duration and convexity eliminate the need to sum the present values of the weighted discounted values of future cash flows and hence constitute a more efficient procedure for calculating these measures. Although a number of closed-form solutions for duration and convexity have been suggested in the literature, here we offer a general approach that allows the derivation of these solutions both at the coupon payment dates and between the coupon payment dates.

Duration and Convexity Formulas for Regular Bonds

Consider a bond that makes a periodic coupon payment of C dollars k times a year. The face value of the bond is F dollars, and its continuously compounded annualized yield equals y. The bond has a total of N cash flows remaining. Let s define the time elapsed since the last coupon payment date *in the units of the time interval between coupon payments*. At the coupon payment dates, $s = 0$. Further, define $c = C/F$ as the periodic coupon rate, and $i = y/k$, the continuously compounded annualized yield divided by k. The formula for the duration of a regular bond between coupon payment dates is given as follows:

$$D = \frac{c\left[e^{Ni}\left(e^{i}(1-s)+s\right)-e^{i}\right]+\left(e^{i}-1\right)(N-s)\left(e^{i}-1-c\right)}{k\left[c\left(e^{i}-1\right)\left(e^{Ni}-1\right)+\left(e^{i}-1\right)^{2}\right]} \tag{2.24}$$

For the special case of $s = 0$, the above formula simplifies to:

$$D_{s=0} = \frac{ce^{i}\left(e^{Ni}-1\right)+N\left(e^{i}-1\right)\left(e^{i}-1-c\right)}{k\left[c\left(e^{i}-1\right)\left(e^{Ni}-1\right)+\left(e^{i}-1\right)^{2}\right]} \tag{2.25}$$

The duration formulas given in equations 2.24 and 2.25 adjust for compounding frequency, and are given in annualized units (i.e., number of years). Hence, they can be directly used for approximating the percentage price change in equation 2.16, given a change Δy in the continuously compounded annualized yield.

The formula for the convexity of a regular bond between coupon payment dates is given as follows:

$$\begin{aligned} CON = {} & \frac{c\left\{e^{Ni}\left[\left(e^{i}(1-s)+s\right)^{2}+e^{i}\right]-e^{i}\left[2\left(1+(N-s)\left(e^{i}-1\right)\right)+e^{i}-1\right]\right\}}{k^{2}\left[c\left(e^{i}-1\right)^{2}\left(e^{Ni}-1\right)+\left(e^{i}-1\right)^{3}\right]} \\ & + \frac{\left(e^{i}-1\right)^{2}(N-s)^{2}\left(e^{i}-1-c\right)}{k^{2}\left[c\left(e^{i}-1\right)^{2}\left(e^{Ni}-1\right)+\left(e^{i}-1\right)^{3}\right]} \end{aligned} \tag{2.26}$$

For the special case of $s = 0$, the earlier formula simplifies to:

$$CON_{s=0} = \frac{c\left\{e^i\left(1+e^i\right)\left(e^{Ni}-1\right)-2\times N\times e^i\left(e^i-1\right)\right\}+N^2\left(e^i-1\right)^2\left(e^i-1-c\right)}{k^2\left[c\left(e^i-1\right)^2\left(e^{Ni}-1\right)+\left(e^i-1\right)^3\right]} \tag{2.27}$$

The convexity formulas given previously also adjust for compounding frequency, and are given in annualized units (i.e., number of years squared). Hence, they can be directly used for approximating the percentage price change in equation 2.19, given a squared change $(\Delta y)^2$ in the continuously compounded annualized yield.

Duration and Convexity Formulas for Annuities and Perpetuities

Consider an annuity with a periodic cash flow of C dollars made k times a year, a continuously compounded annualized yield equal to y, and N cash flows remaining. Let s define the time elapsed since the last annuity payment date *in the units of the time interval between the annuity payments.* So, at the annuity payment dates, $s = 0$. Let $i = y/k$, the continuously compounded annualized yield divided by k. The formula for the duration of an annuity between the payment dates is:

$$D = \left[\frac{e^i}{e^i-1} - \frac{N}{e^{Ni}-1} - s\right] / k \tag{2.28}$$

For the special case of $s = 0$, the equation 2.28 simplifies to:

$$D_{s=0} = \left[\frac{e^i}{e^i-1} - \frac{N}{e^{Ni}-1}\right] / k \tag{2.29}$$

The formula for the convexity of an annuity between coupon payment dates is:

$$CON = \left[\frac{(e^i(1-s)+s)^2+e^i}{(e^i-1)^2} + \frac{(e^i-1)(s^2-(N-s)^2)-2Ne^i}{(e^i-1)(e^{Ni}-1)}\right] / k^2 \tag{2.30}$$

For the special case of $s = 0$, the above formula simplifies to:

$$CON_{s=0} = \left[\frac{e^i(1+e^i)}{(e^i-1)^2} + \frac{-Ne^i(N+2)+N}{(e^i-1)(e^{Ni}-1)} \right] / k^2 \tag{2.31}$$

A *perpetuity* is an annuity with an infinite number of cash flows. The duration and convexity formulas for perpetuity at and between coupon payment dates can be obtained by a simple inspection of equations 2.28, 2.29, and 2.31, and substitution of N = infinity as follows:

$$D = \left[\frac{e^i}{e^i-1} - s \right] / k \tag{2.32}$$

$$D_{s=0} = \left[\frac{e^i}{e^i-1} \right] / k \tag{2.33}$$

$$CON = \left[\frac{(e^i(1-s)+s)^2 + e^i}{(e^i-1)^2} \right] / k^2 \tag{2.34}$$

$$CON_{s=0} = \left[\frac{e^i(1+e^i)}{(e^i-1)^2} \right] / k^2 \tag{2.35}$$

Similar to the case of regular bonds, the duration and convexity formulas given in equations 2.28 through 2.35 adjust for compounding frequency, and are given in annualized units.

Example 2.5 Reconsider the five-year, 10 percent annual coupon bond A with a continuously compounded yield of 5 percent given in Example 2.2. In that example, we obtained the bond's duration as 4.251 years. In Example 2.4, we obtained the same bond's convexity as 19.797. These values can be computed using the closed-form formulas given above. Since the bond matures in *exactly* five years, the closed-form formulas with $s = 0$ are applied.

Using equation 2.25, the bond A's duration is calculated as:

$$D_{s=0} = \frac{0.1 \times e^{0.05}\left(e^{0.05\times5} - 1\right) + 5\left(e^{0.05} - 1\right)\left(e^{0.05} - 1.1\right)}{0.1\left(e^{0.05} - 1\right)\left(e^{0.05\times5} - 1\right) + \left(e^{0.05} - 1\right)^2} = 4.251 \text{ years}$$

Using equation 2.27, bond A's convexity is calculated as:

$$CON_{s=0} = \frac{0.1\left\{e^{0.05}\left(1 + e^{0.05}\right)\left(e^{0.05\times5} - 1\right) - 10 \times e^{0.05}\left(e^{0.05} - 1\right)\right\} + 5^2\left(e^{0.05} - 1\right)^2\left(e^{0.05} - 1.1\right)}{0.1\left(e^{0.05} - 1\right)^2\left(e^{0.05\times5} - 1\right) + \left(e^{0.05} - 1\right)^3}$$

$$= 19.797$$

As expected, the two formulas give the same values obtained in earlier examples.

Now, consider the duration and convexity of this bond after nine months. Assume that the yield to maturity is still 5 percent. Since the bond has not paid any coupons, the number of coupons before maturity remains 5 ($N = 5$), and the first coupon is due in three months. The time elapsed since the date of the last coupon relative to time between two coupon payments is $s = 9$ months/12 months $= 0.75$ years. To calculate the duration and convexity, we use the formulas given in equations 2.24 and 2.26, respectively, as follows:

$$D = \frac{0.1\left[e^{0.05\times5}\left(0.25 \times e^{0.05} + 0.75\right) - e^{0.05}\right] + 4.25 \times \left(e^{0.05} - 1\right)\left(e^{0.05} - 1.1\right)}{0.1\left(e^{0.05} - 1\right)\left(e^{0.05\times5} - 1\right) + \left(e^{0.05} - 1\right)^2}$$

$$= 3.501 \text{ years}$$

$$CON = \frac{0.1\left\{e^{0.05\times5}\left[\left(0.25 \times e^{0.05} + 0.75\right)^2 + e^{0.05}\right] - e^{0.05}\left[2\left(1 + 4.25\left(e^{0.05} - 1\right)\right) + e^{0.05} - 1\right]\right\}}{0.1\left(e^{0.05} - 1\right)^2\left(e^{0.05\times5} - 1\right) + \left(e^{0.05} - 1\right)^3}$$

$$+ \frac{\left(e^{0.05} - 1\right)^2 4.25^2\left(e^{0.05} - 1.1\right)}{0.1\left(e^{0.05} - 1\right)^2\left(e^{0.05\times5} - 1\right) + \left(e^{0.05} - 1\right)^3}$$

$$= 13.982$$

The new values of duration and convexity are lower than those obtained previously due to the time elapsed.

APPENDIX 2.1: OTHER FALLACIES CONCERNING DURATION AND CONVEXITY

Other fallacies found in the fixed-income literature regarding duration and convexity area are as follows:

1. Duration is based on the assumption of infinitesimal and parallel yield curve shifts, therefore, is not a useful risk measure when yield curve shifts are large and nonparallel.
2. Since duration is not derived using the framework of the modern portfolio theory, it does not relate risk to return.
3. Convexity is based on the assumption of large and parallel yield curve shifts, which imply the existence of arbitrage profits, and hence convexity is a theoretically invalid measure for interest rate risk analysis.

The first and third fallacies can be traced back to an influential critique of duration and convexity by Ingersoll, Skelton, and Weil (1978). The second fallacy resulted from comments of Sharpe (1983), which questioned whether duration is consistent with a risk-return equilibrium. A resolution to all of the above fallacies was provided by Nawalkha and Chambers (1999) and is outlined next.

The duration risk measure is consistent with a specific arbitrage-free term structure model of Heath, Jarrow, and Morton (HJM; 1992). This model is discussed in detail in the second part of the book. Under this model, only the "unexpected" portion of the yield curve shift remains parallel. The expected portion of the yield curve shift is always nonparallel and is determined by the "forward rate drift restriction" imposed by the HJM model. Duration reflects the risk resulting only from the unexpected yield curve shifts, which are assumed to be parallel. However, when even the unexpected yield curve shifts are nonparallel, duration risk measure allows interest rate risk hedging against only the shifts in the *height* of the yield curve. Under this scenario, duration becomes a *partial* risk measure, and other higher order measures may be needed to hedge against shifts in the slope, curvature, and other higher order changes in the yield curve. Even as a partial risk measure, duration explains roughly 70 percent of the ex-post return differentials among bonds, and so remains the most important bond risk measure.

Further, the duration risk measure is consistent with Merton's (1973a) intertemporal capital asset pricing model (ICAPM), and, hence, with continuous-time modern portfolio theory. Assuming that the entire investment opportunity set is represented by the changes in the instantaneous short rate, a simplified form of the two-parameter ICAPM can be obtained for securities subject to default risk (e.g., stocks and default-prone bonds). However, the two-parameter ICAPM reduces to a single-factor model for all default-free securities. Interestingly, the appropriate equilibrium measure of the systematic risk of a default-free security is its *duration* and not its bond beta as derived by Alexander (1980); Boquist, Racette, and Schlarbaum (1975); Jarrow (1978); and Livingston (1978), under more restrictive assumptions. Intuitively, the above result obtains because under the two-parameter ICAPM, every default-free bond can serve as a hedge portfolio that is used to hedge against unexpected changes in the interest rates by risk-averse investors.

Finally, using the continuous-time HJM framework, the effect of convexity on the bond return can be shown to cancel out by a portion of the *theta* of the bond. Bond theta measures the drift of the bond price due to the passage of time. Due to this *convexity-theta trade-off,* bond convexity is not priced under the single factor forward rate models of HJM. However, bond convexity may be priced under a two-factor HJM model that allows both level and slope shifts in the term structure of forward rates. The relation of convexity with slope shifts in the yield curve is the subject of Chapter 4.

NOTES

1. Duration was discovered more than half a century ago by Macaulay (1938) and Hicks (1939), and then rediscovered a number of times by researchers including Samuelson (1945) and Redington (1952).
2. Under discrete compounding, equation 2.15 leads to modified duration, which is different from duration. However, with continuous compounding, the definition of duration given in equation 2.15 is *identical* to the definition of duration given by equation 2.13.
3. Under nonparallel shifts in the yield curve, one can use the generalized duration vector models introduced in Chapter 5 or the key rate duration models introduced in Chapter 9.
4. Under discrete compounding, equation 2.18 leads to modified convexity, which is different from convexity. However, with continuous compounding, the definition of convexity given in equation 2.18 is *identical* to the definition of convexity given by equation 2.17.
5. See the following: Cole and Young (1995, p. 1); Fabozzi (1996, pp. 66, 73); Fabozzi, Pitts, and Dattatreya (1995, pp. 97–98, p. 101, p. 109); Johnson (1990, p. 73); Kritzman (1992, p. 19); and Livingston (1990, p. 70).
6. See Nawalkha (1995) for analytical details of the pricing and duration of this callable bond—we are assuming (in his notation) that volatility of returns to the bond is $V = 0.01$.
7. Since $\partial \ln P/\partial y = (\partial P/\partial y)/P$ is the slope, it follows from the definition of D that the slope equals $-D$.

8. Consider an initial price P^* at yield y^* and a new price P at a new yield y. The vertical distance is $\ln P - \ln P^* = \ln(P/P^*) = \ln(1 + \text{Rate of instantaneous return})$, as stated.
9. The slope or the first derivative of the plot at the initial yield y^* equals $[\partial[(P - P^*)/P^*]/\partial y]_{y=y^*} = [(\partial P/\partial y)_{y=y^*}]/P^* = -D$. The curvature (i.e., change in slope) or the second derivative of the plot at the initial yield y^* equals $[\partial[\partial[(P - P^*)/P^*]/\partial y]/\partial y]_{y=y^*} = [(\partial^2 P/\partial y^2)_{y=y^*}]/P^* = CON$.
10. If Figure 2.5 were for a zero-coupon bond, the slopes and curvatures would be identical as initial yield changes.

CHAPTER 3

Estimation of the Term Structure of Interest Rates

The duration model introduced in the previous chapter assumes infinitesimal and parallel shifts in a flat yield curve. In order to consider nonparallel shifts in a nonflat yield curve, we need to model the yields corresponding to different maturities. The *term structure of interest rates* gives the relationship between the yield on an investment and the term to maturity of the investment. This chapter focuses on how to estimate the default-free term structure of interest rates using cross-sectional U.S. Treasury bond data. The term structure obtained in this chapter will serve as an input in many chapters that follow, which introduce more complex risk measures for hedging against nonparallel term structure shifts (such as, M-absolute, M-square, duration vector, key rate durations, principal component durations). The term structure will also be an important input in various chapters in the second and third volumes of this book series. Since the valuation of default-free fixed-income securities and the derivatives based on these securities must fit an empirically observable term structure, estimation of the term structure using cross-sectional data is essential for the valuation process.

The default-free term structure generally rises with maturity, because investors generally demand higher rates of interest on longer maturity investments, both due to a preference for liquidity and as an aversion to interest rate risk. The term structure is typically measured using default-free, continuously compounded, annualized zero-coupon yields. Since coupon bonds are portfolios of zero-coupon bonds, the term structure can be used to value both coupon bonds and zero-coupon bonds. The term structure is not directly observable from the published coupon bond prices and yields. Though default-free zero-coupon prices (such as the U.S. Treasury STRIPS) can be directly used for obtaining the term structure, the lack of liquidity in these markets, and the unavailability of a continuum of maturities, make the use of coupon bond prices necessary for obtaining more robust estimates of the term structure.

This chapter reviews three methods of term structure estimation: the bootstrapping method, the McCulloch cubic-spline method, and the Nelson and Siegel method. We consider various extensions to these methods based on error-weighing schemes that lead to more robust estimates of the term structure. Before introducing these methods however, we review some notation and concepts.

BOND PRICES, SPOT RATES, AND FORWARD RATES

The Discount Function

Under continuous compounding, the price of a zero-coupon bond with a face value of \$100 and a term to maturity of t years can be written as:

$$P(t) = \frac{100}{e^{y(t)t}} = 100\, e^{-y(t)t} = 100\, d(t) \tag{3.1}$$

where $y(t)$ is the continuously compounded rate corresponding to the maturity term t. The equation 3.1 is a generalization of the present value rule given in equation 2.7 in the previous chapter, which assumed a constant rate y. The function $y(t)$ defines the continuously compounded term structure based upon zero-coupon rates. The expression $e^{-y(t)t}$ is referred to as the discount function $d(t)$. The typical shape of the discount function is shown in Figure 3.1. This function starts at 1, since the current value of a \$1

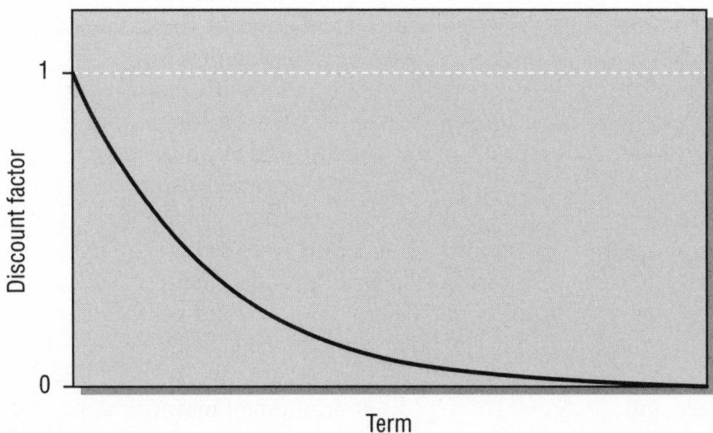

FIGURE 3.1 The Discount Function

payable today is \$1, and it decreases with increasing maturity due to the time value of money.

If a series of default-free zero-coupon bonds exist for differing maturities, then it is possible to extract the term structure by simply inverting equation 3.1 to obtain $y(t)$. Unfortunately, due to the lack of liquidity and unavailability of zero-coupon bonds for all maturities, the term structure cannot be simply obtained by using zero-coupon bonds such as U.S. Treasury STRIPS.

Accrued Interest

Since a coupon bond can be viewed as a portfolio of zero-coupon bonds, the term structure can be used to price the coupon bond as follows. Let the price of a coupon-bearing bond that makes a total of N coupon payments, k times a year at times $t_1, t_2, \ldots, t_N$, and a face value F, be given as:[1]

$$P = \sum_{j=1}^{N} \frac{C}{e^{y(t_j)t_j}} + \frac{F}{e^{y(t_N)t_N}} \tag{3.2}$$

where C is the periodic coupon paid k times a year. Equivalently, we have:

$$P = \sum_{j=1}^{N} C \times d(t_j) + F \times d(t_N) \tag{3.3}$$

Equation 3.3 gives what is called the *cash price* of a bond. This is the price that purchaser pays when buying the bond. However, bond prices are not quoted as cash prices. The quoted prices are *clean prices,* which exclude the accrued interest. Accrued interest is the interest accumulated between the most recent interest payment and the present time. If t_0 denotes the current time, t_p denotes the date of the previous coupon payment, and t_q denotes the date of the next coupon payment, then the formula for accrued interest is given as:

$$AI = C\left(\frac{t_0 - t_p}{t_q - t_p}\right) \tag{3.4}$$

and the bond's quoted price is then expressed as:

$$\text{Quoted Price} = P - AI = \sum_{j=1}^{N} \frac{C}{e^{y(t_j)t_j}} + \frac{F}{e^{y(t_N)t_N}} - C\left(\frac{t_0 - t_p}{t_q - t_p}\right) \tag{3.5}$$

Computation of accrued interest requires the *day-count basis* used in the market. The day-count basis defines how to measure the number of days:

1. Between the current date and the date of the previous coupon payment, or $t_0 - t_p$, and
2. Between the coupon payment dates before and after the current date, or $t_q - t_p$.

The most widely used day-count bases are given as follows:

- Actual/Actual: both $t_0 - t_p$ and $t_q - t_p$ are measured using the actual number of days between the dates.
- Actual/360: $t_0 - t_p$ is measured using the actual number of days between t_0 and t_p, and $t_q - t_p$ equals $360/k$, where k is the number of coupon payments made in one year.
- 30/360: $t_0 - t_p$ is measured as 30 × number of remaining and complete months + actual number of days remaining between the dates t_0 and t_p, and $t_q - t_p$ equals $360/k$, where k is the number of coupon payments made in one year.

The Actual/Actual basis is used for Treasury bonds, the Actual/360 basis is used for U.S. Treasury bills and other money market instruments, and the 30/360 basis is used for U.S. corporate and municipal bonds.

Example 3.1 Consider a semiannual coupon bond with a \$1,000 face value and a 5 percent annualized coupon rate with coupon payments on June 1 and December 1. Suppose we wish to calculate the accrued interest earned from the date of the last coupon payment to the current date, November 3.

If we use the Actual/Actual day count basis to measure the number of days between dates, then,

$t_0 - t_p$ = The actual number of days between June 1 and November 3 = 155, and
$t_q - t_p$ = The actual number of days between June 1 and December 1 = 183

The accrued interest is given as:

$$AI = C\frac{t_0 - t_p}{t_q - t_p} = 25\left(\frac{155}{183}\right) = \$21.17$$

where C = 50/2 = $25, is the semiannual coupon payment.

If we used the Actual/360 convention, then,

$t_0 - t_p$ = The actual number of days between June 1 and November 3 = 155, and
$t_q - t_p = 360/k = 360/2 = 180$

The accrued interest is given as:

$$AI = C\frac{t_0 - t_p}{t_q - t_p} = 25\left(\frac{155}{180}\right) = \$21.53$$

Finally, if we used the 30/360 convention, then,

$t_0 - t_p = 30 \times 5$ (five complete months times 30 days each month) + 2 (number of actual days from November 1 to November 3) = 152, and
$t_q - t_p$ = Equals $360/k = 360/2 = 180$

The accrued interest is given as:

$$AI = C\frac{t_0 - t_p}{t_q - t_p} = 25\left(\frac{152}{180}\right) = \$21.11$$

Now, assume that the bond in the previous example is a U.S. Treasury bond quoted at the price of 95-08 on November 3. Since Treasury bonds are quoted with the accuracy of 32 seconds to a dollar, a quoted price of $95.08 corresponds to a price of $95.25 on a $100 face value, and hence a price of $952.50 for the $1,000 face value. Using an Actual/Actual day count basis, the accrued interest on November 3 is $21.17, giving a cash price equal to:

$$P = \text{Quoted Price} + AI = 952.5 + 21.17 = \$973.67$$

It is not the cash price, but the quoted price that depends on the specific day-count convention being applied. Any increase (decrease) in the accrued interest due to a specific day-count convention used is exactly offset by a corresponding decrease (increase) in the quoted price, so that the cash price remains unchanged. Since the TISR is computed using cash prices, it is also independent of the day-count convention used. It is necessary to know the day-count convention in order to obtain the cash price using the quoted price and the accrued interest.

Yield to Maturity

The yield to maturity is given as that discount rate that makes the sum of the discounted values of all future cash flows (either of coupons or principal) from the bond equal to the cash price of the bond, that is:[2]

$$P = \sum_{j=1}^{N} \frac{C}{e^{y \times t_j}} + \frac{F}{e^{y \times t_N}} \tag{3.6}$$

Equation 3.6 is a tautology. Comparing equations 3.6 and 3.2, the yield to maturity can be seen as a complex weighted average of zero-coupon rates. Given a nonflat term structure of zero-coupon rates, bonds with same maturity but different coupon rates will generally have different yields to maturity, due to the *coupon effect*. The coupon effect makes the term structure of yields on coupon bonds lower (higher) than the term structure of zero-coupon rates, when the latter is sloping upward (downward).

Spot Rates versus Forward Rates

The forward rate between the future dates t_1 and t_2 is the annualized interest rate that can be contractually locked in today on an investment to be made at time t_1 that matures at time t_2. The forward rate is different from the future rate in that the forward rate is known with certainty today, while the future rate can be known only in the future.

Consider two investment strategies. The first strategy requires making a riskless investment of \$1 at a future date t_1, which is redeemed at future date t_2 for an amount equal to:

$$1 \times e^{f(t_1, t_2)(t_2 - t_1)} \tag{3.7}$$

The variable $f(t_1, t_2)$ which is *known today* is defined as the continuously compounded annualized forward rate, between dates t_1 and t_2.

Now consider a second investment strategy that requires shorting today (which is the same as borrowing and immediately selling) a $1 face value riskless zero-coupon bond that matures at time t_1 and investing the proceeds from the short sale in a two-year riskless investment maturing at time t_2. The proceeds of the short sale equal $P(t_1)$, the current price of $1 face value riskless zero-coupon bond that matures at time t_1. This investment costs nothing today, requires covering the short position at time t_1 by paying $1, and receiving the future value of the proceeds from the short sale, which at time t_2 equals:

$$P(t_1)e^{y(t_2)\times t_2} = \frac{e^{y(t_2)\times t_2}}{e^{y(t_1)\times t_1}} \tag{3.8}$$

where $y(t_1)$ and $y(t_2)$ are zero-coupon rates for terms t_1 and t_2. Since both riskless investment strategies require $1 investment at time t_1, and cost nothing today, the value of these investment strategies at time t_2 must be identical. This implies that the compounded value in expression 3.7 must equal the compounded value in equation 3.8, or:

$$e^{f(t_1,t_2)(t_2-t_1)} = \frac{e^{y(t_2)\times t_2}}{e^{y(t_1)\times t_1}} \tag{3.9}$$

Taking logarithms on both sides of the equation 3.9 and further simplification we obtain:

$$f(t_1,t_2) = \frac{y(t_2)t_2 - y(t_1)t_1}{t_2 - t_1} \tag{3.10}$$

Rearranging the terms:

$$f(t_1,t_2) = y(t_2) + \frac{y(t_2) - y(t_1)}{t_2 - t_1} t_1 \tag{3.11}$$

Equation 3.11 implies that if the term structure of zero-coupon rates is upward (downward) sloping, then forward rates will be higher (lower) than zero-coupon rates.

TABLE 3.1 Computing Implied Forward Rates

Maturity t	Spot Rates $y(t)$	Forward Rates $f(t-1, t)$
1	5.444	
2	5.762	6.080
3	5.994	6.457
4	6.165	6.679
5	6.294	6.811
6	6.393	6.888
7	6.471	6.934
8	6.532	6.961
9	6.581	6.977
10	6.622	6.987

Example 3.2 Table 3.1 illustrates the calculation of forward rates. The second column of the table shows the continuously compounded zero-coupon rates for terms ranging from 1 to 10 years. The third column gives the one-year forward rates implied by the zero-coupon rates.

For example the forward rate $f(2, 3)$ is computed using equation 3.10 as follows:

$$f(2,\ 3) = \frac{0.05994 \times 3 - 0.05762 \times 2}{3 - 2} = 0.06457 = 6.457\% \tag{3.12}$$

All forward rates derived in the previous example apply over the discrete time interval of one year. In general, forward rates can be computed for any arbitrary interval length. *Instantaneous forward rates* are obtained when the interval length becomes infinitesimally small. Mathematically, the instantaneous forward rate $f(t)$, is the annualized rate of return locked in today, on money to be invested at a future time t, for an infinitesimally small interval $dt \to 0$, and can be derived using equation 3.11, by substituting $t_2 = t + dt$ and $t_1 = t$:

$$f(t) = \lim_{dt \to 0} f(t,\ t + dt) = y(t) + \frac{\partial y(t)}{\partial t} t \tag{3.13}$$

The instantaneous forward rates can be interpreted as the marginal cost of borrowing for an infinitesimal period of time beginning at time t. Using equation 3.13, the term structure of instantaneous forward rates (or simply forward rates, from here on) can be derived from the term structure of zero-coupon rates.

Equation 3.14 can be expressed in an integral form as follows:[3]

$$y(t) \times t = \int_0^t f(s)ds \tag{3.14}$$

or

$$y(t) = \frac{\int_0^t f(s)ds}{t} \tag{3.15}$$

Equation 3.15 gives a nice relationship between zero-coupon rates and forward rates. It implies that the zero-coupon rate for term t is an average of the instantaneous forward rates beginning from term 0 to term t. This relationship suggests that forward rates should be in general *more volatile* than zero-coupon rates, especially at the longer end. Lekkos (1999) finds this to be empirically true. An excellent visual exposition of the difference in the volatilities of the zero-coupon yields and those of the instantaneous forward rates is given by the Excel term structure "movie," based on McCulloch and Kwon (1993) term structure data in the spreadsheet model for this chapter. The high volatility of long-maturity forward rates has important implications for advanced term structure models, such as the Heath, Jarrow, and Morton (HJM; 1992) forward rate model given in the second volume of this book series.

Term Structure Hypotheses

Figure 3.2 shows different shapes of the term structure of zero-coupon yields. The steep shape of the term structure typically occurs at the trough of a business cycle, when after many interest rate reductions by the central bank, the economy seems poised for a recovery in the future, making the longer maturity rates significantly higher than the shorter maturity rates. The inverted shape of the term structure typically occurs at the peak of a business cycle, when after many interest rate increases by the central bank, the economic boom or a bubble may be followed by a recession or a depression, making the longer interest rates lower than the shorter rates. The

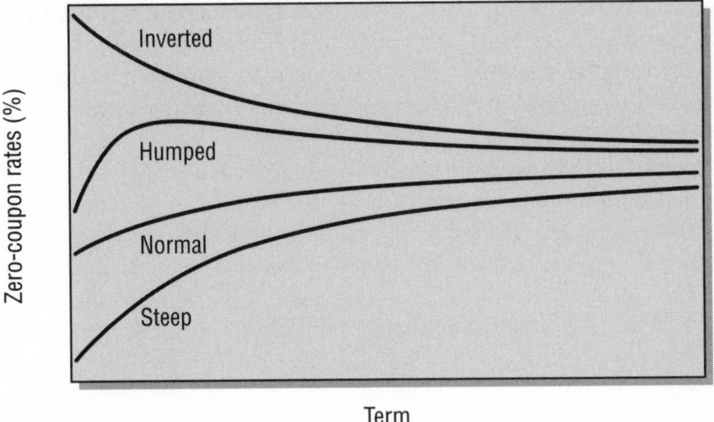

FIGURE 3.2 Basic Shapes of the Term Structure

humped shape typically occurs when the market participants expect a short economic recovery followed by another recession. The normal shape is generally indicative of an economy that is expanding normally.

The previous discussion relating economic expectations to the shapes of the term structure suggests that these shapes contain information about the expectations of the evolution of future interest rates. For example, a steep term structure suggests that future short rates will be higher than the current short rates. However, expectations don't fully explain why term structures have different shapes at different times. Other important variables are risk and liquidity premiums demanded by fixed-income investors in order to invest in bonds of different maturities. Finally, the demand and supply variables in different maturity segments may also explain the shape of the term structure. Since many variables affect the shape of the term structure, alternative hypotheses have been advanced in the fixed-income literature that highlight the individual roles played by these variables.

The four basic term structure hypotheses are given as (1) the expectation hypothesis, (2) the liquidity premium hypothesis, (3) the market segmentation hypothesis, and (4) the preferred habitat hypothesis. More than a century ago, Fisher (1896) introduced the *expectation hypothesis,* and many versions of this hypothesis have appeared since then. Two basic ideas behind expectations hypothesis are (1) expectations about future short rates are reflected in current forward rates and (2) expected holding period returns are the same for bonds of different maturities. As pointed out by Cox, Ingersoll, and Ross (CIR; 1981), these statements are not consistent, and at least four different versions of expectations hypothesis exist in the literature.

The *unbiased* expectations hypothesis states that current forward rates are equal to the expectations of future short rates. The *return-to-maturity* expectations hypothesis states that the total return on a bond maturing at a given future date is equal to the expected return on the investment in a money market account until that date. The *yield-to-maturity* expectations hypothesis states that the yield to maturity of a bond is equal to the expected return per period on an investment in the money market account until the bond maturity date. Finally, the *local* expectations hypothesis states that the instantaneous return on all bonds are equal to the current short rate. CIR demonstrate that all four versions of the expectations hypothesis are consistent with each other in a world of certainty, but they become inconsistent in a world of uncertainty. Further, they show that only the local expectations hypothesis is consistent with an *arbitrage-free* equilibrium under uncertainty. The local expectations hypothesis is consistent with virtually all continuous-time term structure models discussed in the second volume of this book series.[4] The above four versions of expectations hypothesis are the *pure* versions of this theory. Campbell (1986) shows that under the more general expectations hypothesis, the term premiums can be constant (and not zero as under the pure expectations hypothesis) across maturity.

Hicks (1939) introduced the *liquidity premium hypothesis,* which postulates that the return on long-term bonds must exceed the expected returns on short-term bonds in order to compensate the investors for the higher price volatility of long-term bonds. Consequently, even when the market expects the future short rates to remain at the current levels, the term structure should be an increasing function of maturity. The liquidity premium hypothesis can explain the normal and steep shapes of the term structure in Figure 3.2 even if the forward rates are not unbiased expectations of the future short rates.

The *market segmentation hypothesis,* suggested by Culbertson (1957), states that different market participants have a preference for bonds with maturities within different maturity buckets. Due to the segmentation of the demand and supply conditions in the different maturity market segments, the bond prices and interest rates in the different segments become relatively independent. As a consequence, the term structures and the discount function are not necessarily smooth and continuous between the different segments and so the implied forward rates at these points have little informative content.

Modigliani and Sutch (1966) introduced the *preferred habitat hypothesis,* according to which even though investors might prefer bonds with specific maturities, they should be willing to shift to other maturities if the differences in yields compensate them. Therefore, the different market segments are interdependent and the term structure and the discount function are smooth functions. The preferred habitat hypothesis is consistent with all shapes of the term structure shown in Figure 3.2.

Many researchers have tested the general expectations hypothesis and found it to be false. For example, Campbell and Shiller (1991) and Fama and Bliss (1987) find that term premiums are not constant, but predictable using forward rates and term spreads. These finding support the main implications of the liquidity premium hypothesis and/or the preferred habitat hypothesis.

TERM STRUCTURE ESTIMATION: THE BASIC METHODS

Estimation of the term structure involves obtaining zero-coupon rates, or forward rates, or discount functions from a set of coupon bond prices. Generally, this requires fitting a parsimonious functional form that is flexible in capturing stylized facts regarding the shape of the term structure. A good term structure estimation method should satisfy the following requirements:

- The method ensures a suitable fitting of the data.
- The estimated zero-coupon rates and the forward rates remain positive over the entire maturity spectrum.
- The estimated discount functions, and the term structures of zero-coupon rates and forward rates are continuous and smooth.
- The method allows asymptotic shapes for the term structures of zero-coupon rates and forward rates at the long end of the maturity spectrum.

The commonly used term structure estimation methods are given as the bootstrapping method, the polynomial/exponential spline methods of McCulloch (1971, 1975) and Vasicek and Fong (1982), and the exponential functional form methods of Nelson and Siegel (1987) and Svensson (1994). Extensions of the above methods are given as the heteroscedastic error correction based model of Chambers, Carleton, and Waldman (1984), and the error weighing models such as the B-spline method of Steely (1991) and the penalized spline methods of Fisher, Nychka, and Zervos (1995) and Jarrow, Ruppert, and Yu (2004). In the following section, we focus on three commonly used term structure estimation methods given as the bootstrapping method, the McCulloch polynomial cubic-spline method, and the Nelson and Siegel exponential-form method.

Bootstrapping Method

The bootstrapping method consists of iteratively extracting zero-coupon yields using a sequence of increasing maturity coupon bond prices. This method requires the existence of at least one bond that matures at each bootstrapping date. To illustrate this method, consider a set of K bonds that pay semiannual coupons. The shortest maturity bond is a six-month bond, which by definition does not have any intermediate coupon payments between now and six months, since coupons are paid semiannually. Using equation 3.2, the price of this bond is given as:

$$P(0.5) = \frac{C_{0.5} + F_{0.5}}{e^{y(0.5)0.5}} \tag{3.16}$$

where $F_{0.5}$ is the face value of the bond payable at the maturity of 0.5 years, $C_{0.5}$ is the semiannual coupon payment at the maturity, and $y(0.5)$ is the annualized six-month zero-coupon yield (under continuously compounding). The six-month zero-coupon yield can be calculated by taking logarithms of both sides of equation 3.16, and simplifying as follows:

$$y(0.5) = \frac{1}{0.5}\ln\left[\frac{F_{0.5} + C_{0.5}}{P(0.5)}\right] \tag{3.17}$$

To compute the one-year zero-coupon yield, we can use the price of a one-year coupon bond as follows:

$$P(1) = \frac{C_1}{e^{y(0.5)0.5}} + \frac{F_1 + C_1}{e^{y(1)}} \tag{3.18}$$

where F_1 is the face value of the bond payable at the bond's one-year maturity, C_1 is the semiannual coupon, which is paid at the end of 0.5 years and one year, and $y(1)$ is the annualized one-year zero-coupon yield. By rearranging the terms in equation 3.18 and taking logarithms, we get the one-year zero-coupon yield as follows:

$$y(1) = \ln\left[\frac{F_1 + C_1}{P(1) - \dfrac{C_1}{e^{y(0.5)0.5}}}\right] \tag{3.19}$$

Since we already know the six-month yield, $y(0.5)$ from equation 3.17, this can be substituted in equation 3.19 to solve for the one-year yield. Now, continuing in this manner, the six-month yield, $y(0.5)$, and the one-year yield, $y(1)$, can both be used to obtain the 1.5-year yield, $y(1.5)$, given the price of a 1.5-year maturity coupon bond. Following the same approach, the zero-coupon yields of all of the K maturities (corresponding to the maturities of the bonds in the sample) are computed iteratively using the zero-coupon yields of the previous maturities. The zero-coupon yields corresponding to the maturities that lie between these K dates can be computed by using linear or quadratic interpolation. Generally, about 15 to 30 bootstrapping maturities are sufficient in producing the whole term structure of zero-coupon yields.

Instead of solving the zero-coupon yields sequentially using an iterative approach as shown above, the following matrix approach can be used for obtaining a direct solution. Consider K bonds maturing at dates $t_1, t_2, \ldots, t_K$, and let CF_{it} be the total cash flow payments of the ith (for $i = 1, 2, 3, \ldots, K$) bond on the date t (for $t = t_1, t_2, \ldots, t_K$). Then the prices of the K bonds are given by the following system of K simultaneous equations:

$$\begin{pmatrix} P(t_1) \\ P(t_2) \\ \vdots \\ P(t_K) \end{pmatrix} = \begin{pmatrix} CF_{1t_1} & 0 & \cdots & 0 \\ CF_{2t_1} & CF_{2t_2} & \cdots & 0 \\ \vdots & \vdots & \vdots & \vdots \\ CF_{Kt_1} & CF_{Kt_2} & \cdots & CF_{Kt_K} \end{pmatrix} \begin{pmatrix} d(t_1) \\ d(t_2) \\ \vdots \\ d(t_K) \end{pmatrix} \tag{3.20}$$

Note that the upper triangle of the cash flow matrix on the right side of equation 3.20 has zero values. By multiplying both sides of equation 3.20 by the inverse of the cash flow matrix, the discount functions corresponding to maturities $t_1, t_2, \ldots, t_K$ can be computed as follows:

$$\begin{pmatrix} d(t_1) \\ d(t_2) \\ \vdots \\ d(t_K) \end{pmatrix} = \begin{pmatrix} CF_{1t_1} & 0 & \cdots & 0 \\ CF_{2t_1} & CF_{2t_2} & \cdots & 0 \\ \vdots & \vdots & \vdots & \vdots \\ CF_{Kt_1} & CF_{Kt_2} & \cdots & CF_{Kt_K} \end{pmatrix}^{-1} \begin{pmatrix} P(t_1) \\ P(t_2) \\ \vdots \\ P(t_K) \end{pmatrix} \tag{3.21}$$

This solution requires that the number of bonds equal the number of cash-flow maturity dates. The zero-coupon rates can be computed from the corresponding discount functions using equation 3.1.

TABLE 3.2 Bond Data for Bootstrapping Method

Bond #	Price ($)	Maturity (years)	Annual Coupon Rate (%)
1	96.60	1	2
2	93.71	2	2.5
3	91.56	3	3
4	90.24	4	3.5
5	89.74	5	4
6	90.04	6	4.5
7	91.09	7	5
8	92.82	8	5.5
9	95.19	9	6
10	98.14	10	6.5

Example 3.3 This example demonstrates the bootstrapping method using the 10 bonds given in Table 3.2. For expositional simplicity all bonds are assumed to make annual coupon payments.

Bond 1's price is given as follows:

$$96.60 = (2 + 100)e^{-y(1)\times 1}$$

which gives the one-year zero-coupon yield as:

$$y(1) = \ln\left[\frac{100 + 2}{96.60}\right] = 0.05439 = 5.439\%$$

Using the one-year yield of 5.439 percent to discount the first coupon payment from the two-year bond, the price of the two-year bond is given as:

$$93.71 = 2.5 \times e^{-0.05439\times 1} + (2.5 + 100)e^{-y(2)\times 2}$$

Solving for $y(2)$, we get,

$$y(2) = \frac{1}{2}\left[\frac{2.5 + 100}{93.71 - 2.5 \times e^{-0.05439\times 1}}\right] = 0.05762 = 5.762\% \qquad (3.22)$$

Following this iterative procedure, the zero-coupon rates for all 10 maturities can be computed. More directly, we can use the matrix solution given by equation 3.21, as follows:

$$\begin{pmatrix} d(1) \\ d(2) \\ d(3) \\ d(4) \\ d(5) \\ d(6) \\ d(7) \\ d(8) \\ d(9) \\ d(10) \end{pmatrix} = \begin{pmatrix} 102 & 0 & 0 & 0 & 0 & 0 & 0 & 0 & 0 & 0 \\ 2.5 & 102.5 & 0 & 0 & 0 & 0 & 0 & 0 & 0 & 0 \\ 3 & 3 & 103 & 0 & 0 & 0 & 0 & 0 & 0 & 0 \\ 3.5 & 3.5 & 3.5 & 103.5 & 0 & 0 & 0 & 0 & 0 & 0 \\ 4 & 4 & 4 & 4 & 104 & 0 & 0 & 0 & 0 & 0 \\ 4.5 & 4.5 & 4.5 & 4.5 & 4.5 & 104.5 & 0 & 0 & 0 & 0 \\ 5 & 5 & 5 & 5 & 5 & 5 & 105 & 0 & 0 & 0 \\ 5.5 & 5.5 & 5.5 & 5.5 & 5.5 & 5.5 & 5.5 & 105.5 & 0 & 0 \\ 6 & 6 & 6 & 6 & 6 & 6 & 6 & 6 & 106 & 0 \\ 6.5 & 6.5 & 6.5 & 6.5 & 6.5 & 6.5 & 6.5 & 6.5 & 6.5 & 106.5 \end{pmatrix}^{-1} \begin{pmatrix} 96.60 \\ 93.71 \\ 91.56 \\ 90.24 \\ 89.74 \\ 90.04 \\ 91.09 \\ 92.82 \\ 95.19 \\ 98.14 \end{pmatrix}$$

Multiplying the two matrices gives the solution as:

$$\begin{pmatrix} d(1) \\ d(2) \\ d(3) \\ d(4) \\ d(5) \\ d(6) \\ d(7) \\ d(8) \\ d(9) \\ d(10) \end{pmatrix} = \begin{pmatrix} 0.947 \\ 0.891 \\ 0.835 \\ 0.781 \\ 0.730 \\ 0.681 \\ 0.636 \\ 0.593 \\ 0.553 \\ 0.516 \end{pmatrix}$$

The zero-coupon rates are obtained from the corresponding discount functions by the following relationship derived from equation 3.1:

$$y(t) = \frac{-\ln d(t)}{t} \tag{3.23}$$

The zero-coupon rates are displayed in Figure 3.3. The points between the estimated zero-coupon yields are obtained by simple linear or quadratic interpolation, and thus the whole term structure of zero-coupon rates is obtained.

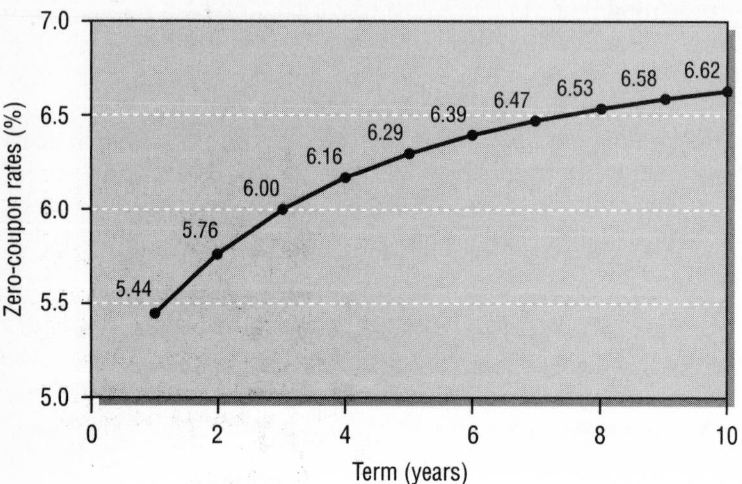

FIGURE 3.3 Zero-Coupon Rate Estimated Using the Bootstrapping Method

The bootstrapping method has two main limitations. First, since this method does not perform optimization, it computes zero-coupon yields that *exactly* fit the bond prices. This leads to overfitting since bond prices often contain idiosyncratic errors due to lack of liquidity, bid-ask spreads, special tax effects, and so on, and, hence, the term structure will not be necessarily smooth as shown in Figure 3.3. Second, the bootstrapping method requires ad-hoc adjustments when the number of bonds are not the same as the bootstrapping maturities, and when cash flows of different bonds do not fall on the same bootstrapping dates. In the following section, we consider alternatives to the bootstrapping method that impose specific functional forms on the term structure of zero-coupon yields or the discount functions.

Cubic-Spline Method

Consider the relationship between the *observed* price of a coupon bond maturing at time t_m, and the term structure of discount functions. Using equations 3.1 and 3.3, the price of this bond can be expressed as:

$$P(t_m) = \sum_{j=1}^{m} CF_j \times d(t_j) + \varepsilon \tag{3.24}$$

where CF_j is the total cash flow from the bond (i.e., coupon, face value, or both) on date t_j ($j = 1, 2, \ldots, m$). Since bond prices are observed with idiosyncratic errors, we need to estimate some functional form for the discount function that minimizes these errors. We face two problems in doing this. First, the discount functions may be highly nonlinear, such that we may need a high-dimensional function to make the approximation work. Second, the error terms in equation 3.24 may increase with the maturity of the bonds, since longer maturity bonds have higher bid-ask spreads, lower liquidity, and so on. Due to this heteroscedasticity of errors, estimation of the discount function using approaches such as least squares minimization, generally fits well at long maturities, but provides a very poor fit at short maturities (see McCulloch, 1971, and Chambers, Carleton, and Waldman, 1984).

The cubic-spline method addresses the first issue by dividing the term structure in many segments using a series of points that are called *knot points*. Different functions of the same class (polynomial, exponential, etc.) are then used to fit the term structure over these segments. The family of functions is constrained to be continuous and smooth around each knot point to ensure the continuity and smoothness of the fitted curves, using spline methods. McCulloch pioneered the application of splines to term structure estimation by using quadratic polynomial splines in 1971 and cubic polynomial splines in 1975. The cubic-spline method remains popular among practitioners and is explained next.

Consider a set of K bonds with maturities of $t_1, t_2, \ldots, t_K$ years. The range of maturities is divided into $s - 2$ intervals defined by $s - 1$ knot points $T_1, T_2, \ldots, T_{s-1}$, where $T_1 = 0$ and $T_{s-1} = t_K$. A cubic polynomial spline of the discount function $d(t)$ is defined by the following equation:

$$d(t) = 1 + \sum_{i=1}^{s} \alpha_i g_i(t) \tag{3.25}$$

where $g_1(t), g_2(t), \ldots, g_s(t)$ define a set of s basis piecewise cubic functions and $\alpha_1, \ldots, \alpha_s$ are unknown parameters that must be estimated.

Since the discount factor for time 0 is 1 by definition, we have:

$$g_i(0) = 0 \quad i = 1, 2, \ldots, s \tag{3.26}$$

The continuity and smoothness of the discount function within each interval is ensured by the polynomial functional form of each $g_i(t)$. The continuity and smoothness at the knot points is ensured by the requirement that the polynomial functions defined over adjacent intervals (T_{i-1}, T_i)

and (T_i, T_{i+1}) have a common value and common first and second derivatives at T_i. These constraints lead to the following definitions for the set of basis functions $g_1(t), g_2(t), \ldots, g_s(t)$:

Case 1: $i < s$

$$g_i(t) = \begin{cases} 0 & t < T_{i-1} \\ \dfrac{(t-T_{i-1})^3}{6(T_i - T_{i-1})} & T_{i-1} \le t < T_i \\ \dfrac{(T_i - T_{i-1})^2}{6} + \dfrac{(T_i - T_{i-1})(t-T_i)}{2} + \dfrac{(t-T_i)^2}{2} - \dfrac{(t-T_i)^3}{6(T_{i+1} - T_i)} & T_i \le t < T_{i+1} \\ (T_{i+1} - T_{i-1})\left(\dfrac{2T_{i+1} - T_i - T_{i-1}}{6} + \dfrac{t - T_{i+1}}{2}\right) & t \ge T_{i+1} \end{cases} \quad (3.27)$$

Case 2: $i = s$

$$g_i(t) = t$$

Substituting equation 3.25 into equation 3.24, we can rewrite the price of the bond maturing at date t_m as follows:

$$P(t_m) = \sum_{j=1}^{m} CF_j \left(1 + \sum_{i=1}^{s} \alpha_i g_i(t_j)\right) + \varepsilon \quad (3.28)$$

By rearranging the terms, we obtain:

$$P(t_m) - \sum_{j=1}^{m} CF_j = \sum_{i=1}^{s} \alpha_i \sum_{j=1}^{m} CF_j g_i(t_j) + \varepsilon \quad (3.29)$$

The estimation of the discount function requires searching the unknown parameters, $\alpha_1, \alpha_2, \ldots, \alpha_s$ to minimize the sum of squared errors across all bonds. Since equation 3.29 is linear with respect to the parameters $\alpha_1, \alpha_2, \ldots, \alpha_s$, this can be achieved by an ordinary least squares (OLS) regression.[5]

The above approach uses $s - 2$ number of maturity segments, $s - 1$ number of knotpoints, and s number of cubic polynomial functions. An intuitive choice for the maturity segments may be short-term, intermediate-term, and long-term, which gives three maturity segments of 0 to 1 years, 1 to 5 years, and 5 to 10 years, four knot points given as, 0, 1, 5, and 10 years, and five cubic polynomial functions.

McCulloch recommends choosing knot points such that there are approximately an equal number of data points (number of bonds' maturities) within each maturity segment. Using this approach, if the bonds are arranged in ascending order of maturity, that is, $t_1 \le t_2 \le t_3 \ldots \le t_K$, then the knot points are given as follows:

$$T_i = \begin{cases} 0 & i = 1 \\ t_h + \theta(t_{h+1} - t_h) & 2 \le i \le s-2 \\ t_K & i = s-1 \end{cases} \tag{3.30}$$

where h is an integer defined as:

$$h = INT\left[\frac{(i-1)K}{s-2}\right] \tag{3.31}$$

and the parameter θ is given as:

$$\theta = \frac{(i-1)K}{s-2} - h \tag{3.32}$$

McCulloch also suggests that the number of basis functions may be set to the integer nearest to the square root of the number of observations, that is:

$$s = Round\left[\sqrt{K}\,\right] \tag{3.33}$$

This choice of s has two desired properties. First, as the number of observations (bonds) increases, the number of basis functions increases. Second, as the number of observations increases, the number of observations within each interval increases, too.

Example 3.4 Consider the 15 bonds in Table 3.3. This set includes five more bonds with maturities ranging from 11 to 15 years in addition to the 10 bonds given in Example 3.3.

According to the McCulloch criterion, the number of basis function is given as:

TABLE 3.3 Bond Data for Cubic-Spline Method

Bond #	Price ($)	Maturity (years)	Annual Coupon Rate (%)
1	96.60	1	2
2	93.71	2	2.5
3	91.56	3	3
4	90.24	4	3.5
5	89.74	5	4
6	90.04	6	4.5
7	91.09	7	5
8	92.82	8	5.5
9	95.19	9	6
10	98.14	10	6.5
11	101.60	11	7
12	105.54	12	7.5
13	109.90	13	8
14	114.64	14	8.5
15	119.73	15	9

$$s = Round\left[\sqrt{15}\ \right] = 4$$

which implies that the number of knot points is $s - 1 = 3$, and the number of intervals for the maturity range that extends from 0 to 15 years is $s - 2 = 2$.

According to equation 3.30, the first knot point, $T_1 = 0$, and the last knot point $T_3 = 15$ years. The second knot point, T_2, is obtained as follows:

$$T_2 = t_h + \theta(t_{h+1} - t_h) \tag{3.34}$$

where using equations 3.31 and 3.32, h and θ are given as:

$$h = INT\left[\frac{(i-1)K}{s-2}\right] = INT\left[\frac{(2-1)\times 15}{4-2}\right] = INT[7.5] = 7$$

and

$$\theta = \frac{(i-1)K}{s-2} - h = \frac{(2-1)\times 15}{4-2} - 7 = 0.5$$

Also, using Table 3.3, $t_7 = 7$ and $t_8 = 8$. Substituting the values of h, θ, t_7, and t_8, given above in equation 3.34, we get,

$$T_2 = 7 + 0.5 \times (8-7) = 7.5$$

Hence, the three knot points are $T_1 = 0$, $T_2 = 7.5$, and $T_3 = 15$. The three knot points divide the maturity spectrum into two segments, 0 to 7.5 year and 7.5 years to 15 years. The number of basis functions is given as $s = 4$. Using equation 3.27, these functions are given as follows:

$$g_1(t) = \begin{cases} \dfrac{t^2}{2} - \dfrac{t^3}{6T_2} & T_1 \le t < T_2 \\ T_2\left(\dfrac{T_2}{3} + \dfrac{t-T_2}{2}\right) & t \ge T_2 \end{cases}$$

$$g_2(t) = \begin{cases} \dfrac{t^3}{6T_2} & T_1 \le t < T_2 \\ \dfrac{T_2^2}{6} + \dfrac{T_2(t-T_2)}{2} + \dfrac{(t-T_2)^2}{2} - \dfrac{(t-T_2)^3}{6(T_3-T_2)} & T_2 \le t \le T_3 \end{cases}$$

$$g_3(t) = \begin{cases} 0 & t < T_2 \\ \dfrac{(t-T_2)^3}{6(T_3-T_2)} & T_2 \le t \le T_3 \end{cases}$$

$$g_4(t) = t \quad \text{for all } t$$

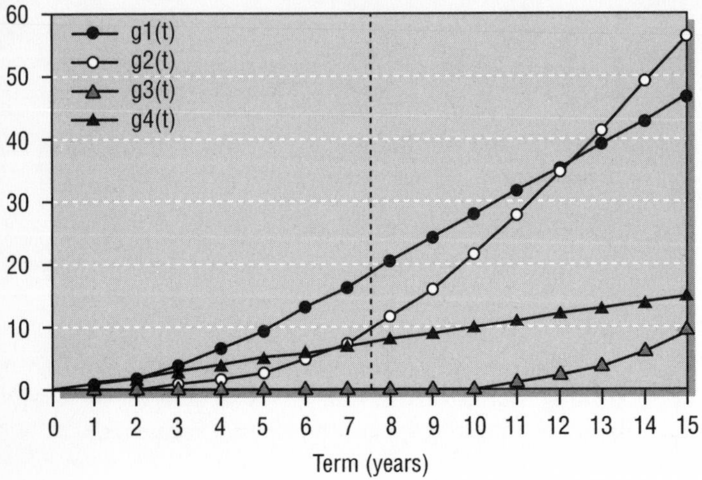

FIGURE 3.4 Basis Functions of the Discount Function

The shapes of these basis functions are shown in Figure 3.4. The vertical line divides the maturity range into the two segments. As can be seen, these basis functions ensure continuity and smoothness at the knot points. The discount function is given as a linear weighted average of the basis functions as follows:

$$d(t) = 1 + \alpha_1 g_1(t) + \alpha_2 g_2(t) + \alpha_3 g_3(t) + \alpha_4 g_4(t)$$

The parameters α_1, α_2, α_3, and α_4 are estimated using an OLS linear regression model given as:

$$P(t_m) - \sum_{j=1}^{m} CF_j = \alpha_1 \left[\sum_{j=1}^{m} CF_j g_1(t_j) \right] + \alpha_2 \left[\sum_{j=1}^{m} CF_j g_2(t_j) \right] + \alpha_3 \left[\sum_{j=1}^{m} CF_j g_3(t_j) \right] + \alpha_4 \left[\sum_{j=1}^{m} CF_j g_4(t_j) \right] + \varepsilon$$

Using the bond data in Table 3.3, the estimated values of the parameters are:

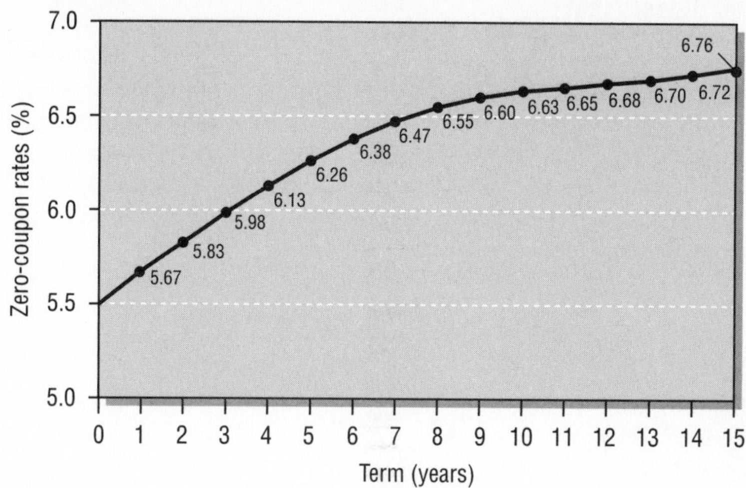

FIGURE 3.5 Estimated Zero-Coupon Rates Using Cubic-Spline Method

$$\alpha_1 = -0.00035 \qquad \alpha_2 = 0.00347$$

$$\alpha_3 = 0.00095 \qquad \alpha_4 = -0.05501$$

The discount function is obtained using the above four parameter values and the four basis functions. The zero-coupon rates are obtained from the discount function using equation 3.23, and are displayed in Figure 3.5.

A potential criticism of the cubic-spline method is the sensitivity of the discount function to the location of the knot points. Different knot points result in variations in the discount function, which can be sometimes significant. Also, too many knot points may lead to overfitting of the discount function. So, one must be careful in the selection of both the number and the placing of the knot points. Another shortcoming of cubic-splines is that they give unreasonably curved shapes for the term structure at the long end of the maturity spectrum, a region where the term structure must have very little curvature. Finally, the OLS regression used for the estimation of the parameters in equation 3.29, gives the same weights to the price errors of the bonds with heterogeneous characteristics, such as liquidity, bid-ask spreads, maturity. Some of these criticisms are addressed in the last section of this chapter, which introduces more advanced term structure estimation models.

Nelson and Siegel Model

The Nelson and Siegel (1987) model uses a single exponential functional form over the entire maturity range. An advantage of this model is that it allows the estimated term structure to behave asymptotically over the long end. Due to the asymptotic behavior of the term structure, many academics and practitioners prefer the Nelson and Siegel model to the cubic-spline models. Nelson and Siegel suggest a parsimonious parameterization of the instantaneous forward rate curve given as follows:

$$f(t) = \alpha_1 + \alpha_2 e^{-t/\beta_1} + \alpha_3 e^{-t/\beta_2} \tag{3.35}$$

Finding this model to be overparameterized, Nelson and Siegel consider a special case of this model given as:[6]

$$f(t) = \alpha_1 + \alpha_2 e^{-t/\beta} + \alpha_3 \frac{t}{\beta} e^{-t/\beta} \tag{3.36}$$

The zero-coupon rates consistent with the forward rates given by the above equation can be solved using equation 3.15, as follows:

$$y(t) = \alpha_1 + (\alpha_2 + \alpha_3)\frac{\beta}{t}\left(1 - e^{-t/\beta}\right) - \alpha_3 e^{-t/\beta} \tag{3.37}$$

The Nelson and Siegel model is based on four parameters. These parameters can be interpreted as follows:

- $\alpha_1 + \alpha_2$ is the instantaneous short rate, that is, $\alpha_1 + \alpha_2 = y(0) = f(0)$.
- α_1 is the consol rate. It gives the asymptotic value of the term structure of both the zero-coupon rates and the instantaneous forward rates, that is, $\alpha_1 = y(\infty) = f(\infty)$.
- The spread between the consol rate and the instantaneous short rate is $-\alpha_2$, which can be interpreted as the slope of the term structure of zero-coupon rates as well as the term structure of forward rates.
- α_3 affects the curvature of the term structure over the intermediate terms. When $\alpha_3 > 0$, the term structure attains a maximum value leading to a concave shape, and when $\alpha_3 < 0$, the term structure attains minimum value leading to a convex shape.
- ß > 0, is the speed of convergence of the term structure toward the consol rate. A lower ß value accelerates the convergence of the term

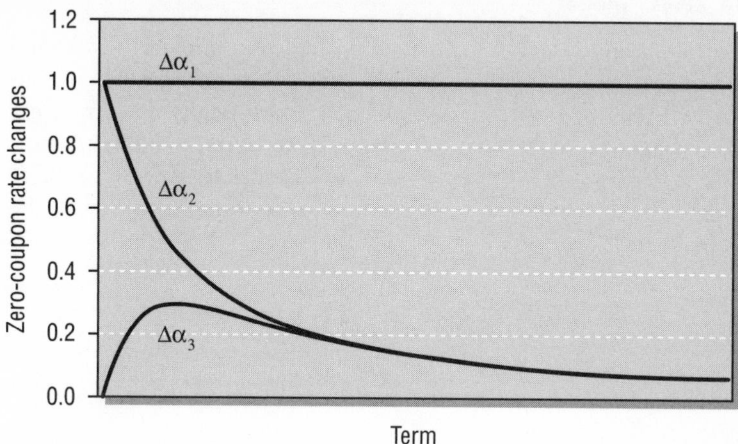

FIGURE 3.6 Influence of the Alpha Parameters of Nelson and Siegel on the Term Structure of Zero-Coupon Rates

structure toward the consol rate, while a higher ß value moves the hump in the term structure closer to longer maturities.

Figure 3.6 illustrates how the parameters α_1, α_2, and α_3, affect the shape of the term structure of zero-coupon rates (given a constant ß = 1). A change in α_1 can be interpreted as the height change, a change in α_2 can be interpreted as the slope change (though this parameter also affects the curvature change slightly), and a change in α_3 can be interpreted as the curvature change in the term structure of zero-coupon rates.

Figure 3.7 demonstrates that Nelson and Siegel method is consistent with a variety of term structure shapes, including monotonic and humped, and allows asymptotic behavior of forward and spot rates at the long end.

The discount function associated with the term structures in 3.36 and 3.37 is given as:

$$d(t) = e^{-\alpha_1 t - \beta(\alpha_2+\alpha_3)\left(1-e^{-t/\beta}\right)+\alpha_3 t e^{-t/\beta}} \tag{3.38}$$

Substituting this functional form into the pricing formula for a coupon-bearing bond, we have:

$$P(t_m) = \sum_{j=1}^{m} CF_j e^{-\alpha_1 t_j - \beta(\alpha_2+\alpha_3)\left(1-e^{-t_j/\beta}\right)+\alpha_3 t_j e^{-t_j/\beta}} \tag{3.39}$$

where t_m is the bond's maturity and CF_j is the cash flow of the bond at time t_j.

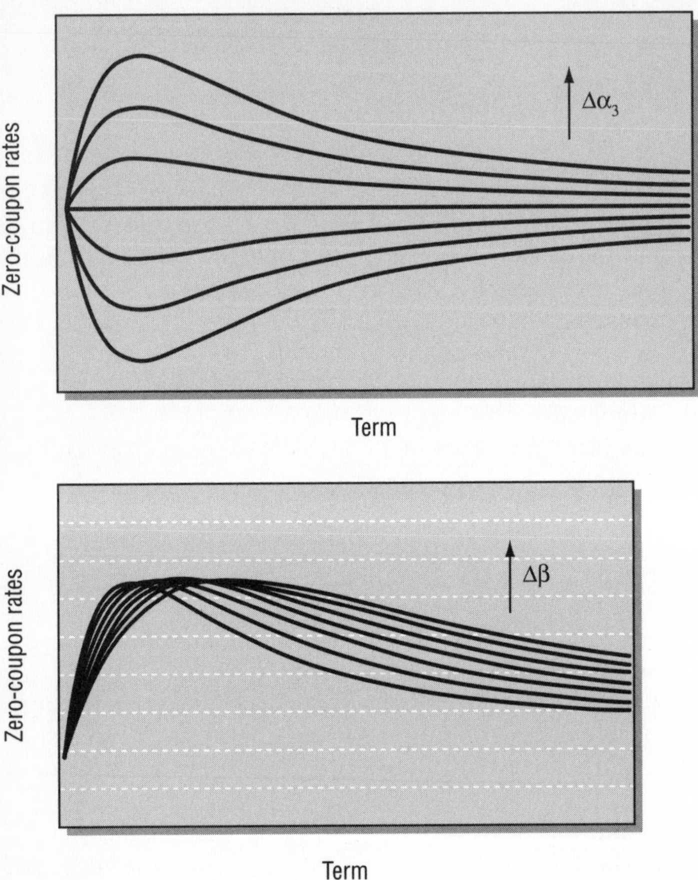

FIGURE 3.7 Influence of the Curvature and Hump Positioning Parameters of Nelson and Siegel on the Spot Curve

The parameters in equation 3.39 can be estimated by minimizing the sum of squared errors, that is:

$$\underset{\alpha_1,\alpha_2,\alpha_3,\beta}{Min} \sum_{i=1}^{K} \varepsilon_i^2 \tag{3.40}$$

subject to the following constraints:

$$\begin{aligned} \alpha_1 &> 0 \\ \alpha_1 + \alpha_2 &> 0 \\ \beta &> 0 \end{aligned} \tag{3.41}$$

where ε_i is the difference between the ith bond's market price and its theoretical price given by equation 3.39. The first constraint in equation 3.41 requires that the consol rate remain positive; the second constraint requires that the instantaneous short rate remain positive; finally, the third constraint ensures the convergence of the term structure to the consol rate.

Since the bond pricing equation 3.39 is a nonlinear function, the four parameters are estimated using a nonlinear optimization technique. As nonlinear optimization techniques are usually sensitive to the starting values of the parameters, these values must be carefully chosen.

Example 3.5 Reconsider the bond data in Table 3.3. The initial values of the parameters may be guessed using some logical approximations. For example, the starting value for the parameter α_1, which indicates the asymptotic value of the term structure of zero-coupon rates, may be set as the yield to maturity of the longest bond in the sample. In Table 3.3, the longest bond is Bond 15, whose continuously compounded yield to maturity can be calculated using the "solver" function in Excel and is given as 6.629 percent.[7]

The starting value for the parameter α_2, which is the difference between the instantaneous short rate and the consol rate, may be set as the difference between the yields to maturity of the shortest maturity bond and the longest maturity bond in the sample. In Table 3.3, this corresponds to the difference between the yields to maturity of Bond 1 and Bond 15, given as $5.439 - 6.629 = -1.19$ percent.

The starting values of the other two parameters, α_3 and ß, which are associated with the curvature of the term structure and the speed of convergence toward the consol rate, respectively, are difficult to guess. Therefore, it might be necessary to consider a grid of different starting values. The feasible range for these parameters for realistic term structure data are $-10 \le \alpha_3 \le 10$, and ß ranging from the shortest maturity and the longest maturity in the sample of bonds. Hence, using Table 3.3, $1 \le ß \le 15$.

Using the data in Table 3.3, we obtain the following values of the parameters using nonlinear optimization:

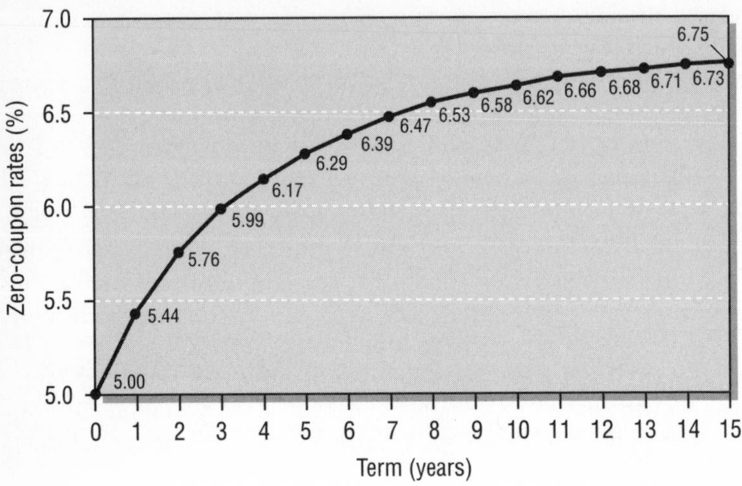

FIGURE 3.8 Estimated Zero-Coupon Rates Using the Nelson and Siegel Method

$$\alpha_1 = 0.07000 \quad \alpha_2 = -0.01999$$
$$\alpha_3 = 0.00129 \quad \beta = 2.02881$$

The corresponding term structure of zero-coupon rates is shown in Figure 3.8.

ADVANCE METHODS IN TERM STRUCTURE ESTIMATION

The advances in term structure estimation have centered around two issues. The first issue centers on the filtering criteria for the selection of bonds in the sample. Bond selection should be from the same risk class, so that maturity is the only distinguishing characteristic across bonds. If multiple bonds are available, then bonds with very low liquidity or unusually high bid-ask errors may be ignored. Also, bonds should be selected in such a way that the tax treatment is as homogenous as possible. Finally, bonds with distortions arising due to embedded options, such as call or put features should be excluded. The filtering criteria based on the discussed variables cannot be defined so tightly that the data reduction seriously compromises the estimation process.

The second issue deals with the pricing error-weighing schemes in the optimization process. Both the estimation of the cubic-spline model using the OLS regression in equation 3.29, and the estimation of the Nelson and Siegel model in equations 3.39 through 3.41, was done by the minimization of the sum of squared pricing errors. However, many alternative error-weighing schemes exist which lead to more robust estimates of the term structure.

Chambers, Carleton, and Waldman (1984) demonstrate that the errors between the fitted and actual prices increase with bond maturity, and so weighing the errors by the inverse of bond maturity after adjusting for a sample dependent parameter, allows the term structure of zero-coupon rates to be fitted well both at the long end and the short end. They found that using a single polynomial of sixth degree for the entire maturity range together with the heteroscedastic error correction, leads to a good fit of the term structure. However, since a sixth-degree polynomial has high instability at the long end (explodes to infinity for infinite maturity), researchers have looked for other alternatives to this model. For example, the heteroscedastic error correction suggested by Chambers, Carleton, and Waldman can also be applied to the exponential model of Nelson and Siegel, which remains stable at the long end.

It is well known that bond maturity is not an adequate measure of the relationship between price changes and yield changes. The percentage change in price is given as the *duration* of the bond times the change in its yield. Hence, given a price error, the corresponding yield error is reduced in proportion to the duration of the bond. So, instead of using bond maturity, Bliss (1997b) suggests weighting the price error by the inverse of the bond's duration. The weight assigned to the jth bond's price error can be expressed as follows:

$$\frac{D(j)^{-1}}{\sum_{i=1}^{K} D(i)^{-1}} \tag{3.42}$$

where K is the number of bonds in the sample, $D(i)$ is the duration of the ith bond.

Other error weighting schemes have focused on the bid-ask spreads, which also tend to be higher for longer maturity bonds. These alternatives can be applied both to the cubic-spline models and models similar to Nelson and Siegel's that use a single functional form for the term structure.

For example, instead of using errors defined as the difference between the true mean prices and the fitted prices, the errors can be defined as follows:

$$\varepsilon' = \begin{cases} P_A - P^* & P^* > P_A \\ P_B - P^* & P^* < P_B \\ 0 & \text{otherwise} \end{cases} \tag{3.43}$$

where P_A, P_B, and P^* are the bid quote, ask quote, and the fitted price, respectively. Using this definition, the errors will be nonzero, only if the fitted prices lie outside the bid-ask quotes.

An alternative consist of dividing the error of each bond's price by its bid-ask spread and raising this quotient to a penalty parameter λ with a value higher than 1 (typically 2), that is,

$$\varepsilon' = \left(\frac{P_i - P_i^*}{P_A - P_B}\right)^{\lambda} \tag{3.44}$$

where the sum of squares of the "penalized" error terms ε's across different bonds is minimized. If the error term in the numerator and the bid-ask spread in the denominator are equal, then the value of the quotient (i.e., the expression in the brackets) equals 1, and, hence, the penalty parameter does not alter the error term. If instead, the error is greater than the bid-ask spread, then the penalty parameter will increase the size of the error and more weight will be given to it in the estimation process. On the contrary, if the error is smaller than the bid-ask spread, then the penalty parameter will decrease the size of the error and less weight will be given to it in the estimation process.

Other penalty functions can also be considered. For example, Fisher, Nychka, and Zervos (1995) consider a nonparametric estimation method using a penalized spline model with the following objective function:

$$\sum_{i=1}^{K}\left(P_i - P_i^*\right)^2 + \lambda\int_0^{t_K} h''(t)dt \tag{3.45}$$

where K is the number of bonds in the sample data, t_K is the maximum terminal maturity of the bonds in the sample, $h(t)$ is the function to be fitted (the discount function, the forward curve or the spot curve) and λ is a positive penalty parameter. The parameter λ controls the trade-off between the smoothness of the fitted function and the goodness of fit. Jarrow, Ruppert, and Yu (2004) extend this model to the estimation of the term structures of corporate yields.

NOTES

1. When compounding is discrete, each $e^{y(t)t}$ is replaced by $(1 + APR(t)/k)^{tk}$, where $APR(t)$ is the annual percentage rate for term t compounded k times a year.

2. When compounding is discrete, each e^{yt} is replaced by $(1 + y/k)^{tk}$. Since cash price is used in equation 3.6, sometimes the discount rate is also called the "adjusted" yield to maturity.
3. Equation 3.14 is the solution to the first order differential equation given in 3.13. This can be verified by taking the partial derivative of both sides of equation 3.14, with respect to t.
4. Though more recently McCulloch (1993) and Fisher and Gilles (1998) have constructed economies in which various versions of the expectations hypothesis may be consistent even in a world of uncertainty, the empirically implausible nature of the short rate processes assumed in these papers suggest that these results are of interest only from a purely theoretical point of view.
5. As explained in the last section of this chapter, other functions can be optimized. McCulloch, indeed, proposed to weight the errors by the inverse of the buy-ask spread. This, however, precludes the use of OLS techniques.
6. The new function resembles a constant plus a Laguerre function, which consists of polynomials multiplied by exponentially decaying terms. This indicates a method for generalization to higher-order models.
7. Generally, the yield to maturity is reported using discrete compounding. This yield may be used as the starting value too, since it is quite close in value to its continuously compounded counterpart.

CHAPTER 4

M-Absolute and M-Square Risk Measures

Chapter 2 analyzed duration and convexity, the two commonly used risk measures for fixed-income securities. These measures are based on the restrictive assumption of parallel shifts in the term structure of interest rates. This chapter introduces two new risk measures that allow nonparallel shifts in the term structure of interest rates. Unlike Chapter 2 that derived risk measures using a flat term structure, these new risk measures allow interest rate movements to be consistent with empirically realistic shapes of the term structures illustrated in Chapter 3.

The first risk measure called *M-absolute* is both simple and powerful. It is simple in that only one risk measure is used to manage interest rate risk. It is powerful in that it reduces by more than half the residual interest rate risk not captured by the traditional duration model.

The second risk measure called *M-square* is a second-order risk measure similar to convexity. Though convexity leads to higher returns for large and parallel shifts in the term structure of interest rates, as pointed out in Chapter 2, this convexity view is somewhat naïve and has been challenged both theoretically and empirically in the fixed-income literature. An alternative view of convexity, which is based on a more realistic economic framework, relates convexity to *slope shifts* in the term structure of interest rates. This view of convexity is proposed by Fong and Vasicek (1983, 1984) through the introduction of the new risk measure, M-square, which is a linear transformation of convexity. Though both measures give similar information about the riskiness of a bond or a bond portfolio (since one is a linear function of the other), the developments of these two risk measures follow different paths. Convexity emphasizes the *gain* in the return on a portfolio, against large and parallel shifts in the term structure of interest rates. On the other hand, M-square emphasizes the *risk exposure* of a portfolio due to slope shifts in the term structure of interest rates. Hence, even though M-square is a linear function of convexity, the convexity view and the M-square view have different implications for bond risk analysis and portfolio management. This chapter shows how to reconcile the two different views, and investigates which view is supported by the empirical data.

MEASURING TERM STRUCTURE SHIFTS

Reconsider the price of a bond with a periodic coupon C paid k times a year, and face value F, given in equation 2.8 in Chapter 2, as follows:

$$P = \frac{C}{e^{yt_1}} + \frac{C}{e^{yt_2}} + \frac{C}{e^{yt_3}} + \cdots + \frac{C}{e^{yt_N}} + \frac{F}{e^{yt_N}} \tag{4.1}$$

where $t_1, t_2, t_3, \ldots, t_N$ are the N cash flow payment dates of the bond, and y is the continuously compounded *yield* of the bond. To derive general interest rate risk measures that allow large and nonparallel shifts in the term structure of interest rates the assumption of a single *yield* must be relaxed. As shown in Chapter 3, the term structure of interest rates can be defined in two equivalent ways—the term structure of *zero-coupon yields* and the term structure *of instantaneous forward rates*. The following two sections consider the shifts in these term structures of interest rates and show an equivalence of the relationship between them.

Shifts in the Term Structure of Zero-Coupon Yields

The term structure of zero-coupon yields can be applied to price the bond given in equation 4.1 as follows:

$$P = \frac{C}{e^{y(t_1)t_1}} + \frac{C}{e^{y(t_2)t_2}} + \frac{C}{e^{y(t_3)t_3}} + \cdots + \frac{C}{e^{y(t_N)t_N}} + \frac{F}{e^{y(t_N)t_N}} \tag{4.2}$$

where each cash flow is discounted by the zero-coupon yield $y(t)$ corresponding to its maturity t. The term structure of zero-coupon yields can be estimated from the quoted yields on coupon bonds (see Chapter 3 for details). We assume a simple polynomial form for the term structure of zero-coupon yields, as follows:[1]

$$y(t) = A_0 + A_1 \times t + A_2 \times t^2 + A_3 \times t^3 + \cdots + \tag{4.3}$$

where parameters A_0, A_1, A_2, and A_3, are the height, slope, curvature, and the rate of change of curvature (and so on) of the term structure. Though about five to six terms on the right side of equation 4.3 may be needed for adequately capturing the shape of the term structure of zero-coupon yields, the height, slope, and curvature parameters are the most important. Example 4.1 demonstrates how the term structure of zero-coupon yields can be used to price bonds.

Example 4.1 Assume the following values for the shape parameters:

$$A_0 = 0.06$$
$$A_1 = 0.01$$
$$A_2 = -0.001$$
$$A_3 = 0.0001$$

Substituting these in equation 4.3, the term structure is given as:

$$y(t) = 0.06 + 0.01 \times t - 0.001 \times t^2 + 0.0001 \times t^3$$

Using the previous equation, the different maturity yields can be given as:

$$y(0) = 0.06 + 0.01 \times 0 - 0.001 \times 0^2 + 0.0001 \times 0^3 = 0.06 = 6.00\% = A_0$$

Similarly, one, two, three, four, and five-year yields are given as follows:

$$y(1) = 0.06 + 0.01 \times 1 - 0.001 \times 1^2 + 0.0001 \times 1^3 = 0.0691 = 6.91\%$$
$$y(2) = 0.06 + 0.01 \times 2 - 0.001 \times 2^2 + 0.0001 \times 2^3 = 0.0768 = 7.68\%$$
$$y(3) = 0.06 + 0.01 \times 3 - 0.001 \times 3^2 + 0.0001 \times 3^3 = 0.0837 = 8.37\%$$
$$y(4) = 0.06 + 0.01 \times 4 - 0.001 \times 4^2 + 0.0001 \times 4^3 = 0.0904 = 9.04\%$$
$$y(5) = 0.06 + 0.01 \times 5 - 0.001 \times 5^2 + 0.0001 \times 5^3 = 0.0975 = 9.75\%$$

The assumed parameters define a rising shape for the term structure of zero-coupon yields. By changing the values of the shape parameters, one can define different types of shapes (e.g., rising, falling, humped) for the term structure.

We can price a \$1,000 face value, five-year, 10 percent annual coupon bond, by substituting these yields in equation 4.2:

$$P = \frac{100}{e^{0.0691}} + \frac{100}{e^{2\times 0.0768}} + \frac{100}{e^{3\times 0.0837}} + \frac{100}{e^{4\times 0.0904}} + \frac{100}{e^{5\times 0.0975}} + \frac{1000}{e^{5\times 0.0975}}$$

$$P = 93.32 + 85.76 + 77.79 + 69.66 + 61.42 + 614.16 = \$1{,}002.11$$

Now, let the term structure experience a noninfinitesimal and a nonparallel shift given as:

$$y'(t) = A_0' + A_1' \times t + A_2' \times t^2 + A_3' \times t^3 + \cdots + \tag{4.4}$$

where $A_0' = A_0 + \Delta A_0$
$A_1' = A_1 + \Delta A_1$
$A_2' = A_2 + \Delta A_2$
$A_3' = A_3 + \Delta A_3$

and ΔA_0, ΔA_1, ΔA_2, and ΔA_3, are the changes in the shape parameters.

Equation 4.4 can be rewritten as follows:

$$y'(t) = y(t) + \Delta y(t) \tag{4.5}$$

where

$$\Delta y(t) = \Delta A_0 + \Delta A_1 \times t + \Delta A_2 \times t^2 + \Delta A_3 \times t^3 + \cdots + \tag{4.6}$$

Equation 4.6 defines the shift in the term structure of zero-coupon yields as a function of the changes in height, slope, curvature, and other parameters.

Example 4.2 Reconsider the initial term structure of zero-coupon yields as defined in Example 4.1. Assume that the central bank increases the short rate ($y(0)$ may proxy for the short rate) by 50 basis points. This increase in the short rate signals a slowing down of the economy to the bond traders. Expecting slower growth and, hence, a lower inflation in the future, the bond traders start buying the medium term bonds (for simplicity, in our case, one year is a short term, and three to five years is a medium term). This leads to a negative slope shift of 20 basis points per year. The changes in curvature and other higher order parameters are zero. The shift in the term structure is given as follows (see equation 4.6):

$$\Delta y(t) = 0.005 - 0.002 \times t$$

The new term structure is given as follows:

$$\begin{aligned} y'(t) &= y(t) + \Delta y(t) \\ &= (0.06 + 0.01 \times t - 0.001 \times t^2 + 0.0001 \times t^3) + (0.005 - 0.002 \times t) \\ &= 0.065 + 0.008 \times t - 0.001 \times t^2 + 0.0001 \times t^3 \end{aligned}$$

Substituting different maturity values in these equations, the new zero-coupon yields and the changes in zero-coupon yields can be easily computed. These are given as follows:

$$\begin{array}{ll} y'(0) = 0.065 & \Delta y'(0) = 0.005 \\ y'(1) = 0.0721 & \Delta y'(1) = 0.003 \\ y'(2) = 0.0778 & \Delta y'(2) = 0.001 \\ y'(3) = 0.0827 & \Delta y'(3) = -0.001 \\ y'(4) = 0.0874 & \Delta y'(4) = -0.003 \\ y'(5) = 0.0925 & \Delta y'(5) = -0.005 \end{array}$$

The new bond price consistent with the new term structure of zero-coupon yields equals \$1,019.84. Hence, the bond price change equals (the original bond price in Example 4.1 was \$1,002.11):

$$\Delta P = \$1019.84 - \$1002.11 = \$17.73$$

Though the central bank increased the instantaneous short rate by 50 basis points, the five-year bond *gained* in value by approximately \$17.73. This happened because the long rates fell even as the short rates rose, leading to an overall increase in the bond price. This example demonstrates the inadequacy of using the simple duration model, which would have falsely predicted a decrease in the five-year bond's price, given an increase in the short rate (since it would assume a parallel increase in all yields). The percentage increase in the bond price is:

$$\Delta P/P = 17.73/1002.11 = 1.769\%$$

Shifts in Term Structure of Instantaneous Forward Rates

An alternate characterization of the term structure can be given by the instantaneous forward rates. In many instances, it is easier to work with instantaneous forward rates as certain interest rate risk measures and fixed-income derivatives are easier to model using forward rates. Though any shift in the term structure of zero-coupon yields corresponds to a *unique* shift in the term structure of instantaneous forward rates, the instantaneous forward rates are a lot more volatile than the zero-coupon yields, especially at the long end of the maturity spectrum. An intuitive reason behind this is that longer term zero-coupon yields are averages of instantaneous forward rates, and as is well known from statistics, an "average" of a set of variables has a lower volatility than the average volatility of the variables. A visual exposition of the difference in the volatility of zero-coupon yields and instantaneous forward rates is given by the Excel term structure *movie* in Chapter 3, based on McCulloch's term structure data.

As mentioned, a one-to-one correspondence exists between the term structure of zero-coupon yields and the term structure of instantaneous forward rates. The relationship between the two term structures can be given as follows (see Chapter 3):

$$y(t) \times t = \int_0^t f(s)ds \tag{4.7}$$

where $y(t)$ is the zero-coupon yield for term t, and $f(t)$ is the instantaneous forward rate for term t (which is the same as the forward rate that can be locked in at time zero for an infinitesimally small interval, t to $t + dt$). Hence, given the term structure of instantaneous forward rates, the term structure of zero-coupon yields can be obtained. It is also possible to obtain the term structure of instantaneous forward rates, given the term structure of zero-coupon yields, by taking the derivative of both sides of equation 4.7 as follows:

$$f(t) = t \times \partial y(t) / \partial t + y(t) \tag{4.8}$$

If the term structure of zero-coupon yields is rising, then $\partial y(t)/\partial t > 0$, and instantaneous forward rates will be higher than zero-coupon yields. Similarly, if the term structure of zero-coupon yields is falling, then $\partial y(t)/\partial t < 0$, and instantaneous forward rates will be lower than zero-coupon yields.

Equation 4.7 can be used to express the bond price in equation 4.2 as follows:

$$P = \frac{C}{e^{\int_0^1 f(s)ds}} + \frac{C}{e^{\int_0^2 f(s)ds}} + \frac{C}{e^{\int_0^3 f(s)ds}} + \cdots + \frac{C}{e^{\int_0^N f(s)ds}} + \frac{F}{e^{\int_0^N f(s)ds}} \tag{4.9}$$

To compute the bond price, we need an expression for the forward rates. Substituting equation 4.3 into equation 4.8, and taking the derivative of $y(t)$ with respect to t, the instantaneous forward rate can be given as:

$$f(t) = t(A_1 + 2A_2 \times t + 3A_3 \times t^2 + \cdots +) + (A_0 + A_1 \times t + A_2 \times t^2 + A_3 \times t^3 + \cdots +) \tag{4.10}$$

or

$$f(t) = A_0 + 2A_1 \times t + 3A_2 \times t^2 + 4A_3 \times t^3 + \cdots + \tag{4.11}$$

Substituting the forward rates given in equation 4.11 in equation 4.9 and computing the respective integrals, the bond price can be obtained using the term structure of instantaneous forward rates.

Both the term structure of zero-coupon yields and the term structure of instantaneous forward rates have the same height, but the term structure of forward rates has twice the slope, and thrice the curvature (and four times the rate of change of curvature, and so on) of the term structure of zero-coupon yields. This makes the term structure of forward rates more volatile, especially for longer maturities.

Using equation 4.11, the shift in the term structure of instantaneous forward rates can be given as follows:

$$\Delta f(t) = \Delta A_0 + 2\Delta A_1 \times t + 3\Delta A_2 \times t^2 + 4\Delta A_3 \times t^3 + \cdots + \tag{4.12}$$

where the new term structure is given as:

$$f'(t) = f(t) + \Delta f(t) \tag{4.13}$$

Example 4.3 In this example, we price the \$1,000 face value, five-year, 10 percent annual coupon bond using the instantaneous forward rates with the same term structure parameter values given in Example 4.1. Then, we obtain the new price of this bond using the instantaneous forward rates corresponding to the new parameter values given in Example 4.2. We expect to find the same prices as in Example 4.1 and Example 4.2, which used zero-coupon yields, demonstrating how instantaneous forward rates are used in practice.

Substituting the term structure parameter values from Example 4.1 into equation 4.11, we get:

$$f(t) = 0.06 + 0.02 \times t - 0.003 \times t^2 + 0.0004 \times t^3$$

This equation can be used to compute the following integral:

$$\begin{aligned}\int_0^t f(s)ds &= 0.06 \times t + 0.02 \times t^2 / 2 - 0.003 \times t^3 / 3 + 0.0004 \times t^4 / 4 \\ &= 0.06 \times t + 0.01 \times t^2 - 0.001 \times t^3 + 0.0001 + t^4\end{aligned}$$

Using the previous equation, the following five integrals can be computed:

$$\int_0^1 f(s)ds = 0.06 \times 1 + 0.01 \times 1^2 - 0.001 \times 1^3 + 0.0001 \times 1^4 = 0.0691$$
$$\int_0^2 f(s)ds = 0.06 \times 2 + 0.01 \times 2^2 - 0.001 \times 2^3 + 0.0001 \times 2^4 = 0.1536$$
$$\int_0^3 f(s)ds = 0.06 \times 3 + 0.01 \times 3^2 - 0.001 \times 3^3 + 0.0001 \times 3^4 = 0.2511$$
$$\int_0^4 f(s)ds = 0.06 \times 4 + 0.01 \times 4^2 - 0.001 \times 4^3 + 0.0001 \times 4^4 = 0.3616$$
$$\int_0^5 f(s)ds = 0.06 \times 5 + 0.01 \times 5^2 - 0.001 \times 5^3 + 0.0001 \times 5^4 = 0.4875$$

Substituting these integrals in equation 4.9:

$$P = \frac{\$100}{e^{0.0691}} + \frac{\$100}{e^{0.1536}} + \frac{\$100}{e^{0.2511}} + \frac{\$100}{e^{0.3616}} + \frac{\$100}{e^{0.4875}} + \frac{\$1000}{e^{0.4875}} = \$1002.11$$

The bond price is the same as Example 4.1. Similarly, we can obtain the new bond price using the new instantaneous forward rates. Substituting the values of $\Delta A_0 = 0.0050$, $\Delta A_1 = -0.0020$, $\Delta A_2 = 0.0$, and $\Delta A_3 = 0.0$, from Example 4.2 into equation 4.12 we get:

$$\Delta f(t) = 0.005 - 0.004 \times t$$

The new term structure of instantaneous forward rates is given as:

$$\begin{aligned} f'(t) &= f(t) + \Delta f(t) \\ &= (0.06 + 0.02 \times t - 0.003 \times t^2 + 0.0004 \times t^3) + (0.005 - 0.004 \times t) \\ &= 0.065 + 0.016 \times t - 0.003 \times t^2 + 0.0004 \times t^3 \end{aligned}$$

The previous equation can again be used to compute the integral:

$$\begin{aligned} \int_0^t f'(s)ds &= 0.065 \times t + 0.016 \times t^2 / 2 - 0.003 \times t^3 / 3 + 0.0004 \times t^4 / 4 \\ &= 0.065 \times t + 0.008 \times t^2 - 0.001 \times t^3 + 0.0001 \times t^4 \end{aligned}$$

Using this equation, the five integrals can be computed for $t = 1, 2, 3, 4$, and 5. Substituting these integrals in the bond price equation, the new price of the bond can be obtained as $1,019.84, which is identical to the new price given in Example 4.2 using zero-coupon yields.

M-ABSOLUTE VERSUS DURATION

Recall that duration is defined as the weighted average of the maturities of the cash flows of a bond, where weights are the present values of the cash flows, given as proportions of the bond's price:

$$D = \sum_{t=t_1}^{t=t_N} t \times w_t \tag{4.14}$$

Duration was defined in Chapter 2 using the bond's yield to maturity. Duration can be defined more generally using the entire term structure of interest rates, with the following weights in equation 4.14:

$$w_t = \left[\frac{CF_t}{e^{\int_0^t f(s)ds}} \right] / P = \left[\frac{CF_t}{e^{y(t) \cdot t}} \right] / P \tag{4.15}$$

where, CF_t is the cash flow occurring at time t. Duration computed using the yield to maturity is often known as the Macaulay duration, while duration computed using the entire term structure of interest rates, as in equations 4.14 and 4.15, is known as the Fisher and Weil (1971) duration. For brevity, we will refer to both duration definitions as simply "duration," though in this chapter we will be using the latter definition.

Duration gives the planning horizon, at which the *future value* of a bond or a bond portfolio remains immunized from an instantaneous, parallel shift in the term structure of interest rates. By setting a bond portfolio's duration to the desired planning horizon, the portfolio's future value is immunized against parallel term structure shifts. The M-absolute risk measure is defined as the weighted average of the absolute differences between cash flow maturities and the planning horizon, where weights are the present values of the bond's (or a bond portfolio's) cash flows, given as proportions of the bond's (or the bond portfolio's) price:

$$M^A = \sum_{t=t_1}^{t=t_N} |t - H| \times w_t \tag{4.16}$$

Unlike duration, the M-absolute measure is specific to a given planning horizon. The M-absolute risk measure selects the bond that minimizes the M-absolute of the bond portfolio. For the special case, when planning horizon is equal to zero, the M-absolute converges to the duration of the bond. To get more insight regarding the M-absolute risk measure, consider the lower bound on the change in the target future value of a bond portfolio $\Delta V_H = V_H' - V_H$, given as follows:[2]

$$\frac{\Delta V_H}{V_H} \geq -K_3 \times M^A \tag{4.17}$$

where V_H is the target future value of the bond portfolio at the planning horizon H, given as:

$$V_H = V_0 \times \exp\left[\int_0^H f(s)ds\right]$$

and V_H' is the realized future value of the bond portfolio at time H, given an instantaneous change in the forward rates from $f(t)$ to $f'|(t)$, and V_0 is the current price of the bond portfolio.

Equation 4.17 puts a lower bound on the change in the target future value of the bond portfolio, which is a function of a constant K_3 and the portfolio's M-absolute. The term K_3 depends on the term structure movements and gives the maximum absolute deviation of the term structure of the initial forward rates from the term structure of the new forward rates. Mathematically, K_3 can be defined as follows:

$$K_3 = \text{Max}\left(|K_1|,\ |K_2|\right),\ \textit{where}, K_1 \leq \Delta f(t) \leq K_2 \tag{4.18}$$

for all t such that, $0 \leq t \leq t_N$.

The term K_3 is outside of the control of a portfolio manager. A portfolio manager can control the portfolio's M-absolute, however, by selecting a particular bond portfolio. The smaller the magnitude of M-absolute, the lower the immunization risk exposure of the bond portfolio. Only a zero-coupon bond maturing at horizon H has zero M-absolute, which implies that only this bond is completely immune from interest rate risk. An implicit condition required for the inequality 4.17 to hold is that the bond portfolio *does not contain any short positions* (see Appendix 4.1). The immunization objective of the M-absolute model is to select a bond portfolio that minimizes the portfolio's M-absolute. We call this objective the *M-absolute immunization approach.*

Both the duration model and the M-absolute model are single risk-measure models. An important difference between them arises from the nature of the stochastic processes assumed for the term structure movements. The difference between duration and M-absolute can be illustrated using two cases.

Case 1: *The term structure of instantaneous forward rates experiences an instantaneous, infinitesimal, and parallel shift (i.e., slope, curvature, and other higher order shifts are not allowed).* In this case, the model leads to a perfect immunization performance (with duration equal to the planning horizon date). In contrast, the M-absolute model leads to a reduction in immunization risk but not to a complete elimination of immunization risk except in certain trivial situations.[3] Hence, the performance of the duration model would be superior to that of the M-absolute model under the case of small parallel shifts.

Case 2: *The term structure of instantaneous forward rates experiences a general shift in the height, slope, curvature, and other higher order term structure shape parameters, possibly including large shifts.* Because the traditional duration model focuses on immunizing against small and parallel shifts in the term structure of instantaneous forward rates, the presence of shifts in the slope, curvature, and other higher order term structure shape parameters may result in a "stochastic process risk" for the duration model. The effects of the stochastic process risk are especially high for a "barbell" portfolio as compared to a "bullet" portfolio.

Although the use of M-absolute does not entirely eliminate the risk of small and parallel interest rate shifts, it does offer enhanced protection against nonparallel shifts. Equation 4.17 gives the lower bound on the target future value of the bond portfolio as a product of its M-absolute and the parameter K_3, which gives the maximum absolute deviation of the term structure of new forward rates from the term structure of initial forward rates. In general, the value of K_3 depends on the shifts in the height, slope, curvature, and other relevant higher order term structure shape parameters.

The essential difference between the duration model and the M-absolute model can be summarized as follows.

The duration model completely immunizes against the height shifts but ignores the impact of slope, curvature, and other higher order term structure shifts on the future target value of a bond portfolio. This characteristic allows the traditional duration model to be neutral toward selecting a barbell or a bullet portfolio. In contrast, the M-absolute model immunizes only partially against the height shifts, but it also reduces the immunization risk caused by the shifts in the slope, curvature, and all other term structure shape parameters by selecting a bond portfolio with cash flows clustered around its planning horizon date.

The relative desirability of the duration model or the M-absolute model depends on the nature of term structure shifts expected. If height shifts completely dominate the slope, curvature, and other higher order term structure shifts, then the duration model will outperform the M-absolute model. If, however, slope, curvature, and other higher order shifts are relatively significant—in comparison with the height shifts—then the M-absolute model may outperform the traditional duration model.

Example 4.4 The M-absolute of a bond portfolio is computed identically to the duration of a bond portfolio, except that the longevity of each cash flow is reduced by *H* and then its absolute value is taken. For example, consider a bond portfolio *A* consisting of equal investments in two zero-coupon bonds maturing in two years and three years, respectively. The duration of this portfolio would be equal to 2.5 years; that is,

$$D_A = (50\% \times 2.0 \text{ years}) + (50\% \times 3.0 \text{ years}) = 2.5 \text{ years}$$

The M-absolute of this portfolio, however, would depend upon the investor's time horizon. For an investor with a time horizon of 2.5 years, the portfolio M-absolute would be equal to 0.5; that is,

$$M_A^A = \left(50\% \times |2.0 - 2.5|\right) + \left(50\% \times |3.0 - 2.5|\right) = 0.5 \text{ years}$$

Now, consider bond portfolio *B*, consisting of equal investments in two zero-coupon bonds maturing in one year and four years, respectively. The duration of this portfolio would also be equal to 2.5 years; that is,

$$D_B = \left(50\% \times 1.0 \text{ years}\right) + \left(50\% \times 4.0 \text{ years}\right) = 2.5 \text{ years}$$

Note that both bond portfolios have equal durations and, based upon duration alone, would appear to be equally risky. Portfolio *A*, however, offers generally superior immunization because its cash flows are closer to the horizon and therefore are less subjected to the effects of large and nonparallel term structure shifts. This difference in riskiness is captured by the M-absolute risk measures of the two portfolios. Note that the M-absolute of portfolio B is greater than the M-absolute of portfolio A:

$$M_B^A = \left(50\% \times |1.0 - 2.5|\right) + \left(50\% \times |4.0 - 2.5|\right) = 1.5 \text{ years}$$

Because M-absolute is a single-risk-measure model, it does not generally provide perfect interest rate risk protection. For example, the M-absolute of portfolio *A* is equal to 0.5 years for any value of investment horizon *H* from two to three years. Ultimately, the usefulness of M-absolute must be resolved empirically.

Nawalkha and Chambers (1996) test the M-absolute risk measure against the duration risk measure using McCulloch's term structure data over the observation period 1951 through 1986. On December 31 of each year, 31 annual coupon bonds are constructed with seven different maturities (1, 2, 3, . . . , 7 years) and five different coupon values (6, 8, 10, 12, and 14 percent) for each maturity.[4]

For December 31, 1951, two different bond portfolios are constructed corresponding to the duration strategy and the M-absolute strategy. Under the duration strategy, an infinite number of portfolios exist that would set the portfolio duration equal to the investment horizon *H*. To determine a unique portfolio, the following quadratic objective function is minimized:[5]

$$\text{Min}\left[\sum_{i=1}^{J} p_i^2\right] \tag{4.19}$$

subject to:

$$\sum_{i=1}^{J} p_i D_i = H$$

$$\sum_{i=1}^{J} p_i = 1$$

$$p_i \geq 0, \text{ for all } i = 1, 2, \ldots, J$$

where p_i gives the weight of the *i*th bond in the bond portfolio, and D_i defines the duration of the *i*th bond. The objective function of the M-absolute strategy is to minimize the portfolio's M-absolute:

$$\text{Min}\left[\sum_{i=1}^{J} p_i M_i^A\right] \tag{4.20}$$

subject to:

$$\sum_{i=1}^{J} p_i = 1$$

$$p_i \geq 0, \text{ for all } i = 1, 2, \ldots, J$$

where M_i^A defines the M-absolute of the *i*th bond.

The planning horizon, *H*, is assumed to equal four years. The two portfolios are rebalanced on December 31 of each of the next three years (i.e., 1952, 1953, 1954) when annual coupons are received. At the end of the four-year horizon (i.e., December 31, 1955), the returns of the two bond portfolios are compared with the return on a hypothetical four-year zero-coupon bond (computed at the beginning of the planning horizon). The differences between the actual values and the target value are defined as deviations in the interest rate, risk-hedging performance. The immunization procedure is repeated over 32 overlapping four-year periods: 1951 to 1955, 1952 to 1956, . . . , 1982 to 1986. Because interest rate volatility in the 1950s and 1960s was lower than in the 1970s and 1980s, and to test the robustness of these models against the possible nonstationarities in the stochastic processes for the term structure, results for these two periods are analyzed separately.

Table 4.1 reports the sum of absolute deviations of the M-absolute hedging strategy as a percentage of the sum of absolute deviations of the duration strategy, for the two separate time periods. The M-absolute strategy reduces the immunization risk inherent in the duration model by more than half in both time periods. This finding implies that the changes in the height of the term structure of instantaneous forward rates must be accompanied by significant changes in the slope, curvature, and other higher order term structure shape parameters.

M-SQUARE VERSUS CONVEXITY

Recall that convexity is defined as the weighted average of the maturity-squares of the cash flows of a bond, where weights are the present values of the cash flows, given as proportions of the bond's price:

$$CON = \sum_{t=t_1}^{t=t_N} t^2 \times w_t \tag{4.21}$$

The weights are defined using the entire term structure of interest rates as in equation 4.15. Convexity measures the gain in a bond's (or a bond portfolio's) value due to the second order effect of a large and parallel shift in the term structure of interest rates.

TABLE 4.1 Deviations of Actual Values from Target Values for the Duration and M-Absolute Strategies

	Sum of Absolute Deviations	As a Percentage of the Duration Strategy
Observation period 1951–1970		
Duration strategy	0.10063	100.00
M-absolute strategy	0.03560	35.37
Observation period 1967–1986		
Duration strategy	0.28239	100.00
M-absolute strategy	0.11604	41.09

The M-square risk measure is defined as the weighted average of the squared differences between cash flow maturities and the planning horizon, where weights are the present values of the bond's (or a bond portfolio's) cash flows, given as proportions of the bond's (or the bond portfolio's) price:

$$M^2 = \sum_{t=t_1}^{t=t_N} (t-H)^2 \times w_t \tag{4.22}$$

Unlike convexity, the M-square measure is specific to a given planning horizon. The M-square model selects the bond portfolio that minimizes the M-square of the bond portfolio, subject to the duration constraint (i.e., Duration = Planning horizon). For the special case, when planning horizon is equal to zero, the M-square converges to the convexity of the bond. To get more insight regarding the M-square risk measure, consider the following inequality.[6]

$$\frac{\Delta V_H}{V_H} \geq -(D-H) \times \Delta f(H) - \frac{1}{2} K_4 \times M^2 \tag{4.23}$$

where V_H is the target future value of the bond portfolio at the planning horizon H.

Unlike the M-absolute model, the M-square model is based upon two risk measures. If the portfolio is immunized with respect to duration (i.e., $D = H$), then equation 4.23 puts a lower bound on the target future value, which is a function of a constant K_4 and the portfolio's M-square. The term K_4 depends on term structure movements and gives the maximum slope of the shift in the term structure of instantaneous forward rates across the maturity term t.[7] Mathematically, K_4 can be defined as follows:

$$K_4 \geq \partial[\Delta f(t)] / \partial t \tag{4.24}$$

for all t such that, $0 \leq t \leq t_N$.

The term K_4 is outside of the control of a portfolio manager. A portfolio manager can control the portfolio's M-square, however, by selecting a particular duration-immunized bond portfolio. The smaller the magnitude of M-square, the lower the risk exposure of the bond portfolio. A portfolio that has cash flows centered closer to its planning horizon has a lower M-square. However, only a zero-coupon bond maturing at horizon H has a zero M-square, which implies that only this bond is completely immune from interest rate risk. An implicit condition required for the inequality (4.23) to hold is that the bond portfolio *does not contain any short positions* (see Appendix 4.1). The immunization objective of the M-square model is to select a bond portfolio that minimizes the portfolio's M-square, subject to the duration constraint $D = H$.

A linear relationship exists between M-square and convexity, given as follows:

$$M^2 = CON - 2 \times D \times H + H^2 \tag{4.25}$$

If duration is kept constant, then M-square is an increasing function of convexity. Equation 4.25 leads to the well-known *convexity-M-square paradox*.[8] As shown in equation 3.18 in the previous chapter, higher convexity is beneficial since it leads to higher returns. On the other hand, equation 4.23 suggests that M-square should be minimized, in order to minimize immunization risk. These two statements contradict each other since increasing convexity is equivalent to increasing M-square (see equation 4.25). This convexity-M-square paradox can be resolved by noting that the "convexity view" assumes parallel term structure shifts, while the "M-square view" assumes nonparallel term structure shifts. Obviously, *perfect* parallel shifts in the term structure are not possible. Hence, which view is valid, depends on the extent of the violation of the parallel term structure shift assumption (i.e., Is this violation slight or significant?).

Before we address this issue using empirical data, note that the convexity view is not consistent with bond market equilibrium, because a riskless positive return with zero initial investment can be guaranteed by taking a long position in a barbell or high positive-convexity portfolio along with a simultaneous and equal short position in a bullet or low-convexity portfolio, each portfolio having equal durations. Hence, to avoid riskless arbitrage opportunities, bond convexity must be priced in equilibrium. Specifically, if convexity is desirable, the price of the barbell portfolio will be bid up much like the expected bid-up in the price of a stock portfolio with positive skewness. This conclusion is at odds with the convexity view that bond portfolio returns can be increased through higher portfolio convexity.

However, since the M-square view is based on risk minimization conditions against nonparallel shifts in the term structure of interest rates, this view is consistent with equilibrium conditions, as it requires no specific assumptions regarding the shape of these shifts.

In the following subsection, we provide a unified framework, which allows both the convexity view and the M-square view as special cases of the general framework. Then we show the empirical relationship between bond convexity (which is linear in M-square) and ex ante bond returns. We also investigate whether higher convexity portfolios lead to higher immunization risk.

Resolving the Convexity/M-Square Paradox

Unlike the lower bound approach to the M-square model given earlier, Fong and Fabozzi (1985) and Lacey and Nawalkha (1993) suggest an alternative two-term Taylor-series-expansion approach to the M-square model. This approach leads to a generalized framework for resolving the convexity/M-square paradox.

Consider a bond portfolio at time $t = 0$ that offers the amount C_t at time $t = t_1, t_2, \ldots, t_N$. The return $R(H)$ on this portfolio between $t = 0$ and $t = H$ (an investment horizon) can be given as:

$$R(H) = \frac{\left[V_H' - V_0\right]}{V_0} \tag{4.26}$$

where as shown in equation 4.17, V_H' is the realized future value of the portfolio at the planning horizon H after the term structure of forward rates shifts to $f'(t)$, and V_0 is the current value of the portfolio using the current term structure of forward rates $f(t)$. As shown in Appendix 4.2, using a two-term Taylor series expansion, equation 4.26 can be simplified as:

$$R(H) = R_F(H) + \gamma_1 \times \left[D - H\right] + \gamma_2 \times M^2 + \varepsilon \tag{4.27}$$

where, $R_F(H)$ is the riskless-return on any default-free zero-coupon bond with maturity H given as:

$$R_F(H) = \exp\left[\int_0^H f(s)ds\right] - 1 \tag{4.28}$$

and ε is the error term due to higher order Taylor series terms.

The duration coefficient in equation 4.28 is defined as follows:

$$\gamma_1 = -\Delta f(H) \times (1 + R_F(H)) \tag{4.29}$$

and the M-square coefficient in equation 4.27 is defined as a difference of two effects as follows:

$$\gamma_2 = \text{CE} - \text{RE} \tag{4.30}$$

where

$$\text{CE} = \text{Convexity Effect} = \frac{1}{2}\left(1 + R_F\left(H\right)\right)\left(\Delta f\left(H\right)\right)^2 \tag{4.31}$$

and

$$\text{RE} = \text{Risk Effect} = \frac{1}{2}\left(1 + R_F\left(H\right)\right)\left[\frac{\partial\left(\Delta f(t)\right)}{\partial t}\right]_{t=H} \tag{4.32}$$

The convexity effect (CE) is positive for any term structure shift such that an increase in convexity (i.e., same as increase in M-square) enhances return regardless of the direction of the shift. This demonstrates the traditional view of convexity. The risk effect (RE) can be either positive or negative, depending on whether the instantaneous forward rate at the planning horizon H experiences a positive or a negative slope shift. A positive slope shift will decrease the value of the M-square coefficient (see equation 4.30) such that a higher-M-square portfolio (i.e., the same as a higher convexity portfolio) will result in a decline in portfolio return. A negative slope shift will increase the value of the M-square coefficient such that a higher-M-square portfolio (i.e., the same as a higher convexity portfolio) will result in an increase in portfolio return.

The convexity view assumes an insignificant risk effect (i.e., parallel shifts) such that only the convexity effect matters. Within this view, higher convexity always leads to higher return, which is inconsistent with the equilibrium conditions as outlined in Ingersoll, Skelton, and Weil (1978). Conversely, the equilibrium-consistent M-square view assumes an insignificant convexity effect such that only the risk effect matters. Within this view, the desirability of convexity depends on whether the risk effect is positive, negative, or insignificantly different from zero.

Example 4.5 Reconsider the \$1,000 face value, five-year, 10 percent annual coupon bond that was priced in Example 4.3. In this example, the initial term structure of instantaneous forward rates is given as:

$$f\left(t\right) = 0.06 + 0.02 \times t - 0.003 \times t^2 + 0.0004 \times t^3$$

The instantaneous shift in the forward rates and the new term structure of forward rates were given in that example as:

$$\Delta f(t) = 0.005 - 0.004 \times t$$

and

$$f'(t) = 0.065 + 0.016 \times t - 0.003 \times t^2 + 0.0004 \times t^3$$

Consider the instantaneous return on this bond (at $H = 0$) using equation 4.27. Substituting $H = 0$, equation 4.27 simplifies to the following equation:

$$R(0) = \frac{V_0' - V_0}{V_0} = -D \times \Delta f(0) + CON \times [CE - RE] + \varepsilon$$

where D is the duration, and CON is the convexity of the bond.[9] The convexity effect and the risk effect are given as follows:

$$\text{CE} = \text{Convexity Effect} = \frac{1}{2}\left(\Delta f(0)\right)^2 = \frac{1}{2}(0.005)^2 = 0.0000125$$

$$\text{RE} = \text{Risk Effect} = \frac{1}{2}\left[\frac{\partial(\Delta f(t))}{\partial t}\right]_{t=0} = \frac{1}{2}[-0.004] = -0.002$$

The M-square (or convexity) coefficient is equal to CE – RE = 0.0020125. The risk effect completely dominates the convexity effect in this example. This could be because in this example, the slope change is high, equal to –0.004 or negative 40 basis points per year. However, note that even if slope change were only 1 basis point per year, the risk effect would still be equal to ½(0.0001) = 0.00005, which is four times the convexity effect of 0.0000125 *produced by 50 basis points shift in the height of the term structure.* What this suggests is that even very small changes in the slope (or curvature, etc.) of the term structure of forward rates can violate the assumption of parallel term structure shifts sufficiently, such that the risk effect dominates the convexity effect. This is also consistent with a number of empirical studies that show that convexity adds risk but not extra return to option-free bond portfolios.

From Example 4.3, the instantaneous return on the bond can be given as:

$$R(0) = \frac{V_0' - V_0}{V_0} = \frac{1019.84 - 1002.11}{1002.11} = \frac{17.73}{1002.11} = 1.769\%$$

Approximating this return using the two-term Taylor series expansion given earlier we get:

$$R(0) = \frac{V_0' - V_0}{V_0} = -D \times 0.005 + CON \times 0.0020125 + \varepsilon$$

where

$$D = \frac{\frac{1 \times 100}{e^{0.0691}} + \frac{2 \times 100}{e^{0.1536}} + \frac{3 \times 100}{e^{0.2511}} + \frac{4 \times 100}{e^{0.3616}} + \frac{5 \times 100}{e^{0.4875}} + \frac{5 \times 1000}{e^{0.4875}}}{1002.11} = 4.146$$

and

$$CON = \frac{\frac{1^2 \times 100}{e^{0.0691}} + \frac{2^2 \times 100}{e^{0.1536}} + \frac{3^2 \times 100}{e^{0.2511}} + \frac{4^2 \times 100}{e^{0.3616}} + \frac{5^2 \times 100}{e^{0.4875}} + \frac{5^2 \times 1000}{e^{0.4875}}}{\$1002.11} = 19.1$$

Substituting duration and convexity in the Taylor series expansion, we get:

$$R(0) = \frac{V_0' - V_0}{V_0} = -4.146 \times 0.005 + 19.1 \times 0.0020125 + \varepsilon$$

or

$$R(0) \cong 1.771\%$$

The approximation of 1.771 percent is extremely close to the actual return of 1.769 percent (the difference equals 0.002 percent).

Note that the approximation is good because it considers the *risk effect* consistent with the M-square view. Suppose, we assumed perfect parallel shifts consistent with the convexity view, instead. Then the risk effect would be assumed to be zero, and the approximation would be given as follows:

$$R(0) = \frac{V_0' - V_0}{V_0} = -4.146 \times 0.005 + 19.1 \times 0.0000125 + \varepsilon$$

or

$$R(0) \cong -2.049\%$$

The return of –2.049 percent is consistent with the convexity view outlined in the previous chapter, and is very different from the actual return of 1.769 percent (the difference equals –3.818 percent).

Convexity, M-Square, and Ex-Ante Returns

Lacey and Nawalkha (1993) test a modified version of equation 4.27 in order to empirically distinguish between the risk effect (caused by slope changes) and the convexity effect (caused by second-order effect of height changes). The equation tested is obtained from equation 4.27 by substituting the linear relationship between M-square and convexity given in equation 4.25 as follows:

$$R(H) - R_F(H) = \beta_0 + \beta_1 \times D + \gamma_2 \times CON + \varepsilon \tag{4.33}$$

where

$$\beta_0 = -\gamma_1 \times H + \gamma_2 \times H^2 \text{ and } \beta_1 = \gamma_1 - 2\gamma_2 \times H \tag{4.34}$$

An *ex-ante* version of equation 4.33 is tested with CRSP government bond data using pooled cross-sectional time-series regressions of two-month excess holding period returns of U.S. Treasury bonds on their duration and convexity measures over the period January 1976 through November 1987. The results of these tests over the whole sample period as well as over selected five-year periods are reported in Table 4.2.

The convexity coefficient (same as the M-square coefficient in equation 4.27) is negative in all eight subperiods, and is negative and statistically significant over two of these periods. In general, high positive convexity is not

TABLE 4.2 Ex Ante Bond Returns and Convexity Exposure

Test Period	β_1	γ_2	Number of Observations
Jan. 1976–Nov. 1987	0.00039	−0.000026	3,881
Jan. 1976–Dec. 1981	−0.00083	−0.000048	1,553
Jan. 1982–Nov. 1987	0.00126[a]	−0.000034	2,328
Jan. 1977–Dec. 1982	0.00029	−0.000043	1,682
Jan. 1978–Dec. 1983	−0.00004	−0.000057	1,808
Jan. 1979–Dec. 1984	0.00057	−0.000075[c]	1,942
Jan. 1980–Dec. 1985	0.00109[c]	−0.000071[c]	2,097
Jan. 1981–Dec. 1986	0.00120[b]	−0.000041	2,263

[a] Indicates significant at the 0.001 level.
[b] Indicates significant at the 0.05 level.
[c] Indicates significant at the 0.10 level.

Note: The number of observations in each period test is determined by (1) the number of two-month holding periods in the particular test period, and (2) the number of bonds within each two-month holding period.

associated with positive excess returns, a conclusion that rejects the "convexity view," consistent with the theoretical criticisms of bond convexity given by Ingersoll, Skelton, and Weil (1978), among others.

However, the statistically significant negative values of the convexity coefficient over two subperiods provide some evidence that convexity is priced, and that increasing the level of positive convexity *reduces* the ex-ante excess return on a bond portfolio. The negative relationship between the convexity exposure and excess holding-period bond returns is not inconsistent with the results of Fama (1984), which imply a positive slope, but a *negative curvature* for the term structure of excess holding-period returns.

Convexity, M-Square, and Immunization Risk

The previous section demonstrated that increasing convexity (or M-square) does not increase *ex-ante* returns on bonds. This section shows that holding duration constant, and increasing the absolute size of convexity (or M-square) leads to higher immunization risk for bond portfolios. Bond portfolios are constructed (using CRSP bond data) to have different levels of convexity exposure, while keeping the duration equal to two months (i.e., 0.16667 years). The standard deviation of the excess returns over two-month holding periods is measured for each of these portfolios. The excess returns are defined as the portfolio's duration-immunized return less the riskless return.

Table 4.3 reports the standard deviation of the excess holding period returns for portfolios with different levels of convexity exposures, for the full sample period and the two subperiods, 1976 through 1981 and 1982 through 1987. Figure 4.1 illustrates these standard deviations graphically.

A clear relationship is shown between portfolio convexity and immunization risk, where risk is defined by the standard deviation of the portfolio's excess return. High-convexity portfolios (both positive and negative) have the highest risk, while low-convexity portfolios (both positive and negative) have the lowest risk. Although the degree of tilt between convexity and risk is not constant through time—the tilt is steeper over 1976 through 1981 than it is over 1982 through 1987—a monotonic relationship between convexity and risk holds for each period under examination. Thus, these results demonstrate that the magnitude of convexity exposure increases immunization risk.

CLOSED-FORM SOLUTIONS FOR M-SQUARE AND M-ABSOLUTE

In this section, we present closed-form solutions of M-square and M-absolute that remove much of the computational burden associated with

TABLE 4.3 Convexity Exposure and Immunization Risk

Convexity Exposure	Immunization Risk		
	Jan. 76–Nov. 87	Jan. 76–Dec. 81	Jan. 82–Nov. 87
−50	4.842	6.379	2.414
−40	3.944	5.200	1.962
−30	3.051	4.026	1.516
−20	2.170	2.862	1.085
−10	1.323	1.734	0.699
0	0.659	0.803	0.479
+10	0.872	1.052	0.633
+20	1.652	2.096	1.001
+30	2.518	3.241	1.426
+40	3.406	4.409	1.870
+50	4.301	5.585	2.322

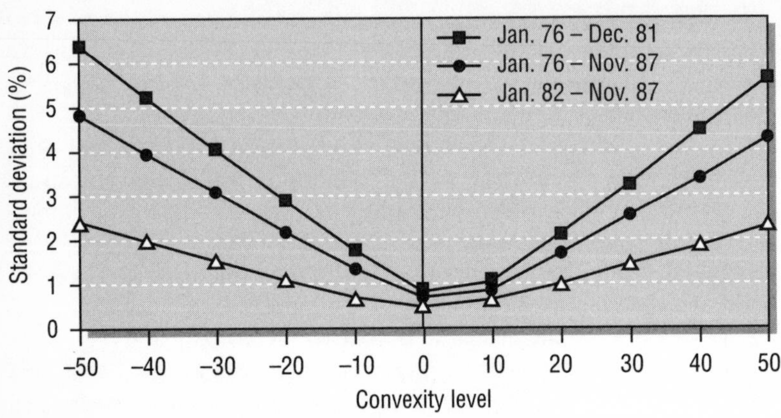

FIGURE 4.1 Relationship between Convexity and Risk

summing quantities over time. The closed forms are valid both at coupon payment dates and between coupon payment dates.

The expression for M-square of a security between cash flow payment dates, with cash flows paid k times a year at regular intervals, is given as:

$$M^2 = \left(\frac{\displaystyle\sum_{j=1}^{N} \frac{(j-s-H)^2 \, CF_j}{e^{i(j-s)}}}{\displaystyle\sum_{j=1}^{N} \frac{CF_j}{e^{i(j-s)}}} \right) / \, k^2 \tag{4.35}$$

where $i = y/k$ is the continuously compounded yield of the bond divided by k, CF_i is the ith of the cash flow payment ($i = 1, 2, \ldots, N$), N is the total number of cash flows, s is the time elapsed since the date of last cash flow payment in the units of time interval between coupon payment dates, and H is the planning horizon in the units of time interval between coupon payment dates. At the coupon payment dates, $s = 0$.

The M-square formula in equation 4.35 applies to all fixed-income securities with fixed regular cash flows, such as bonds, annuities, and perpetuities. The division of the bracketed expressions by k^2 on the right hand side of equation 4.35 gives the M-square value in annualized units. Even though the derivation of M-square risk measure uses the whole forward rate curve, the equation 4.35 uses the continuously compounded yield per period of the security. It has been shown that the error by using a single yield versus the whole yield curve in calculating the M-square is insignificant for portfolio immunization and other hedging applications. Simplifying equation 4.35 gives:

$$M^2 = \left(\begin{array}{l} \left[\sum_{j=1}^{N} \frac{(j-s)^2 CF_j}{e^{i(j-s)}} \right] \Big/ \left[\sum_{j=1}^{N} \frac{CF_j}{e^{i(j-s)}} \right] \\ -2H \left[\sum_{j=1}^{N} \frac{(j-s) CF_j}{e^{i(j-s)}} \right] \Big/ \left[\sum_{j=1}^{N} \frac{CF_j}{e^{i(j-s)}} \right] \\ +H^2 \left[\sum_{j=1}^{N} \frac{CF_j}{e^{i(j-s)}} \right] \Big/ \left[\sum_{j=1}^{N} \frac{CF_j}{e^{i(j-s)}} \right] \end{array} \right) / k^2 \tag{4.36}$$

which can be rewritten in an alternative form as:

$$M^2 = CON - 2 \times D \times H + H^2 \tag{4.37}$$

where D is the duration and CON is the convexity as defined in Chapter 2.

Equation 4.37 expresses M-square in terms of duration and convexity. Hence, substituting the closed-form solutions of D and CON obtained in Chapter 2 into equation 4.37 gives the closed-form formula of M-square. Since Chapter 2 obtained the formulas of D and CON, both between coupon payment dates and at coupon payment dates, for three types of securities (i.e., regular bonds, annuities, and perpetuities), appropriate substitutions of D and CON in equation 4.37 lead to the corresponding M-square formulas.

The M-absolute is given in the summation form as:

$$M^A = \left(\frac{\sum_{j=1}^{N} \frac{|j-s-H| CF_j}{e^{i(j-s)}}}{\sum_{j=1}^{N} \frac{CF_j}{e^{i(j-s)}}} \right) / k \tag{4.38}$$

where all variables are as defined above and $|x|$ refers to the absolute value of x. The division of the bracketed expressions by k on the right hand side of equation 4.38 gives the M-absolute value in annualized units.

A closed-form formula for M-absolute between cash flow payment dates is given as follows:

$$M^A = \left[(D-H)I_A + 2\left(H - \frac{e^i}{e^i-1} + \frac{L}{e^{Li}-1} + s\right)\left(\frac{CF_1}{(e^i-1)}\left[\frac{1}{e^{-is}} - \frac{1}{e^{(L-s)i}}\right]\right)\frac{I_B}{P}\right] / k \quad (4.39)$$

where P = Price of the underlying security *with the accrued interest* (the security may be a regular fixed-coupon bond, an annuity, or a perpetuity)
D = Duration of the underlying security
CF_1 = First cash flow of the underlying security
$L = \text{INT}(H+s)$
$\text{INT}(x)$ = Integer function defined as the closest integer less than or equal to x

I_A and I_B are indicator functions defined as:

$$I_A = \begin{cases} 1 & \text{if } H+s<N \\ -1 & \text{if } H+s \geq N \end{cases}$$

$$I_B = \begin{cases} 1 & \text{if } 1<H+s<N \\ 0 & \text{else} \end{cases}$$

By substituting the appropriate formulas of the price and duration from the previous chapter, either at coupon payment dates or between coupon payment dates, into equation 4.39, the M-absolute of a regular bond, or an annuity, or a perpetuity, can be calculated, easily.

Example 4.6 Consider 12 bonds, all of which have a \$1,000 face value and a 10 percent annual coupon rate, but different maturities ranging from 1 year to 3.75 years in increments of 0.25 years. Assume that the yields to maturity of all bonds are identical and equal 5 percent and the planning horizon is set to two years. Table 4.4 gives the M-square and M-absolute of the

TABLE 4.4 M-Square and M-Absolute for All Twelve Bonds

Bond's Maturity	N	s	M-Square	M-Absolute
1	1	0	1.000	1.000
1.25	2	0.75	0.781	0.837
1.5	2	0.5	0.424	0.587
1.75	2	0.25	0.193	0.337
2	2	0	0.087	0.087
2.25	3	0.75	0.354	0.416
2.5	3	0.5	0.418	0.584
2.75	3	0.25	0.607	0.752
3	3	0	0.920	0.920
3.25	4	0.75	1.497	1.179
3.5	4	0.5	1.949	1.349
3.75	4	0.25	2.526	1.520

nine bonds obtained by applying the closed-form solutions presented previously. All the figures are expressed in years.

APPENDIX 4.1: DERIVATION OF THE M-ABSOLUTE AND M-SQUARE MODELS

Consider a bond portfolio at time $t = 0$ with CF_t as the payment on the portfolio at time t ($t = t_1, t_2, \ldots, t_N$). Let the continuously compounded term structure of instantaneous forward rates be given by $f(t)$. The value of the bond portfolio at time 0 is:

$$V_0 = \sum_{t=t_1}^{t=t_N} CF_t \times e^{-\int_0^t f(s)ds} \tag{4.40}$$

and the expected value of the portfolio at the planning horizon H is:

$$V_H = V_0 \times e^{\int_0^H f(s)ds} = \sum_{t=t_1}^{t=t_N} CF_t \times e^{\int_t^H f(s)ds} \tag{4.41}$$

Now, allow an instantaneous shift in the forward rates from $f(t)$ to $f'(t)$ such that $f'(t) = f(t) + \Delta f(t)$. The realized future value of the portfolio at time H is:

$$V_H' = \sum_{t=t_1}^{t=t_N} CF_t \times e^{\int_t^H f'(s)ds} = \sum_{t=t_1}^{t=t_N} CF_t \times e^{\int_t^H f(s)ds} e^{\int_t^H \Delta f(s)ds} \tag{4.42}$$

The change in the expected terminal value of the bond portfolio caused by the instantaneous change in the forward rates is given as:

$$\Delta V_H = V_H' - V_H = \sum_{t=t_1}^{t=t_N} CF_t \times e^{\int_t^H f(s)ds} [e^{\int_t^H \Delta f(s)ds} - 1] \tag{4.43}$$

Using equations 4.41 and 4.43, the percentage change in the expected terminal value of the bond portfolio can be given as:

$$\frac{\Delta V_H}{V_H} = \frac{1}{V_0} \sum_{t=t_1}^{t=t_N} CF_t \times e^{-\int_0^t f(s)ds} [e^{h(t)} - 1] \tag{4.44}$$

where

$$h(t) = \int_t^H \Delta f(s)ds$$

To derive the M-absolute model, consider the following two cases:

Case 1: $H \geq t$. Define a constant K_1, subject to $\Delta f(t) \geq K_1$, for all $t \geq 0$. Therefore,

$$\int_t^H \Delta f(s)ds \geq \int_t^H K_1 ds = K_1 (H - t) = K_1 |H - t| \tag{4.45}$$

which implies:

$$h(t) \geq K_1 |H - t| \tag{4.46}$$

where $|x|$ refers to the absolute value of x.

Case 2: $H \leq t$. Define a constant K_2, subject to $\Delta f(t) \leq K_2$, for all $t \geq 0$. Therefore,

$$\int_H^t \Delta f(s)ds \leq \int_H^t K_2 ds = K_2\left(t - H\right) \tag{4.47}$$

or alternatively,

$$\int_t^H \Delta f(s)ds \geq -K_2\left(t - H\right) = -K_2\left|H - t\right| \tag{4.48}$$

which implies:

$$h(t) \geq -K_2\left|H - t\right| \tag{4.49}$$

Combining equations 4.46 and 4.49 produces:

$$h(t) \geq \left|H - t\right| \times \text{Min}\left[K_1, -K_2\right], \text{ for all } t \geq 0 \tag{4.50}$$

Equation 4.50 can be rewritten as:

$$h(t) \geq -K_3 \times \left|H - t\right|, \text{ for all } t \geq 0 \tag{4.51}$$

where $K_3 = -\text{Min}\left[K_1, -K_2\right] = \text{Max}\left[\left|K_1\right|, \left|K_2\right|\right]$, because $K^1 \leq K^2$ for all $t \geq 0$.

Because $e^x \geq 1 + x$, then

$$e^{h(t)} \geq 1 - K_3\left|H - t\right| \tag{4.52}$$

Assuming short positions are restricted such that $CF_t \geq 0$ for all $t \geq 0$, then by substituting the value of $e^{h(t)}$ from equation 4.52 into equation 4.44, we obtain a lower bound on the change in the terminal value of the bond portfolio given as:

$$\frac{\Delta V_H}{V_H} \geq -K_3 \times M^A \tag{4.53}$$

where M^A is the M-absolute of the bond portfolio defined as:

$$M^A = \frac{1}{V_0} \sum_{t=t_1}^{t=t_N} CF_t \times e^{-\int_0^t f(s)ds} |H - t| \tag{4.54}$$

or equivalently,

$$M^A = \frac{1}{V_0} \sum_{t=t_1}^{t=t_N} CF_t \times e^{-\int_0^t f(s)ds} |t - H| \tag{4.55}$$

To derive the M-square model, let us define:

$$g(t) = \frac{\partial \Delta f(t)}{\partial t} \tag{4.56}$$

Then:

$$\Delta f(H) - \Delta f(t) = \int_t^H g(u)du \tag{4.57}$$

which implies:

$$\begin{aligned} h(t) &= \int_t^H \Delta f(s)ds \\ &= \int_t^H \Delta f(H)\,ds - \int_t^H \left(\int_s^H g(u)du \right) ds \\ &= -\Delta f(H)(t - H) - \int_t^H (u - t)\, g(u)\, du \end{aligned} \tag{4.58}$$

Assume that the maximum slope of the shift in the term structure of instantaneous forward rates across the maturity term t is given by a constant K_4 such as $g(t) \leq K_4$ for all $t \geq 0$. Consider the following two cases.

Case 1: $H \geq t$. We have:

$$\int_t^H (u - t)\, g(u)\, du \leq \int_t^H (u - t)\, K_4\, du = \frac{1}{2} K_4 (H - t)^2 \tag{4.59}$$

Case 2: $H \leq t$. We have:

$$\int_t^H (u-t)\,g(u)\,du = \int_H^t (t-u)\,g(u)\,du \leq \int_H^t (t-u)\,K_4\,du = \frac{1}{2} \tag{4.60}$$

Combining equations 4.59 and 4.60 gives:

$$\int_t^H (u-t)\,g(u)\,du \leq \frac{1}{2}K_4\,(t-H)^2 \tag{4.61}$$

for all $t \geq 0$ and, therefore:

$$h(t) \geq -\Delta f(H)(t-H) - \frac{1}{2}K_4\,(t-H)^2, \text{ for all } t \geq 0 \tag{4.62}$$

We then have:

$$e^{h(t)} \geq 1 - \Delta f(H)(t-H) - \frac{1}{2}K_4\,(t-H)^2 \tag{4.63}$$

Substituting this result into equation 4.44, we obtain the following lower bound on the change in the terminal value of the bond portfolio:

$$\frac{\Delta V_H}{V_H} \geq -(D-H) \times \Delta f(H) - \frac{1}{2}K_4 \times M^2 \tag{4.64}$$

where M^2 is the M-square of the bond portfolio defined as:

$$M^2 = \frac{1}{V_0}\sum_{t=t_1}^{t=t_N} CF_t \times e^{-\int_0^t f(s)ds}\,(t-H)^2 \tag{4.65}$$

APPENDIX 4.2: TWO-TERM TAYLOR-SERIES-EXPANSION APPROACH TO THE M-SQUARE MODEL

Consider a bond portfolio at time $t = 0$ that offers the amount CF_t at time t ($t = t_1, t_2, \ldots, t_N$). Let the continuously compounded term structure of instantaneous forward rates be given by $f(t)$. Now allow an instantaneous shift in the forward rates from $f(t)$ to $f'(t)$ such that $f'(t) = f(t) + \Delta f(t)$. The return on the bond portfolio between $t = 0$ and $t = H$ can be given as:

$$R(H) = \frac{\left[V_H' - V_0\right]}{V_0} \tag{4.66}$$

where V_0 is the value of the bond portfolio at time 0, before the shift in the forward rates:

$$V_0 = \sum_{t=t_1}^{t=t_N} CF_t \times e^{-\int_0^t f(s)ds} \tag{4.67}$$

and V_H' is the realized future value of the portfolio at the planning horizon, after the term structure of forward rates have shifted to $f'(t)$:

$$V_H' = \sum_{t=t_1}^{t=t_N} CF_t \times e^{\int_t^H f'(s)ds} \tag{4.68}$$

Substituting the definitions of V_0 and V_H' into equation 4.66 gives:

$$R(H) = \left[e^{\int_0^H f(s)ds} \left[\sum_{t=t_1}^{t_N} CF_t \times e^{-\int_0^t f(s)ds} \times k(t) \right] - V_0 \right] / V_0 \tag{4.69}$$

where

$$k(t) = e^{\int_t^H \Delta f(s)ds} \tag{4.70}$$

If the forward rate function does not change between time 0 and H, then $k(t) = 1$, and equation 4.69 reduces to:

$$R_F(H) = e^{\int_0^H f(s)ds} - 1 \tag{4.71}$$

where $R_{F(H)}$ is the riskless return on any default-free zero-coupon bond with maturity H.

If forward rates do change, the bond portfolio return will be different from the riskless return. Equation 4.69 can be simplified further using a two-term Taylor series expansion of $k(t)$ around time $t = H$:

$$k(t) = 1 - (t-H) \times \Delta f(H) - \frac{1}{2}(t-H)^2 \left[\frac{\partial(\Delta f(t))}{\partial t} - (\Delta f(t))^2 \right]_{t=H} + \varepsilon(t) \qquad (4.72)$$

where $\varepsilon(t)$ is the error term due to higher order Taylor series terms.

Substituting the value of $k(t)$ from equation 4.72 into equation 4.69 and simplifying gives:

$$R(H) = R_F(H) + \gamma_1 \times [D - H] + \gamma_2 \times M^2 + \varepsilon \qquad (4.73)$$

where ε is the error term, the duration coefficient is defined as:

$$\gamma_1 = -\Delta f(H) \times (1 + R_F(H)) \qquad (4.74)$$

and the M-square coefficient is defined as:

$$\gamma_2 = -\frac{1}{2}(1 + R_F(H)) \left\{ \left[\frac{\partial(\Delta f(t))}{\partial t} \right]_{t=H} - (\Delta f(H))^2 \right\} \qquad (4.75)$$

As done in subsection 0, the M-square coefficient can be divided into two components:

$$\gamma_2 = \text{CE} - \text{RE} \qquad (4.76)$$

where:

$$\text{CE} = \text{Convexity Effect} = \frac{1}{2}(1 + R_F(H))(\Delta f(H))^2 \qquad (4.77)$$

and

$$\text{RE} = \text{Risk Effect} = \frac{1}{2}\left(1 + R_F\left(H\right)\right)\left[\frac{\partial\left(\Delta f(t)\right)}{\partial t}\right]_{t=H} \tag{4.78}$$

NOTES

1. See Chambers et al. (1984). Assuming a polynomial form for the term structure of zero-coupon yields is not necessary, but doing so leads to many insights on the nature of the nonparallel term structure shifts.
2. The proof of inequality in equation 4.17 is given in Appendix 4.1.
3. Only a single zero-coupon bond maturing on the planning horizon date has a zero M-absolute (because short positions are restricted).
4. Since coupons are paid annually, all the one-year maturity coupon bonds collapse to a single one-year zero-coupon bond regardless of the coupon rate.
5. The objective function "spreads out" the investment among available bonds. Diversification across bonds tends to minimize the effects of unsystematic interest rate risk.
6. The proof of inequality in equation 4.23 is given in Appendix 4.1.
7. The expression $\partial\Delta f(t)/\partial t$ is not the same as $2\Delta s$ in equation 4.12. The expression $\partial\Delta f(t)/\partial t$ defines the slope of the shift in the term structure of forward rates at term t, and will generally change with t. The changing slope will result whenever curvature and other higher-order shape changes are nonzero.
8. See Lacey and Nawalkha (1993).
9. Recall that M-square converges to the convexity of a bond when the planning horizon $H = 0$ (see equation 4.25).

CHAPTER 5

Duration Vector Models

Though both M-absolute and M-square risk measures provide significant enhancement in the immunization performance over the traditional duration model, perfect immunization is not possible using either of the two measures except for the trivial case in which the portfolio consists of a zero-coupon bond maturing at the horizon date. Further gains in immunization performance have been made possible by the duration vector model, which using a vector of higher order duration measures immunize against changes in the shape parameters (i.e., height, slope, curvature, and so on) of the term structure of interest rates. Various derivations to the duration vector model have been given in the literature that assume a polynomial form for the shifts in the term structure of interest rates.[1] The duration vector model provides a high level of immunization performance using only three to five risk measures.

In this chapter, we give a more general derivation to the duration vector model that does not require the term structure shifts to be of a particular functional form.[2] Using an example, we demonstrate the application of the duration vector model when the term structure is estimated using the exponential functional form of the Nelson and Siegel (1987) model introduced in Chapter 3.

This chapter also derives a new class of *generalized duration vector models.* Since the shifts in the height, slope, curvature, and other parameters of the term structure of interest rate shifts are generally larger at the shorter end of the maturity spectrum, it is possible that an alternative set of duration measures that are linear in $g(t)$, $g(t)^2$, $g(t)^3$, and so on, and which put relatively more weight at the shorter end of the maturity spectrum due to the specific choice of the function $g(t)$, may provide enhanced immunization performance. Consistent with this intuition, this chapter gives a new class of generalized duration vector models using a Taylor series expansion of the bond return function with respect to specific *functions* of the cash

---

This chapter coauthored with Donald Chambers and Jun Zhang.

flow maturities. Using a change of variable for the Taylor series expansion, the generalized duration vector model leads to duration measures that are linear in $g(t)$, $g(t)^2$, $g(t)^3$, and so on. The generalized duration vector models subsume the traditional duration vector models by considering the special case, $g(t) = t$.

We consider a polynomial class of generalized duration vector models based upon the functional form $g(t) = t^{\alpha}$. Different values of the parameter α result in different generalized duration vector models. The value of $\alpha = 1$ corresponds to the case of the traditional duration vector, where the higher order duration measures are linear in t, t^2, t^3, and so on. Other values of α are equivalent to cases where the higher order duration measures are linear in some polynomial function of the maturity raised to integer powers [e.g., $\alpha = 0.5$ produces $t^{0.5}$, $(t^{0.5})^2$, $(t^{0.5})^3$].

Two other types of multifactor models that have become popular with bond practitioners are given as the *key rate duration models* and the *principal component models*.[3] Though these models will be considered in detail in Chapters 9 and 10, some fundamental distinctions between them and the generalized duration vector models must be pointed out briefly. Both the generalized duration vector models and the key rate duration models are based upon *the assumption of smoothness* in the shift of the term structure of interest rates.[4] These models do not require any assumptions regarding the stationarity of the covariance structure of interest rate changes. For example, the interest rate risk hedging conditions and portfolio formation do not change depending upon whether short rates and long rates have a positive correlation or a negative correlation under these models. This explains why these models can hedge with a high level of accuracy, even over periods in which the covariance structure of interest rate changes is nonstationary. However, the number of risk measures to be used and the corresponding division of the term structure into different key rates remain quite arbitrary under the key rate duration models. For example, Ho (1992) proposes as many as *eleven* key rate durations to effectively hedge against interest rate risk. The principal component models, however, *require* a stationary covariance structure of interest rate changes and, hence, their performance can be poor if the stationarity assumption is violated.

THE DURATION VECTOR MODEL

This section derives the duration vector model, which captures the interest rate risk of fixed-income securities under nonparallel and noninfinitesimal shifts in a nonflat yield curve. This model is a generalization of the traditional duration model. Under the duration vector model, the riskiness of bonds is captured by a vector of risk measures, given as $D(1)$, $D(2)$, $D(3)$, and so on. Generally, the first three to five duration vector measures are sufficient to capture all of the interest rate risk inherent in default-free bonds and bond portfolios.

To derive the duration vector model, consider a bond portfolio at time $t = 0$ with CF_t as the payment on the portfolio at time t ($t = t_1, t_2, \ldots, t_N$). Let the continuously compounded term structure of instantaneous forward rates be given by $f(t)$. Now allow an instantaneous shift in the forward rates from $f(t)$ to $f'(t)$ such that $f'(t) = f(t) + \Delta f(t)$. The instantaneous percentage change in the current value of the portfolio is given as:

$$
\begin{aligned}
\frac{\Delta V_0}{V_0} = & -D(1)\left[\Delta f(0)\right] \\
& - D(2)\left[\frac{1}{2}\left(\frac{\partial(\Delta f(t))}{\partial t} - (\Delta f(0))^2\right)\right]_{t=0} \\
& - D(3)\left[\frac{1}{3!}\left(\frac{\partial^2(\Delta f(t))}{\partial t^2} - 3 \times \Delta f(0)\frac{\partial(\Delta f(t))}{\partial t} + (\Delta f(0))^3\right)\right]_{t=0} \\
& \vdots \\
& - D(M)\left[\frac{1}{M!}\left(\frac{\partial^{M-1}(\Delta f(t))}{\partial t^{M-1}} + \cdots + (\Delta f(0))^M\right)\right]_{t=0}
\end{aligned}
\tag{5.1}
$$

where

$$
\begin{aligned}
D(m) &= \sum_{t=t_1}^{t=t_N} w_t \times t^m, \quad \text{for } m = 1, 2, \ldots, M, \text{ and,} \\
w_t &= \left[\frac{CF_t}{e^{\int_0^t f(s)ds}}\right] / V_0
\end{aligned}
\tag{5.2}
$$

Equation 5.1 expresses the percentage change in the bond portfolio value as a product of a duration vector and a shift vector. The duration vector depends on the maturity characteristics of the portfolio, while the shift vector depends on the nature of the shifts in the term structure of instantaneous forward rates. The elements of the duration vector are defined by equation 5.2. The duration vector elements are linear in the integer powers of the maturity of the cash flows of the bond portfolio (i.e., t, t^2, t^3). The first element of the duration vector is the traditional duration measure given as the weighted-average time to maturity. Higher order duration measures are computed similarly as weighted averages of the times to maturity squared, cubed, and so forth.

The first shift vector element captures the change in the level of the forward rate curve for the instantaneous term, given by $\Delta f(0)$; the second shift vector element captures the difference between the square of this change and the slope of the change in the forward rate curve (given by $\partial \Delta f(t)/\partial t$ at $t = 0$); and finally the third shift vector element captures the effect of the third power of the change in the level of the forward rate curve, the interaction between the change in the level and the slope of the change in the forward rate curve, and the curvature of the change in the forward rate curve (given by $\partial^2 \Delta f(t)/\partial t^2$ at $t = 0$).

Generally, it has been found that the magnitudes of the higher order derivatives in the shift vector elements dominate the magnitudes of higher powers. For example, in the second shift vector element, the magnitude of $\partial \Delta f(t)/\partial t$ evaluated at $t = 0$ generally dominates the magnitude of $\Delta f(0)^2$. In fact, this is the reason why the second-order duration measure $D(2)$ (which is the same as bond convexity when using continuous compounding) mostly measures the sensitivity of the bond portfolio to the changes in the slope of the forward rate curve (defined as the *risk effect* in the previous chapter), and not as much the sensitivity of the bond portfolio to *large* changes in the height of the forward rate curve (defined as the *convexity effect* in the previous chapter). Similarly, the third-order duration measure $D(3)$ mostly measures the sensitivity of the bond portfolio to the changes in the curvature (and to some extent the product of the changes in the height and the slope) of the forward rate curve, and not as much the sensitivity of the bond portfolio to *large* changes in the height of the forward rate curve.

To immunize a portfolio at a planning horizon of H years, the duration vector model requires setting the portfolio duration vector to the duration vector of a hypothetical default-free zero-coupon bond maturing at H. Since the duration vector elements of a zero-coupon bond are given as its maturity, maturity squared, maturity cubed, and so on, the immunization constraints are given as follows:

$$
\begin{aligned}
D(1) &= \sum_{t=t_1}^{t=t_N} w_t \times t = H \\
D(2) &= \sum_{t=t_1}^{t=t_N} w_t \times t^2 = H^2 \\
D(3) &= \sum_{t=t_1}^{t=t_N} w_t \times t^3 = H^3 \\
&\vdots \\
D(M) &= \sum_{t=t_1}^{t=t_N} w_t \times t^M = H^M
\end{aligned}
\tag{5.3}
$$

The duration vector of a bond portfolio is obtained as the weighted average of the duration vectors of individual bonds, where the weights are defined as the proportions of investment of the bonds in the total portfolio. If p_i $(I = 1, 2, \ldots, J)$ is the proportion of investment in the ith bond, and $D_i(m)$ $(m = 1, 2, \ldots, M)$ is the duration vector of the ith bond, the duration vector of a portfolio of bonds is given by:

$$D(m) = p_1 \times D_1(m) + p_2 \times D_2(m) + \cdots + p_J \times D_J(m) \quad m = 1, 2, \ldots, M \tag{5.4}$$

where

$$\sum_{i=1}^{J} p_i = 1$$

To immunize a bond portfolio, proportions of investments in different bonds are chosen such that the duration vector of the portfolio is set equal to a horizon vector as follows:

$$\begin{aligned} D(1) &= p_1 \times D_1(1) + p_2 \times D_2(1) + \cdots + p_J \times D_J(1) = H \\ D(2) &= p_1 \times D_1(2) + p_2 \times D_2(2) + \cdots + p_J \times D_J(2) = H^2 \\ &\vdots \\ D(M) &= p_1 \times D_1(M) + p_2 \times D_2(M) + \cdots + p_J \times D_J(M) = H^M \\ & p_1 + p_2 + \cdots + p_J = 1 \end{aligned} \tag{5.5}$$

If the number of bonds J equals the number of constraints $M + 1$, then a unique solution exists for the bond proportions $p_1, p_2, \ldots, p_J$. If $J < M + 1$, then the system shown in equation 5.5 does not have any solution. If $J > M + 1$ (which is the most common case), the system of equations has an infinite number of solutions. To select a unique immunizing solution in this case, we optimize the following quadratic function:

$$\text{Min}\left[\sum_{i=1}^{J} p_i^2\right] \tag{5.6}$$

subject to the set of constraints given in equation 5.5. The objective function (5.6) is used for achieving diversification across all bonds, and reduces bond-specific idiosyncratic risks that are not captured (e.g., liquidity risk) by the systematic term structure movements.

A solution to the constrained quadratic optimization problem given previously can be obtained by deriving the first order conditions using the Lagrange method. The solution requires multiplying the inverse of a $J + M + 1$ dimensional square matrix with a column vector containing $J + M + 1$ elements as follows:

$$\begin{bmatrix} 2 & 0 & \cdots & 0 & D_1(1) & D_1(2) & \cdots & D_1(M) & 1 \\ 0 & 2 & \cdots & 0 & D_2(1) & D_1(2) & \cdots & D_1(M) & 1 \\ 0 & 0 & \cdots & 0 & \vdots & \vdots & \vdots & \vdots & \vdots \\ \vdots & \vdots & \vdots & \vdots & \vdots & \vdots & \vdots & \vdots & \vdots \\ 0 & 0 & \cdots & 2 & D_J(1) & D_J(2) & \cdots & D_J(M) & 1 \\ D_1(1) & D_2(1) & \cdots & D_J(1) & 0 & 0 & \cdots & 0 & 0 \\ D_1(2) & D_2(2) & \cdots & D_J(2) & 0 & 0 & \cdots & 0 & 0 \\ \vdots & \vdots & \vdots & \vdots & \vdots & \vdots & \vdots & \vdots & \vdots \\ D_1(M) & D_2(M) & \cdots & D_J(M) & 0 & 0 & \cdots & 0 & 0 \\ 1 & 1 & \cdots & 1 & 0 & 0 & \cdots & 0 & 0 \end{bmatrix}^{-1} \times \begin{bmatrix} 0 \\ 0 \\ \vdots \\ \vdots \\ 0 \\ H \\ H^2 \\ \vdots \\ H^M \\ 1 \end{bmatrix} = \begin{bmatrix} p_1 \\ p_2 \\ \vdots \\ \vdots \\ p_J \\ \lambda_1 \\ \lambda_2 \\ \vdots \\ \lambda_M \\ \lambda_{M+1} \end{bmatrix} \tag{5.7}$$

The first J elements of the column vector on the right-hand side of equation 5.7 give the proportions to be invested in the different bonds in the portfolio. The rest of the $M + 1$ elements of the column vector on the right-hand side of equation 5.7 can be ignored. The matrix inversion and matrix multiplication can be done on any popular software programs such as Excel or Matlab.

This duration vector model has been derived under very general assumptions that do not require the term structure shifts to be of a particular functional form. This derivation follows from the M-vector model (1997) as shown in Appendix 5.1.[5] All previous approaches to the duration vector model were more restrictive and based on a *polynomial functional form* for the term structure shifts.[6]

Though more restrictive, a polynomial form for the term structure shifts is insightful for understanding the return decomposition of a portfolio using the duration vector model. Recall from Chapter 4 (see equations 4.6 and 4.12) that under a polynomial functional form, the instantaneous shifts in the term structure of zero-coupon yields and the term structure of instantaneous forward rates are given as follows:

$$\Delta y(t) = \Delta A_0 + \Delta A_1 \times t + \Delta A_2 \times t^2 + \Delta A_3 \times t^3 + \cdots + \tag{5.8}$$

and

$$\Delta f(t) = \Delta A_0 + 2\Delta A_1 \times t + 3\Delta A_2 \times t^2 + 4\Delta A_3 \times t^3 + \cdots + \tag{5.9}$$

where
ΔA_0 = Change in the height parameter
ΔA_1 = Change in the slope parameter
ΔA_2 = Change in the curvature parameter
$\Delta A_3, \Delta A_4, \ldots$ = Changes in other higher order shape parameters

Substituting equation 5.9 into equation 5.1, the percentage change in the portfolio value is given as:

$$\begin{aligned}\frac{\Delta V_0}{V_0} &= -D(1)\left[\Delta A_0\right] \\ &\quad -D(2)\left[\Delta A_1 - \frac{(\Delta A_0)^2}{2}\right] \\ &\quad -D(3)\left[\Delta A_2 - \Delta A_0 \Delta A_1 + \frac{(\Delta A_0)^3}{3!}\right] \\ &\quad \vdots \\ &\quad -D(M)\left[\Delta A_{Q-1} + \cdots + \frac{(\Delta A_0)^M}{M!}\right]\end{aligned} \tag{5.10}$$

It can be seen that the shift vector elements simplify considerably under the assumption of polynomial shifts. However, since our earlier derivation ensures that the duration vector model does not require the assumption of polynomial shifts, the model performs well even when the shifts are given by other functional forms. This is demonstrated by the following two examples that apply the duration vector model to the term structure given in the exponential form by Nelson and Siegel (1987).

Example 5.1 Consider five bonds all of which have a $1,000 face value and a 10 percent annual coupon rate, but with different maturities as shown in Table 5.1.

Assume that the term structure of instantaneous forward rates is estimated using Nelson and Siegel's exponential form:

$$f(t) = \alpha_1 + \alpha_2 \times e^{-t/\beta} + \alpha_3 \times e^{-t/\beta} \times \frac{t}{\beta} \tag{5.11}$$

TABLE 5.1 Description of the Bonds

Bond #	Face Value ($)	Maturity (years)	Annual Coupon Rate (%)
1	1,000	1	10
2	1,000	2	10
3	1,000	3	10
4	1,000	4	10
5	1,000	5	10

Chapter 3 showed that the zero-coupon yield curve consistent with this structure is:

$$y(t) = \alpha_1 + (\alpha_2 + \alpha_3)\frac{\beta}{t}\left[1 - e^{-t/\beta}\right] - \alpha_3 e^{-t/\beta} \tag{5.12}$$

Now, consider the following parameter values: $\alpha_1 = 0.07$, $\alpha_2 = -0.02$, $\alpha_3 = 0.001$, and $ß = 2$. The corresponding instantaneous forward rate curve and zero-coupon yield curve are shown in Figure 5.1.

Table 5.2 illustrates the computation of the first, second, and third order duration risk measures of bond 5.

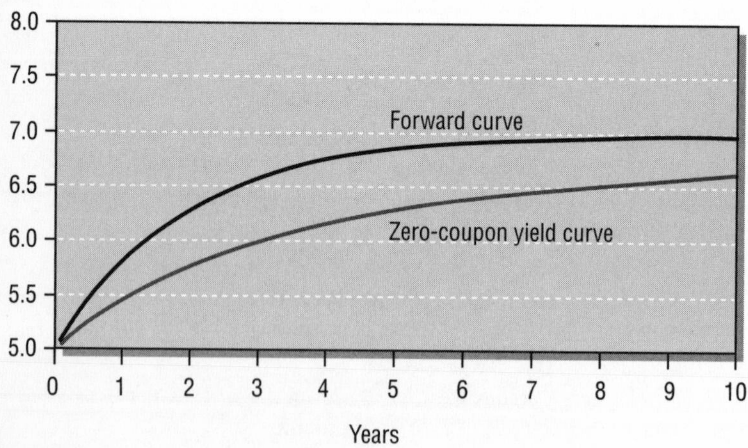

FIGURE 5.1 Term Structure of Instantaneous Forward Rates and Zero-Coupon Yields

TABLE 5.2 Computing the Price and the Duration Risk Measures of Bond 5

Maturity	Cash Flows ($)	Zero-Coupon Yield (%)	Present Value ($)	Computing $D_5(1)$	Computing $D_5(2)$	Computing $D_5(3)$
T	CF	$y(t)$	$CF/e^{t\,y(t)}$	$PV \times t$	$PV \times t^2$	$PV \times t^3$
1	100	5.444	94.70	94.70	94.70	94.70
2	100	5.762	89.11	178.23	356.46	712.92
3	100	5.994	83.54	250.63	751.89	2,255.66
4	100	6.165	78.15	312.58	1,250.32	5,001.29
5	1,100	6.294	803.00	4,015.01	20,075.04	100,375.18
Total			P = 1,148.51	4,851.15	22,528.41	108,439.75
				$D_5(1) =$ 4.224	$D_5(2) =$ 19.615	$D_5(3) =$ 94.418

The first column of Table 5.2 gives the maturities of the cash flows; the second column gives the dollar values of the cash flows; the third column gives the zero-coupon yields obtained from Nelson and Siegel's formula given in equation 5.12; the fourth column gives the present values of the cash flows, and the remaining three columns give the value of the product of the present value of each cash flow and the corresponding maturity raised to the power one, two, and three, respectively.

The sum of the present values of the cash flows gives the bond price. The first-, second-, and third-order duration risk measures are computed by dividing the sums in the last three columns, respectively, by the bond price, or:

$$D_5(1) = \frac{4851.15}{1148.51} = 4.224$$

$$D_5(2) = \frac{22528.41}{1148.51} = 19.615$$

$$D_5(3) = \frac{108439.75}{1148.51} = 94.418$$

Similar calculations give the first-, second-, and third-order duration measures for bonds 1, 2, 3, and 4 in Table 5.3.

TABLE 5.3 Prices and Duration Risk Measures for All Five Bonds

Bond #	Price ($)	Duration Measures		
1	1,041.72	$D_1(1) = 1.000$	$D_1(2) = 1.000$	$D_1(3) = 1.000$
2	1,074.97	$D_2(1) = 1.912$	$D_2(2) = 3.736$	$D_2(3) = 7.383$
3	1,102.79	$D_3(1) = 2.747$	$D_3(2) = 7.909$	$D_3(3) = 23.232$
4	1,126.96	$D_4(1) = 3.516$	$D_4(2) = 13.272$	$D_4(3) = 51.535$
5	1,148.51	$D_5(1) = 4.224$	$D_5(2) = 19.615$	$D_5(3) = 94.418$

The duration vector of a bond portfolio is simply the weighted average of the duration vectors of individual bonds, where the weights are defined as the proportions invested in the bonds. To illustrate the computation of portfolio duration vector, consider a bond portfolio with an initial value of \$10,000 composed of an investment of \$2,000 in each of the five bonds. The proportion of investment in each bond is then 0.2 and the duration vector of the bond portfolio is computed as follows:

$$D_{PORT}(1) = 0.2 \times 1 + 0.2 \times 1.912 + 0.2 \times 2.747 + 0.2 \times 3.516 + 0.2 \times 4.224 = 2.680$$
$$D_{PORT}(2) = 0.2 \times 1 + 0.2 \times 3.736 + 0.2 \times 7.909 + 0.2 \times 13.272 + 0.2 \times 19.615 = 9.106$$
$$D_{PORT}(3) = 0.2 \times 1 + 0.2 \times 7.383 + 0.2 \times 23.232 + 0.2 \times 51.535 + 0.2 \times 94.418 = 35.514$$

This portfolio with equal weights in all bonds was arbitrarily selected and does not provide an immunized return over a given planning horizon. Suppose an institution desires to create an *immunized portfolio* consisting of bonds 1, 2, 3, 4, and 5 over a planning horizon of three years using the first-, second-, and third-order duration measures. The immunization constraints given by equation 5.5 lead to the following equations:

$$D_{PORT}(1) = p_1 \times 1 + p_2 \times 1.912 + p_3 \times 2.747 + p_4 \times 3.516 + p_5 \times 4.224 = 3$$
$$D_{PORT}(2) = p_1 \times 1 + p_2 \times 3.736 + p_3 \times 7.909 + p_4 \times 13.272 + p_5 \times 19.615 = 3^2$$
$$D_{PORT}(3) = p_1 \times 1 + p_2 \times 7.383 + p_3 \times 23.232 + p_4 \times 51.535 + p_5 \times 94.418 = 3^3$$
$$p_1 + p_2 + p_3 + p_4 + p_5 = 1$$

The previous system of four equations leads to an infinite number of solutions, because the number of unknowns (five portfolio weights) is greater than the number of equations. To select a unique immunizing solution, we optimize the quadratic objective function given as:

$$\text{Min}\left[\sum_{i=1}^{J} p_i^2\right]$$

subject to the four constraints given.

The solution using equation 5.7 is:

$$p_1 = -0.187;\ p_2 = 0.294;\ p_3 = 0.558;\ p_4 = 0.456;\ p_5 = -0.122$$

Multiplying these proportions by the portfolio value of $10,000, bonds 1 and 5 must be shorted in the amounts of $1,871.40 and $1,215.25, respectively. Adding the proceeds from the short positions to the initial portfolio value of $10,000, the investments in bonds 2, 3, and 4 must be $2,939.94, $5,582.55, and $4,564.17, respectively. Dividing these amounts by the respective bond prices, the immunized portfolio is composed of –1.796 number of bonds 1, 2.735 number of bonds 2, 5.062 number of bonds 3, 4.050 number of bonds 4, and –1.058 number of bonds 5.

Example 5.2 Consider a shift in the instantaneous forward rate curve given in Example 5.1. Let the new parameters measuring the forward rate curve be given as $\alpha_1 = 0.075$, $\alpha_2 = -0.01$, $\alpha_3 = 0.002$, and $\beta = 2$. The instantaneous forward rates before and after the shock are shown in Figure 5.2.

The instantaneous forward rate curve shifts upward, while its shape flattens. This is consistent with a positive height change, negative slope change, and a positive curvature change. Though the magnitude of curvature decreases, the sign of the change is positive, since it is from a high negative curvature to a less negative curvature. The hypothesized signs of the changes in the shape of the forward rate curve are confirmed later in this example. As a result of the shift in the instantaneous forward rate curve, the values of the bonds 1, 2, 3, 4, 5, and the equally weighted portfolio comprised of these bonds analyzed in Example 5.1 change to $1,028.21 (bond 1), $1,051.28 (bond 2), $1,071.09 (bond 3), $1,088.65 (bond 4), $1,104.53 (bond 5), and $9,727.98 (bond portfolio).[7]

As a result of the change in forward rates, the instantaneous return on the portfolio is given as follows:

$$\frac{\Delta V_0}{V_0} = \frac{9727.98 - 10000}{10000} = -0.02720 = -2.72\%$$

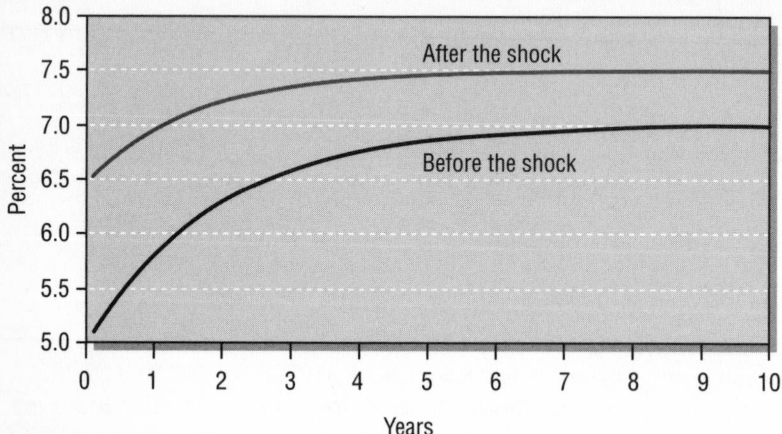

FIGURE 5.2 Shock in the Term Structure of Instantaneous Forward Rates

According to equation 5.1, the return on the portfolio can be estimated using three duration risk measures, as follows:

$$\frac{\Delta V_0}{V_0} \approx D(1) \times Y_1 + D(2) \times Y_2 + D(3) \times Y_3$$

where

$$Y_1 = -\Delta f(0)$$

$$Y_2 = -\frac{1}{2} \times \left[\frac{\partial(\Delta f(t))}{\partial t} - (\Delta f(0))^2 \right]_{t=0}$$

$$Y_3 = -\frac{1}{3!} \times \left[\frac{\partial^2(\Delta f(t))}{\partial t^2} - 3 \times \Delta f(0) \frac{\partial(\Delta f(t))}{\partial t} + (\Delta f(0))^3 \right]_{t=0}$$

Since the initial forward rate curve is given as:

$$f(t) = 0.07 - 0.02 \times e^{-t/2} + 0.001 \times e^{-t/2} \times \frac{t}{2}$$

and the new forward rate curve after the shock is given as:

$$f'(t) = 0.075 - 0.01 \times e^{-t/2} + 0.002 \times e^{-t/2} \times \frac{t}{2}$$

we can compute the following expressions:

$$\Delta f(0) = f'(0) - f(0) = 0.065 - 0.05 = 0.015$$

$$\left[\frac{\partial(\Delta f(t))}{\partial t}\right]_{t=0} = \left[\frac{\partial(f'(t))}{\partial t}\right]_{t=0} - \left[\frac{\partial(f(t))}{\partial t}\right]_{t=0} = 0.006 - 0.0105 = -0.0045$$

$$\left[\frac{\partial^2(\Delta f(t))}{\partial t^2}\right]_{t=0} = \left[\frac{\partial^2(f'(t))}{\partial t^2}\right]_{t=0} - \left[\frac{\partial^2(f(t))}{\partial t^2}\right]_{t=0} = -0.0035 - (-0.0055) = 0.002$$

As conjectured in Figure 5.2, the forward rate curve experiences a positive height change, a negative slope change, and a positive curvature change. Substituting the previous expressions into the shift vector elements, gives:

$$Y_1 = -0.015$$

$$Y_2 = -\frac{1}{2} \times \left[-0.0045 - 0.015^2\right] = 0.00236$$

$$Y_3 = -\frac{1}{3!} \times \left[0.015^3 - 3 \times 0.015 \times (-0.0045) + 0.002\right] = -0.00037$$

The returns on the bond portfolio estimated from the model for the three cases, when $M = 1$, $M = 2$, and $M = 3$, are given as:

$$R^{M=1} \cong 2.680 \times (-0.015) = -0.04020 = -4.020\%$$

$$R^{M=2} \cong 2.680 \times (-0.015) + 9.106 \times 0.00236 = -0.01868 = -1.868\%$$

$$R^{M=3} \cong 2.680 \times (-0.015) + 9.106 \times 0.00236 + 35.514 \times (-0.00037) = -0.03174 = -3.174\%$$

The estimated returns approach the actual return on the bond portfolio (−2.72 percent) as M increases. As Figure 5.3 shows, when $M = 3$ the difference between the estimated and the actual return has reduced to a third of the corresponding difference when $M = 1$. Further, as Figure 5.3 demonstrates, the differences between the estimated returns and actual returns decline further as M increases. Though adding higher order duration measures

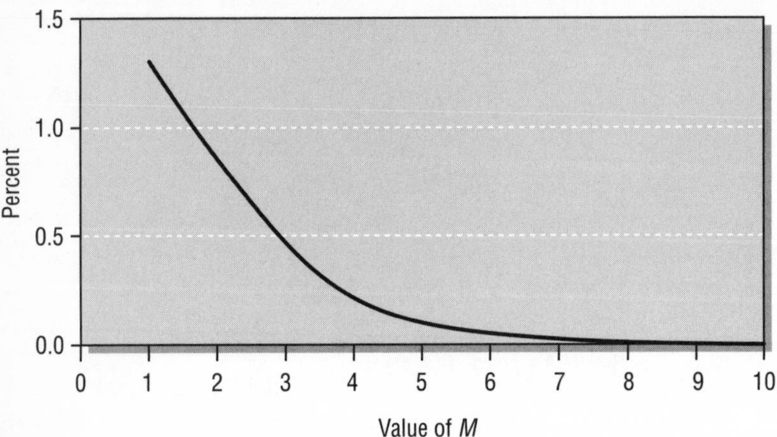

FIGURE 5.3 Absolute Differences between Actual and Estimated Returns for Different Values of *M*

(i.e., by using higher values of *M*) leads to lower errors between the estimated and the actual returns, the appropriate number of duration measures to be used for portfolio immunization is an empirical issue, since the marginal decline in the errors has to be traded off against higher transaction costs associated with portfolio rebalancing.

Nawalkha and Chambers (1997) perform an extensive set of empirical tests over the observation period 1951 through 1986 to determine an appropriate value of *M* for the duration vector model. Using McCulloch term structure data, they simulate coupon bond prices as follows. On December 31 of each year (1951 through 1986), 31 annual coupon bonds are constructed with seven different maturities (1, 2, 3, . . . , 7 years) and five different coupon values (6, 8, 10, 12, and 14 percent) for each maturity.[8]

On December 31, 1951, five different bond portfolios are constructed corresponding to five alternative immunization strategies corresponding to five different values of $M = 1, 2, 3, 4$, and 5. For each value of *M*, the following quadratic objective function is minimized, subject to the immunization constraints:

$$\text{Min}\left[\sum_{i=1}^{J} p_i^2\right]$$

subject to:

$$\sum_{i=1}^{J} p_i \, D_i(m) = H^m, \text{ for all } m = 1, 2, \ldots, M$$

$$\sum_{i=1}^{J} p_i = 1$$

where p_i gives the weight of the *i*th bond in the bond portfolio, and $D_i(m)$ defines the duration vector for the *i*th bond. The solution to this constrained optimization problem is given by equation 5.7.

The initial investment is set to $1 and the planning horizon is assumed to equal four years. The five portfolios are rebalanced on December 31 of each of the next three years when annual coupons are received. At the end of the four-year horizon, the returns of all five bond portfolios are compared with the return on a hypothetical four-year zero-coupon bond (computed at the beginning of the planning horizon). The differences between the actual values and the target value are defined as deviations in the interest rate risk hedging performance. The tests are repeated over 32 overlapping four-year periods given as 1951 to 1955, 1952 to 1956, . . . , 1982 to 1986.

Because interest rate volatility in the 1950s and 1960s was lower than in the 1970s and 1980s, and to test the robustness of these models against possible nonstationarities in the stochastic processes for the term structure, results for the periods 1951 to 1970 and 1967 to 1986 are shown separately in Table 5.4. Panels A and B report the sums of absolute deviations of actual portfolio values from target values of the five hedging strategies for each of the two subperiods.[9] These deviations are also reported as a percentage of the deviations of the simple duration strategy (i.e., with $M = 1$) for the two subperiods.

TABLE 5.4 Deviations of Actual Values from Target Values for the Duration Vector Strategies

	$M = 1$	$M = 2$	$M = 3$	$M = 4$	$M = 5$
Panel A: Observation period 1951–1970					
Sum of absolute deviations	0.10063	0.03445	0.01085	0.00305	0.00136
As percentage of $M = 1$	100.00	34.23	10.78	3.03	1.35
Panel B: Observation period 1967–1986					
Sum of absolute deviations	0.28239	0.06621	0.03228	0.01412	0.01082
As percentage of $M = 1$	100.00	23.45	11.43	4.99	3.83

The figures show that the immunization performance of the duration vector strategies improves steadily as the length of the duration vector is increased. The strategy with $M = 5$ leads to near-perfect interest rate risk hedging performance, eliminating more than 95 percent of the interest rate risk inherent in the simple duration strategy over both subperiods. The results of the tests are similar over both subperiods, providing empirical confirmation that the duration vector model is independent of the particular stochastic processes for term structure movements.

Hedging Strategies Based on the Duration Vector Model

Though portfolio immunization is the most common application of the duration vector model, other applications include bond index replication, duration gap analysis of financial institutions, and active trading strategies. Bond index replication consists of replicating the risk-return characteristics of some underlying bond index. Under the duration vector model, this involves equating the duration measures of the portfolio to those of the bond index. For replicating a bond index, the relevant constraints on the duration measures are:

$$\begin{aligned} D(1)_{PORT} &= D(1)_{INDEX} \\ D(2)_{PORT} &= D(2)_{INDEX} \\ &\vdots \\ D(M)_{PORT} &= D(M)_{INDEX} \end{aligned} \tag{5.13}$$

Another application of the duration vector model is controlling the interest rate risk of financial institutions by eliminating or reducing the duration measure gaps. For example, the duration gaps can be defined as follows with respect to the first- and second-order duration measures:

$$\begin{aligned} D(1)_{Gap} &= D(1)_{Assets} - \left(V^L/V^A\right) \times D(1)_{Liabilities} \\ D(2)_{Gap} &= D(2)_{Assets} - \left(V^L/V^A\right) \times D(2)_{Liabilities} \end{aligned} \tag{5.14}$$

where V^A is the value of the assets and V^L the value of the liabilities.

To immunize the equity value of the financial institution from the changes in the term structure, the managers can eliminate the duration gaps by imposing the following constraints:

$$V^A D(1)_{Assets} = V^L D(1)_{Liabilities}$$
$$V^A D(2)_{Assets} = V^L D(2)_{Liabilities} \quad (5.15)$$

Highly leveraged financial institutions such as Fannie Mae and Freddie Mac are generally very concerned about their interest rate risk exposure. Though these institutions typically aim to make their first-order duration gap equal to zero, they could use a gap model for the first- and second-order duration measures as shown in equation 5.15.

Finally, the duration vector models allow speculative bond trading strategies that are of interest to many fixed-income hedge funds. To obtain the desired portfolio return, the duration risk measures can be set to any values.

Example 5.3 Suppose a hedge-fund manager predicts that the forward rate yield curve will evolve as in Example 5.2. Hence, the shift vector under the duration vector model is given as $Y_1 = -0.015$, $Y_2 = 0.00236$, and $Y_3 = -0.00037$. To benefit from such a yield-curve shift, the manager can select a portfolio with a negative value of $D(1)$, a positive value of $D(2)$, and a negative value of $D(3)$. Let us assume that the target values for the three duration measures are:

$$D(1) = -0.5;\ D(2) = 1;\ D(3) = -5$$

The instantaneous return on the bond portfolio, given the previous yield-curve shift, is approximately equal to:

$$\begin{aligned} R &\approx D(1)\times Y_1 + D(2)\times Y_2 + D(3)\times Y_3 + \cdots + D(M)\times Y_M \\ &= (-0.5)\times(-0.015) + 1\times 0.00236 + (-5)\times(-0.00037) \\ &= 0.01171 = 1.171\% \end{aligned}$$

To obtain this return from the bond portfolio comprised of the bonds 1, 2, 3, 4, and 5 introduced in Example 5.1, the manager will have to determine the proportion of investment in the five bonds by performing the following constrained quadratic minimization:

$$\text{Min}\left[\sum_{i=1}^{J} p_i^2\right]$$

subject to:

$$D_{PORT}(1) = p_1 \times 1 + p_2 \times 1.912 + p_3 \times 2.747 + p_4 \times 3.516 + p_5 \times 4.224 = -0.5$$
$$D_{PORT}(2) = p_1 \times 1 + p_2 \times 3.736 + p_3 \times 7.909 + p_4 \times 13.272 + p_5 \times 19.615 = 1$$
$$D_{PORT}(3) = p_1 \times 1 + p_2 \times 7.383 + p_3 \times 23.232 + p_4 \times 51.535 + p_5 \times 94.418 = -5$$
$$p_1 + p_2 + p_3 + p_4 + p_5 = 1$$

The solution is given as follows:

$$p_1 = 6.712;\ p_2 = -9.120;\ p_3 = -0.747;\ p_4 = 7.447;\ p_5 = -3.292$$

Closed-Form Formulas for Duration Measures

Though the higher order duration measures given in equation 5.2 are computed as summations, significant saving in computation time results by using closed-form formulas for these measures instead of the summations. The derivations of closed-form formulas require using the bond-specific yield to maturity to compute the duration measures, instead of the whole yield curve. It has been observed by Chambers et al. (1988) that the duration measures computed by using the bond-specific yield-to-maturities lead to virtually identical immunization performance as achieved by the duration measures computed using the whole yield curve. From a practical perspective, this means that all duration measures can be computed using a simple calculator or a spreadsheet using information that is widely available.[10]

Nawalkha and Lacey (1990) show how to compute higher order duration measures, both at coupon payment dates, and between coupon payment dates. The expression for the mth order duration risk measure of a bond, between coupon payment dates, with coupons paid k times a year is given as:

$$D(m) = \left(\frac{\displaystyle\sum_{j=1}^{N} \frac{(j-s)^m C}{e^{i(j-s)}} + \frac{(N-s)^m F}{e^{i(N-s)}}}{\displaystyle\sum_{j=1}^{N} \frac{C}{e^{i(j-s)}} + \frac{F}{e^{i(N-s)}}} \right) / k^m \qquad (5.16)$$

where $i = y/k$ is the continuously compounded yield of the bond divided by k, C is periodic coupon payment given as the annual coupon payment divided by k, F is the face value, N is the total number of cash flows, and s is the time elapsed since the date of last cash flow payment in the units of time interval between coupon payment dates. The division of the bracketed expressions by k^m on the right side of equation 5.16 gives the mth order duration measure in annualized units.

The closed-form solution for the mth order duration measure is given as:

$$D(m) = \left(\frac{\left(e^{i}-1\right)\left[c \times S_{m} \times e^{i(N-s)} + (N-s)^{m}\right]}{c\left(e^{iN}-1\right)+\left(e^{i}-1\right)} \right) / k^{m} \tag{5.17}$$

where $c = C/F$, and S_m is given in closed form as follows:

$$S_{m} = \frac{1}{\left(e^{i}-1\right)} \left[(1-s)^{m} e^{is} + \sum_{t=0}^{m-1} {}_{m}K_{t} S_{t} - \frac{(1+N-s)^{m}}{e^{i(N-s)}} \right] \quad \text{for all } m \geq 1 \tag{5.18}$$

and

$${}_{m}K_{t} = \frac{m!}{(m-t)!t!} \quad \text{and } S_{0} = \frac{e^{is}}{\left(e^{i}-1\right)}\left[1 - \frac{1}{e^{iN}}\right]$$

Although in principle this approach can be used to obtain the closed-form solution of all higher order elements of the duration vector, the formulas become complicated and cumbersome to report as we move to higher orders beyond three. Table 5.5 gives the closed-form solutions of the first three elements of the duration vector. Bond practitioners frequently use these three duration measures.

Example 5.4 Reconsider the five-year, 10 percent coupon bond in Example 5.1. The first three duration measures of this bond were given as, $D(1) = 4.224$, $D(2) = 19.615$, and $D(3) = 94.418$. We now compute these duration measures using the closed-form formulas given in Table 5.5. Since this bond gives annual coupons, its *quoted* yield to maturity is based upon annual compounding and must be equal to 6.433 percent as shown next:

$$1148.51 = \frac{100}{(1+r)} + \frac{100}{(1+r)^{2}} + \frac{100}{(1+r)^{3}} + \frac{100}{(1+r)^{4}} + \frac{1100}{(1+r)^{5}}$$

$$= \frac{100}{e^{y}} + \frac{100}{e^{y\times 2}} + \frac{100}{e^{y\times 3}} + \frac{100}{e^{y\times 4}} + \frac{1100}{e^{y\times 5}}$$

which gives $r = 6.433\%$ and $y = i = 6.234\%$.

Assuming y is the continuously compounded yield, it is equal to $\ln(1 + r) = \ln(1.06433) = 6.234$ percent, and can be easily obtained from the quoted discrete annual yield.

TABLE 5.5 Closed-Form Solutions for $D(1)$, $D(2)$, and $D(3)$

Between Coupon Payment Dates

$$D(1)=\frac{c\left[e^{iN}\left(e^{i}(1-s)+s\right)-e^{i}\right]+\left(e^{i}-1\right)(N-s)\left(e^{i}-1-c\right)}{\left(c\left(e^{i}-1\right)\left(e^{iN}-1\right)+\left(e^{i}-1\right)^{2}\right)k}$$

$$D(2)=\frac{c\left\{e^{iN}\left[\left(e^{i}(1-s)+s\right)^{2}+e^{i}\right]-e^{i}\left[2\left(1+(N-s)\left(e^{i}-1\right)\right)+e^{i}-1\right]\right\}+\left(e^{i}-1\right)^{2}(N-s)^{2}\left(e^{i}-1-c\right)}{\left(c\left(e^{i}-1\right)^{2}\left(e^{iN}-1\right)+\left(e^{i}-1\right)^{3}\right)k^{2}}$$

$$D(3)=\frac{c\left\{(e^{i}-1)^{3}\times\left[e^{iN}\times(1-s)^{3}-(1+N-s)^{3}\right]-3N(e^{i}-1)^{2}\times(3+N-2s)+(e^{iN}-1)\times\left[6+6\times(e^{i}-1)\times(2-s)+(e^{i}-1)^{2}\times(7-9s+3s^{2})\right]-6N(e^{i}-1)\right\}+(N-s)^{3}\times(e^{i}-1)^{4}}{\left(c\times(e^{i}-1)^{3}\times(e^{iN}-1)+(e^{i}-1)^{4}\right)k^{3}}$$

At Coupon Payment Dates

$$D_{s=0}(1)=\frac{ce^{i}\left(e^{iN}-1\right)+N\left(e^{i}-1\right)\times\left(e^{i}-1-c\right)}{\left(c\left(e^{i}-1\right)\times\left(e^{iN}-1\right)+\left(e^{i}-1\right)^{2}\right)k}$$

$$D_{s=0}(2)=\frac{c\left\{e^{i}\left(1+e^{i}\right)\left(e^{iN}-1\right)-2Ne^{i}\left(e^{i}-1\right)\right\}+N^{2}\left(e^{i}-1\right)^{2}\left(e^{i}-1-c\right)}{\left(c\left(e^{i}-1\right)^{2}\left(e^{iN}-1\right)+\left(e^{i}-1\right)^{3}\right)k^{2}}$$

$$D_{s=0}(3)=\frac{c\left\{(e^{i}-1)^{3}\left[e^{iN}-(1+N)^{3}\right]-3N(e^{i}-1)^{2}\times(3+N)+(e^{iN}-1)\times(1-2e^{i}+7e^{2i})-6N(e^{i}-1)\right\}+N^{3}\times(e^{i}-1)^{4}}{\left(c(e^{i}-1)^{3}\times(e^{iN}-1)+(e^{i}-1)^{4}\right)k^{3}}$$

Since the bond matures in exactly five years, the closed-form formulas with $s = 0$ given in Table 5.5 can be used to compute the three duration measures. The first-, second-, and third-order duration measures of this bond are computed as follows:

$$D_{s=0}(1) = \frac{0.1 \times e^{0.06234} \times \left(e^{0.06234\times 5} - 1\right) + 5 \times \left(e^{0.06234} - 1\right) \times \left(e^{0.06234} - 1.1\right)}{0.1 \times \left(e^{0.06234} - 1\right) \times \left(e^{0.06234\times 5} - 1\right) + \left(e^{0.06234} - 1\right)^2} = 4.230$$

$$D_{s=0}(2) = \frac{0.1 \times \left\{e^{0.06234}\left(1 + e^{0.06234}\right) \times \left(e^{0.06234\times 5} - 1\right) - 10 \times e^{0.06234} \times \left(e^{0.06234} - 1\right)\right\} + 25 \times \left(e^{0.06234} - 1\right)^2 \times \left(e^{0.06234} - 1.1\right)}{0.1 \times \left(e^{0.06234} - 1\right)^2 \times \left(e^{0.06234\times 5} - 1\right) + \left(e^{0.06234} - 1\right)^3} = 19.656$$

$$D_{s=0}(3) = \frac{0.1 \times \left(e^{0.06234} - 1\right)^3 \times \left[e^{0.06234\times 5} - 216\right] - 0.1 \times 120 \times \left(e^{0.06234} - 1\right)^2}{0.1 \times \left(e^{0.06234} - 1\right)^3 \times \left(e^{0.06234\times N} - 1\right) + \left(e^{0.06234} - 1\right)^4}$$
$$+ \frac{0.1 \times \left(e^{0.06234\times 5} - 1\right) \times \left(1 - 2 \times e^{0.06234} + 7 \times e^{2\times 0.06234}\right) - 0.1 \times 30 \times \left(e^{0.06234} - 1\right) + 125 \times \left(e^{0.06234} - 1\right)^4}{0.1 \times \left(e^{0.06234} - 1\right)^3 \times \left(e^{0.06234\times N} - 1\right) + \left(e^{0.06234} - 1\right)^4}$$
$$= 94.647$$

The three values obtained using the closed-form formulas are virtually identical to the values to these duration measures obtained using the summation form earlier, the slight differences being due to the use of the single rate i instead of the whole yield curve. The slight differences are so insignificant, that immunization performance is virtually identical using either of these duration measures.

Now consider the computation of the first-, second-, and the third-order duration measures after nine months, so that the bond now matures in four years and three months. Also, assume that the yield to maturity is still 6.234 percent. Since the bond has not paid any coupons yet, the number of coupons before maturity is still 5 ($N = 5$), but the first coupon is due in three months. The time elapsed since the date of the last coupon relative to time between two coupon payments is $s = 9$ months/12 months $= 0.75$

$$
\begin{array}{rcrcr}
 & & S_0 = 4.163 & & \\
S_0, S_1 & \xrightarrow{Eq.(5.18)} & S_1 = 11.971 & \xrightarrow{Eq.(5.17)} & D(1) = 4.230 \\
S_0, S_1, S_2 & \xrightarrow{Eq.(5.18)} & S_2 = 42.709 & \xrightarrow{Eq.(5.17)} & D(2) = 19.656 \\
S_0, S_1, S_2, S_3 & \xrightarrow{Eq.(5.18)} & S_3 = 171.793 & \xrightarrow{Eq.(5.17)} & D(3) = 94.647 \\
S_0, S_1, S_2, S_3, S_4 & \xrightarrow{Eq.(5.18)} & S_4 = 739.359 & \xrightarrow{Eq.(5.17)} & D(4) = 462.820 \\
S_0, S_1, S_2, S_3, S_4, S_5 & \xrightarrow{Eq.(5.18)} & S_5 = 3316.800 & \xrightarrow{Eq.(5.17)} & D(5) = 2281.012
\end{array}
$$

FIGURE 5.4 Calculating Higher Order Duration Measures

years. To compute the duration measures, we use the formulas in the top section of Table 5.5, which yield:

$$D(1) = 3.480; \; D(2) = 13.874; \; D(3) = 57.136$$

As expected, the duration measures between coupon payment dates are lower than those obtained earlier. The significant differences between the duration measures at coupon payment dates and those between payment dates as we move to higher order measures, show that ignoring the time elapsed between coupon payment dates can introduce significant errors in portfolio formation when higher order duration strategies are used.

When duration measures of orders higher than three are needed, we suggest the approach illustrated in Example 5.5 for efficiency of calculation. The approach consists of computing the values of S_m for every m from 0 to the length chosen for the duration vector. According to equation 5.18, S_0 is used in the calculation of S_1, S_0 and S_1 are used in the calculation of S_2, and so on. As we are obtaining the value of each S_m, it can be substituted into equation 5.17 to obtain each duration measure $D(m)$.

Example 5.5 Consider again the five-year, 10 percent coupon bond priced to yield 6.234 percent. The method used for computing the five elements of the duration vector of this bond is shown by Figure 5.4.

GENERALIZED DURATION VECTOR MODELS

Although increasing the length of the duration vector improves the immunization performance, it also tends to produce more extreme portfolio holdings than is produced by the duration vector of a shorter length. As a result, the portfolio becomes increasingly exposed to *nonsystematic* risks (i.e., bond-specific) and incurs high transactions costs. For this reason, instead of increasing the length of the duration vector, we propose a polynomial class of *generalized duration vector models,* which seems to be more effective in protecting against immunization risk than the traditional duration vector model, without increasing the vector length.[11] These models are obtained using a generalized Taylor series expansion of the portfolio return given in Appendix 5.1.

The generalized duration vector model is given as follows:

$$\frac{\Delta V_0}{V_0} \approx D^*(1)\, Y_1^* + D^*(2)\, Y_2^* + D^*(3)\, Y_3^* + \cdots + D^*(M)\, Y_M^* \qquad (5.19)$$

where

$$D^*(M) = \sum_{t=t_1}^{t=t_N} w_t \times g(t)^m, \text{ for } m = 1, 2, \ldots, M \qquad (5.20)$$

and

$$w_t = \left[\frac{CF_t}{e^{\int_0^t f(s)ds}} \right] / V_0$$

Equation 5.20 defines the *generalized duration risk measures* $D^*(1)$, $D^*(2)$, $D^*(3)$, . . . , $D^*(M)$. The generalized duration risk measures are similar to the traditional duration risk measures, except that the weighted averages are computed with respect to $g(t)$, $g(t)^2$, $g(t)^3$, and so on, instead of t, t^2, t^3, and so on. Hence, the generalized duration risk measure $D^*(1)$ is the weighted average of $g(t)$, the generalized duration risk measure $D^*(2)$ is the weighted average of $g(t)^2$, and so on. The shift vector elements in equation 5.19 depend only on the nature of term structure shifts, and not on the portfolio characteristics. These elements are defined in Appendix 5.1.

For immunizing a bond portfolio, the first-, second-, third-, and higher order generalized duration risk measures of the portfolio are set equal to $g(H)$, $g(H)^2$, $g(H)^3$, and so on, which is similar to the traditional duration vector models in which the first-, second-, third-, and higher order duration measures of the bond portfolio are set equal to H, H^2, H^3, and so on. The immunization constraints are given as follows:

TABLE 5.6 Computing the Generalized Duration Risk Measures of Bond 5

Maturity	Cash Flows ($)	Zero-Coupon Yield (%)	Present Value ($)	Computing $D_5^*(1)$	Computing $D_5^*(2)$	Computing $D_5^*(3)$
t	CF	$y(t)$	$CF/e^{t\,y(t)}$	$PV \times t^{0.25}$	$PV \times t^{0.25 \times 2}$	$PV \times t^{0.25 \times 3}$
1	100	5.444	94.70	94.70	94.70	94.70
2	100	5.762	89.11	105.98	126.03	149.87
3	100	5.994	83.54	109.95	144.70	190.44
4	100	6.165	78.15	110.51	156.29	221.03
5	1,100	6.294	803.00	1,200.77	1,795.57	2,685.00
Total			$P =$ 1,148.51	1,621.91	2,317.29	3,341.04
				$D_5^*(1) =$ 1.412	$D_5^*(2) =$ 2.018	$D_5^*(3) =$ 2.909

$$
\begin{aligned}
D^*(1) &= \sum_{t=t_1}^{t=t_N} w_t \times g(t) = g(H) \\
D^*(2) &= \sum_{t=t_1}^{t=t_N} w_t \times g(t)^2 = g(H)^2 \\
D^*(3) &= \sum_{t=t_1}^{t=t_N} w_t \times g(t)^3 = g(H)^3 \\
&\vdots \\
D^*(M) &= \sum_{t=t_1}^{t=t_N} w_t \times g(t)^M = g(H)^M
\end{aligned}
\tag{5.21}
$$

Example 5.6 Consider the polynomial functions given as $g(t) = t^{\alpha}$ for the generalized duration vector models. Reconsider the five bonds and the bond portfolio given in Example 5.1. Assuming that $\alpha = 0.25$ and thus, $g(t) = t^{0.25}$, Table 5.6 shows how to compute the generalized duration risk measures of bond 5 up to the third order.

The first four columns of Table 5.6 give the cash flow maturities, the dollar value of the cash flows, the zero-coupon yield, and the present values of the cash flows, respectively. The remaining three columns of the table

TABLE 5.7 Prices and Duration Risk Measures for Each Bond

Bond #	Price ($)	Generalized Duration Measures		
1	1,041.72	$D_1^*(1) = 1.000$	$D_1^*(2) = 1.000$	$D_1^*(3) = 1.000$
2	1,074.97	$D_2^*(1) = 1.173$	$D_2^*(2) = 1.378$	$D_2^*(3) = 1.622$
3	1,102.79	$D_3^*(1) = 1.279$	$D_3^*(2) = 1.644$	$D_3^*(3) = 2.121$
4	1,126.96	$D_4^*(1) = 1.354$	$D_4^*(2) = 1.850$	$D_4^*(3) = 2.543$
5	1,148.51	$D_5^*(1) = 1.412$	$D_5^*(2) = 2.018$	$D_5^*(3) = 2.909$

compute the first-, second-, and third-order generalized duration measures by summing the products of the present value of cash flows and the corresponding maturities raised to different powers. These powers are obtained by multiplying the value of $\alpha = 0.25$ by the successive integer values of one, two and three, respectively.

The first-, second-, and third-order generalized duration risk measures are computed by dividing the sums in the last three columns, respectively, by the bond price, or:

$$D_5^*(1) = \frac{1621.91}{1148.51} = 1.412$$

$$D_5^*(2) = \frac{2317.29}{1148.51} = 2.018$$

$$D_5^*(3) = \frac{3341.04}{1148.51} = 2.909$$

Similar calculations for bond 1, 2, 3, and 4 give the generalized duration risk measures for these bonds shown in Table 5.7.

Using Table 5.7, the generalized duration vector of an equally weighted bond portfolio, invested in the five bonds, is given as follows:

$$D_{PORT}^*(1) = 0.2 \times 1 + 0.2 \times 1.173 + 0.2 \times 1.279 + 0.2 \times 1.354 + 0.2 \times 1.412 = 1.244$$
$$D_{PORT}^*(2) = 0.2 \times 1 + 0.2 \times 1.378 + 0.2 \times 1.644 + 0.2 \times 1.850 + 0.2 \times 2.018 = 1.578$$
$$D_{PORT}^*(3) = 0.2 \times 1 + 0.2 \times 1.622 + 0.2 \times 2.121 + 0.2 \times 2.543 + 0.2 \times 2.909 = 2.039$$

This portfolio with equal weights in all bonds was arbitrarily selected and does not provide an immunized return over a given planning horizon.

Suppose an institution desires to create an *immunized portfolio* consisting of bonds 1, 2, 3, 4, and 5 over a planning horizon of three years using the first-, second-, and third-order generalized duration measures. The immunization constraints given by equation 5.21 lead to the following equations:

$$D^*_{PORT}(1) = p_1 \times 1 + p_2 \times 1.173 + p_3 \times 1.279 + p_4 \times 1.354 + p_5 \times 1.412 = 3^{0.25}$$
$$D^*_{PORT}(2) = p_1 \times 1 + p_2 \times 1.378 + p_3 \times 1.644 + p_4 \times 1.850 + p_5 \times 2.018 = 3^{0.25\times 2}$$
$$D^*_{PORT}(3) = p_1 \times 1 + p_2 \times 1.622 + p_3 \times 2.121 + p_4 \times 2.543 + p_5 \times 2.909 = 3^{0.25\times 3}$$
$$p_1 + p_2 + p_3 + p_4 + p_5 = 1$$

This system of four equations leads to an infinite number of solutions, because the number of unknowns (five portfolio weights) is greater than the number of equations. To select a unique immunizing solution, we optimize the quadratic objective function given as:

$$\text{Min}\left[\sum_{i=1}^{J} p_i^2\right]$$

subject to the four constraints given here.

The solution is similar to that shown in equation 5.7, but with two modifications. First, generalized duration measures given in Table 5.7 are used instead of traditional duration measures. Second, $g(H) = 3^{0.25}$, $g(H)^2 = (3^{0.25})^2$, $g(H)^3 = (3^{0.25})^3$, and so on, are substituted instead of H, H^2, H^3, and so on in the *column vector* on the left-hand side of equation 5.7. Quadratic optimization gives the following solution for the bonds' proportions:

$$p_1 = -0.120;\ p_2 = 0.107;\ p_3 = 0.664;\ p_4 = 0.541;\ p_5 = -0.192$$

Multiplying these proportions by the portfolio value of \$10,000, bonds, 1 and 5 must be shorted in the amounts of \$1,202.73 and \$1,923.12, respectively. Adding the proceeds from the short positions to the initial portfolio value of \$10,000, the investments in bonds 2, 3, and 4 must be \$1,072.81, \$6,641.98, and \$5,411.05. Dividing these amounts by the respective bond prices, the immunized portfolio is composed of −1.155 number of bonds 1, 0.998 number of bonds 2, 6.023 number of bonds 3, 4.801 number of bonds 4, and −1.674 number of bonds 5.

Not surprisingly, the immunized portfolio under the generalized duration vector with $g(t) = t^{0.25}$ is different from the immunized portfolio under

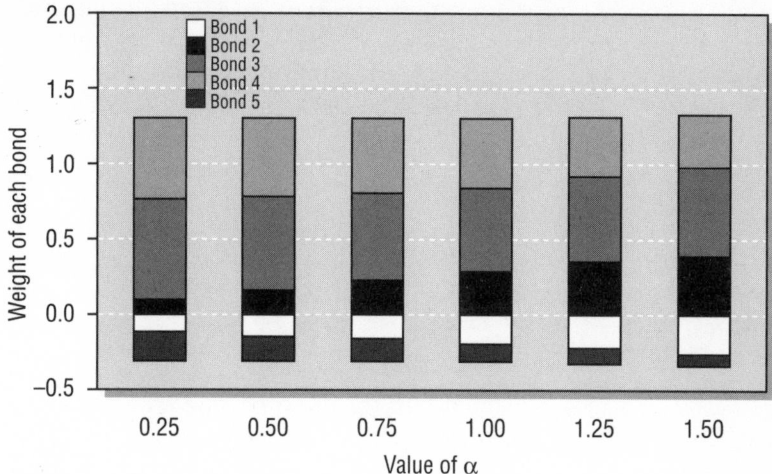

FIGURE 5.5 Weights of Each Bond in the Portfolios Immunized with the Generalized Duration Vector for Different Values of α

the traditional duration vector model (i.e., when $g(t) = t$). Other different values of α lead to different portfolio weights. This is shown in Figure 5.5, which gives the weights of each of the five bonds in the immunized portfolio for values of α ranging from 0.25 to 1.5.

Figure 5.5 shows that a lower value of α comes with a higher bond portfolio concentration in bonds 3 and 4, where as a high value of α comes with investments spread out in bonds 2, 3, and 4. Nawalkha, Soto, and Zhang (2003) examine the immunization performance of the generalized duration vector model corresponding to $g(t) = t^\alpha$ with six different values of α: 0.25, 0.5, 0.75, 1, 1.25, and 1.5. Different lengths of the generalized duration vectors (i.e., the value of M ranging from 1 to 5) are used to test which functional forms converge faster. Nawalkha, Soto, and Zhang (2003) find that the lower α generalized duration strategies significantly outperform higher α strategies, when higher order duration constraints are used.

APPENDIX 5.1: DERIVATION OF THE GENERALIZED DURATION VECTOR MODELS

Consider a bond portfolio at time $t = 0$ with CF_t as the payment on the portfolio at time $t(t = t_1, t_2, \ldots, t_N)$. Let the continuously compounded term structure of instantaneous forward rates be given by $f(t)$. Now allow an instantaneous shift in the forward rates from $f(t)$ to $f'(t)$ such that $f'(t) = f(t) + \Delta f(t)$. The return on the bond portfolio between $t = 0$ and $t = H$ can be given as:

$$R(H) = \frac{\left[V_H' - V_0\right]}{V_0} \tag{5.22}$$

where V_0 is the value of the bond portfolio at time 0, before the shift in the forward rates:

$$V_0 = \sum_{t=t_1}^{t=t_N} CF_t e^{-\int_0^t f(s)ds} \tag{5.23}$$

and V_H' is the realized future value of the portfolio at the planning horizon, after the term structure of forward rates have shifted to $f'(t)$:

$$V_H' = \sum_{t=t_1}^{t=t_N} CF_t e^{\int_t^H f'(s)ds} \tag{5.24}$$

Substituting the definitions of V_0 and V_H' into equation 5.22 gives:

$$R(H) = \left[e^{\int_0^H f(s)ds} \left[\sum_{t=t_1}^{t_N} CF_t \times e^{-\int_0^t f(s)ds} \times k(t) \right] - V_0 \right] / V_0 \tag{5.25}$$

where

$$k(t) = e^{\int_t^H \Delta f(s)ds} \tag{5.26}$$

Using a change of variable, let the forward rate function $f(t)$ be represented by a chain function given as:

$$f(t) = h\left(g(t)\right) \tag{5.27}$$

where $g(t)$ is a continuously differentiable function of t. Further assume that $g(t)$ is monotonic and the inverse function of $g(t)$ exists and is given as:

$$t = g^{-1}(g) = q(g) \tag{5.28}$$

The instantaneous change in the forward rate function can be given as:

$$\Delta f(t) = \Delta h\big(g(t)\big) \tag{5.29}$$

Using equations 5.28 and 5.29, we have:

$$k(t) = e^{\int_t^H \Delta f(s)ds} = e^{\int_{g(t)}^{g(H)} p(\gamma)d\gamma} \tag{5.30}$$

where

$$p(g(t)) = \Delta h(g(t)) \frac{\partial(q(g))}{\partial g} \tag{5.31}$$

Doing a Taylor series expansion of $r(g(t))$ around $g(H)$, $k(t)$ can be represented as:

$$\begin{aligned}
k(t) = {} & 1 - \left[g(t) - g(H)\right] \times p(g(H)) \\
& - \frac{1}{2}[g(t) - g(H)]^2 \times \left[\frac{\partial(p(g))}{\partial g} - [p(g)]^2\right]_{g=g(H)} \\
& - \frac{1}{3!}[g(t) - g(H)]^3 \times \left[[p(g)]^3 - 3 \times p(g)\frac{\partial(p(g))}{\partial g} + \frac{\partial^2(p(g))}{\partial g^2}\right]_{g=g(H)} \\
& + \ldots + \\
& - \frac{1}{M!}[g(t) - g(H)]^M \times \left[(-1)^{M+1}[p(g)]^M + \cdots + \frac{\partial^{M-1}(p(g))}{\partial g^{M-1}}\right]_{g=g(H)} \\
& + \cdots + \text{remainder}
\end{aligned} \tag{5.32}$$

For a reasonably large number M, the first $M + 1$ terms of the above equation may approximate the value of $k(t)$ well. Equation 5.32 can be written in a simplified form as:

$$k(t) = 1 + \sum_{m=1}^{M} [g(t) - g(H)]^{m} \times Z_{m}^{*} + \varepsilon(t) \tag{5.33}$$

where

$$Z_1^* = -p(g(H))$$

$$Z_2^* = -\frac{1}{2} \times \left[\frac{\partial(p(g))}{\partial g} - [p(g)]^2 \right]_{g=g(H)}$$

$$Z_3^* = -\frac{1}{3!} \times \left[[p(g)]^3 - 3 \times p(g) \frac{\partial(p(g))}{\partial g} + \frac{\partial^2(p(g))}{\partial g^2} \right]_{g=g(H)}$$

$$\vdots$$

$$Z_M^* = -\frac{1}{M!} \times \left[(-1)^{M+1} [p(g)]^M + \ldots + \frac{\partial^{M-1}(p(g))}{\partial g^{M-1}} \right]_{g=g(H)}$$

and expression $\varepsilon(t)$ is the error term due to higher order Taylor series terms.

Equation 5.31 shows that the value of $p(g)$ depends on the change in the forward rate function. In particular, if the forward rate function does not change, $p(g(H))$ equals zero and, therefore, $Z_m^* = 0$ for all $m = 1, 2, \ldots, M$. In this case, $k(t) = 1$, and the return on the portfolio is riskless. Substituting $k(t) = 1$ into equation 5.25, the riskless return between time 0 and H is given as:

$$R_F(H) = e^{\int_0^H f(s)ds} - 1 \tag{5.34}$$

If forward rates do change, the bond portfolio return will be different from the riskless return. The bond portfolio return can be obtained by substituting equation 5.33 into equation 5.25, which gives:

$$R(H) = R_F(H) + [1 + R_F(H)] \times \sum_{m=1}^{M} M^{*m} Z_m^* + \varepsilon \tag{5.35}$$

where ε is the error term due to higher order Taylor series terms, $R_F(H)$ is the riskless return defined in equation 5.34, and M^{*m} is the mth measure of the generalized M-vector corresponding to a given function $g(t)$ for all $m = 1, 2, \ldots, M$. The mth measure is of the following form:

$$M^{*m} = \left[\sum_{t=t_1}^{t_N} CF_t \times e^{-\int_0^t f(s)ds} \left[g(t) - g(H) \right]^m / V_0 \right] \tag{5.36}$$

Defining the generalized shift vector elements for all $m = 1, 2, \ldots, M$, as:

$$Y_m^* = \left(1 + R_F(H)\right) \times Z_m^* \tag{5.37}$$

where

$$Y_1^* = -\left(1 + R_F(H)\right) \times p(g(H))$$

$$Y_2^* = -\frac{1}{2} \times \left(1 + R_F(H)\right) \times \left[\frac{\partial(p(g))}{\partial g} - \left[p(g)\right]^2 \right]_{g=g(H)}$$

$$Y_3^* = -\frac{1}{3!} \times \left(1 + R_F(H)\right) \times \left[[p(g)]^3 - 3 \times p(g) \frac{\partial(p(g))}{\partial g} + \frac{\partial^2(p(g))}{\partial g^2} \right]_{g=g(H)}$$

$$\vdots$$

$$Y_M^* = -\frac{1}{M!} \times \left(1 + R_F(H)\right) \times \left[(-1)^{M+1} \left[p(g)\right]^M + \cdots + \frac{\partial^{M-1}(p(g))}{\partial g^{M-1}} \right]_{g=g(H)}$$

Assuming $H = 0$, equation 5.35 reduces to the generalized duration vector model given by equation 5.19:

$$R(0) = \frac{\Delta V_0}{V_0} \approx D^*(1)\, Y_1^* + D^*(2)\, Y_2^* + D^*(3)\, Y_3^* + \cdots + D^*(M)\, Y_M^* \tag{5.38}$$

The duration vector model introduced in equation 5.1 can be obtained as a special case of the generalized duration vector model given in equation 5.38, when $g(t) = t$.

NOTES

1. For example, see Chambers, Carleton, and McEnally (1988), Grandville (2003), Granito (1984), Nawalkha (1995), and Prisman and Tian (1994).
2. This derivation is based upon the M-vector model of Nawalkha and Chambers (1997) and the generalized M-vector model of Nawalkha, Soto, and Zhang (2003).

3. A review of different multifactor models can be found in Soto (2001b). For an empirical comparison of various recent approaches, see Soto (2004a).
4. The generalized duration vector models require the assumption of smoothness in the shift of the term structure of interest rates in order to perform a generalized Taylor series expansion. The key rate durations require the same assumption in order to divide the shift in the term structure of interest into many approximately linear segments.
5. The M-Vector model was derived by Nawalkha and Chambers (1997). The derivation of equation 5.1 follows from the M-Vector model, under the assumption of an instantaneous planning horizon, or $H = 0$.
6. See Chambers, Carleton, and McEnally (1988), Grandville (2003), Granito (1984), and Nawalkha (1995).
7. To compute the prices, note that the new zero-coupon yields for maturities from one year to five years are: $y(1) = 6.749\%$, $y(2) = 6.921\%$, $y(3) = 7.041\%$, $y(4) = 7.127\%$, and $y(5) = 7.190\%$.
8. Since coupons are paid annually, all the one-year maturity coupon bonds collapse to a single one-year zero-coupon bond regardless of the coupon rate.
9. Each of these two periods includes 16 four-year overlapping holding periods.
10. Yield to maturity given in discrete frequencies (annual, semiannual, etc.) can be turned into continuously compounded yields using the results shown in Chapter 2.
11. See Nawalkha, Chambers, Soto, and Zhang (2003) and Nawalkha, Soto, and Zhang (2003).

CHAPTER 6

Hedging with Interest-Rate Futures

For centuries futures contracts traded primarily on physical commodities such as precious metals, agriculture, wood products, and oil. The introduction of exchange-traded derivative contracts on financial securities in the 1970s coincided with the publications of highly influential papers on how to value these derivatives. A futures contract is an agreement between two parties to trade an asset at some future date for a fixed price agreed upon today. Due to features such as standardization, marking to market, and so forth, futures contracts are more liquid and easier to trade than forward contracts. Popular interest rate futures contracts in the United States and Europe include Eurodollar futures, and futures on Treasury bonds, notes, and bills. Short-term interest rate futures contracts, such as T-bill and Eurodollar, trade on the Chicago Mercantile Exchange (CME), while long-term contracts such as T-note and T-bond, trade on the Chicago Board of Trade (CBOT). Table 6.1 displays the denomination, the name of the exchange, and the open interest (the number of contracts outstanding) on December 10, 2003, for the different interest rate futures contracts. As can be seen from this table, the explosive growth of the Eurodollar futures contract has come at the expense of the T-bill futures contract, which has virtually faded to extinction, even though the T-bill cash market continues to be the most liquid short-term fixed-income market in the world. In 2003, less than 20 futures contracts traded daily on T-bills compared to roughly 800,000 contracts on Eurodollar time deposits. The number of contracts outstanding on T-notes and T-bonds are less than 1.5 million, while the number of contracts outstanding on Eurodollars are 5.2 million on December 10, 2003.

This chapter describes the contractual details and pricing of the interest rate futures contracts listed in Table 6.1. The chapter also shows how to hedge and speculate against interest rate movements using these futures contracts. In order to capture the effects of nonparallel rate changes, we derive

This chapter coauthored with Iuliana Ismailescu.

TABLE 6.1 Interest Rate Futures

Contract	Denomination ($)	Exchange	Open Interest December 10, 2003
U.S. T-Bills	1,000,000	CME	0
Eurodollars	1,000,000	CME	5,203,120
U.S. T-Bonds	100,000	CBOT	490,968
U.S. T-Notes	100,000	CBOT	986,595

Note: CME = Chicago Mercantile Exchange; CBOT = Chicago Board of Trade.
Source: The *Wall Street Journal.*

the duration vectors of these contracts (see Chapter 5 for more details on the duration vector model), which allow hedging against the changes in height, slope, curvature, and so on of the term structure of interest rates.

EURODOLLAR FUTURES

A Eurodollar deposit is a deposit denominated in U.S. dollars in an American or foreign bank located outside the United States. The interest rate on the Eurodollar deposit is given as the *London* Interbank Offer Rate (LIBOR), which is the *ask* rate at which large international banks lend U.S. dollars to each other.[1] The three-month Eurodollar futures contract is based on a hypothetical three-month (90-day) Eurodollar CD with a face value of $1 million. The contract expires in the months of March, June, September, and December, as well as all four nearest months, with maturities extending up to 10 years into the future. The Eurodollar futures contract is settled in cash on the second London business day prior to the third Wednesday of the delivery month.

The three-month Eurodollar futures is the most liquid and actively traded futures contracts in the world, its success largely resulting from complimentary growth of the over-the-counter LIBOR-based derivative products, such as interest rates swaps, interest rate options (caps, floors, etc.), and forward rate agreements (FRAs). Traders often use Eurodollar futures to hedge against the exposure in interest rate swaps and other LIBOR-based products. Compared to the notional amount of about $5.2 trillion for the Eurodollar futures contracts at the end of 2003 (see Table 6.1), the notional amounts of dollar-denominated derivative such as interest rate swaps, interest rate options, and FRAs are about $31 trillion, $5.2 trillion, and $3.6 trillion, respectively.

Arguably, even though Eurodollar futures is the most successful exchange traded contract ever, its price does not converge to any spot market instrument in the Eurodollar market. The CME designed the contract so that its price converges to 100 *minus* $q/4$ at expiration, where q is the annualized rate on a 90-day Eurodollar time deposit (using quarterly compounding and 360 days in a year). Hence, though the futures contract is priced as if the underlying Eurodollar time deposit is a discount instrument (similar to T-bills), in reality the Eurodollar time deposits are add-on instruments. Specifically, given the annualized rate q on a 90-day Eurodollar time deposit observed at the futures expiration date, an investment of \$100 in the Eurodollar time deposit grows to 100 *plus* $q/4$ after 90 days, even though futures price converges to 100 *minus* $q/4$ at the expiration date. Due to the absence of convergence of the Eurodollar futures contract to the underlying spot price, the sensitivities of Eurodollar futures prices to changes in LIBOR have a slightly different form than the sensitivities of T-bill futures prices to changes in the U.S. Treasury rates.

Futures Prices and Futures Interest Rates

Let Q be the quoted or the settlement price for a Eurodollar futures contract with an expiration date s. The relationship between the settlement price and the futures interest rate is given as follows:

$$q = 100 - Q \tag{6.1}$$

where q is the 90-day LIBOR futures rate expressed in percentage with quarterly compounding and an actual/360 day-count convention (see Chapter 3 for details on the three different day-count conventions). Conceptually, the futures rate q is the quarterly compounded annualized rate that can be locked in on a Eurodollar deposit to be made at time s for a period of 90 days. Of course, Eurodollar futures are settled in cash, so the exercise of the futures contract does not lead to an actual investment in Eurodollars on the delivery date. The discrete rate q can be transformed into a continuously compounded annualized rate that uses *actual/365 day count convention* as follows:

$$1 + \frac{q/4}{100} = e^{f^*(s, s+90/365)\times(90/365)} \tag{6.2}$$

where $f^*(s, s + 90/365)$ is the continuously compounded futures rate expressed in decimal form, which can be locked in on a Eurodollar deposit to be made at time s for a period of 90 days. By taking logarithms of both sides of equation 6.2 and simplifying, we get:

$$f^*(s, s + 90/365) = \frac{365}{90}\ln\left(1 + \frac{q}{400}\right) \quad (6.3)$$

The futures interest rate is different from forward interest rate. The difference arises because futures contracts are marked-to-market every day, which makes these contracts more volatile than the corresponding forward contracts. Though the exact relationship between the futures rates and forward rates is dependent on the assumptions of a specific term structure model, the following approximation based on Ho and Lee (1986) can be used:

$$f(s, s + t) = f^*(s, s + t) - \frac{1}{2}\sigma^2 s(s + t) \quad (6.4)$$

where, $f(s, s + t)$ is the annualized forward rate with continuous compounding, t is the maturity of the underlying asset at the delivery date s (for the Eurodollar futures contracts, $t = 90/365$), and σ is the annual standard deviation of the change in the short-term interest rate. The term $\frac{1}{2}\sigma^2 s(s + t)$ is known as the *convexity adjustment*. For short maturities, convexity adjustment is close to zero, and the Eurodollar futures interest rates can be assumed to be the same as the corresponding forward interest rate. For long maturity Eurodollar futures, a convexity adjustment must be used for obtaining the implied forward rates. If the default risk associated with Eurodollar deposits in foreign countries is small, then Eurodollar forward rates should be only slightly higher than the corresponding U.S. Treasury forward rates. Hence, the deviations of the Eurodollar futures rates from the forward rates in the U.S. Treasury markets should be due to two reasons: the convexity adjustment and the default risk.

Example 6.1 Consider a five-year maturity Eurodollar futures contract with a quoted or settlement price of 96. The quarterly compounded annualized futures rate, q, can be calculated *in percentage* using equation 6.1:

$$q = 100 - 96 = 4$$

Using equation 6.3, the continuously compounded annualized futures rate $f^*(5, 5 + 90/365)$ based on an actual/365 day-count convention is computed as follows:

$$f^*(5,\ 5+90/365) = \frac{365}{90}\ln\left(1+\frac{4}{400}\right) = 0.04035$$

Finally, the continuously compounded annualized *forward* rate, $f(5, 5 + 90/365)$ is computed using equation 6.4 as follows:

$$f(5,5+90/365) = f^*(5,5+90/365) - \frac{1}{2}\sigma^2 \times 5 \times (5+90/365)$$

Using a standard deviation of 1.2 percent, the forward rate is equal to:

$$f(5.5+90/365) = 0.04035 - \frac{1}{2}\times(0.012)^2 \times 5 \times (5+90/365) = 0.03846 = 3.846\%$$

Due to marking-to-market, futures contracts are riskier investments than forward contracts and, hence, it is natural that the futures rate is higher than the forward rate.

An investor with a long position in the Eurodollar futures expects to gain (lose) when interest rates go down (up), while an investor with a short position expects to gain (lose) when interest rates go up (down). Due to marking-to-market, the gains or losses are settled on a daily basis. Gains and losses incurred by the holders of futures positions are equal to the changes in the contract price. To compute the gains and losses, we need to convert the settlement price of the futures contract Q, into a contract price.

The contract price (CP) corresponding to the settlement price Q, is given as:

$$\begin{aligned} CP &= 10,000\left[100 - \frac{90}{360}(100-Q)\right] \\ &= 10,000\left[100 - 0.25(100-Q)\right] \\ &= 750,000 + 2,500Q \end{aligned} \tag{6.5}$$

Thus, a settlement price of 96 in the previous example corresponds to a contract price of:

$$CP = 10,000[100 - 0.25(100 - 96)] = \$990,000$$

This can be alternatively computed as follows:

$$CP = 750,000 + 2,500 \times 96 = \$990,000 \tag{6.6}$$

Due to the linear relationship in equation 6.1, a change of one basis point in the settlement price Q, corresponds to a change of one basis point in the quoted futures rate q. Further, the contract price changes by $25 for every one basis point change in either the settlement price or the futures rate. For example, if the settlement price Q changes to 96.01 from 96, then quoted futures rate q will change to 3.99 from 4 (using equation 6.1, and the contract price will increase by $25 to become $990,025, using equation 6.5). Finally, substituting equation 6.1 into equation 6.5, the contract price can also be expressed as a linear function of the quoted futures rate q as follows:

$$CP = 1{,}000{,}000 - 2{,}500 \times q = 10{,}000(100 - q/4) \tag{6.7}$$

Hedging with Eurodollar Futures

Due to the availability of Eurodollar futures with expiration dates up to 10 years, these contracts are useful in capturing the effects of the changes in the various shape parameters that measure the term structure of interest rates. Since the contract prices of Eurodollar futures are linear in the quoted futures rates (see equation 6.7), Eurodollar futures are effective in hedging against the changes in interest rates, without introducing the nonlinear effects of convexity, and so forth. Since many instruments in the LIBOR-based derivative markets, such as interest rate swaps and interest rate options are also linear in interest rates, Eurodollar futures are effective in hedging these products.

In the following section we show that Eurodollars may be effective in hedging even fixed-income securities such as regular bonds that are nonlinear functions of interest rates.

As pointed out in Chapters 4 and 5, the nonlinear effects of rate changes are extremely small compared to the linear effects of the nonparallel rate changes, such as shifts in the height, slope, curvature, and so on of the term structure of interest rates. In this section, we extend the duration vector model developed in Chapter 5 to Eurodollar futures, by making two assumptions:

1. We use a linear approximation for the derivation of the duration vector of Eurodollar futures, unlike the nonlinear approximation used in Chapter 5 for regular bonds.
2. We assume that the difference between forward rates and futures rates (see equation 6.4) is time homogenous and stationary over time.

Recall from Chapter 4 (see equations 4.6 and 4.12) that under a polynomial functional form, the instantaneous shifts in the term structure of zero-coupon yields and the term structure of instantaneous forward rates are given as follows:

$$\Delta y(t) = \Delta A_0 + \Delta A_1 \times t + \Delta A_2 \times t^2 + \Delta A_3 \times t^3 + \cdots + \tag{6.8}$$

and

$$\Delta f(t) = \Delta A_0 + 2\Delta A_1 \times t + 3\Delta A_2 \times t^2 + 4\Delta A_3 \times t^3 + \cdots + \tag{6.9}$$

where ΔA_0 = Change in the height parameter
ΔA_1 = Change in the slope parameter
ΔA_2 = Change in the curvature parameter
$\Delta A_3, \Delta A_4, \ldots$ = Changes in other higher order shape parameters

For expositional simplicity we are using the same notation for instantaneous forward rates in the Eurodollar market (given by equation 6.9) as we did for the corresponding rates in the U.S. Treasury market in equation 4.12 in Chapter 4. Using the same notation does not create any confusion when hedging Eurodollar-based derivative products using Eurodollar futures. However, when cross-hedging fixed-income products based on the U.S. Treasury curve using Eurodollar futures, we assume that the spread of the Eurodollar forward rate curve over the U.S. Treasury forward rate curve is constant over time, such that the *changes* in both forward rate curves are identical and are given by equation 4.12 in Chapter 4 and equation 6.9 in this chapter. The percentage change in the contract price of a Eurodollar futures can be linearly approximated using the duration vector model as follows (see Appendix 6.1 for a proof):

$$\frac{\Delta CP}{CP} = -D^f(1) \times \Delta A_0 - D^f(2) \times \Delta A_1 - D^f(3) \times \Delta A_2 + \cdots + \tag{6.10}$$

where

$$\begin{aligned} D^f(1) &= K(Q) \times (90/365) \\ D^f(2) &= K(Q) \times \left[(s + 90/365)^2 - s^2\right] \\ D^f(3) &= K(Q) \times \left[(s + 90/365)^3 - s^3\right] \end{aligned} \tag{6.11}$$

and $K(Q)$ is defined as follows:

$$K(Q) = \left(1 + \left(\frac{100 - Q}{400}\right)\right) / \left(1 - \left(\frac{100 - Q}{400}\right)\right) = \frac{500 - Q}{300 + Q} \tag{6.12}$$

The definitions of the duration vector elements in equation 6.11 are similar to the duration vector elements of T-bill futures (as shown later), except for the term $K(Q)$.

The term $K(Q)$ is required since the Eurodollar futures does not converge to an underlying spot instrument in the Eurodollar market. The Eurodollar futures is priced as if the underlying Eurodollar deposit is a discount instrument, and yet the Eurodollar deposit is an add-on instrument. The expression $K(Q)$ remains close to 1 for low levels of interest rates, but as interest rates become high, $K(Q)$ becomes significantly larger than 1, leading to higher duration vector values. This implies that the *percentage* change in the contract price of a Eurodollar futures contract is higher for the same magnitude of rate change, when the initial rates are higher.

The duration vector model for Eurodollar futures contracts given by equation 6.10 is different from the duration vector model for regular bonds given by equation 5.10 in Chapter 5. Since the contract price of a Eurodollar futures is linear in futures rates, the nonlinear terms related to changes in the rates (e.g., square of the changes in the height and slope of the term structure) are absent in equation 6.10. However, since the magnitudes of the nonlinear terms are extremely small relative to the linear terms, the duration vectors of U.S. Treasury bonds and the duration vectors of Eurodollar futures can be combined for designing hedging strategies. These cross-hedging strategies are based on the assumption that the spread between Eurodollar forward rates and U.S. Treasury forward rates remains stationary over time. The following example shows how to compute the duration vector of a Eurodollar futures contract.

Example 6.2 Assume that the settlement price quote of a Eurodollar futures contract with 100 days until maturity is 95. Then $Q = 95$ and $s =$ 100/360 or 0.2778 years. The contract price is computed using equation 6.5 and equals:

$$CP = 10{,}000[100 - 0.25(100 - 95)] = 987{,}500 \tag{6.13}$$

The variable $K(Q)$ and the duration vector of this contract can be computed as follows:

$$K(95) = \left(1 + \frac{100-95}{400}\right) / \left(1 - \frac{100-95}{400}\right) = \frac{500-95}{300+95} = 1.025316$$

$$D^f(1) = 1.025316 \times (90/365) = 0.2528$$

$$D^f(2) = 1.025316 \times \left[(0.2778 + 90/365)^2 - 0.2778^2\right] = 0.2028$$

$$D^f(3) = 1.025316 \times \left[(0.2778 + 90/365)^3 - 0.2778^3\right] = 0.1259$$

We now show how to design a cross-hedging strategy where Eurodollar futures can be added to a U.S. Treasury bond portfolio to eliminate interest rate risk arising from nonparallel rate changes. Consider the M duration vector elements of the bond portfolio given in equation 5.4 as follows:

$$D_{PORT}(m) = p_1 \times D_1(m) + p_2 \times D_2(m) + \cdots + p_J \times D_J(m), \; m = 1, 2, \ldots, M \quad (6.14)$$

where, p_i $(i = 1, 2, \ldots, J)$ is the proportion of investment in the ith bond, and $D_i(m)$ $(m = 1, 2, \ldots, M)$ is the mth order duration vector element of the ith bond.

Unlike in Chapter 5, we assume that the bond proportions given previously are *known,* and we wish to hedge the earlier bond portfolio with M duration vector constraints using M number of Eurodollar futures. Let the number of ith bond in the portfolio be given as n_i, and the price of the ith bond be P_i. Then the proportion of investment in the ith bond equals:

$$p_i = \frac{n_i P_i}{\sum_{i=1}^{J} n_i P_i} \quad (6.15)$$

where by definition the sum of the proportions equals 1. Let the number of ith Eurodollar futures contracts be given as n_i^f, and the contract price of the ith Eurodollar futures be given as CP_i. Define the proportion of the ith $(i = 1, 2, \ldots, M)$ Eurodollar futures contract with respect to the total dollar investment in the bond portfolio as follows:

$$p_i^f = \frac{n_i^f CP_i}{\sum_{i=1}^{J} n_i P_i} \quad (6.16)$$

The M duration vector constraints can be given as follows:

$$
\begin{aligned}
&D_{PORT}(1) + p_1^f D_1^f(1) + p_2^f D_2^f(1) + \cdots + p_M^f \; D_M^f(1) = H \\
&D_{PORT}(2) + p_1^f D_1^f(2) + p_2^f D_2^f(2) + \cdots + p_M^f \; D_M^f(2) = H^2 \\
&\vdots \\
&D_{PORT}(M) + p_1^f D_1^f(M) + p_2^f D_2^f(M) + \cdots + p_M^f \; D_M^f(M) = H^M
\end{aligned}
\tag{6.17}
$$

where $D_i^f(m)$, for $i = 1, 2, \ldots, M$, and $m = 1, 2, \ldots, M$, gives the mth order duration vector element for the ith Eurodollar futures contract, and H is the immunization planning horizon of the bond portfolio. Equation 6.17 has an intuitive interpretation. The left side of equation 6.17 gives the duration vector of the *total* portfolio, which includes the duration vector of the cash bond portfolio plus the duration vectors of the Eurodollar futures. Similar to equation 5.3, the duration vector of the total portfolio is set equal to a horizon vector. This allows replicating a zero-coupon bond maturing at the horizon date H, and hence dynamically immunizes the total portfolio.

If H is set to zero, then the portfolio is hedged with respect to instantaneous price changes.

The proportions in the Eurodollar futures contracts which are defined relative to the investment in the cash bond portfolio (see equation 6.16) give the magnitude of positions undertaken (long or short), *but do not require any cash investment.*[2] Since equation 6.17 gives M equations in M unknowns, the proportions $p_1^f, p_2^f, \ldots, p_M^f$, can be solved as follows:

$$
\begin{bmatrix} p_1^f \\ p_2^f \\ \vdots \\ p_M^f \end{bmatrix}
=
\begin{bmatrix} D_1^f(1) & D_2^f(1) & \ldots & D_M^f(1) \\ D_1^f(2) & D_2^f(2) & \ldots & D_M^f(2) \\ \vdots & & & \\ D_1^f(M) & D_2^f(M) & \ldots & D_M^f(M) \end{bmatrix}^{-1}
\times
\begin{bmatrix} H - D_{PORT}(1) \\ H^2 - D_{PORT}(2) \\ \vdots \\ H^M - D_{PORT}(M) \end{bmatrix}
\tag{6.18}
$$

Equation 6.18 can be understood as follows: If the cash bond portfolio is already immunized, then equation 5.3 holds, and the last column vector on the right side of equation 6.18 consists of a vector of zeros (since $D_{PORT}(1) = H$, $D_{PORT}(2) = H^2, \ldots, D_{PORT}(M) = H^M$). In this case, the positions in the Eurodollar futures are equal to zero, which intuitively makes sense since the cash portfolio is *already immunized.* However, if the last column vector has nonzero terms, then some positions in the Eurodollar futures may be required to immunize the portfolio. In general, larger are the

TABLE 6.2 Delivery Dates for Eurodollar Futures

Futures Contract	Delivery Date	Maturity (in years)
June 2004	June 14, 2004	0.53 = 189/360
December 2005	December 19, 2005	2.03 = 211/360
December 2008	December 15, 2008	5.02 = 7/360

deviations of the duration vector values of the cash portfolio from the horizon vector values, larger will be the positions in the Eurodollar futures to immunize the portfolio. The actual number of Eurodollar futures contracts can be computed once the proportions are known from equation 6.18, by inverting equation 6.16 as follows:

$$n_i^f = \frac{p_i^f}{CP_i} \sum_{i=1}^{J} n_i P_i \tag{6.19}$$

Example 6.3 Consider a trader who has a bond portfolio consisting of one thousand 3.375-percent, November 2008 Treasury notes (T-note). On December 8, 2003, the quoted price of this T-note is 100:16, or 100 + 16/32 = 100.50 percent of the face value, which equals \$1,005 on the \$1,000 face value. The trader expects an increase in the interest rates and she wants to hedge her bond portfolio against this risk over the instantaneous interval. She selects three Eurodollar futures contracts expiring in June 2004, December 2005, and December 2008, respectively. On December 8, 2003, the settlement prices of these futures contracts are 98.42, 96.18, and 94.42, respectively. The contract prices corresponding to these settlement prices are given by equation 6.5 as follows:

$$\begin{aligned}
\text{June 2004 contract: } CP_1 &= 10{,}000[100 - 0.25(100 - 98.42)] = \$996{,}050 \\
\text{December 2005 contract: } CP_2 &= 10{,}000[100 - 0.25(100 - 96.18)] = \$990{,}450 \\
\text{December 2008 contract: } CP_3 &= 10{,}000[100 - 0.25(100 - 94.42)] = \$986{,}050
\end{aligned}$$

The Eurodollar futures contracts are settled in cash two days prior to the third Wednesday of the delivery month. The delivery dates and times to maturity of the three Eurodollar futures contracts are given in Table 6.2, and the duration vectors are shown in Table 6.3.

TABLE 6.3 Duration Vector Values of Eurodollar Futures and T-Note

Futures Contract	$D(1)$	$D(2)$	$D(3)$	Price[a] ($)
June 2004	0.2485	0.3222	0.3171	996,050
December 2005	0.2513	1.0827	3.5016	990,450
December 2008	0.2536	2.6079	20.1215	986,050
Treasury Note	4.5804	21.9946	107.0826	1,007.144

[a] This column gives the contract price for futures contracts and cash price for the T-Note.

The ask yield to maturity of the Treasury note is 3.25 percent per year with semiannual compounding. The corresponding continuously compounded yield to maturity per payment period (half a year) is $i = y/2 = \ln(1 + 0.0325/2) = 1.6119$ percent. Since the government note matures on November 15, 2008, a coupon of \$16.875 is paid on May 15 and November 15, every year until maturity. The number of days elapsed since the date of the last coupon payment equals 23, and, thus, the accrued interest equals $\$16.875 \times 23/181 = \$2.144$. Hence, the cash price of the bond on December 8, 2003 is equal to:

$$P_1 = \$1,005 + \$2.144 = \$1,007.144$$

Using the closed-form solutions of the duration measures given in Table 5.5, the first-, second-, and third-order duration measures of the Treasury note can be computed with $c = \$16.875/1000 = 1.6875\%$, $i = y/2 = 1.6119\%$, $N = 10$, and $s = 0.127$. Similarly, using equation 6.11, the first-, second-, and third-order duration measures of the three Eurodollar futures given previously, can be computed as shown in Table 6.3.

If the trader uses all three futures contracts, she can hedge against the linear effects of changes in the height, slope, and curvature of the term structure, using three duration vector constraints. The proportions in the three Eurodollar futures contracts can be computed using equation 6.18, for an instantaneous horizon of zero, as follows:

$$\begin{bmatrix} p_1^f \\ p_2^f \\ p_3^f \end{bmatrix} = \begin{bmatrix} 0.2485 & 0.2513 & 0.2536 \\ 0.3222 & 1.0827 & 2.6079 \\ 0.3171 & 3.5016 & 20.1215 \end{bmatrix}^{-1} \times \begin{bmatrix} 0 - 4.5804 \\ 0^2 - 21.9946 \\ 0^3 - 107.0826 \end{bmatrix}$$

TABLE 6.4 Eurodollar Futures and Treasury Note Quoted Prices on December 9, 2003

Futures Contract	Quoted Price Dec. 9	Price[a] Dec. 9 ($)	Price Change ($)
June 2004	98.38	995,950	−100
December 2005	96.09	990,225	−225
December 2008	94.31	985,775	−275
Treasury Note	100.02	1,002.863	−4.281

[a] This column gives the contract price for futures contracts and cash price for the T-Note.

The solution is given as:

$$\begin{bmatrix} p_1^f \\ p_2^f \\ p_3^f \end{bmatrix} = \begin{bmatrix} -3.6651 \\ -11.2679 \\ -3.3032 \end{bmatrix}$$

The number of futures contracts can be computed using equation 6.19 to hedge one thousand Treasury notes as follows:

$$n_1^f = \frac{-3.6651}{996050} \times 1000 \times 1007.144 = -3.7059$$

$$n_2^f = \frac{-11.2679}{990450} \times 1000 \times 1007.144 = -11.4578$$

$$n_3^f = \frac{-3.3032}{986050} \times 1000 \times 1007.144 = -3.3738$$

To assess the performance of the immunization strategy, consider the prices of the T-note and Eurodollar futures contracts on December 9, 2003, one day after the trader entered this strategy. The quoted prices on this day, along with the futures contract prices, and changes in the contract price are given in Table 6.4.

The loss on the portfolio of one thousand Treasury notes equals:

$$(1{,}002.863 - 1{,}007.144) \times 1{,}000 = -4.281 \times 1{,}000 = -\$4{,}281$$

This loss is offset by a gain on the futures positions equal to:

$$(-3.7059) \times (-100) + (-11.4578) \times (-225) + (-3.3738) \times (-275) = \$3{,}876.41$$

The residual loss not captured by the immunization strategy is \$405.36, which is less than 10 percent of the loss on the cash portfolio of T-notes.

Though the immunization technique given in equations 6.14 through 6.19 is derived in the context of cross-hedging U.S. Treasury bonds with Eurodollar futures, the same technique applies when using T-bill futures, T-note futures, and T-bond futures to hedge U.S. Treasury bonds. We now turn to these instruments as alternative instruments for hedging interest rate risk.

TREASURY BILL FUTURES

The asset underlying a Treasury bill futures contract is the 90-day U.S. Treasury bill worth \$1 million in face value. Treasury bill (T-bill) futures trade on the CME, with contract's expiration months in March, June, September, and December, and maturities extending up to a year and a half. Despite the large size of the U.S. T-bill market, the T-bill futures market has shrunk considerably, losing market share to the Eurodollar futures market. In recent years, T-bill futures have settled via cash, rather than physical delivery that used to be the norm when these contracts were first introduced.

Treasury Bill Pricing

The price of a T-bill is quoted with a discount assuming \$100 face value and 360 days in a year as follows:

$$P = 100 - \frac{t}{360} d \qquad (6.20)$$

where d is the quoted discount rate, and t is the number of days until maturity of the T-bill. Using equation 6.20, the quoted ask discount rate gives the T-bill ask price at which the trader sells and the quoted bid discount rate gives the T-bill bid price at which the trader buys. Suppose the quoted ask discount rate equals 5.9325 on a T-bill maturing in 91 days. Then, the asking price for the T-bill is given as:

$$P = 100 - \frac{91}{360} \times 5.9325 = \$98.50 \qquad (6.21)$$

If the face value of the T-bill is \$1,000, the buyer of one T-bill pays 98.50×10 = \$985 to the trader to purchase one T-bill. T-bills can be bought with face values ranging from \$1,000 to \$1,000,000.

Futures Prices and Futures Interest Rates

Using the same notation for Eurodollar futures, let q define the quoted futures rate and Q define the quoted settlement price of a T-bill futures contract. Then similar to equation 6.1 we have:

$$q = 100 - Q \tag{6.22}$$

Since the 90-day T-bill underlying the T-bill futures contract is a *discount* instrument, the relationship between the quoted futures rate q and the continuously compounded futures rate is given as:

$$1 - \left(\frac{90}{360}\right)\frac{q}{4} = 1 - \frac{q/4}{100} = \frac{1}{e^{f^*(s,s+90/365)\times(90/365)}} \tag{6.23}$$

The relationship between q and $f^*(s, s + 90/365)$ for T-bill futures in equation 6.23 is different from a similar relationship for Eurodollar futures in equation 6.2. This difference arises because the Eurodollar deposit underlying the Eurodollar futures contract is priced as an add-on instrument, while the cash T-bill underlying the T-bill futures contract is priced as a discount instrument.

The contract price of a T-bill future is defined in the same way as that of the Eurodollar futures and is given by equations 6.5 and 6.7, assuming q and Q are the quoted futures rate and the quote settlement price of the T-bill futures contract. On July 2, 2003, the settlement price for the September Treasury bill futures contract was $Q = 99.14$. According to equation 6.22, the quoted futures rate q equals 100 – 99.14 = 0.86. Also, the contract price is similar to the Eurodollar futures contract and is given by equation 6.5 as 10,000(100 – 0.25 × (100 – 99.14)) = \$997,850. Similar to Eurodollar futures contract, a one basis point change in the T-bill futures quoted rate corresponds to a \$25 change in the futures contract price.

Assuming that the changes in the Treasury forward rates are also defined by equation 6.9, the duration vector of T-bill futures contracts can be obtained as follows:[3]

$$\frac{\Delta CP}{CP} = -D^f(1)\times\Delta A_0 - D^f(2)\times\Delta A_1 - D^f(3)\times\Delta A_2 + \cdots \tag{6.24}$$

where

$$\begin{aligned} D^f(1) &= 90/365 \\ D^f(2) &= (s + 90/365)^2 - s^2 \\ D^f(3) &= (s + 90/365)^3 - s^3 \end{aligned} \tag{6.25}$$

The definition of the duration vector elements in equation 6.25 is similar to the duration vector elements of Eurodollar futures except for the term $K(Q)$. $K(Q)$ is absent in equation 6.25, since unlike Eurodollar futures, the price of the T-bill futures converges to the underlying 90-day cash bill, which is a discount instrument. The duration vector of T-bill futures is identical to that obtained by Chambers, Carleton, and Waldman (1984) and others. Hedging short-term U.S. Treasury securities with T-bill futures can be accomplished using the duration vector by the technique outlined in equations 6.14 through 6.19. However, using T-note futures and T-bond futures may be essential when hedging long-term U.S. Treasury securities.

TREASURY BOND FUTURES

Treasury bond futures are the most popular long-term interest rate futures. These futures trade on the Chicago Board of Trade (CBOT) and expire in the months of March, June, September, and December in addition to extra months scheduled by the CBOT based on the demand for these contracts. The last trading day for these contracts is the business day prior to the last seven days of the expiration month. Delivery can take place any time during the delivery month and is initiated by the short side. The first delivery day is the first business day of the delivery month. As with most other futures contracts, delivery seldom takes place. The uncertainty about the delivery date poses a risk to the futures buyer that cannot be hedged away.

The underlying asset in a Treasury bond (T-bond) futures contract is any \$100,000 face value government bond with more than 15 years to maturity on the first day of delivery month and which is noncallable for 15 years from this day. The quoted price of the T-bond futures contract is based on the assumption that the underlying bond has a 6 percent coupon rate, but the CBOT also permits delivery of bonds with coupon rates different than 6 percent. In fact, a wide range of coupons and maturities qualify for delivery. To put all eligible bonds on a more or less equal footing, the CBOT has developed comprehensive tables to compute an adjustment factor, called *conversion factor,* that converts the quoted futures price to an invoice price applicable for delivery. The invoice price for the deliverable bond (not including accrued interest) is the bond's conversion factor times the futures price.

$$\text{Invoice price} = \text{FP} \times \text{CF} \tag{6.26}$$

where FP = Quoted futures price
CF = Conversion factor

Similarly to Treasury bond prices, Treasury bond futures prices are quoted in dollars and 32nd of a dollar on a \$100 face value. Thus, a quoted futures price of 98.04 represents 98 + 4/32, or \$98,125 on a \$100,000 face-value contract.

T-bond futures price quotes do not include accrued interest. Therefore, the delivery cash price is always higher than the invoice price by the amount of the accrued interest on the deliverable bond.

$$\begin{aligned} \text{CP} &= \text{Invoice price} + \text{Accrued interest} \\ &= \text{FP} \times \text{CF} + \text{AI} \end{aligned} \tag{6.27}$$

where AI is the accrued interest.

Example 6.4 Suppose on November 12, 2003, the quoted price of the 10 percent coupon bond maturing on August 5, 2019, is 97.08 (or \$97,250 on a \$100,000 face value). Since government bonds pay coupons semiannually, a coupon of \$5,000 would be paid on February 5 and August 5 of each year. The number of days between August 5, 2003, and November 12, 2003 (not including August 5, 2003, and including November 12, 2003), is 99, whereas the number of days between August 5, 2003, and February 5, 2004 (not including August 5, 2003, and including February 5, 2004), is 181 days. Therefore, with the actual/actual day-count convention used for Treasury bonds, the accrued interest from August 5, 2003, to November 12, 2003, is

$$AI = \$5,000 \times \frac{99}{181} = \$2,734.81$$

If this bond is the deliverable bond underlying the futures contract, then the cash price in equation 6.27 will be greater than the invoice price by an amount equal to the accrued interest of \$2,734.81.

Conversion Factor

A bond's conversion factor is the price at which the bond would yield 6 percent to maturity or to the first call date (if callable), on the first delivery date of the T-bond futures expiration month. The bond maturity is rounded down to the nearest zero, three, six, or nine months. If the maturity of the bond is rounded down to zero months, then the conversion factor is:

$$CF_0 = \frac{c}{2}\left[\frac{1}{0.03} - \frac{1}{0.03(1.03)^{2n}}\right] + \frac{1}{(1.03)^{2n}} \tag{6.28}$$

where c is the coupon rate and n is the number of years to maturity. If the maturity of the bond is rounded down to three months, the conversion factor is:

$$CF_3 = \frac{CF_0 + \frac{c}{2}}{(1.03)^{\frac{1}{2}}} - \frac{c}{4} \tag{6.29}$$

If the maturity of the bond is rounded down to six months, the conversion factor is:

$$CF_6 = \frac{c}{2}\left[\frac{1}{0.03} - \frac{1}{0.03(1.03)^{2n+1}}\right] + \frac{1}{(1.03)^{2n+1}} \tag{6.30}$$

And, finally, if the maturity of the bond is rounded down to nine months, the conversion factor is:

$$CF_9 = \frac{CF_6 + \frac{c}{2}}{(1.03)^{\frac{1}{2}}} - \frac{c}{4} \tag{6.31}$$

CF_0 and CF_6 have the same format, and so do CF_3 and CF_9. Therefore, we can combine equations 6.28 and 6.30 into a single equation:

$$CF_0 = \frac{c}{2}\left[\frac{1}{0.03} - \frac{1}{0.03(1.03)^{m}}\right] + \frac{1}{(1.03)^{m}} \tag{6.32}$$

where m is the number of semiannual periods to maturity.

Thus, instead of rounding the bond's maturity down to zero, three, six, or nine months, we can just round it down to zero or three months. If the result is zero, use equation 6.32, otherwise, use equation 6.29. The conversion factor always increases with the coupon rate, holding the maturity constant. If the coupon rate is more than 6 percent, the conversion factor increases with maturity, but if the coupon rate is less than 6 percent, the conversion factor decreases with maturity. The conversion factor equals one when the coupon rate equals 6 percent, regardless of the maturity.

Example 6.5 Consider a futures contract expiring in the month of December with the underlying deliverable bond given in Example 6.4. Assume that the bond is delivered on the first day of the expiration month, December 1, 2003. On this day, the bond has 15 years 8 months and 5 days to maturity. Rounding the bond's maturity on the delivery day down to the nearest zero or three months, the maturity is 15 years and 6 months. We treat this as 31 six-month periods. Applying equation 6.32 for $m = 31$:

$$CF_0 = \frac{0.10}{2}\left[\frac{1}{0.03} - \frac{1}{0.03(1.03)^{31}}\right] + \frac{1}{(1.03)^{31}} = 1.4$$

Suppose the quoted futures price on this bond is 96.04 (or \$96,125 on a \$100,000 face value contract). The time elapsed since the previous coupon payment date, August 5, 2003, to the expiration date of the futures contract, December 1, 2003, equals 118 days. Hence, the accrued interest on the bond equals:

$$\$5,000 \times \frac{118}{181} = \$3,259.67$$

Using equation 6.27, the delivery cash price of the T-bond futures contract is:

$$CP = \$96,125 \times 1.4 + \$3,259.67 = \$137,835.49$$

Cheapest-to-Deliver Bond

The party with the short position in the T-bond futures contract can deliver any government bond with more than 15 years to maturity and which is noncallable for 15 years from the delivery date. At any given day of the delivery month, there are about 30 bonds that the short side can deliver. Which bond should the seller choose to deliver? The answer to this question can be understood as follows.

On the delivery date, the seller receives:

$$\text{Quoted futures price} \times \text{Conversion factor} + \text{Accrued interest}$$

TABLE 6.5 Deliverable Bonds for the T-Bond Futures Contract

Bond	Coupon (%)	Quoted Bond Price P	Conversion Factor CF
1	7.50	98–23	1.0138
2	6.00	97–16	1.0000
3	8.00	99–12	1.0204
4	6.25	97–30	1.0049

The cost of purchasing a bond to deliver is:

Quoted bond price + Accrued interest

Hence, the seller will choose the *cheapest-to-deliver* bond, which is the bond for which the cost of delivery is lowest, where the cost of delivery is defined as:

$$\begin{aligned}\text{Cost of delivery} &= \text{Quoted bond price} - \text{Quoted futures price} \times \text{Conversion factor} \\ &= P - FP \times CF\end{aligned} \tag{6.33}$$

Example 6.6 illustrates the selection of the cheapest-to-deliver bond.

Example 6.6 Assume that the T-bond quoted futures price on the delivery day is 97.09 and that the party with the short position in the contract can choose to deliver from the bonds given in Table 6.5.

The cost of delivering each of these bonds is given in Table 6.6. It gives the quoted bond price and quoted futures price in decimal form. Using equation 6.33, the cheapest-to-deliver bond is bond 1.

TABLE 6.6 Cost of Delivery

Bond	Quoted Bond Price (P)	Quoted Futures Price (FP)	Conversion Factor (CF)	Cost of Delivery ($P - (FP \times CF)$)
1	98.72	97.28	1.0138	**0.10**
2	97.50	97.28	1.0000	0.22
3	99.38	97.28	1.0204	0.11
4	97.94	97.28	1.0049	0.18

Options Embedded in T-Bond Futures

A variety of options are embedded in T-bond futures. We have already discussed the cheapest-to-deliver option. The seller of the futures contract can also choose when to deliver the bond on the designated days in the delivery month. Another option known as the *wild card play* makes the T-bond futures price lower than it would be without this option. This option arises from the fact that the T-bond futures market closes at 2:00 P.M. Chicago time, while the bonds continue trading until 4:00 P.M. Moreover, the short side of the futures contract does not have to notify the clearing house about her intention to deliver until 8:00 P.M. Thus, if the bond prices declines between 2 and 4 P.M., the seller can notify the clearing house about her intention to deliver using the 2:00 P.M. futures price, and make the delivery by buying the cheapest-to-deliver bond at a lower price after 2 P.M. Otherwise, the party with the short position keeps the position open and applies the same strategy the next day.

Treasury Bond Futures Pricing

The uncertainty regarding the many delivery options makes the T-bond futures contract difficult to price. In the following analysis, we assume that both the deliverable bond and delivery date are known, and the wild card play option is not significant in the pricing of T-bond futures. Under these assumptions, the Treasury bond futures price can be approximated by its forward price, and is given as:

$$FP = (P - I)e^{s \times y(s)} \tag{6.34}$$

where P is the current price of the deliverable T-bond, I is the present value of the coupons during the life of the futures contract, s is the expiration date of the futures contract, and $y(t)$ is the zero-coupon yield for the term t.

In the following analysis, we assume that the delivery date is the first day of the expiration month of the futures contract, and use the following notations:

T = Current maturity of the cheapest-to-deliver bond
C = Coupon payment of cheapest-to-deliver bond
F = Face value of cheapest-to-deliver bond
CF = Conversion factor of cheapest-to-deliver bond
τ = Length of time between expiration date of the futures contract and first cash flow payment after the futures' expiration date
n = number of coupon payments between current time and futures' expiration date

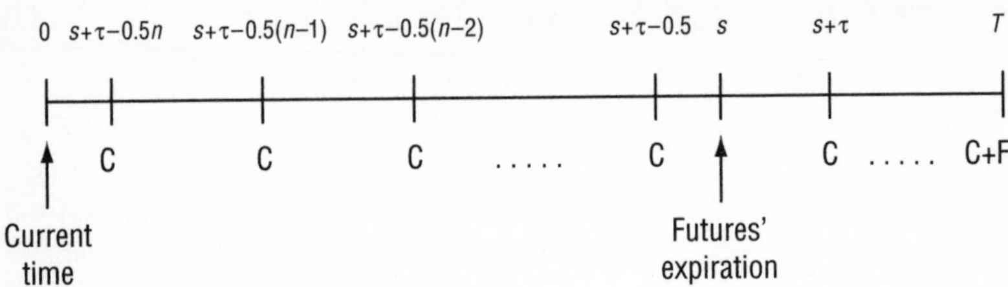

FIGURE 6.1 Timeline for T-Bond Futures

In addition, assume that there are two coupon payments per year, so that by definition $0 \le \tau \le 0.5$.

The timeline is shown in Figure 6.1. The price of a futures contract depends only on cash flows received after the T-bond is delivered. The delivery cash price of the futures contract is given as:[4]

$$CP = \left[\sum_{t=0}^{2(T-s-\tau)} \frac{Ce^{s \times y(s)}}{e^{(s+\tau+t\times 0.5)\times y(s+\tau+t\times 0.5)}} + \frac{Fe^{s\times y(s)}}{e^{T\times y(T)}} \right] \tag{6.35}$$

Using equation 6.27, the quoted price of the futures contract is given as:

$$FP = \frac{1}{CF}(CP - AI) \tag{6.36}$$

Substituting equation 6.35 and the definition of accrued interest in equation 6.36, we get,

$$FP = \frac{1}{CF}\left[\sum_{t=0}^{2(T-s-\tau)} \frac{Ce^{s \times y(s)}}{e^{(s+\tau+t\times 0.5)\times y(s+\tau+t\times 0.5)}} + \frac{Fe^{s\times y(s)}}{e^{T\times y(T)}} \right] - \frac{C}{CF} \times \left(\frac{0.5-\tau}{0.5} \right) \tag{6.37}$$

Example 6.7 Reconsider the cheapest-to-deliver bond in Example 6.5 with the delivery date of December 1, 2003. Assume that the bond's quoted price is not given, but that the term structure of zero-coupon yields has the polynomial form defined in Chapter 3, as follows:

$$y(t) = A_0 + A_1 t + A_2 t^2$$

where for expositional simplicity the height, slope, and curvature are assumed to be the only parameters of the term structure of interest rates. Further, assume that these parameters are defined as:

$$A_0 = 0.02$$
$$A_1 = 0.005$$
$$A_2 = -0.0001$$

For the futures contract written on this T-bond, the variables are $T = 15$ years, 8 months, and 23 days; $C = \$5$ on a \$100 face value (or \$5,000 on a \$100,000 face value); $F = \$100$; $CF = 1.4$ (see Example 6.4); $s = 18$ days; $\tau = 66$ days; and $n = 0$ (no coupon payments between current time and futures' expiration date). Though the asset underlying the Treasury bond futures contract is a \$100,000 face-value government bond, we do all calculations assuming a \$100 face value. All final prices can be multiplied by 1,000 later. The timeline of the cash flows associated with this futures contract is shown in Figure 6.2.

$$\begin{aligned} s &= 18 \text{ days} = 0.05 \text{ years} \\ \tau &= 66 \text{ days} = 0.18 \text{ years} \\ s+\tau &= 84 \text{ days} = 0.23 \text{ years} \\ T &= 15 \text{ years, 8 months, and 23 days} = 15.73 \text{ years} \\ T-(s+\tau) &= 15 \text{ years and 6 months} = 15.5 \text{ years} \end{aligned}$$

Using equation 6.37, the quoted futures price is given as:

$$FP = \frac{e^{0.05\times y(0.05)}}{1.4}\left[\sum_{t=0}^{31}\frac{5}{e^{(0.23+t\times 0.5)\times y(0.23+t\times 0.5)}}+\frac{100}{e^{15.73\times y(15.73)}}\right]-\frac{5}{1.4}\times\frac{0.5-0.18}{0.5} \quad (6.38)$$

The yields for different maturities are computed using the following equation and are displayed in Table 6.7.

$$y(t) \approx A_0 + A_1 t + A_2 t^2 = 0.02 + 0.005t - 0.0001t^2 \quad (6.39)$$

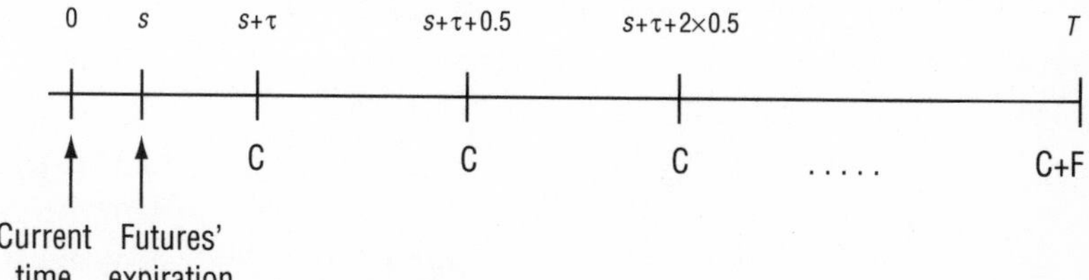

FIGURE 6.2 Timeline for T-Bond Futures

Substituting the zero-coupon yields from Table 6.7 into equation 6.38, the quoted price of the futures contract based on a \$100 face value is equal to \$95.10. The cash price is derived from the quoted futures price using equation 6.36 and is equal to \$136.33.

Duration Vector of T-Bond Futures

Assuming that the changes in the zero-coupon yields and the instantaneous forward rates are given by equations 6.8 and 6.9, respectively, the percentage change in the T-bond futures quoted price is given as follows:[5]

$$\frac{\Delta FP}{FP} = -D(1)\Delta A_0 - D(2)\Delta A_1 - D(3)\Delta A_2 - \cdots - D(M)\Delta A_{M-1} \tag{6.40}$$

TABLE 6.7 Zero-Coupon Yields

Maturity $(0.23 + t \times 0.5)$	Yield $y(0.23 + t \times 0.5)$	Maturity $(0.23 + t \times 0.5)$	Yield $y(0.23 + t \times 0.5)$
$t = 0$	0.0211	$t = 16$	0.0544
$t = 1$	0.0236	$t = 17$	0.0560
$t = 2$	0.0260	$t = 18$	0.0576
$t = 3$	0.0284	$t = 19$	0.0592
$t = 4$	0.0307	$t = 20$	0.0607
$t = 5$	0.0329	$t = 21$	0.0621
$t = 6$	0.0351	$t = 22$	0.0635
$t = 7$	0.0373	$t = 23$	0.0649
$t = 8$	0.0394	$t = 24$	0.0662
$t = 9$	0.0414	$t = 25$	0.0674
$t = 10$	0.0434	$t = 26$	0.0686
$t = 11$	0.0454	$t = 27$	0.0698
$t = 12$	0.0473	$t = 28$	0.0709
$t = 13$	0.0491	$t = 29$	0.0720
$t = 14$	0.0509	$t = 30$	0.0730
$t = 15$	0.0527	$t = 31$	0.0739

where

$$D(m) = \frac{e^{s\times y(s)}}{CF \times CP}\left[\sum_{t=0}^{2(T-s-\tau)} \frac{C\left(\left(s+\tau+t\times 0.5\right)^m - s^m\right)}{e^{(s+\tau+t\times 0.5)\times y(s+\tau+t\times 0.5)}} + \frac{F(T^m - s^m)}{e^{T\times y(T)}}\right] \tag{6.41}$$

for $m = 1, 2, 3, \ldots, M$.

Hedging using the duration vector of T-bond futures can be accomplished in the same manner as hedging using the duration vector of Eurodollar futures and T-bill futures. These hedging conditions are outlined in equations 6.14 through 6.19. Unlike T-bill futures, T-bond futures can be used for hedging long-term bond portfolios, since the deliverable bonds underlying the T-bond futures have longer maturities.

Example 6.8 Consider the T-bond futures contract in Example 6.5. The contract is initiated on November 12, 2003 and expires on December 1, 2003. The cheapest-to-deliver bond is a 10 percent coupon, $100,000 face-value government bond that matures on August 5, 2019. The conversion factor of this bond is 1.4. The timeline of the cash flows associated with this futures contract and all other variables are given in Example 6.6. These cash flows are given as shown in Figure 6.3.

$$\begin{aligned}
s &= 18 \text{ days} = 0.05 \text{ years} \\
\tau &= 66 \text{ days} = 0.18 \text{ years} \\
s + \tau &= 84 \text{ days} = 0.23 \text{ years} \\
T &= 15 \text{ years } 8 \text{ months and } 23 \text{ days} = 15.73 \text{ years} \\
T - (s + \tau) &= 15 \text{ years and } 6 \text{ months} = 15.5 \text{ years}
\end{aligned}$$

Reconsider the term structure of zero-coupon yields given in Example 6.7, as $y(t) = 0.02 + 0.005t - 0.0001t^2$, and suppose that the term structure parameters change instantaneously as shown in Table 6.8.

The original and the new zero-coupon yields based on the parameters in Table 6.8 are given in Table 6.9 on page 169.

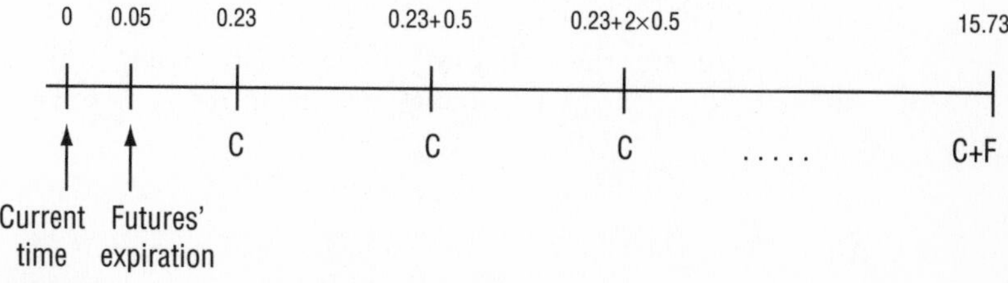

FIGURE 6.3 Timeline for T-Bond Futures

TABLE 6.8 Changes in the Term Structure Parameters

	Original Parameters	Change	New Parameters
A_0	0.02	0.005	0.025
A_1	0.005	−0.0001	0.0049
A_2	−0.0001	0	−0.0001

Substituting the new zero-coupon yields into equation 6.35, the new quoted price of the futures contract equals $92.02, which is a decline of 3.24 percent from the original price of $95.10. This change is approximated by the first three elements of the duration vector model. The duration vector elements are given as:

$$D(m) = \frac{e^{0.05\times y(0.05)}}{1.4\times 95.10}\left[\sum_{t=0}^{31}\frac{5\left((0.23+t\times 0.5)^m - 0.05^m\right)}{e^{(0.23+t\times 0.5)\times y(0.23+t\times 0.5)}} + \frac{100(15.73^m - 0.05^m)}{e^{15.73\times y(15.73)}}\right] \quad (6.42)$$

Using the zero-coupon yields given in Table 6.9, we obtain the first three elements of the duration vector as follows:

$$D(1) = 8.73$$
$$D(2) = 105.97$$
$$D(3) = 1442.99$$

Using only the duration, the percentage change in the cash price is given as:

$$\frac{\Delta FP}{FP} = -D(1)\Delta A_0 = -8.73\times 0.005 = -0.0437$$

or a decline of 4.37 percent. Since the actual percentage change is −3.24 percent, duration overestimates the magnitude of the change. Using a three-element duration vector model, the percentage change in the cash price is given as:

$$\frac{\Delta FP}{FP} = -D(1)\Delta A_0 - D(2)\Delta A_1 - D(3)\Delta A_2 = -8.73\times 0.005 - 105.97\times(-0.0001)$$
$$= -0.0331$$

TABLE 6.9 Original Yields and the New Yields

Maturity $(0.23 + t \times 0.5)$	Original Yield $y(0.23 + t \times 0.5)$	New Yield $y'(0.23 + t \times 0.5)$	Maturity $(0.23 + t \times 0.5)$	Original Yield $y(0.23 + t \times 0.5)$	New Yield $y'(0.23 + t \times 0.5)$
$t = 0$	0.0211	0.0261	$t = 16$	0.0544	0.0586
$t = 1$	0.0236	0.0285	$t = 17$	0.0560	0.0602
$t = 2$	0.0260	0.0309	$t = 18$	0.0576	0.0617
$t = 3$	0.0284	0.0332	$t = 19$	0.0592	0.0632
$t = 4$	0.0307	0.0354	$t = 20$	0.0607	0.0647
$t = 5$	0.0329	0.0376	$t = 21$	0.0621	0.0661
$t = 6$	0.0351	0.0398	$t = 22$	0.0635	0.0674
$t = 7$	0.0373	0.0419	$t = 23$	0.0649	0.0687
$t = 8$	0.0394	0.0439	$t = 24$	0.0662	0.0700
$t = 9$	0.0414	0.0459	$t = 25$	0.0674	0.0712
$t = 10$	0.0434	0.0479	$t = 26$	0.0686	0.0723
$t = 11$	0.0454	0.0498	$t = 27$	0.0698	0.0734
$t = 12$	0.0473	0.0516	$t = 28$	0.0709	0.0745
$t = 13$	0.0491	0.0534	$t = 29$	0.0720	0.0755
$t = 14$	0.0509	0.0552	$t = 30$	0.0730	0.0764
$t = 15$	0.0527	0.0569	$t = 31$	0.0739	0.0773

or a decline of 3.31 percent. Using only duration gives an immunization risk error of:

$$-4.37\% - (-3.24\%) = -1.13\%$$

while using the three-element duration vector model gives an immunization risk error of only:

$$-3.31\% - (-3.24\%) = -0.07\%$$

which is less than one tenth of the error of the duration model.

TREASURY NOTE FUTURES

Three kinds of Treasury note (T-note) futures are transacted on the CBOT given as two-year, five-year, and 10-year T-note futures. The two-year T-note futures is not as actively traded as the five-year and the 10-year T-note futures, because both T-bill futures and short-term Eurodollar futures are close competitors of the two-year T-note futures. The asset underlying the 10-year T-note futures contract is any \$100,000 face-value Treasury note maturing between six and 10 years from the first calendar day of the delivery month. The asset underlying the five-year T-note futures contract is any \$100,000 face-value T-note maturing between four and five years from the first calendar day of the delivery month. The five-year Treasury note issued after the last trading day of the contract month is not eligible for delivery into that month's contract. The least active of the three T-note futures, the two-year Treasury note futures contract is based on a \$200,000 face-value U.S. Treasury note with an original maturity of not more than five years and a remaining maturity of not less than one years from the first day of the delivery month but not more than two years from the last day of the delivery month.

Delivery months for the T-note futures are March, June, September, and December, and the first delivery day is the first business day of the delivery month. While five-year and 10-year T-note futures can be delivered any time during the delivery month, the delivery day of the two-year T-note futures contract is any day up to the third business day following the last trading day. The last trading day for the two-year T-note futures is the earlier of either (1) the second business day prior to the issue day of the two-year note auctioned in the current month or (2) the last business day of the calendar month, whereas for the other two futures contracts it is the seventh business day preceding the last business day of the delivery month.

Since Treasury notes with different maturities and coupons are eligible for delivery on the T-note futures contract, the CBOT adjusts the invoice price and the cash price of the T-note futures in the same manner as it adjusts those for T-bond futures (see equations 6.26 and 6.27). Even the definition of the conversion factor is similar for T-note futures and for T-bond futures, and is given by equations 6.28 through 6.31. The only difference between T-note futures and T-bond futures is the range of maturities of the deliverable bonds. Hence, all results derived for pricing and hedging using the T-bond futures hold for T-note futures by considering the appropriate range of maturities of deliverable bonds applicable to the specific T-note futures.

APPENDIX 6.1: THE DURATION VECTOR OF THE EURODOLLAR FUTURES

The relation between the continuously compounded forward rate over a *discrete* interval and the continuously compounded *instantaneous* forward rates is given as follows:

$$f\left(s,\ s+t\right)\times t = \int_{s}^{s+t} f(v)dv \tag{6.43}$$

The relationship between the instantaneous changes in both forward rates is given as follows:

$$\Delta f(s,\ s+t)\times t = \int_{s}^{s+t} \Delta f(v)dv \tag{6.44}$$

Substituting equation 6.9 into (6.44) gives:

$$\Delta f(s,\ s+t)\times t = \int_{s}^{s+t} \left(\Delta A_0 + 2\Delta A_1 v + 3\Delta A_2 v^2 + \cdots\right) dv \tag{6.45}$$

or

$$\begin{aligned}\Delta f(s,\ s+t)\times t = \Delta A_0 \times t + \Delta A_1 \times\left[\left(s+t\right)^2 - s^2\right] + \Delta A_2 \\ \times\left[\left(s+t\right)^3 - s^3\right] + \cdots\end{aligned} \tag{6.46}$$

where A_0, A_1, and A_2 are the height, slope, and curvature of the change in the term structure of zero-coupon yields, as shown in equation 6.8.

Since the futures rates underlying the Eurodollar futures contract are based on a 90-day Eurodollar deposit, we substitute $t = 90/365$ in equation 6.46, which gives:

$$\Delta f(s,\ s+90/365)\times 90/365 = \Delta A_0[90/365] + \Delta A_1\left[(s+90/365)^2 - s^2\right] + \Delta A_2\left[(s+90/365)^3 - s^3\right] + \cdots \tag{6.47}$$

Using equation 6.4, the instantaneous change in the forward rate equals the instantaneous change in the futures rate. Hence, replacing the forward rate with the futures rate in equation 6.47 gives:

$$\Delta f^*(s,\ s+90/365)\times 90/365 = \Delta A_0[90/365] + \Delta A_1\left[(s+90/365)^2 - s^2\right] + \Delta A_2\left[(s+90/365)^3 - s^3\right] + \cdots \tag{6.48}$$

Using equation 6.5, the change in the contract price is given as:

$$\Delta \mathit{Contract\ Price} = 2{,}500 \times \Delta Q \tag{6.49}$$

Since $q = 100 - Q$, in equation 6.1, it follows that:

$$\Delta Q = -\Delta q \tag{6.50}$$

Rearranging equation 6.2 gives:

$$q = \left(e^{f^*(s,s+90/365)\times(90/365)} - 1\right)\times 400 \tag{6.51}$$

If the discrete futures rate q changes to q', and the corresponding continuously compounded rate $f^*(s,\ s + 90/365)$ changes to $f^{*\prime}(s,\ s + 90/365)$, then the relationship between these changes is given using equation 6.51 as follows:

$$\Delta q = \left(e^{f^{*\prime}(s,s+90/365)\times(90/365)} - e^{f^*(s,s+90/365)\times(90/365)}\right)\times 400 \tag{6.52}$$

By defining,

$$f^{*\prime}(s,\ s+90/365) = f^*(s,\ s+90/365) + \Delta f^*(s,\ s+90/365) \tag{6.53}$$

equation 6.52 becomes:

$$\Delta q = e^{f^*(s,s+90/365)\times(90/365)}\left(e^{\Delta f^*(s,s+90/365)\times(90/365)} - 1\right)\times 400 \tag{6.54}$$

and by using equation 6.50, we get:

$$\Delta Q = -e^{f^*(s,s+90/365)\times(90/365)}\left(e^{\Delta f^*(s,s+90/365)\times(90/365)} - 1\right)\times 400 \tag{6.55}$$

Using a first-order Taylor series approximation for the exponential function, $\exp(x) \approx 1 + x$, for small values of x, in equation 6.55 and applying equation 6.49 we obtain the change in the contract price as follows:

$$\Delta CP = -2,500\times e^{f^*(s,s+90/365)\times(90/365)}\times\Delta f^*(s,\ s+90/365)\times(90/365)\times 400 \tag{6.56}$$

Substituting equation 6.2 and equation 6.1 into equation 6.56 we get,

$$\Delta CP = -1,000,000\times\left(1+\frac{100-Q}{400}\right)\times\Delta f^*(s,\ s+90/365)\times(90/365) \tag{6.57}$$

Substituting equation 6.48 into equation 6.57 and rearranging the terms gives:

$$\begin{aligned}\Delta CP = &-1,000,000\times\left(1+\frac{100-Q}{400}\right)\\ &\times\begin{pmatrix}\Delta A_0[90/365]+\Delta A_1\left[(s+90/365)^2-s^2\right]\\ +\Delta A_2\left[(s+90/365)^3-s^3\right]+\ \ldots\end{pmatrix}\end{aligned} \tag{6.58}$$

Dividing both sides by the contract price, and redefining the terms, we get,

$$\frac{\Delta CP}{CP} = -D^f(1)\times\Delta A_0 - D^f(2)\times\Delta A_1 - D^f(3)\times\Delta A_2 + \ \ldots \tag{6.59}$$

where

$$\begin{aligned}D^f(1) &= K(Q)\times(90/365),\\ D^f(2) &= K(Q)\times\left[(s+90/365)^2-s^2\right],\\ D^f(3) &= K(Q)\times\left[(s+90/365)^3-s^3\right],\end{aligned} \tag{6.60}$$

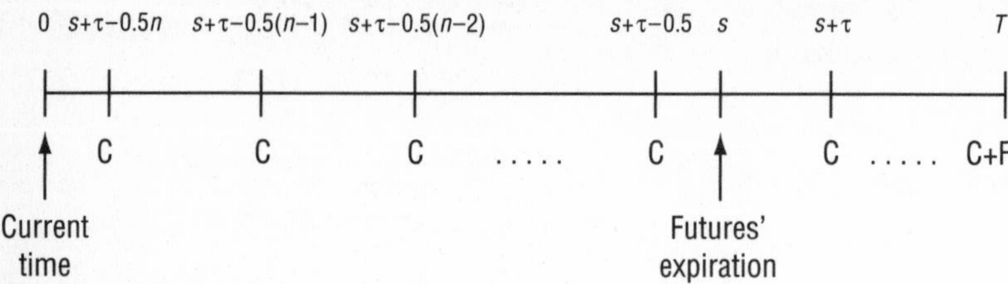

FIGURE 6.4 Timeline for T-Bond Futures

and $K(Q)$ is defined as follows:

$$K(Q) = \frac{1{,}000{,}000}{CP} \times \left(1 + \frac{100 - Q}{400}\right) \qquad (6.61)$$

Substituting the value of CP from equation 6.5 into equation 6.61 gives the definition of $K(Q)$ in equation 6.12, as shown next:

$$K(Q) = \frac{1{,}000{,}000}{750{,}000 + 2{,}500Q} \times \left(1 + \frac{100 - Q}{400}\right) = \frac{500 - Q}{300 + Q} \qquad (6.62)$$

APPENDIX 6.2: THE DURATION VECTOR OF THE T-BOND FUTURES

Consider a futures contract on a Treasury bond with a given cheapest-to-deliver bond and a given delivery date. The variables of the futures contract are defined as follows:

T = The maturity of the cheapest-to-deliver bond
C = Coupon payment of the cheapest-to-deliver bond
F = Face value of the cheapest-to-deliver bond
CF = Conversion factor of the cheapest-to-deliver bond
τ = Length of time between the expiration date of the futures contract and the first cash flow payment made after the futures' expiration date
n = Number of coupon payments between current time and the futures' expiration date

Given semiannual payments, the timeline of the cash flows is given in Figure 6.4.

The current price of the cheapest-to-deliver bond to be delivered at time s and maturing at time T is given as follows:

$$P_c = \frac{\displaystyle\sum_{t'=1}^{2(T-s-\tau+0.5n)} \frac{C}{e^{0.5t\times f^*(s+\tau-0.5n,s+\tau-0.5n+0.5t')}} + \frac{F}{e^{(T-s-\tau+0.5n)\times f^*(s+\tau-0.5n,T)}}}{e^{(s+\tau-0.5n)\times y(s+\tau-0.5n)}} \tag{6.63}$$

where: $f^*(s, t)$ = continuously compounded futures rate from time s to time t.

For expositional simplicity, we assume that the futures rate $f^*(s, t)$ and the forward rate $f(s, t)$ are equal. In reality, all we require is that the *instantaneous changes* in the futures rate and the forward rate are equal. Thus, equation 6.63 becomes:

$$\begin{aligned} P_c = &\sum_{t'=1}^{2(T-s-\tau+0.5n)} \frac{C}{e^{0.5t\times f(s+\tau-0.5n,s+\tau-0.5n+0.5t')}e^{(s+\tau-0.5n)\times y(s+\tau-0.5n)}} \\ &+\frac{F}{e^{(T-s-\tau+0.5n)\times f(s+\tau-0.5n,T)}e^{(s+\tau-0.5n)\times y(s+\tau-0.5n)}} \end{aligned} \tag{6.64}$$

If $f(t_1, t_2)$ is the forward rate between time t_1 and t_2, $y(t_1)$ is the zero-coupon yield maturing at time t_1 and $y(t_2)$ is the zero-coupon yield maturing at time t_2, then, the relationship between $f(t_1, t_2)$, $y(t_1)$, and $y(t_2)$ is given by equation 6.65:

$$e^{t_1 y(t_1)} e^{(t_2-t_1)f(t_1,t_2)} = e^{t_2 y(t_2)} \tag{6.65}$$

Substituting equation 6.65 into equation 6.64 we obtain:

$$P_c = \sum_{t'=1}^{2(T-s-\tau+0.5n)} \frac{C}{e^{(s+\tau-0.5n+0.5t')y(s+\tau-0.5n+0.5t')}} + \frac{F}{e^{Ty(T)}} \tag{6.66}$$

The present value of the coupons during the life of the futures contract, I, is:

$$I = \sum_{t'=1}^{n-1} \frac{C}{e^{(s+\tau-0.5n+0.5t')y(s+\tau-0.5n+0.5t')}} \tag{6.67}$$

Subtracting (6.67) from (6.66) and multiplying by $e^{sy(s)}$, we obtain the futures cash price at delivery:

$$\sum_{t'=n}^{2(T-s-\tau+0.5n)} \frac{C}{e^{(s+\tau-0.5n+0.5t')y(s+\tau-0.5n+0.5t')}} + \frac{F}{e^{Ty(T)}} \tag{6.68}$$

To make equation 6.68 more intuitive let us change the summation index from t' to $t = t' - n$. With the new summation index, the futures cash price at delivery becomes:

$$\sum_{t=0}^{2(T-s-\tau)} \frac{C}{e^{(s+\tau+0.5t)y(s+\tau+0.5t)}} + \frac{F}{e^{Ty(T)}} \tag{6.69}$$

The above gives the cash price of the cheapest-to-deliver bond at delivery. Once we have the cash futures price, we can calculate the invoice price at delivery by deducting the accrued interest on the first coupon payment that is distributed after the futures contract expires, or:

$$\sum_{t=0}^{2(T-s-\tau)} \frac{C}{e^{(s+\tau+0.5t)y(s+\tau+0.5t)}} + \frac{F}{e^{Ty(T)}} - C\frac{0.5-\tau}{0.5} \tag{6.70}$$

Further, using equation 6.26, we obtain the quoted futures price given in equation 6.37, or:

$$FP = \frac{1}{CF}\left[\sum_{t=0}^{2(T-s-\tau)} \frac{Ce^{s\times y(s)}}{e^{(s+\tau+t\times 0.5)\times y(s+\tau+t\times 0.5)}} + \frac{Fe^{s\times y(s)}}{e^{T\times y(T)}} - C\frac{0.5-\tau}{0.5}\right] \tag{6.71}$$

For a given change in the zero-coupon yields, the old and new zero-coupon yields are given by equations 4.3 and 4.4, respectively. Then, the old (quoted) futures price is given by equation 6.71 and the new price can be given as follows:

$$FP' = \frac{1}{CF}\left[\sum_{t=0}^{2(T-s-\tau)} \frac{Ce^{s\times y'(s)}}{e^{(s+\tau+t\times 0.5)\times y'(s+\tau+t\times 0.5)}} + \frac{Fe^{s\times y'(s)}}{e^{T\times y'(T)}} - C\frac{0.5-\tau}{0.5}\right] \tag{6.72}$$

Subtracting (6.71) from (6.72) we obtain the change in the futures price:

$$\Delta FP = FP' - FP = \frac{1}{CF}\sum_{t=0}^{2(T-s-\tau)}\left[\frac{Ce^{s\times y'(s)}}{e^{(s+\tau+t\times 0.5)\times y'(s+\tau+t\times 0.5)}} - \frac{Ce^{s\times y(s)}}{e^{(s+\tau+t\times 0.5)\times y(s+\tau+t\times 0.5)}}\right] + \frac{1}{CF}\left[\frac{Fe^{s\times y'(s)}}{e^{T\times y'(T)}} - \frac{Fe^{s\times y(s)}}{e^{T\times y(T)}}\right] \quad (6.73)$$

Substituting $y'(t)$ by $y(t) + \Delta y(t)$, into the above equation:

$$\Delta FP = \frac{1}{CF}\sum_{t=0}^{2(T-s-\tau)}\left[\frac{Ce^{s\times[y(s)+\Delta y(s)]}}{e^{(s+\tau+t\times 0.5)\times[y(s+\tau+t\times 0.5)+\Delta y(s+\tau+t\times 0.5)]}} - \frac{Ce^{s\times y(s)}}{e^{(s+\tau+t\times 0.5)\times y(s+\tau+t\times 0.5)}}\right] + \frac{1}{CF}\left[\frac{Fe^{s\times[y(s)+\Delta y(s)]}}{e^{T\times[y(T)+\Delta y(T)]}} - \frac{Fe^{s\times y(s)}}{e^{T\times y(T)}}\right]$$

or

$$\Delta FP = \frac{1}{CF}\sum_{t=0}^{2(T-s-\tau)}\frac{Ce^{s\times y(s)}}{e^{(s+\tau+t\times 0.5)\times y(s+\tau+t\times 0.5)}}\left[e^{s\times\Delta y(s)-(s+\tau+t\times 0.5)\times\Delta y(s+\tau+t\times 0.5)} - 1\right] + \frac{1}{CF}\times\frac{Fe^{s\times y(s)}}{e^{T\times y(T)}}\left[e^{s\times\Delta y(s)-T\times\Delta y(T)} - 1\right] \quad (6.74)$$

Using the first-order approximation of the exponential function's expansion $e^x = 1 + x + x^2/2! + x^3/3! + \ldots$ in equation 6.74, we get:

$$\Delta FP = \frac{1}{CF}\sum_{t=0}^{2(T-s-\tau)}\frac{Ce^{s\times y(s)}}{e^{(s+\tau+t\times 0.5)\times y(s+\tau+t\times 0.5)}} \times\left[s\times\Delta y(s) - (s+\tau+t\times 0.5)\times\Delta y(s+\tau+t\times 0.5)\right] + \frac{1}{CF}\times\frac{Fe^{s\times y(s)}}{e^{T\times y(T)}}\left[s\times\Delta y(s) - T\times\Delta y(T)\right] \quad (6.75)$$

The shift in the term structure of zero-coupon yields as a function of changes in height, slope, curvature, and other parameters is given as follows:

$$\Delta y(t) = \Delta A_0 + \Delta A_1 \times t + \Delta A_2 \times t^2 + \cdots$$

Substituting this equation into equation 6.75, the change in the futures price is:

$$
\begin{aligned}
\Delta FP &= \frac{1}{CF} \sum_{t=0}^{2(T-s-\tau)} \frac{Ce^{s\times y(s)}}{e^{(s+\tau+t\times 0.5)\times y(s+\tau+t\times 0.5)}} \\
&\times \begin{bmatrix} \Delta A_0 \left(s-(s+\tau+t\times 0.5)\right) + \Delta A_1 \left(s^2 - (s+\tau+t\times 0.5)^2\right) \\ +\Delta A_2 \left(s^3 - (s+\tau+t\times 0.5)^3\right) + \ \cdots \end{bmatrix} \\
&+ \frac{1}{CF} \times \frac{Fe^{s\times y(s)}}{e^{T\times y(T)}} \left[\Delta A_0 (s-T) + \Delta A_1 (s^2 - T^2) + \Delta A_2 (s^3 - T^3) + \ \cdots\right]
\end{aligned} \tag{6.76}
$$

Dividing both sides of equation 6.76 by the futures (quoted) price, we obtain:

$$
\begin{aligned}
\frac{\Delta FP}{FP} &= -\Delta A_0 \left\{ \frac{1}{CF} \begin{bmatrix} \sum_{t=0}^{2(T-s-\tau)} \frac{\frac{Ce^{s\times y(s)}}{e^{(s+\tau+t\times 0.5)\times y(s+\tau+t\times 0.5)}}}{FP} \\ \times\left((s+\tau+t\times 0.5) - s\right) + \frac{Fe^{s\times y(s)}}{FP\times e^{T\times y(T)}} (T-s) \end{bmatrix} \right\} \\
&-\Delta A_1 \left\{ \frac{1}{CF} \begin{bmatrix} \sum_{t=0}^{2(T-s-\tau)} \frac{\frac{Ce^{s\times y(s)}}{e^{(s+\tau+t\times 0.5)\times y(s+\tau+t\times 0.5)}}}{FP} \\ \times\left((s+\tau+t\times 0.5)^2 - s^2\right) + \frac{Fe^{s\times y(s)}}{FP\times e^{T\times y(T)}} (T^2-s^2) \end{bmatrix} \right\} \\
&-\Delta A_2 \left\{ \frac{1}{CF} \begin{bmatrix} \sum_{t=0}^{2(T-s-\tau)} \frac{\frac{Ce^{s\times y(s)}}{e^{(s+\tau+t\times 0.5)\times y(s+\tau+t\times 0.5)}}}{FP} \\ \times\left((s+\tau+t\times 0.5)^3 - s^3\right) + \frac{Fe^{s\times y(s)}}{FP\times e^{T\times y(T)}} (T^3-s^3) \end{bmatrix} \right\} \\
&\cdots
\end{aligned} \tag{6.77}
$$

If we denote

$$D(m) = \frac{1}{CF}\left[\sum_{t=0}^{2(T-s-\tau)} \frac{\dfrac{Ce^{s\times y(s)}}{e^{(s+\tau+t\times 0.5)\times y(s+\tau+t\times 0.5)}}}{FP} \times \left((s+\tau+t\times 0.5)^m - s^m\right) + \frac{Fe^{s\times y(s)}}{FP\times e^{T\times y(T)}}(T^m - s^m)\right]$$

equation 6.77 becomes:

$$\frac{\Delta FP}{FP} = -D(1)\Delta A_0 - D(2)\Delta A_1 - D(3)\Delta A_2 - \cdots$$

which is the percentage change of T-bond futures cash price expressed in equation 6.40.

NOTES

1. The Bid Rate is known as the London Interbank Bid Rate, or LIBID.
2. We have ignored the margin requirements that do require some cash investment.
3. For expositional simplicity, we are using the same notation for the forward rate changes in both the LIBOR market and the Treasury market. For cross-hedging, we assume that the changes in both markets are identical even if the initial forward rates in the two markets are different.
4. Full proof of equation 6.35 is given in Appendix 6.2.
5. The proof of equation 6.40 is given in Appendix 6.2.

CHAPTER 7

Hedging with Bond Options: A General Gaussian Framework

This chapter derives the duration vector risk measures of bond options using a general multifactor Gaussian framework. This framework allows arbitrary nonparallel shifts in the yield curve assuming that interest rates have a normal or a Gaussian distribution. Though the model is quite general and is consistent with a variety of single and multiple factor Gaussian term structure models (given by Ho and Lee, 1986; Vasicek, 1977; extensions of Vasicek model by Hull and White, 1993; multifactor affine and nonaffine models of Heath, Jarrow, and Morton, 1992, and others), the results of this chapter are not restricted to any one of these models.

Though we do not provide the specific details of the Gaussian term structure models, which are covered in detail in the second book of this series, we ensure that the duration measures are consistent with a general framework that applies to all of these models. It is well known that an option on a zero-coupon bond can be considered a portfolio consisting of the underlying zero-coupon bond and another zero-coupon bond maturing on the expiration date of the option. Since the duration vector of a portfolio of securities is a weighted average of the duration vectors of the securities in the portfolio, the duration vector of an option on a zero-coupon bond is obtained by using the duration vectors of zero-coupon bonds that replicate the option. We also derive the duration vector measures of a callable zero-coupon bond by considering it as a portfolio of a noncallable zero-coupon bond and an option on the noncallable zero-coupon bond.

Though this chapter derives the results for European options on zero-coupon bonds, the framework given here applies even to other options such as interest rate caps and floors, which can be considered portfolios of European puts and calls, respectively, on zero-coupon bonds. Hence, the results of this chapter can be generalized to derive the duration vectors of interest rate caps and floors under the multifactor Gaussian framework.

This chapter uses an empirical approach for the estimation of the duration vector of bond options using the *implied volatility* methodology. An advantage of the implied volatility methodology is that it incorporates all of the currently available information and thus avoids the errors contained in the estimation of future volatility using the historical full-rank covariance structure of bond returns. This approach allows the general Gaussian model to be calibrated not only to the observed bond prices (or yield curve), but also the observed option prices at the current date. Since minimal theoretical assumptions are made about the volatility structure, the framework is consistent with a variety of Gaussian term structure models.

This chapter also introduces a more general approach to the estimation of the duration vector of a bond option, which holds under non-Gaussian term structure models. However, this approach requires the knowledge of specific term structure models to estimate the implied volatilities and the hedge ratios for the computation of the duration vector.

Unfortunately, the duration vector model cannot be easily extended to options on coupon bonds. This is because an option on a coupon bond cannot be given as a sum of the options on the zero-coupon bonds comprising the coupon bond, in a setting that allows multiple factors. The numerical methods in the second book of this series may be applied to obtain the duration vectors of options on coupon bonds under such a general framework.

The final part of this chapter derives a general duration model for European options on default-free coupon bonds assuming a single affine interest rate factor. The models in this category are Ho and Lee (1986), Vasicek (1977), Cox, Ingersoll, and Ross (CIR; 1985), and the single-factor affine extensions of the Vasicek model and the CIR model given by Hull and White (1993). The Hull and White model allows calibrating the interest rate process to the observed market bond prices. Though we will not provide all of the term structure mathematics in this chapter, we give enough information to understand and apply these term structure models to compute the durations of options on coupon bonds and callable coupon bonds. Also, the applications given here hold for European options only. The second book in this series covers term structure mathematics and numerical techniques in more detail, which can be used to derive the durations of American options on coupon bonds and callable coupon bonds.

A GENERAL GAUSSIAN FRAMEWORK FOR PRICING ZERO-COUPON BOND OPTIONS

Consider a European call option with an expiration date of S, written on a default-free zero-coupon bond maturing at time T ($S \leq T$). Assume that the bond has a face value of F and the exercise price of the option is K. Further, assume that $P(t, T)$ is the time t price of a zero-coupon bond that pays \$1 at time T. At the option expiration date S, the terminal value of this option can be given as follows:

$$c(S) = Max\left[P(S, T)F - K, 0\right] \tag{7.1}$$

The time t price of this option $c(t)$, can be obtained using a variety of term structure models given in the fixed-income literature. In this chapter, we restrict our attention to the Gaussian term structure models. These models assume that the underlying continuously compounded interest rates, such as the short rate, zero-coupon rates, or the forward rates, have a normal or Gaussian distribution. A variety of single and multiple factor Gaussian term structure models exist in the literature given by Merton (1973b), Vasicek (1977), extensions of Vasicek model by Hull and White (1993), Ho and Lee (1986), and the multifactor affine and nonaffine forward rate models of Heath, Jarrow, and Morton (1992). The current price of this option $c(t)$, under all the above models has the following functional form:

$$c(t) = N(d_1)P(t, T)F - N(d_2)P(t, S)K \tag{7.2}$$

where

$N(x)$ = the cumulative probability that a standard normal variable is less than x (the popular spreadsheet program Microsoft Excel gives the value of $N(x)$ using the command function, "=NORMSDIST(x)"),

$$d_1 = \frac{\ln\left[\dfrac{P(t, T)F}{P(t, S)K}\right] + V/2}{\sqrt{V}}$$

$$d_2 = d_1 - \sqrt{V}$$

$$V = \int_t^S \left[\sigma^2(v, T) + \sigma^2(v, S) - 2\sigma(v, T)\sigma(v, S)\rho(v, S, T)\right] dv$$

$\sigma^2(v, T)\, dv = VaR[dP(v, T)/P(v, T)]$ = the variance at time v ($t \le v \le T$) of the return on the bond maturing on date T, over the infinitesimal interval v to $v + dv$

$\sigma^2(v, S)\,dv = VaR[dP(v, S)/P(v, S)]$ = the variance at time v $(t \le v \le S)$ of the return on the bond maturing on the option expiration date S over the infinitesimal interval v to $v + dv$

$\rho(v, S, T)\,dv = CORR[dP(v, S)/P(v, S), dP(v, T)/P(v, T)]$ = the correlation at time v $(t \le v \le S)$ between the returns on the bond maturing on date T and the bond maturing on the option expiration date S over the infinitesimal interval v to $v + dv$

A property shared by all Gaussians models is that the volatilities of instantaneous bond returns, $\sigma(v, T)$ and $\sigma(v, S)$, and the correlation between the instantaneous bond returns $\rho(v, S, T)$, are *deterministic* functions of current time and the bond maturity. In other words, $\sigma(v, T)$, $\sigma(v, S)$, and $\rho(v, S, T)$, are completely predictable at any time $t \ge 0$ and do not depend upon the evolution of the future interest rates and/or bond prices. These models assume that interest rates have a Gaussian distribution, which leads to a lognormal distribution for bond prices. The deterministic functions $\sigma(v, T)$, $\sigma(v, S)$, and $\rho(v, S, T)$, take on different forms under different Gaussian term structure models.

For the purpose of deriving the duration vector risk measures for these models, we do not need to estimate these functions, as we can use an implied volatility approach, which does not require explicit specification of these functions. To understand the implied volatility approach, note that in equation 7.2, if the market values of $c(t)$, $P(t, T)$, $P(t, S)$, and the values of F and K are known, then we can immediately estimate the *implied* value of the integrated volatility expression V, without explicitly knowing the functions $\sigma(v, T)$, $\sigma(v, S)$, and $\rho(v, S, T)$, which are specific to the term structure models. As we will show later, once the value of V is known, the duration vector of options on bonds are easily calculated.

The terms $N(d_1)$ and $N(d_2)$ in equation 7.2 always lie between 0 and 1, and have two interpretations given as follows:

1. *A replicating portfolio interpretation:* The quantity $N(d_1)$ is the number of zero-coupon bonds maturing on date T, and the quantity $-N(d_2)$ is the number of zero-coupon bonds maturing on date S, which replicate the option on the zero-coupon bond. The replicating portfolio is *self-financing* in that any increase (decrease) in the portfolio holding of the first bond is exactly offset by the decrease (increase) in the portfolio holding of the second bond. According to this interpretation, the call option can be thought of as a leveraged security. Specifically, it represents $N(d_1)$ long positions in the \$$F$ face-value zero-coupon bond underlying the option contract and $N(d_2)$ short positions in a \$$K$ face-value zero-coupon bond maturing on the option expiration date.

2. *A hedging ratio interpretation:* Using equation 7.2, it can be shown that

$$N(d_1) = Delta_1 = \frac{\partial c(t)}{\partial (P(t,\ T)F)}$$

and

$$-N(d_2) = Delta_2 = \frac{\partial c(t)}{\partial (P(t,\ S)K)}$$

Hence, $N(d_1)$ or $Delta_1$ is the hedge ratio of the change in the call price to the change in the price of the $\$F$ face-value zero-coupon bond maturing on date T. Similarly, $-N(d_2)$ or $Delta_2$ is the hedge ratio of the change in the call price to the change in the price of the $\$K$ face-value zero-coupon bond maturing on date S. Note that bond options have two delta measures as opposed to stock options, which only have one delta measure.

Now, consider a European put option with an expiration date of S, written on a default-free zero-coupon bond maturing at time T ($S \leq T$). Assume that the bond has a face value of F and the exercise price of the option is K. At the option expiration date S, the terminal value of this option can be given as follows:

$$p(S) = Max\left[K - P(S,\ T)F, 0\right] \tag{7.3}$$

Similar to equation 7.2, the time t price of this put option can be given as follows:

$$p(t) = \left[1 - N(d_2)\right]P(t,\ S)K - \left[1 - N(d_1)\right]P(t,\ T)F \tag{7.4}$$

where all variables in equation 7.4 are as defined before. The put price can also be obtained directly from the call price using the following put-call parity relationship, when all of the underlying variables are the same:

$$p(t) = c(t) + P(t,\ S)K - P(t,\ T)F \tag{7.5}$$

Example 7.1 Consider the zero-coupon yield curve given as:

$$y(t) = A_0 + A_1 \times t + A_2 \times t^2 + A_3 \times t^3 + \cdots + \tag{7.6}$$

where parameters A_0, A_1, A_2, and A_3 are the height, slope, curvature, and so on of the term structure of zero-coupon yields (see Chapters 3 and 4). Assume the following values for the shape parameters:

$$A_0 = 0.06$$
$$A_1 = 0.01$$
$$A_2 = -0.001$$
$$A_3 = 0.0001$$

Substituting these in equation 7.6, the term structure is given as:

$$y(t) = 0.06 + 0.01\, t - 0.001\, t^2 + 0.0001\, t^3$$

Now consider the price of a call option on a five-year zero-coupon bond (i.e., $T = 5$ years), with an exercise price $K = \$70$, option expiration date $S = 1$ year, and $V = 0.3$. The face value of the five-year bond, $F = \$100$. To get the call option price $c(0)$, we need to know the values of $P(0, 5)$, $P(0, 1)$ in equation 7.2. These values can be computed using the one-year and five-year zero-coupon yields that are obtained as follows:

$$y(1) = 0.06 + 0.01 \times 1 - 0.001 \times 1^2 + 0.0001 \times 1^3 = 0.0691$$

and

$$y(5) = 0.06 + 0.01 \times 5 - 0.001 \times 5^2 + 0.0001 \times 5^3 = 0.0975$$

Hence, the values of \$1 face-value zero-coupon bonds maturing at years 1 and 5 are given as follows:

$$P(0, 1) = 1/e^{0.0691} = 0.93323$$
$$P(0, 5) = 1/e^{(0.0975 \times 5)} = 0.61416$$

Substituting the above values in the expressions for d_1 and d_2, in equation 7.2, we get:

$$d_1 = \frac{\ln\left[\dfrac{0.61416 \times 100}{0.93323 \times 70}\right] + 0.3/2}{\sqrt{0.3}} = 0.16117$$

$$d_2 = 0.16117 - \sqrt{0.3} = -0.38655$$

Using the cumulative normal distribution function in Excel ($N(x)$ is computed using the command "=NORMSDIST(x)"), we get:

$$N(d_1) = N(0.16117) = 0.56402$$
$$N(d_2) = N(-0.38655) = 0.34955$$

Hence, call option price equals:

$$c(t) = 0.56402 \times 0.61416 \times 100 - 0.34955 \times 0.93323 \times 70 = \$11.81$$

Now consider the price of a put option on the same five-year zero-coupon bond, with an exercise price of \$70, option expiration date of one year, and $V = 0.3$. The face value of the five-year bond equals \$100. Since all variables for the call and the put are identical, we can use the put-call parity relationship given in equation 7.5, and get the put price as follows:

$$p(t) = 11.81 + 0.93323 \times 70 - 0.61416 \times 100 = \$15.72$$

THE DURATION VECTORS OF BOND OPTIONS

To obtain the duration vector of a European call option on a zero-coupon bond, note that the value of the call option can be given as a replicating portfolio of two bonds: a long position equal to $N(d_1)\ P(t, T)\ F$ (i.e., $N(d_1)$ number of bonds with a price of $P(t, T)\ F$ per bond), and a short position equal to $-N(d_2)\ P(t, S)\ K$ (i.e., $-N(d_2)$ number of bonds with a price of $P(t, S)\ K$ per bond).

Since the total value of this portfolio is the value of the call option, the portfolio weights are given as:

$$w_{c1} = \left[N(d_1)P(t,\ T)F\right] / c(t) \tag{7.7}$$

and

$$w_{c2} = -\left[N(d_2)P(t,\ S)K\right] / c(t) \tag{7.8}$$

where, by definition $w_{c1} + w_{c2} = 1$.

Since the duration vector of a portfolio of bonds is equal to the weighted average of the duration vectors of the bonds in the portfolio, we can compute the duration vector of the call option by treating it as a replicating portfolio of the two bonds, using the weights given previously.

At time t, the duration vector of the zero-coupon bond maturing at date T is given as follows (using the definition of the duration vector elements from equation 5.2):

$$D(m) = (T - t)^m, \text{ for all } m = 1, 2, \ldots, M \tag{7.9}$$

Similarly, at time t, the duration vector of the zero-coupon bond maturing at date S is given as follows:

$$D(m) = (S - t)^m, \text{ for all } m = 1, 2, \ldots, M \tag{7.10}$$

Hence, the duration vector of the call option is given as follows:

$$D^c(m) = w_{c1}(T - t)^m + w_{c2}(S - t)^m \tag{7.11}$$

where w_{c1} and w_{c2} are defined in equations 7.7 and 7.8, respectively.

Substituting the duration vector of the call option from equation 7.11 into equation 5.10, we can express the percentage change in the call price as follows:

$$\begin{aligned}\frac{\Delta c(t)}{c(t)} &= -D^c(1)\Delta A_0 \\ &\quad - D^c(2)\left[\Delta A_1 - (\Delta A_0)^2/2!\right] \\ &\quad - D^c(3)\left[\Delta A_2 - \Delta A_0 \Delta A_1 + (\Delta A_0)^3/3!\right] \\ &\quad \vdots \\ &\quad - D^c(M)\left[\Delta A_{M-1} + \cdots + \frac{(\Delta A_0)^M}{M!}\right]\end{aligned} \tag{7.12}$$

Similarly, we can obtain the duration vector of a European put option on a zero-coupon bond. Similar to the call option, the put option can also be given as a replicating bond portfolio using equation 7.4. Specifically, it represents a short position equal to $-[1 - N(d_1)]\, P(t, T)\, F$ (i.e., $-[1 - N(d_1)]$ number of bonds with a price of $P(t, T)\, F$, per bond), and a long position equal to $[1 - N(d_2)]\, P(t, S)\, K$ (i.e., $[1 - N(d_2)]$ number of bonds with a price of $P(t, S)\, K$, per bond).

Hence, the portfolio weights in the two bonds are given as follows:

$$w_{p1} = -\left[\left[1 - N(d_1)\right]P(t,\ T)F\right]/\,p(t) \tag{7.13}$$

and

$$w_{p2} = \left[\left[1 - N(d_2)\right]P(t,\ S)K\right]/\,p(t) \tag{7.14}$$

where by definition $w_{p1} + w_{p2} = 1$.

Hence, the duration vector of the put option is given as:

$$D^p(m) = w_{p1}(T-t)^m + w_{p2}(S-t)^m \tag{7.15}$$

for all $m = 1, 2, \ldots, M$.

Substituting the duration vector of the put option from equation 7.15 into equation 5.10, we can express the percentage change in the put price as follows:

$$\begin{aligned} \frac{\Delta p(t)}{p(t)} = & -D^p(1)\Delta A_0 \\ & -D^p(2)\left[\Delta A_1 - (\Delta A_0)^2/2!\right] \\ & -D^p(3)\left[\Delta A_2 - \Delta A_0 \Delta A_1 + (\Delta A_0)^3/3!\right] \\ & \vdots \\ & -D^p(M)\left[\Delta A_{M-1} + \cdots + \frac{(\Delta A_0)^M}{M!}\right] \end{aligned} \tag{7.16}$$

The duration vector of calls and puts obtained in this section allows these options to be used in designing immunization and other hedging strategies such as index replication, duration gap management, and so on, as outlined in Chapter 5. By treating these options as additional securities, all of the results derived in Chapter 5 for hedging against arbitrary nonparallel term structure shifts immediately apply to fixed-income portfolios that include these options. However, unlike using cash bonds and futures, in which portfolio rebalancing can be done at discrete cash flow payment dates, the use of options requires portfolio rebalancing to be done on a daily basis as the hedge ratios and duration vectors change continuously due to the changing *time value* of these options.

Though options on zero-coupon bonds are not that common, a huge market in the interest rate options such as caps, floors, and collars exists. As shown in the next chapter, these interest rate options can be considered portfolios of European zero-coupon bond options. Hence, the duration vector of options obtained above can be generalized to hold for these interest rate options under the general multifactor Gaussian framework.

Example 7.2 In this example, we estimate the percentage change in the price of the call option given in Example 7.1 using the duration vector, and compare it to the actual change caused by a shift in the yield curve. To compute the duration vector of the call option in Example 7.1, we estimate the weights w_{c1} and w_{c2}, given in equation 7.7 and 7.8, as follows:

$$w_{c1} = \left[N(d_1)P(t,\ T)F\right] / c(t) = 0.56402 \times 0.61416 \times 100 / 11.81 = 2.9342$$
$$w_{c2} = -\left[N(d_2)P(t,\ S)K\right] / c(t) = -0.34955 \times 0.93323 \times 70/11.81 = -1.9342$$

In Example 7.1, the maturity of the two zero-coupon bonds that replicate the call option are given as $T - t = 5$ years, and $S - t = 1$ year. Hence, the first two elements of the duration vector are computed using equation 7.11, as follows:

$$D^c(1) = 2.9342 \times 5 - 1.9342 \times 1 = 12.737$$
$$D^c(2) = 2.9342 \times 25 - 1.9342 \times 1 = 71.421$$

Using only the first two elements of the duration vector in equation 7.12, we get:

$$\frac{\Delta c(t)}{c(t)} = -D^c(1)\Delta A_0 - D^c(2)\left[\Delta A_1 - (\Delta A_0)^2 / 2!\right] + error \tag{7.17}$$

Now, consider an instantaneous change in the parameters of the yield curve, as follows:

$$\Delta A_0 = 0.005$$
$$\Delta A_1 = -0.002$$
$$\Delta A_2 = 0$$
$$\Delta A_3 = 0$$

Substituting the above parameters in equation 7.17, we get:

$$\frac{\Delta c(t)}{c(t)} \approx -12.737 \times 0.005 - 71.421 \times (-0.0020125) = 0.0801 = 8.01\%$$

The estimated percentage change given previously can be compared with the actual percentage change in the call price. The yield curve in Example 7.1 was given as follows:

$$y(t) = 0.06 + 0.01\,t - 0.001\,t^2 + 0.0001\,t^3$$

Since we have assumed $\Delta A_0 = 0.005$ and $\Delta A_1 = -0.002$, the new yield curve is given as follows:

$$y(t) = 0.065 + 0.008\,t - 0.001\,t^2 + 0.0001\,t^3$$

The new yield curve gives the following values for the one-year and five-year zero-coupon yields:

$$y(1) = 0.065 + 0.008 \times 1 - 0.001 \times 1^2 + 0.0001 \times 1^3 = 0.0721$$

and

$$y(5) = 0.065 + 0.008 \times 5 - 0.001 \times 5^2 + 0.0001 \times 5^3 = 0.0925$$

Hence, the new values of $1 face-value zero-coupon bonds maturing at years 1 and 5 are given as:

$$P(0, 1) = 1/e^{0.0721} = 0.93044$$
$$P(0, 5) = 1/e^{(0.0925 \times 5)} = 0.62971$$

Substituting the new bond prices, $F = 100$ and $K = 70$ in equation 7.2, and following the procedure given in Example 7.1, the new call price equals $12.77. Since the original call price equals 11.81 in Example 7.1, the *actual* percentage change in the call price equals:

$$(12.77 - 11.81)/11.81 = 0.96/11.81 = 8.16\%$$

The estimated percentage change using the two-element duration vector is 8.01 percent, which is quite close to the actual percentage change of

8.16 percent. The difference is only 0.15 percent, or less than one-sixth of 1 percent of \$11.81, equal to about 2 pennies.

Note that the use of two duration risk measures allowed capturing the effect of both the change in the height (i.e., $\Delta A_0 = 0.005$) and the change in the slope (i.e., $\Delta A_1 = -0.002$) of the zero-coupon yield curve on the call option price. Suppose we ignored the change in the slope and assumed a parallel shift in the yield curve. Then, the estimated percentage change would be given as:

$$\frac{\Delta c(t)}{c(t)} = -D^c(1)\Delta A_0 + D^c(2)\left(\Delta A_0\right)^2 / 2 + error \tag{7.18}$$

Substituting $\Delta A_0 = 0.005$ in equation 7.18, we get:

$$\frac{\Delta c(t)}{c(t)} \approx -12.737 \times 0.005 + 71.421 \times 0.0000125 = -0.0628 = -6.28\%$$

Hence, the estimated percentage change is *negative* 6.28 percent, which is 14.44 percent lower than the actual change of 8.16 percent. Though the results of this example are based upon hypothetical numbers, it is well known that the effects of nonparallel shifts on options written on longer term bonds are significant. The use of a two or three element duration vector model can significantly reduce the basis risk arising from nonparallel shifts in the yield curve.

Bounds on the Duration Vector of Bond Options

A Lower Bound on the Duration Vector of Call Options It can be seen from equations 7.7 and 7.8 that $w_{c1} \geq 0$ and $w_{c2} \leq 0$. Since $w_{c2} \leq 0$ and $(T-t)^m \geq (S-t)^m$ (for all $m = 1, 2, \ldots, M$), it is implied that $w_{c2}(S-t)^m \geq w_{c2}(T-t)^m$. This implies that $D^c(m) = w_{c1}(T-t)^m + w_{c2}(S-t)^m \geq (w_{c1} + w_{c2})(T-t)^m$. Finally, since $w_{c1} + w_{c2} = 1$, the following inequality must always hold:

$$D^c(m) \geq (T-t)^m, \text{ for all } m = 1, 2, \ldots, M \tag{7.19}$$

In other words, the duration vector of the zero-coupon bond underlying the call option defines a *lower bound* of the duration vector of the call

TABLE 7.1 Duration Vector Values of Call and Puts versus Exercise Price

Exercise Price ($)	Panel A: Call Option			Panel B: Put Option		
	$D^c(1)$	$D^c(2)$	$D^c(3)$	$D^p(1)$	$D^p(2)$	$D^p(3)$
0+	5.00	25.00	125.00	$-\infty$	$-\infty$	$-\infty$
40	8.56	46.36	235.35	−317.79	−1,911.75	−9,881.56
80	40.80	239.78	1,234.70	−62.05	−377.31	−1,953.61
120	160.72	959.31	4,952.25	−8.69	−57.14	−299.39
$+\infty$	$+\infty$	$+\infty$	$+\infty$	1.00	1.00	1.00

option. This implies that sensitivity of the call option to interest rate changes is higher than the sensitivity of the underlying bond to these changes. Also, the lower bound on the duration vector of a call option implies that its duration measures of a call option are always positive. The duration vector of a call option does not have an upper bound. Hence, under certain conditions the duration vector of the call option can become infinitely large (e.g., as shown in Panel A of Table 7.1).

An Upper Bound on the Duration Vector of Put Options It can be seen from equations 7.13 and 7.14 that $w_{p1} \leq 0$ and $w_{p2} \geq 0$. Since $w_{p1} \leq 0$ and $(T - t)^m \geq (S - t)^m$ (for all $m = 1, 2, \ldots, M$), it is implied that $w_{p1}(T - t)^m \leq w_{p1}(S - t)^m$. This implies that $D^p(m) = w_{p1}(T - t)^m + w_{p2}(S - t)^m \leq (w_{p1} + w_{p2})(S - t)^m$. Finally, since $w_{p1} + w_{p2} = 1$, the following inequality must always hold:

$$D^p(m) \leq (S - t)^m, \text{ for all } m = 1, 2, \ldots, M \tag{7.20}$$

In other words, the duration vector of the zero-coupon bond maturing at the put option's expiration date, defines an *upper bound* of the duration vector of the put option. Unlike the duration vectors of regular bonds and call options, which are always positive, the duration vector of the put option is generally negative, but can also be positive with an upper bound given in equation 7.20. Since the duration vector of a put option does not have a lower bound, under certain conditions the duration vector of the put option can become infinitely negative (e.g., as shown in Panel B of Table 7.1).

To get additional insights into the duration vectors of call options and put options, the next section performs numerical simulations to analyze the

TABLE 7.2 Duration Vector Values of Call and Puts versus Volatility

Volatility	Panel A: Call Option			Panel B: Put Option		
V	$D^c(1)$	$D^c(2)$	$D^c(3)$	$D^p(1)$	$D^p(2)$	$D^p(3)$
0.25%	59.38	351.30	1,810.86	−161.09	−971.54	−5,023.83
1%	40.80	239.78	1,234.70	−62.05	−377.31	−1,953.61
4%	24.86	144.13	740.53	−25.68	−159.08	−826.10
25%	12.60	70.62	360.69	−7.68	−51.09	−268.14
$+\infty$	5.00	25.00	125.00	1.00	1.00	1.00

relationships between the duration vector values of these options and the underlying variables that define these options.

Numerical Simulations

This section numerically simulates the duration vector values of European options written on zero-coupon bonds. Unless stated otherwise, the following values of the different parameters are assumed:

1. Maturity of the underlying zero-coupon bond equals five years.
2. Option expiration date equals one year.
3. Exercise price, or the face value of the one-year bond equals $80.
4. Price of the five-year bond equals $80.
5. Integrated volatility, V, equals 1 percent.
6. Annualized interest rate (assuming a flat term structure) equals 6 percent.

The comparative static results are reported with respect to the exercise price, the integrated bond volatility, and the interest rate in Tables 7.1, 7.2, and 7.3, respectively.

The Exercise Price Table 7.1 provides the values of the duration vectors of a European call option and a European put option, with respect to different values of the exercise price. Panel A of Table 7.1 gives the first three elements of the duration vector values of the call option. When the exercise price tends to zero, the price of the call option converges to the price of the underlying five-year bond, and the duration vector of the call

TABLE 7.3 Duration Vector Values of Call and Puts versus Interest Rate

Interest	Panel A: Call Option			Panel B: Put Option		
Rate (%)	$D^c(1)$	$D^c(2)$	$D^c(3)$	$D^p(1)$	$D^p(2)$	$D^p(3)$
5	34.10	199.62	1,027.21	−73.19	−444.11	−2,298.76
10	79.18	470.07	2,424.54	−28.11	−173.64	−901.32
15	144.38	861.27	4,445.72	−10.41	−67.48	−352.48
20	219.25	1,310.51	6,766.82	−5.17	−36.00	−190.15

option becomes identical to that of the five-year bond. However, as the exercise price increases, the call option becomes a leveraged security and its duration vector rises rapidly.

Panel B constructed similar to Panel A, gives the values of the first three elements of the duration vector of the put option. As the exercise price tends to zero, the duration vector values of the put option tend to negative infinity. Increases in the exercise price decrease the magnitudes of the duration vector elements of the put option. As shown in Panel A of Table 7.1, that the duration vector of a call option attains its lower bound when the exercise price tends to zero. Similarly, it can be seen from Panel B of Table 7.1, that the duration vector of a put option attains its upper bound when the exercise price tends to infinity.

The Bond Volatility Table 7.2, constructed very similar to Table 7.1, allows the integrated volatility V (see equation 7.2 for the definition) to vary, and assumes the exercise price to be a constant equal to \$80. Table 7.2 demonstrates that the magnitudes of the duration vectors of both the call option and the put option decrease as V increases. As shown in Panel A of Table 7.2, when V becomes infinitely large, the duration vector of the call option converges to its lower bound. Similarly, as shown in Panel B of Table 7.2, when V becomes infinitely large, the duration vector of the put option converges to its upper bound.

The Interest Rate Until now, we have assumed that the five-year zero-coupon bond sells for an \$80 price, with a 6 percent annualized interest rate. This corresponds to a maturity face value of \$107.99, at the end of five years. Table 7.3 assumes this face value to be a given constant, and allows the price of the five-year bond to fluctuate in response to the changes in the level of the interest rates. It can be seen from Panel A of Table 7.3 that the magnitudes of the duration vector elements of the call option are positively related to level of the interest rates. Similarly, it can be seen from Panel B of Table 7.3 that the magnitudes of the duration vector elements of the put option are negatively related to level of the interest rates.

Estimation of the Duration Vectors Using Implied Volatilities

Though we have identified the appropriate formulae for the duration vectors of bond options and callable bonds (see equations 7.11 and 7.15), these formulae remain meaningless unless they can be estimated using empirical data. The main obstacle in the computation of the duration vectors of bond options is the estimation of the integrated volatility V (see equation 7.2). This requires the estimation of the full-rank covariance structure of returns on zero-coupon bonds using historical data. Though this is possible, it remains a complicated task due to the declining maturities of the zero-coupon bonds. Also, using specific functional forms of the volatility V may limit the model to the Gaussian interest rate processes implied by these functions. Since the model given in this chapter is very general and includes all single and multifactor Gaussian models given by Merton (1973b); Vasicek (1977); extensions of Vasicek model by Hull and White (1993); multifactor affine and nonaffine models of Heath, Jarrrow, and Morton (1992); and others; we want to put minimum theoretical constraints on the integrated volatility V.

Hence, we use a direct empirical approach for the estimation of the duration vector of bond options using the *implied volatility* methodology to estimate V. An advantage of the implied volatility methodology is that it incorporates all of the currently available information and thus avoids the errors contained in the estimation of future volatility using the historical full-rank covariance structure of bond returns. This approach allows the general Gaussian model to fit the observed bond prices (or yield curve) at the current date, and also be calibrated to the observed option prices at the current date. Since no theoretical assumption is made about V, it is consistent with a variety of Gaussian term structure models.

To apply this approach note that if the market values of $c(t)$, $P(t, T)$, $P(t, S)$, and the values of F and K are known in equation 7.2, then we can estimate the *implied* value of the integrated volatility V, without explicitly knowing the functions $\sigma(v, T)$, $\sigma(v, S)$, and $\rho(v, S, T)$, contained in V, which are specific to the term structure models. However, since $c(t)$ is a nonlinear function of V and other variables, it is not easy to invert equation 7.2 and express V as a nonlinear function of $c(t)$ and other variables.

However, computing V using $c(t)$ and other variables, is quite an easy task using any programming languages. In fact, both the "Solver" and "Goal Seek" functions in Excel can be used to estimate V in a single step. The value of V will change for options with different underlying variables. However, for a specific call option, once the implied value of V is computed, equations 7.7 through 7.11 can be used to estimate its duration vector.

A similar argument applies for the computation of the duration vector of a put option. In this case, we use equation 7.4 to estimate the implied value of V, and then use this value of V in equations 7.13 through 7.15 to estimate the duration vector of the put option.

In the real world, options on zero-coupon bonds are not that common. However, interest rate options such as caps, floors, and collars are very widely used in many markets (i.e., the interest rate swap market, the mortgage market). Since a cap can be considered a portfolio of a sequence of increasing maturity European put options on a corresponding sequence of zero-coupon bonds with increasing maturities (as shown in the next chapter), an iterative method can be used to estimate different values of V corresponding to different zero-coupon bond options embedded in the cap, by using a sequence of caps of increasing maturities. Using the different values of V corresponding to different zero-coupon bond options, the results given earlier can be applied for estimating the duration vector of a cap, which is represented as a portfolio of European puts. Similarly, the duration vector of a floor can be estimated by expressing the floor as a portfolio of a sequence of increasing maturity call options on a corresponding sequence of zero-coupon bonds with increasing maturities.

THE DURATION VECTOR OF CALLABLE BONDS

Consider a default-free zero-coupon callable bond maturing at time T with a face value \$1. The time t price of this bond is $P^c(t, T)$. The price of this bond with \$$F$ of face value equals $P^c(t, T)F$. Assume that the \$$F$ face-value callable bond is callable at time S ($t < S < T$) for an exercise price of K. This means that at time S, the issuer of the callable bond can buy the bond back at a fixed price equal to K dollars. Let $P(t, T)F$ be the price of the corresponding zero-coupon noncallable bond maturing at time T with a face value F.

The relationship between the callable and the noncallable bond can be given as:

$$P(t, T)F = P^c(t, T)F + c(t) \tag{7.21}$$

where $c(t)$ is the price of a call option. This call option gives the option holder the right to buy the zero-coupon bond maturing at date T, at time S for an exercise price equal to \$$K$. The price of the call option $c(t)$ is defined in equation 7.2. The short position in the call option embedded in the callable bond is exactly offset by explicitly adding a long position in the same call option on the right-hand side of equation 7.21, resulting in the price of a noncallable bond. Equation 7.21 can be rewritten:

$$P^c(t,\ T)F = P(t,\ T)F - c(t) \tag{7.22}$$

Hence, the callable bond represents a portfolio of a long position in the underlying noncallable bond, and a short position in the call option.

The call option price is given in equation 7.2 as:

$$c(t) = N(d_1)P(t,\ T)F - N(d_2)P(t,\ S)K$$

Substituting equation 7.2 into equation 7.22, we get:

$$P^c(t,\ T)F = \left[1 - N(d_1)\right]P(t,\ T)F + N(d_2)P(t,\ S)K \tag{7.23}$$

To obtain the duration vector of the callable bond, note that the value of the callable bond $P^c(t, T)F$, can be given as a portfolio of two bonds:

1. A long position equal to $[1 - N(d_1)]\ P(t, T)F$, or $[1 - N(d_1)]$ number of bonds with a price of $P(t, T)F$ for each \$$F$ face-value bond maturing at time T.
2. A long position equal to $N(d_2)\ P(t, S)K$, or $N(d_2)$ number of bonds with a price of $P(t, S)K$ for each \$$K$ face-value bond maturing at time S.

Since the total value of this portfolio is the value of the callable bond, the portfolio weights are given as:

$$w_{cB1} = \left[\left(1 - N(d_1)\right)P(t,\ T)\right] / P^c(t,\ T) \tag{7.24}$$

and

$$w_{cB2} = \left[N(d_2)P(t,\ S)K\right] / \left[P^c(t,\ T)F\right] \tag{7.25}$$

Note that $w_{cB1} + w_{cB2} = 1$, and $w_{cB1} \geq 0$, $w_{cB2} \geq 0$.

The duration vector of the callable bond can be obtained as a weighted average of the duration vectors of zero-coupon bonds maturing at dates T and S, where the weights are given in equations 7.24 and 7.25, respectively. Substituting the duration vectors of the two zero-coupon bonds maturing at dates T and S from equations 7.9 and 7.10, respectively, the duration vector of the callable bond is given as:

$$D^{cB}(m) = w_{cB1}(T-t)^m + w_{cB2}(S-t)^m \tag{7.26}$$

Since $w_{cB1} + w_{cB2} = 1$, and $w_{cB1} \geq 0$, $w_{cB2} \geq 0$ from the definitions given in equation 7.25, it follows from equation 7.26 that the duration vector of a callable zero-coupon bond always lies between the duration vector of the bond maturing on the call date S and the duration vector of the bond underlying the option contract, maturing on date T. In other words:

$$(S-t)^m \leq D^{cB}(m) \leq (T-t)^m \tag{7.27}$$

To compute the duration vector of a callable zero-coupon bond, a two-step procedure can be followed. First, the price of the embedded call option is calculated as the difference between the market price of the corresponding noncallable bond and the callable bond. Next, the implied value of the volatility expression V is estimated using the price of the embedded call option and other variables. The computation of the duration vector of the callable bond is then straightforward using equation 7.26.

Substituting the duration vector of the callable bond from equation 7.26 into equation 5.10, we can express the percentage change in the callable zero-coupon bond price as follows:

$$\begin{aligned}
\frac{\Delta(P^c(t,\ T)F)}{P^c(t,\ T)F} = \frac{\Delta(P^c(t,\ T))}{P^c(t,\ T)} &= -D^{cB}(1)\Delta A_0 \\
&-D^{cB}(2)\left[\Delta A_1 - (\Delta A_0)^2/2!\right] \\
&-D^{cB}(3)\left[\Delta A_2 - \Delta A_0 \Delta A_1 + (\Delta A_0)^3/3!\right] \\
&\ \vdots \\
&-D^{cB}(M)\left[\Delta A_{M-1} + \cdots + \frac{(\Delta A_0)^M}{M!}\right]
\end{aligned} \tag{7.28}$$

A number of authors in the fixed-income literature derive the duration of the callable bond, assuming infinitesimal parallel term structure shifts. As noted by Nawalkha (1995), the duration measure for callable bonds derived by these authors is incorrect. To see this, consider equation 7.28, for the special case of infinitesimal parallel shift in the term structure of interest rates, as follows:

$$\frac{\Delta(P^c(t, T)F)}{P^c(t, T)F} = -D^{cB}(1)\Delta A_0 \tag{7.29}$$

where $D^{cB}(1)$ is given as:

$$D^{cB}(1) = w_{cB1}(T-t) + w_{cB2}(S-t) \tag{7.30}$$

Many researchers including Dunetz and Mahoney (1988) and Jamshidian and Zhu (1988), and others show the duration of the callable zero-coupon bond to be given as follows:

$$D^{cB}(1) = w_{cB1}(T-t) \tag{7.31}$$

Hence, the duration formula given in equation 7.31 by these authors is incorrect since it ignores the term $w_{cB2}(S-t)$, given in equation 7.30. Ignoring this term can lead to big errors if the call date S is quite distant.

Numerical Simulations

This section numerically simulates the duration vector values of callable zero-coupon bonds. Unless stated otherwise, the following values of the different parameters are assumed:

1. Maturity of the callable zero-coupon bond equals five years.
2. Call date equals one year.
3. Call exercise price, or K is \$80.
4. Price of the noncallable five-year zero-coupon bond equals \$80.
5. Volatility Expression, V is 1 percent.
6. Annualized interest rate (assuming a flat term structure) is 6 percent.

The comparative static results are reported with respect to the call exercise price, the underlying bond volatility, and the interest rate.

TABLE 7.4 Duration Vector Values of Callable Bond versus Call Exercise Price

Call Exercise Price ($)	$D^{cB}(1)$	$D^{cB}(2)$	$D^{cB}(3)$
0+	1.00	1.00	1.00
70	1.11	1.69	4.55
80	2.09	7.68	35.44
90	3.85	18.14	89.54
$+\infty$	5.00	25.00	125.00

The Call Exercise Price Table 7.4 provides the values of the duration vectors of the callable zero-coupon bond with respect to different values of the call exercise price. When the call exercise price is zero, the probability of exercising the call is 100 percent, and hence the duration vector of the callable bond equals the duration vector of the bond maturing at the call date (i.e., the lower bound of the duration vector of the callable bond). For higher call exercise prices, the probability of exercising the call decreases, which increases the duration vector values of the callable bond. In the limit, as the call exercise price becomes infinite, the duration vector of the callable bond equals the duration vector of the noncallable bond (i.e., the upper bound of the duration vector of the callable bond).

The Bond Volatility Table 7.5 investigates the relationship of the duration vector of the callable zero-coupon bond with respect to the changes in the integrated volatility *V*. This table is divided into two panels. Panel A

TABLE 7.5 Duration Vector Values of Callable Bond versus Volatility

Volatility	Panel A (Call Exercise Price = $90)			Panel B (Call Exercise Price = $70)		
V (%)	$D^{cB}(1)$	$D^{cB}(2)$	$D^{cB}(3)$	$D^{cB}(1)$	$D^{cB}(2)$	$D^{cB}(3)$
0.25	4.49	21.97	109.33	1.00	1.00	1.01
1	3.85	18.14	89.54	1.11	1.69	4.55
4	3.44	15.61	76.49	1.71	5.24	22.92
25	3.16	13.99	68.10	2.46	9.75	46.19
$+\infty$	3.00	13.00	63.00	3.00	13.00	63.00

TABLE 7.6 Duration Vector Values of Callable Bond versus Interest Rate

Interest Rate (%)	$D^{cB}(1)$	$D^{cB}(2)$	$D^{cB}(3)$
5	1.65	4.93	21.30
10	4.34	21.07	104.69
15	4.99	24.96	124.81
20	4.99	24.99	124.99

assumes that the call exercise price equals $90, while Panel B assumes that the call exercise price equals $70. The noncallable bond's price equals $80. If the volatility V is very low, and if the call exercise price is significantly higher than the price of the noncallable bond, then it is implied that the probability of the exercise of the call is low, and the duration vector of the callable bond should be closer to the duration vector of the noncallable bond. Similarly, if the volatility V is very low, but the call exercise price is significantly lower than the price of the noncallable bond, then it is implied that the probability of the exercise of the call is high, and the duration vector of the callable bond should be closer to the duration vector of the zero-coupon bond maturing at the call date.

Panel A and Panel B of Table 7.5 demonstrate these results. When the volatility V equals only 0.25 percent, the duration vector values of the callable bond are closer to the duration vector values of the noncallable bond in Panel A, and are closer to the duration vector values of the bond maturing at the call date in Panel B. However, as the volatility increases in Panel A (Panel B), the probability of the exercise of the call increases (decreases), causing the duration vector values of the callable bond to decrease (increase). In the limit, as the volatility becomes infinite, the portfolio weights of the callable bond become half or, $w_{cB1} = w_{cB2} = \frac{1}{2}$, for both Panels A and B, and the duration vector of the callable bond becomes half of the sum of the duration vectors of the five-year noncallable bond and the one-year bond maturing at the call date.

The Interest Rate Until now we have assumed that the five-year noncallable zero-coupon bond sells for an $80 price, with a 6 percent annualized interest rate. This corresponds to a maturity face value of $107.99, at the end of five years. Table 7.6 assumes this face value to be a given constant, and allows the price of the five-year noncallable bond to fluctuate in response to the changes in the level of the interest rates. It can be seen from Table 7.6, that as the interest rate increases, the probability of exercising the call decreases (since the five-year noncallable bond loses in value). Hence, the duration vector values of the callable bond increase and approach the duration vector values of the noncallable bond at high levels of the interest rate.

The duration vector of the callable bond in this section assumed that the underlying zero-coupon bond is called on a given call date. However, most callable bonds are callable anytime after the call protection period, and so the embedded call option in these callable bonds is an *American*-type option that can be exercised at any time after the first call date, using a contractually specified call schedule with deterministically changing call exercise prices. Also, since most callable bonds are also coupon-paying bonds, the embedded call option is written on the underlying noncallable coupon-paying bond. Simple closed-form formulas for options on coupon-paying bonds do not exist in a multifactor setting. Hence, it is difficult to derive simple analytical formulas for the duration vector of callable coupon bonds with American-type option features. A variety of term structure models and the numerical techniques such as binomial and trinomial trees in the second book of this series can be used to derive the interest rate sensitivities of these callable bonds. Later in this chapter, we consider the pricing and durations of European options on coupon bonds, which provide some intuition about the interest rate sensitivities of coupon-bond options.

ESTIMATION OF DURATION VECTORS USING NON-GAUSSIAN TERM STRUCTURE MODELS

The results until now have assumed a general Gaussian framework for the derivation of the duration vectors of bond options and callable bonds. This framework uses the implied volatility V to estimate the duration vectors. This section shows how the results derived in the previous sections may be extended to derive the duration vectors of bond options and callable bonds under non-Gaussian multifactor models, including the general affine models of Dai and Singleton (2000), quadratic models of Ahn, Dittmar, and Gallant (2002), and the jump-affine models of Chacko and Das (2002). The price of a European call option on a zero-coupon bond maturing at date T, with a face value F, under all the above term structure models has the following general form:

$$c(t) = \Pi_1 P(t, T)F - \Pi_2 P(t, S)K \tag{7.32}$$

where all variables except Π_1 and Π_2 are as defined in earlier sections. Though under the Gaussian framework $\Pi_1 = N(d_1)$ and $\Pi_2 = N(d_2)$ (as can be seen from equation 7.2), Π_1 and Π_2 may have more complex functional forms under general non-Gaussian models. For example, under the multi-factor jump-affine models of Chacko and Das, Π_1 and Π_2 are obtained using fourier inversion of the characteristic functions associated with the risk-neutral densities. In general, different term structure models will lead to different functional forms for Π_1 and Π_2.

Using put-call parity given in equation 7.5, the price of the put option with the same characteristic as that of the call option in equation 7.32, is given as:

$$p(t) = [1 - \Pi_2]P(t,\ S)K - [1 - \Pi_1]P(t,\ T)F \tag{7.33}$$

Similarly, the price of a callable bond given in equation 7.23 can be given under the more general framework as follows:

$$P^c(t,\ T)F = \left[1 - \Pi_1\right]P(t,\ T)F + \Pi_2 P(t,\ S)K \tag{7.34}$$

The derivation of functional forms of Π_1 and Π_2 for general multifactor non-Gaussian models are outside the scope of this chapter, but are derived under a variety of multifactor affine and quadratic term structure models in the second book of this series. By substituting Π_1 for $N(d_1)$ and Π_2 for $N(d_2)$, in all equations after equation 7.2, the results related to the duration vectors of calls, puts, and callable bonds (and also interest rate caps and floors which can be given as portfolios of European puts and calls, respectively) given in the previous sections immediately hold under the more general multifactor non-Gaussian term structure models.

THE DURATIONS OF EUROPEAN OPTIONS ON COUPON BONDS AND CALLABLE COUPON BONDS

A default-free coupon bond can be considered a portfolio of default-free zero-coupon bonds. Since an option on a coupon bond cannot be generally priced as a portfolio of options on the underlying zero-coupon bonds (because the portfolio will generally have less volatility than the weighted average of the volatilities of the individual zero-coupon bonds in the portfolio), obtaining closed-form solutions for European options on coupon bonds is difficult if not impossible under a multiple factor setting.

In this section, we derive the interest rate sensitivities of European options on coupon bonds assuming a class of single-factor affine term structure models. A term structure model is affine with respect to the instantaneous short rate if the zero-coupon bond price is exponentially linear in the short rate. The zero-coupon bond prices can be expressed as a decreasing function of the current short rate under all single-factor affine term structure models. Jamshidian (1989) demonstrates a mathematical trick to obtain the European solution of an option on a coupon bond, from the European solutions of options on the underlying zero-coupon bonds, under all single-factor affine term structure models. Jamshidian's result can be demonstrated as follows.

Consider a European call option on a coupon bond, with an expiration date S and exercise price K. The coupon bond has M cash flows given as CF_i at time $T_i \leq S$, for $i = 1, 2, \ldots, M$, maturing before or at the option expiration date S, and $N - M$ cash flows given as CF_i at time $T_i > S$, for $i = M + 1, M + 2, \ldots, N$, maturing *after* the option expiration date S. The present value of the $N - M$ cash flows maturing *after* the option expiration date S is given as:

$$\sum_{i=M+1}^{N} CF_i \times P(t, T_i) \tag{7.35}$$

where using the affine property the time t price $P(t, T_i) = P(r(t),t,T_i)$, of a zero-coupon bond that pays \$1 at time T_i, is a decreasing function of the short rate $r(t)$, at time t. The value of the call option at expiration date S, equals:

$$c(S) = Max\left[\left(\sum_{i=M+1}^{N} CF_i \times P(S, T_i)\right) - K, 0\right] \tag{7.36}$$

where $P(S, T_i) = P(r(S), S, T_i)$ is the time S price of a zero-coupon bond maturing at time T_i. Since all zero-coupon bond prices $P(S, T_i)$ are monotonically decreasing functions of the short rate $r(S)$ under the single-factor term structure models, the sum given in the inside brackets on the right side of equation 7.36 also decreases as $r(S)$ increases.

Consequently, the option will be exercised only if $r(S)$ is below the specific value of short rate equal to $r^*(S)$, which makes the following equation hold:

$$\sum_{i=M+1}^{N} CF_i \times P(r^*(S), S, T_i) = K \tag{7.37}$$

Now define $N - M$, new constants given as:

$$K_i = P(r^*(S), S, T_i), \text{ for } i = M+1, M+2, \ldots, N \tag{7.38}$$

Substituting equation 7.38 into equation 7.37, we get:

$$\sum_{i=M+1}^{N} CF_i \times K_i = K \tag{7.39}$$

By substituting equation 7.39 into equation 7.36, the payoff of the option on the coupon bond at time S can be expressed as:

$$Max\left[\left(\sum_{i=M+1}^{N} CF_i\ P(S,\ T_i)\right) - K, 0\right] = Max\left[\sum_{i=M+1}^{N} CF_i\left(P(S,\ T_i) - K_i\right), 0\right] \tag{7.40}$$

If $r(S) < r^*(S)$, then $P(S, T_i) = P(r(S), S, T_i)$ will be higher than K_i for each i, and thus the payoff of the option becomes:

$$\sum_{i=M+1}^{N} CF_i\left(P(S,\ T_i) - K_i\right) = \sum_{i=M+1}^{N} CF_i \times Max\left[P(S,\ T_i) - K_i, 0\right] \tag{7.41}$$

On the other hand, if $r(S) \geq r^*(S)$, then each term $P(S, T_i) - K_i$ will be nonpositive, and so the option is not exercised and its payoff equals zero. Hence, for all possible values of $r(S)$, the payoff of the option on the coupon bond is given as:

$$\sum_{i=M+1}^{N} CF_i \times Max\left[P(S,\ T_i) - K_i, 0\right] \tag{7.42}$$

In other words, the payoff of the option on the coupon bond equals the payoff on a portfolio of options on zero-coupon bonds comprising the coupon bond. Hence, the time t price of the call option on the coupon bond equals the price of the portfolio of call options on zero-coupon bonds, or

$$c(t) = \sum_{i=M+1}^{N} CF_i \times c_i(t) \tag{7.43}$$

where $c_i(t)$ is the price of the European call option with expiration date S and exercise price K_i, written on a \$1 face-value zero-coupon bond maturing at time T_i. A similar argument can be applied to get the price of a European put option on a coupon bond as follows:

$$p(t) = \sum_{i=M+1}^{N} CF_i \times p_i(t) \tag{7.44}$$

where the put option is based on the same variables as the call option given previously.

Now consider a callable coupon bond with a call date S and a call exercise price K. The callable coupon bond has M cash flows given as CF_i at time $T_i \le S$, for $i = 1, 2, \ldots, M$, maturing before or at the call date S, and $N - M$ cash flows given as CF_i at time $T_i > S$, for $i = M + 1, M + 2, \ldots, N$, maturing *after* the call date S.

The price of a callable coupon bond can be given as:

$$CP^c(t) = CP(t) - c(t) = \sum_{i=1}^{N} CF_i P(t,\ T_i) - \sum_{i=M+1}^{N} CF_i \times c_i(t) \tag{7.45}$$

where, $CP^c(t)$ = price of the callable coupon bond, $CP(t)$ = price of a coupon bond, and all other variables are as defined before.

Equation 7.43 shows that a call option on a coupon bond can be treated as a portfolio of call options on zero-coupon bonds. Similarly, equation 7.44 shows that a put option on a coupon bond can be treated as a portfolio of put options on zero-coupon bonds. Finally, equation 7.45 shows that a callable coupon bond can be treated as a portfolio of long positions in the zero-coupon bonds and another portfolio of short positions in the call options written on zero-coupon bonds.

Hence, equations 7.43, 7.44, and 7.45 can be used to derive the duration vectors of call options on coupon bonds, put options on coupon bonds, and callable coupon bonds, using the duration vectors of the underlying call and put options on zero-coupon bonds given in equations 7.11 and 7.15, respectively. Since the derivation of the coupon bond option formulas in the above equations are based upon the assumption of single-factor affine term structure models, the elements of the duration vector for these securities, measure the sensitivity of these securities to height, slope, curvature shifts in the yield curve, caused by only one factor, and not multiple factors. However, since the first factor is the most important factor in interest rate models, and the shape of the bond volatility function may be nonstationary over time even if driven by only one factor, using two or three elements of the duration vector model may still be useful in designing hedging strategies. The use of a higher number of risk measures to capture risks arising from a smaller number of factors is not that uncommon. For example, Ho (1992) suggests using as many as 11 key rate durations to capture the interest rate risk of fixed-income securities, arising from only three to four factors.

However, the theoretical framework developed in this section is more suitable for the derivation of duration measures corresponding to the single-factor affine term structure models. Though the results of this section can be applied to single-factor affine term structure model (e.g., Cox, Ingersoll, and Ross, 1985; Ho and Lee, 1986; Hull and White, 1993; Vasicek, 1977; and the extensions of the Vasicek and CIR models), we focus our attention on the Vasicek model and the extended Vasicek model given by Hull and White. We do not give a detailed analysis of these models (which are given in the second book of this series), but instead focus on the main results needed to derive the prices and duration risk measures of options on coupon bonds using these models.

Durations of Coupon Bond Options Using Vasicek and Extended Vasicek Models

In order to derive the durations of bond options, we first need the definition of the duration of a zero-coupon bond under both the Vasicek model and the extended Vasicek model.

Duration of a Zero-Coupon Bond Vasicek assumes a mean reverting Ornstein-Uhlenbeck process for the instantaneous short rate of the form:

$$dr(t) = \alpha\big(m - r(t)\big)dt + \sigma dZ(t) \tag{7.46}$$

where $r(t)$ is the instantaneous short rate at time t, m is the long term mean to which r reverts at a speed α, σ is the volatility coefficient and $dZ(t)$ is the standard Wiener process for the short rate. Assuming the price of a default-free zero-coupon bond is a function of the short rate and the bond maturity, applying Ito's lemma, and using absence of arbitrage, Vasicek obtained the following equation for the bond price at time t maturing T periods hence:

$$P(t,\ T) = e^{A(t,T)-B(t,T)r(t)} \tag{7.47}$$

where

$$B(t, T) = \frac{1 - e^{-\alpha(T-t)}}{\alpha}$$

$$A(t, T) = \left(m + \frac{\sigma\gamma}{\alpha} - \frac{\sigma^2}{2\alpha^2}\right)\left[B(t, T) - (T - t)\right] - B(t, T)^2 \frac{\sigma^2}{4\alpha}$$

where γ is the market price of interest rate risk. The affine property of the Vasicek model allows the bond price at any time to be expressed as an exponentially linear function of the short rate at that time in equation 7.47. This property is useful in obtaining the solution of a coupon-bond option as a portfolio of options on zero-coupon bonds as derived by Jamshidian (1989) for all single-factor affine term structure models.

The stochastic bond price process consistent with equation 7.47 is given as follows:

$$\frac{dP(t, T)}{P(t, T)} = \left(r(t) + \gamma\, \sigma B(t, T)\right)dt - \sigma B(t, T)dZ(t) \tag{7.48}$$

The relative basis risk of the default-free zero-coupon bond using equation 7.47 can be given as $-[\partial P(t, T)/\partial r(t)]/P(t, T)$, which defines the duration of the zero-coupon bond under the Vasicek model, given as:

$$D = -\left(\frac{\partial P(t, T)}{\partial r(t)}\right) / P(t, T) = B(t, T) = \frac{1 - e^{-\alpha(T-t)}}{\alpha} \tag{7.49}$$

The asymptotic value of the duration under the Vasicek model as T goes to infinity equals $1/\alpha$. The traditional Macaulay duration can be obtained as a special case of the Vasicek duration by assuming the speed of mean reversion α equals zero. This can be demonstrated by using the L'Hospital's rule to equation 7.49, which gives $D_P(\alpha = 0) = T - t$. Intuitively, this result obtains since a zero mean reversion makes the Vasicek's model consistent with parallel term structure shifts. In general, if the term structure is mean reverting and α is positive, the duration of a zero-coupon bond will be lower than its traditional Macaulay duration.

Duration of a Call Option on a Coupon Bond Since the Vasicek model assumes a Gaussian interest rate process, the general solution of the European call option price given in equation 7.2 holds for this model. By identifying the zero-coupon bond volatility as $\sigma(t, T) = \sigma B(t, T)$, and correlation as $\rho(v, S, T) = 1$ (since the Vasicek model is a one-factor model), from the Vasicek bond price process given in equation 7.48, and substituting it in the expression V in equation 7.2, the time t price of a European call option expiring at time S with an exercise price K_i, written on a \$1 face-value zero-coupon bond with maturity T_i is given as:

$$c_i(t) = N(d_{1i})P(t, T_i) - N(d_{2i})K_i P(t, S) \tag{7.50}$$

where $P(t, T_i)$ is the price at time t of a \$1 face-value zero-coupon bond maturing at time T_i, and $N(x)$ is the cumulative standard normal distribution evaluated at x. The variables d_{1i} and d_{2i} are given as:

$$= \frac{\ln\left[\dfrac{P(t,T_i)}{P(t,S)K_i}\right] + V_i/2}{\sqrt{V_i}}$$

$$d_{2i} = d_{1i} - \sqrt{V_i}$$

$$\begin{aligned} V_i &= \int_t^S \left[\sigma^2(v, T_i) + \sigma^2(v, S) - 2\sigma(v, T_i)\sigma(v, S)\rho(v, S, T_i)\right] dv \\ &= \int_t^S \left[\sigma^2 B(v, T_i)^2 + \sigma^2 B(v, S)^2 - 2\sigma^2 B(v, T_i)B(v, S)\right] dv \\ &= \int_t^S \left(\sigma B(v, T_i) - \sigma B(v, S)\right)^2 dv \end{aligned}$$

By substituting the value of $B(t, T_i)$ from equation 7.49 into expression V_i given previously, we get:

$$V_i = \left(\frac{\sigma}{\alpha}\left(1 - e^{-\alpha(T_i - S)}\right)\right)^2 \left(\frac{1 - e^{-2\alpha(S-t)}}{2\alpha}\right) \tag{7.51}$$

Now reconsider the European call option on a coupon bond with the expiration date S and exercise price K. The coupon bond pays M cash flows given as CF_i at time $T_i \leq S$, for $i = 1, 2, \ldots, M$, maturing before or at the option expiration date S, and $N - M$ cash flows given as CF_i at time $T_i > S$, for $i = M + 1, M + 2, \ldots, N$, maturing *after* the option expiration date S.

Obviously, the M cash flows maturing before the option expiration date S, can be ignored for pricing the coupon bond option.

As shown in the previous section, the price of the call option on the coupon bond can be given as a portfolio of call options on zero-coupon bonds. By substituting the prices of call options written on \$1 face-value zero-coupon bonds from equation 7.50 into equation 7.43, the price of the call option on the coupon bond can be given as follows:

$$c(t) = \sum_{i=M+1}^{N} CF_i \times c_i(t) \tag{7.52}$$

where $c_i(t)$ is defined in equation 7.50, and K_i can be obtained using equations 7.38 and 7.39, for $i = M + 1, M + 2, \ldots, N$ as follows. Guess a value for the short rate $r^*(S)$ at time S, for which:

$$\sum_{i=M+1}^{N} CF_i \ K_i = K \tag{7.53}$$

such that K_i is given as:

$$K_i = P(r^*(S), S, T_i), \text{ for } i = M+1, M+2, \ldots, N \tag{7.54}$$

where using the affine single-factor assumption, the Vasicek's bond price $P(r^*(S), S, T_i) = \exp[A(S, T_i) - B(S, T_i)\ r^*(S)]$ is a decreasing function of $r^*(S)$ as shown in equation 7.47.

Substituting equation 7.50 into equation 7.52, the price of the European call option on the coupon bond can be given as:

$$c(t) = \sum_{i=M+1}^{N} N(d_{1i}) CF_i \ P(t, T_i) - \left(\sum_{i=M+1}^{N} N(d_{2i}) CF_i \ K_i \right) P(t, S) \tag{7.55}$$

The call option on the coupon bond in equation 7.55 is given as a replicating portfolio of long positions in $N - M$ different zero-coupon bonds maturing at dates T_i, for $i = M + 1, M + 2, \ldots, N$, and a short position in the zero-coupon bond maturing at date S. The portfolio weights in the long positions in the $N - M$ different zero-coupon bonds are given as follows:

$$w_{c1i} = \frac{N(d_{1i})CF_i\ P(t,\ T_i)}{c(t)},\ \text{for } i = M+1,\ M+2,\ \ldots,\ N \tag{7.56}$$

The portfolio weight in the short position in the zero-coupon bond maturing at date S is given as follows:

$$w_{c2} = -\frac{\left(\sum_{i=M+1}^{N} N(d_{2i})CF_i\ K_i\right)P(t,\ S)}{c(t)} \tag{7.57}$$

The duration of the call option on the coupon bond is given as the weighted average of the durations of the $N - M + 1$ ($N - M$ long positions and 1 short position) zero-coupon bonds that replicate the option. Using the definition of the duration of a zero-coupon bond from equation 7.49, the duration of the call option on the coupon bond is given as follows:

$$D^c = \sum_{i=M+1}^{N} w_{c1i}\left(\frac{1-e^{-\alpha(T_i-t)}}{\alpha}\right) + w_{c2}\left(\frac{1-e^{-\alpha(S-t)}}{\alpha}\right) \tag{7.58}$$

Example 7.3 Consider a one-year European call option with a strike price of \$96, written on a three-year 4 percent annual coupon bond with a \$100 face value. Assume the following parameters for the Vasicek model:

$$\alpha = 0.3$$
$$m = 7\%$$
$$\sigma = 0.5\%$$

Assume that the market price of risk $\lambda = 0$, and the current value of the short rate equals 5 percent.

At the option expiration date of one year, the bond makes it first coupon payment of \$4, and the bond has two cash flows remaining. Hence, at the end of one year, the bond can be regarded as a portfolio consisting of four \$1 face-value zero-coupon bonds maturing at the end of two years, and 104 \$1 face-value zero-coupon bonds maturing at the end of three years. The coupon bond can be valued as follows:

$$4 \times P(1,\ 2) + 104 \times P(1,\ 3)$$

To determine the strike prices of the options on the zero-coupon bonds, we need to find $r^*(1)$, which is that value of $r(1)$ that makes the coupon bond price at the end of one year, equal to the strike price of $96 (see equation 7.37). Substituting the Vasicek bond price formulas, we estimate $r^*(1)$ from the following equation:

$$4e^{A(1,2)-B(1,2)r^*(1)} + 104e^{A(1,3)-B(1,3)r^*(1)} = \$96$$

or

$$4e^{-r^*\times 0.863939-0.009521} + 104e^{-r^*\times 1.50396-0.034701} = \$96$$

Using the Solver function in excel, we find $r^*(1) = 5.680\%$. Substituting $r^*(1) = 5.680\%$ for the short rate, the zero-coupon bond prices $P(1, 2)$ and $P(1, 3)$ are given as:

$$P(1,\ 2) = e^{-0.0568\times 0.864-0.010} = \$0.9431$$
$$P(1,\ 3) = e^{-0.0568\times 1.504-0.035} = \$0.8868$$

The value of the option on the coupon bond equals the value of the portfolio consisting of four one-year European options with strike price $0.9431 on a zero-coupon that pays $1 at year 2, and 104 one-year European options with strike price $0.8868 on a zero-coupon that pays $1 at year 3. The calculations needed for valuing each of the two European options are shown in Table 7.7.

TABLE 7.7 Calculations for Separate Zero-Coupon European Calls

	Option 1 $i = 2$	Option 2 $i = 3$
Bond face value	$1	$1
Bond maturity, T_i	2 years	3 years
Option strike price, K_i	$0.9431	$0.8868
Option maturity, S	1 year	1 year
$(V_i)^{0.5}$	0.37459%	0.65209%
d_{1i}	0.3795	0.3822
d_{2i}	0.3757	0.3757
$N(d_{1i})$	0.6478	0.6489
$N(d_{2i})$	0.6464	0.6464
Option price, $c_i(0)$	$0.002065	$0.003388

The value of the option on the coupon bond is given as:

$$\begin{aligned} c(0) &= 4\times c_2(0)+104\times c_3(0)=\$0.3606 \\ &= 4\times 0.002065+104\times 0.003388=\$0.3606 \end{aligned}$$

The duration of the European call option on the coupon bond can be computed by using the weights defined in equations 7.56 and 7.57, and the duration formula given in equation 7.58, as follows:

$$\begin{aligned} w_{c1i} &= \frac{N(d_{1i})CF_i\ P(0,T_i)}{c(0)} \\ &= \frac{0.6478\times 4\times 0.8959}{0.3606} = 6.4389, \text{ for } i=2 \\ &= \frac{0.6489\times 104\times 0.8433}{0.3606} = 157.8365, \text{ for } i=3 \\ w_{c2} &= -\frac{\left(\sum_{i=2}^{3} N(d_{2i})CF_i\ K_i\right)P(0,\ 1)}{c(0)} \\ &= -\frac{\left(0.6464\times 4\times 0.9431+0.6464\times 104\times 0.8868\right)\times 0.9486}{0.3606} \\ &= -163.2754 \end{aligned}$$

where $P(0, T_1) = P(0, 1) = 0.9486$, $P(0, T_2) = P(0, 2) = 0.8959$, and $P(0, T_3) = P(0, 3) = 0.8433$, using the Vasicek bond price formula given in equation 7.47 with $r(0) = 5\%$.

Hence, the call option on the coupon bond is equivalent to −163.2754 weight in the zero-coupon bond maturing at time $t = 1$, 6.4389 weight in the zero-coupon bond maturing at time $t = 2$, and 157.8365 weight in the zero-coupon bond maturing at time $t = 3$. The three weights add up to 1, but their huge magnitudes indicate that this option is a highly leveraged security (since it is a deeply out-of-the-money option).

Using equation 7.58 the duration of the call option on the coupon bond is given as:

$$\begin{aligned} D^c &= -163.2754\times\left(\frac{1-e^{-0.3(1-0)}}{0.3}\right)+6.4389\times\left(\frac{1-e^{-0.3(2-0)}}{0.3}\right) \\ &\quad + 157.8365\times\left(\frac{1-e^{-0.3(3-0)}}{0.3}\right) \\ &= -163.2754\times 0.8639+6.4389\times 1.5040+157.8365\times 1.9781 \\ &= 180.84 \text{ years} \end{aligned}$$

Hence, the duration of the call option equals 180.84 years.

Duration of a Put Option on a Coupon Bond Using a similar methodology for the call option, the price of the put option on the coupon bond based on the same underlying variables is given as follows:

$$p(t)=\left(\sum_{i=M+1}^{N}\left[1-N(d_{2i})\right]CF_i\ K_i\right)P(t,\ S)-\sum_{i=M+1}^{N}\left[1-N(d_{1i})\right]CF_i\ P(t,\ T_i) \tag{7.59}$$

The put option on the coupon bond in equation 7.59 is given as a replicating portfolio of short positions in $N-M$ different zero-coupon bonds maturing at dates T_i, for $i=M+1, M+2, \ldots, N$, and a long position in the zero-coupon bond maturing at date S. The portfolio weights in the short positions in the $N-M$ different zero-coupon bonds are given as follows:

$$w_{p1i}=-\frac{\left[1-N(d_{1i})\right]CF_i\ P(t,\ T_i)}{p(t)},\ \text{for } i=M+1,\ M+2,\ \ldots,\ N \tag{7.60}$$

The portfolio weight in the long position in the zero-coupon bond maturing at date S is given as follows:

$$w_{p2}=\frac{\left(\sum_{i=M+1}^{N}\left[1-N(d_{2i})\right]CF_i\ K_i\right)P(t,\ S)}{p(t)} \tag{7.61}$$

The duration of the put option on the coupon bond is given as the weighted average of the durations of the $N-M+1$ ($N-M$ short positions and 1 long position) zero-coupon bonds that replicate the option. Using the definition of the duration of a zero-coupon bond from equation 7.49, the duration of the put option on the coupon bond is given as follows:

$$D^p=\sum_{i=M+1}^{N}w_{p1i}\left(\frac{1-e^{-\alpha(T_i-t)}}{\alpha}\right)+w_{p2}\left(\frac{1-e^{-\alpha(S-t)}}{\alpha}\right) \tag{7.62}$$

Duration of a Callable Coupon Bond Reconsider the callable coupon bond with a call date S and a call exercise price K given earlier. The callable coupon bond has M cash flows given as CF_i at time $T_i \leq S$, for $i=1, 2, \ldots, M$, maturing before or at the call date S, and $N - M$ cash flows given as CF_i at time $T_i > S$, for $i = M + 1, M + 2, \ldots, N$, maturing *after* the call date S.

The price of a callable coupon bond can be given as follows:

$$CP^c(t) = CP(t) - c(t) \tag{7.63}$$

where, $CP^c(t)$ = price of the callable coupon bond, $CP(t)$ = price of a coupon bond, and $c(t)$ = price of the call option on the coupon bond.

Substituting the price formula for the regular coupon bond, and the price of the call option on coupon bond from equation 7.55 in equation 7.63, we get,

$$\begin{aligned} CP^c(t) = & \sum_{i=1}^{M} CF_i \, P(t, T_i) \\ & + \sum_{i=M+1}^{N} [[1 - N(d_{1i})] CF_i \, P(t, T_i) + \left(\sum_{i=M+1}^{N} N(d_{2i}) CF_i \, K_i \right) P(t, S) \end{aligned} \tag{7.64}$$

The callable coupon bond in equation 7.64 is given as a replicating portfolio of long positions in N different zero-coupon bonds maturing at dates T_i, for $i = 1, 2, \ldots, N$, and a long position in the zero-coupon bond maturing at date S. The portfolio weights are given as:

$$w_{cB1i} = \frac{CF_i \, P(t, T_i)}{CP^c(t)}, \text{ for } i = 1, 2, \ldots, M \tag{7.65}$$

$$w_{cB1i} = \frac{[1 - N(d_{1i})] CF_i \, P(t, T_i)}{CP^c(t)}, \text{ for } i = M+1, M+2, \ldots N \tag{7.66}$$

and

$$w_{cB2} = \frac{\left(\sum_{i=M+1}^{N} N(d_{2i}) CF_i \, K_i \right) P(t, S)}{CP^c(t)} \tag{7.67}$$

The duration of the callable coupon bond is given as the weighted average of the durations of the $N + 1$ zero-coupon bonds that replicate this bond.

Using the definition of the duration of a zero-coupon bond from equation 7.49, the duration of the callable coupon bond is given as:

$$D^{cB} = \sum_{i=1}^{N} w_{cB1i}\left(\frac{1-e^{-\alpha(T_i-t)}}{\alpha}\right) + w_{cB2}\left(\frac{1-e^{-\alpha(S-t)}}{\alpha}\right) \tag{7.68}$$

Generalization to the Extended Vasicek Model The Vasicek model assumes that time t prices of a zero-coupon bond is given by equation 7.47. However, these prices may or may not fit the existing set of observable zero-coupon bond prices at time t. If the model prices and market observed prices are different, then option prices and duration measures will be incorrect. To avoid this problem, practitioners often *calibrate* the term structure model to observable prices at some initial date. Typically, calibration is done on a daily basis, assuming the initial date is the current date $t = 0$. Calibrating the model requires using an observable set of zero-coupon bond prices $P(0, T)$, as an input to the model. Since in general the Vasicek model will not fit these observable prices, the short rate process given in equation 7.46 must be modified, so that the model fits the observable prices. The modified short rate process, called the extended Vasicek model, is derived by Hull and White (1993) and is given as:

$$dr(t) = \alpha\big(m(t) - r(t)\big)dt + \sigma dZ(t) \tag{7.69}$$

The only difference between equation 7.46 and equation 7.69 is that the long-term mean in equation 7.69 is a deterministic function of time. The deterministically changing long-term mean is given as follows:

$$m(t) = \frac{1}{\alpha}\left(\frac{\partial f(0,\, t)}{\partial t} + \alpha f(0,\, t) + \frac{\sigma^2}{2\alpha}\left[1 - e^{-2\alpha t}\right] - \gamma\, \sigma\right) \tag{7.70}$$

where, $f(0, t) = -\partial \ln P(0, t)/\partial t$ = initially observed instantaneous forward rate at time 0 for term t. Equation 7.70 requires that the zero-coupon bond prices observed at the initial date $t = 0$, must be twice differentiable with respect to bond maturity. This condition is satisfied by the commonly used models for the estimation of the $P(0, T)$ function (e.g., the cubic-spline model of McCulloch and Kwon, 1993, and the exponential model of Nelson and Siegel, 1987, in Chapter 3).

Since the long-term mean $m(t)$ does not appear in any option pricing formulas or duration formulas, all equations from 7.50 to 7.68, except equations 7.53 and 7.54, continue to hold for calibrated model by simply assuming current time $t = 0$ and using the twice-differentiable observable zero-coupon bond price function $P(0, T)$ instead of the Vasicek model prices given by equation 7.47. Equations 7.53 and 7.54 are used to obtain the exercise prices K_i such that an option on a coupon bond can be treated as a portfolio of options on zero-coupon bonds. Estimation of K_i requires that the zero-coupon bond price $P(r(S), S, T)$ at the future time S, be a function of the future short rate $r(S)$. This relationship between the short rate and zero-coupon bond price is obviously not given by equation 7.47 under the calibrated model, since the long-term mean $m(t)$ is deterministically changing, and equation 7.47 is valid only when the long-term mean is a constant. Hence, one requires the functional relationship between $P(r(S), S, T)$ and $r(S)$ at the future time S under the calibrated model with changing long-term mean $m(t)$, in order to apply equations 7.53 and 7.54 to estimate K_i. This relationship is given as follows under the calibrated model:

$$P(S,\ T) = e^{A(S,T) - B(S,T)r(S)} \tag{7.71}$$

where

$$B(S,\ T) = \frac{1 - e^{-\alpha(T-S)}}{\alpha}$$

$$A(S,\ T) = -\int_S^T \left[\left(\alpha m(t) + \gamma\sigma \right) B(t,\ T) \right] dt + \frac{\sigma^2}{2\alpha^2} \left(T - S - B(S,\ T) - \frac{\alpha B(S,T)^2}{2} \right)$$

Using this relationship to find K_i in equations 7.53 and 7.54, all equations from (7.50) to (7.68), continue to hold for the calibrated model by simply assuming current time $t = 0$ and using the twice-differentiable observable zero-coupon bond price function $P(0, T)$, instead of the Vasicek model prices given by equation 7.47. It can be confirmed that the bond price formula in equation 7.71 reduces to the bond price formula in equation 7.47, for the special case when $m(t) = m$, a constant.

The calibration of the Vasicek model using the above framework allows the model to become consistent with the initially observable prices $P(0, T)$. However, the model is not calibrated to the historical term structure of zero-coupon bond return volatility at time $t = 0$. In fact, bond volatility function equals $\sigma B(t, T)$, which can take only a limited number of shapes. As shown by Hull and White (1993), calibration to the historical term structure of zero-coupon bond return volatility would require that the speed of mean reversion parameter α is also time dependent. Such calibration is covered in the second book of this series.

CHAPTER 8

Hedging with Swaps and Interest Rate Options Using the LIBOR Market Model

An interest rate swap is a contractual agreement between two counterparties under which each agrees to make periodic payment to the other for a prespecified time period based on a notional amount of principal. The principal amount is called *notional* because this amount is not exchanged, but is used as a notional figure to determine the cash flows that are exchanged periodically. In a plain-vanilla interest rate swap, fixed cash flows computed using a fixed interest rate on the notional amount are exchanged for floating cash flows computed using a floating interest rate on the notional amount. The most common floating interest rate used for computing the floating leg of the cash flows is the three-month London Interbank Offer Rate (LIBOR). Most interest rate swaps exchange the floating cash flows every quarter, and the fixed cash flows every six-months. The stream of floating cash flows in a swap agreement is called the *floating leg,* whereas the stream of fixed cash flows constitute the *fixed leg*. The fixed rate in an interest rate swap agreement is known as the *swap rate*. The dates at which the floating rates are observed are called *resets*.

The total notional amount of interest rate swaps was about $111 trillion on December 31, 2003, which was approximately 56 percent of the notional amount of the entire over-the-counter global derivative market, which includes options, forward rate agreements, and other popular swaps such as currency swaps, equity swaps, and so on.[1] The explosive growth of interest rate swaps over the past quarter century suggests that managing interest rate risk remains a chief concern for many financial institutions and other market participants, even as U.S. interest rates have gone down steadily since reaching their peak in 1980 to 1981. With virtually record low interest rates prevailing in November 2004, a change in interest rate regime could lead to a huge exchange of wealth among swap participants, though not necessarily

This chapter coauthored with Iuliana Ismailescu.

creating a panic if the majority of the participants have used interest rate swaps wisely to hedge against the negative effects of interest rate risk.

Interest rate swaps are used by financial institutions and other market participants including corporations with interest rate sensitive assets or liabilities for hedging interest rate risk arising from the maturity mismatches between the assets and the liabilities. For example, a mortgage bank with a high asset duration resulting from holding longer maturity fixed-rate loans, and a low liability duration resulting from short maturity deposits, may initiate an interest rate swap in which it pays the fixed leg of the cash flows and receives the floating leg of the cash flows. The swap-adjusted duration gap of the mortgage bank would be reduced considerably, though this would also mean lower return on its net worth. However, since the mortgage bank specializes in the business of profiting from the services provided in the home-loan business market, and not predicting the future direction of interest rates, initiating such a swap may be consistent with its business model. Similarly, very highly leveraged institutions such as Fannie Mae and Freddie Mac often use interest rate swaps to fine-tune their duration gaps. Virtually, all financial institutions and many corporations with nonfinancial businesses use interest rate swaps to manage the effects of unwanted interest rate risk on their net worth.

In this chapter, we analyze the pricing and duration measures of interest rate swaps by applying the duration vector model to swaps. Since interest rate swaps can often include embedded options such as caps, floors, and collars, we also derive the duration vectors of these interest rate options. To price the interest rate options, we use the LIBOR market model, which has become the industry standard for pricing these options in the swap market. Finally, we derive the duration vectors of interest rate swaps with embedded interest rate options.

The use of the duration vector model allows us to hedge the risks of nonparallel interest rate shifts on the portfolio of assets and liabilities using interest rate swaps, without making restrictive assumptions about the correlation structure of interest rates. This is important because recent research shows the importance of allowing maximum flexibility in the correlation structure of interest rates to consistently price both the interest rate options, such as caps and floors, and *swaptions,* which are options on the underlying swap rate.

A SIMPLE INTRODUCTION TO INTEREST RATE SWAPS

We begin this chapter with an introduction to an example of a plain-vanilla interest rate swap. For expositional simplicity, we assume that the counterparties exchange fixed and floating cash flows every six months.[2]

TABLE 8.1 Cash Flows Exchanged by Firm A

Date	LIBOR Rate (%)	Floating Cash Flow Received ($)	Fixed Cash Flow Paid ($)	Net Cash Flow ($)
September 1, 2003	3.50			
March 1, 2004	3.75	175,000	200,000	–25,000
September 1, 2004	4.00	187,500	200,000	–12,500
March 1, 2005	4.20	200,000	200,000	0
September 1, 2005	4.50	210,000	200,000	+10,000

Example 8.1 Consider a two-year interest rate swap between firms A and B, initiated on September 1, 2003, with an annualized swap rate of 4 percent compounded semiannually, and the floating rate given as the six-month LIBOR. The notional principal of the swap equals $10 million. The LIBOR rates and the exchange of cash flows are displayed in Table 8.1.

Every six months firm A pays 0.02 × $10 million = $200,000 to firm B and receives the six-month LIBOR × $10 million from firm B, observed at the *beginning* of each six-month period. The first exchange occurs on March 1, 2004, six months after the agreement is initiated. Since the annualized six-month LIBOR rate observed six months earlier on September 1, 2003, is 3.5 percent, firm A receives from firm B a floating cash flow equal to:

$$\left(\frac{1}{2}\right) \times 3.5\% \times 10{,}000{,}000 = \$175{,}000$$

and pays to firm B, a fixed cash flow equal to:

$$\left(\frac{1}{2}\right) \times 4\% \times 10{,}000{,}000 = \$200{,}000$$

Since the net difference between these two cash flows is –$25,000, firm A sends $25,000 to firm B on March 1, 2004. The second exchange of cash flows takes place on September 1, 2004. Since the six-month LIBOR rate observed six months earlier on March 1, 2004, is 3.75 percent, firm A receives from firm B a floating cash flow equal to:

$$3.75\% \times \left(\frac{1}{2}\right) \times 10{,}000{,}000 = \$187{,}500$$

on September 1, 2004, and in return pays the fixed cash flow of $200,000, resulting in a net cash flow payment from firm A to firm B of $12,500. The cash flow exchanges on other dates are shown in Table 8.1.

Another way to look at the previous swap transaction is to assume that firm A gives to firm B a fixed-coupon bond in exchange for receiving a floating-coupon bond, where both bonds have a redemption face value equal to the notional principal of $10 million. Hence, a plain-vanilla swap can be considered equivalent to a long position in the floating rate bond together with a short position in the fixed-coupon bond (or vice versa). If one or both counterparties involved in the swap transaction decide to terminate the contract, they must negotiate the cancellation of the contract, called the *unwind,* which involves one of the counterparties to make a payment based upon the mark-to-market value of the swap contract. Another way to terminate the original contract is to enter into a new swap contract by taking exactly opposite positions in the fixed and floating legs, in order to neutralize the interest rate risk of the original swap contract.

For the purpose of expositional simplicity, Example 8.1 abstracted from the many real-world features of interest rate swap contracts. For example, you must consider day-count conventions used for computing the cash flows corresponding to the floating rates and fixed rates. Also, often the number of payments on the floating leg is not necessarily equal to the number of payments on the fixed leg, and cash flows are not exchanged on the same dates. We address all of these issues in this chapter.

Day-Count Conventions

In Example 8.1, we assumed that the floating rate for a six-month period is half as much as the annual rate. In doing this, we disregarded that, as a money market instrument, LIBOR is quoted on an actual/360 basis. However, between March 1 and September 1 there are 184 days, thus, the second cash flow received by firm A should be:

$$3.75\% \times \frac{184}{360} \times \$1{,}000{,}000 = \$191{,}667$$

and firm A's net cash outflow should be $8,334.

The fixed rate and the floating rate may come with different day-count conventions. If the fixed rate comes from a Treasury note or Treasury bond, it is quoted on an actual/365 basis and it cannot be directly compared with LIBOR, which is quoted on an actual/360 basis. To make the two rates comparable, we multiply the fixed rate by 360/365. The fixed rate quote

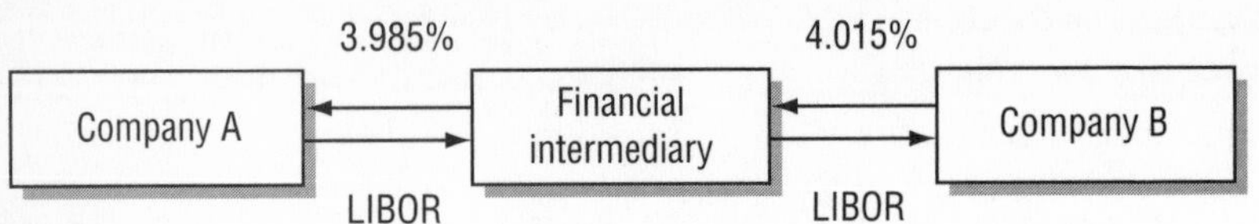

FIGURE 8.1 Interest Rate Swap with a Financial Intermediary

may also be given using a 30/360 day-count basis. A similar adjustment from 30/360 basis to actual/360 basis is needed if the fixed rate is quoted on a 30/360 basis.

The Financial Intermediary

Originally, interest rate swaps were brokered transactions in which the financial intermediary would match customers interested in a swap transaction. Once the transaction was completed, the role of the intermediary ceased as the swap counterparties exchanged payments directly. Today, the swap market is more or less a dealer market dominated by large international banks and financial institutions that act as market makers—they become a counterparty to a swap transaction before a swap player for the other side of the transaction is found.

The plain-vanilla swaps on U.S. interest rates usually yield 2 to 4 basis points to the financial intermediary on a pair of offsetting transactions. Figure 8.1 illustrates the role of the financial intermediary in a transaction similar to that described in Example 8.1.

Note that the simple plain-vanilla swap transaction in Example 8.1 is structured as a pair of offsetting transactions: one between the dealer and firm A and the other between the dealer and firm B. In most instances, firms A and B will never know that the financial institution has engaged in a swap transaction with the other firm. If either of the two firms defaults, it is the financial intermediary that assumes the loss, as it still must honor its agreement with the other firm. The 2- to 4-basis-points fee partly compensates the intermediary against the risk of default. To further control this risk, some swap dealers require counterparties to post collateral, usually high grade securities, that can be used in the case of default.

Significant efforts to ensure smooth trading of swaps have been made by the International Swaps and Derivatives Association (ISDA), a global organization representing leading participants in the swaps and derivatives markets. The ISDA recommends a standardized master agreement to counterparties interested in conducting derivatives business. The master agreement specifies many details including how the mark-to-market of transactions are calculated, what mutual collateral thresholds apply, the types of derivatives that are netted out for margins, and so on.

MOTIVATIONS FOR INTEREST RATE SWAPS

Interest swaps are motivated by either the existence of what is known as *comparative cost advantage* or by the need to hedge interest rate risk. The concept of comparative cost advantage can be understood using Example 8.2.

Example 8.2 Consider issuance of debt by two firms. Firm A needs to issue fixed-coupon debt maturing in T years, while firm B needs to issue floating-coupon debt maturing in T years. The yield or the cost of debt for both these firms in the fixed-coupon debt market and the floating-coupon debt market are given in Table 8.2.

Due to its better credit rating, firm B gets cheaper financing in both the fixed rate market and the floating rate market. However, its advantage in the fixed rate market is 1 percent, which is higher than its advantage in the floating rate market of 0.25 percent. The difference between the cost advantages in the two markets is called the *comparative cost advantage* of firm B over firm A in the fixed rate market compared to the floating rate market and is given as:

$$\text{Comparative cost advantage} = 1\% - 0.25\% = 0.75\% \qquad (8.1)$$

If the comparative cost advantage is not zero, then both firms could benefit by issuing debt securities in the market in which they are relatively better off, and still obtaining their choice of financing by doing an interest rate swap. Specifically, firm A needs to issue fixed-coupon debt, but could issue floating-coupon debt instead, since in the floating rate market its disadvantage is only 0.25 percent. Similarly, firm B needs to issue floating-coupon debt, but could issue fixed-coupon debt instead, since in the fixed

TABLE 8.2 Cost of Debt in Fixed and Floating Debt Markets

Firm	Fixed-Coupon Debt (%)	Floating-Coupon Debt (%)
A	5	LIBOR + 0.50
B	4	LIBOR + 0.25
Cost advantage for B	1	0.25

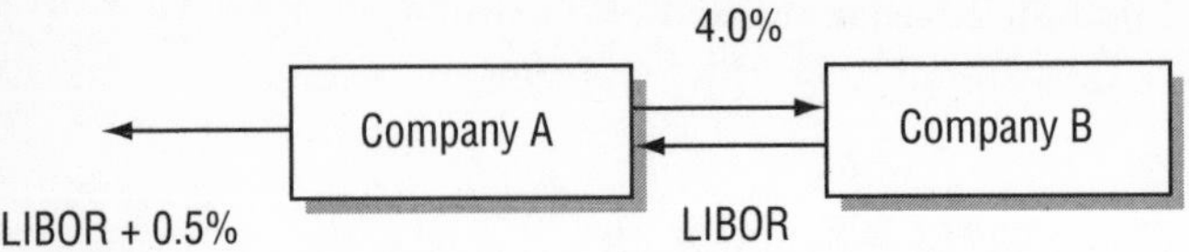

FIGURE 8.2 Cash Payments of Company A

rate market its advantage is 1 percent. Simultaneously, the two firms execute an interest rate swap, which converts firm A's financing from floating rate to fixed rate, and firm B's financing from fixed rate to floating rate.

The issuance of securities by the two firms and the simultaneous execution of the interest rate swap through an intermediary are shown in Figure 8.2. Based on the information in Figure 8.2, we can compute the cost of financing to each firm if they simply obtained the type of financing they needed without doing the swap, and then compare it to the cost of financing to each firm if they obtained financing from the markets in which they are relatively better off with a simultaneous execution of an interest rate swap. We assume that the intermediary charges an annual fee of 4 basis points (or 0.04% = 0.0004), which is divided and paid equally by firms A and B.

The cost of financing to the two firms, using the type of financing they need without using a swap, is given as follows:

Firm A's cost of financing without the swap = 5%
Firm B's cost of financing without the swap = LIBOR + 0.25%

The cost of financing to the two firms, using the financing from the markets in which they are relatively better off with a simultaneous execution of an interest rate swap, is given as follows:

Firm A's cost of financing with the swap (see Figure 8.2):

Payments to financial intermediary = Swap rate + Fee =	4% + 0.02%
+ Payments to the investors in the floating rate debt =	LIBOR + 0.5%
– Payments received from the financial intermediary =	–LIBOR
	4.52%

Firm B's cost of financing with the swap (see Figure 8.2):

Payments to financial intermediary	= LIBOR
+Payments to the investors in the fixed rate debt	= 4%
–Payments received from the financial intermediary	= –(Swap rate – Fee)
	= –(4% – 0.02%)
	LIBOR + 0.02%

TABLE 8.3 Cost of Financing and Savings for Firm A and Firm B

Cost of Financing	A (%)	B (%)
Without the swap	5	LIBOR + 0.25
With the swap	4.52	LIBOR + 0.02
Savings	0.48	0.23

The savings from using the swap are given as the firms' cost of financing without the swap minus the firms' cost of financing with the swap, as shown in Table 8.3.

The savings of firms A and B, and the 4 basis points given to the intermediary add up to the comparative cost advantage of 0.75 percent as shown:

$$\begin{aligned} \text{Savings for firm A} &= 0.48\% \\ \text{Savings for firm B} &= 0.23\% \\ \text{Fee to the intermediary} &= \underline{0.04\%} \\ \text{Total} &= 0.75\% \end{aligned}$$

The fact that the annual savings to the two firms and the fee to the intermediary add up to 0.75 percent is not a coincidence. This was the annual comparative cost advantage computed earlier in equation 8.1. As a general principal the comparative cost advantage represents the pie that can be shared among all swap participants including the fee paid to the intermediary. Of course, the existence of comparative cost advantage should not be necessarily viewed as arbitrage opportunities in the market. The intermediary will require collateral, and so forth, or may engage in better monitoring, some of which can explain a reduction in cost of financing to the swap participants. Occasionally, discrepancies in the relative pricing in different markets may exist temporarily, such that all swap participants can benefit as shown in Example 8.2.

Example 8.2 demonstrated how comparative cost advantage can be exploited by the execution of an interest rate swap. In Example 8.3, we show that hedging interest rate risk is another motivation for engaging in an interest rate swap.

Example 8.3 Consider two firms A and B with the cash flow maturity structure of assets and liabilities as shown in Table 8.4. Firm A's assets are financed with $100 million of floating rate bonds that give an annual interest of LIBOR plus 0.5 percent. Firm B's assets are financed with $100

TABLE 8.4 Cash Flow Structure of Assets and Liabilities of Firm A and Firm B

Firm	Assets	Liabilities
A	Fixed cash inflows	Floating rate bond financed at LIBOR plus 0.5%
B	Floating cash inflows	Fixed rate bond financed at 4%

million of fixed rate bonds that give an annual interest of 4 percent. Firm A's assets are mostly in businesses that provide fixed earnings, which do not fluctuate with interest rates (these could also be long-term *fixed*-coupon bonds held by a financial institution). In contrast, firm B's assets are in businesses that provide floating earnings that fluctuate with the inflation rate and, hence, with the level of the interest rates (e.g., producer of oil or other raw materials tied with inflation).

Obviously, both firms have a mismatched maturity structure of the asset/liability cash flows. Firm A's fixed cash flow earnings are financed by the issuance of floating rate debt, which implies a higher duration for its assets than for its liabilities. In contrast, firm B's floating cash flow earnings are financed by the issuance of fixed rate debt, which implies a higher duration for its liabilities than for its assets.[3] The duration mismatch implies high exposure to interest rate risk for both firms. Firm A gains and firm B loses when interest rates fall, while firm A loses and firm B gains when interest rates rise.

To hedge the duration mismatch caused by the mismatch in cash flow maturity structure, both these firms can pay off their debts and obtain new financing to match their liability cash flow structure with the asset cash flow structure. We assume that if firm A were to pay off its floating rate bond and issue a fixed rate bond, it would have to pay an interest of 5 percent per year on the new bond. Similarly, we assume that if firm B were to pay off its fixed rate bond and issue a floating rate bond, it would have to pay an interest of LIBOR + 0.25 percent per year on the new bond. However, early redemption of bonds is not easy unless the bonds are callable, and issuing new bonds implies the occurrence of issuance costs. So, to save on transactions costs, these two firms do a plain-vanilla interest rate swap based on a $100 million notional principal. Since all numbers assumed in this example are consistent with the numbers used in Example 8.2, the swap details are consistent with those in Example 8.2, and both Figure 8.2 and Table 8.3 apply to this example also.

The swap-transformed balance sheet is given in Table 8.5, and is based on the information given in Table 8.3. Not only does the swap transaction

TABLE 8.5 Swap-Transformed Market Value Balance Sheets of Firm A and Firm B

Firm	Assets	Liabilities
A	Fixed cash inflows	Effective fixed rate financing at 4.52%
B	Floating cash inflows	Effective floating rate financing at LIBOR + 0.02%

allow these two firms to hedge against interest rate risk by matching the asset cash flows to liability cash flows (fixed to fixed, and floating to floating), it also allows them additional savings arising from the comparative cost advantage, as shown in Example 8.2. Firm A saves 0.48 percent in interest cost per year (5% – 4.52% = 0.48%), while firm B saves 0.23 percent in interest cost per year (LIBOR + 0.25% – LIBOR + 0.02% = 0.23%). In general, savings due to comparative cost advantage, and hedging interest rate risk are the two main motivations for the use of interest rate swaps.

PRICING AND HEDGING WITH INTEREST RATE SWAPS

This section shows how to price and hedge using interest rate swaps. A swap can be considered an exchange of a fixed-coupon bond and a floating rate bond with face values of both bonds equal to the notional principal of the swap. The coupon rate on the floating rate bond can be considered as the floating rate that is used for obtaining the floating leg of the swap, while coupon rate on the fixed-coupon bond can be considered as the fixed *swap rate* that is used for obtaining the fixed cash flows of the swap. The payment frequency of the fixed and floating coupons may or may not be the same. In the Eurodollar swap market, the floating rate is generally given as the three-month LIBOR, and the fixed rate is quoted as the swap rate. The fixed payments based on the swap rate are made semiannually and floating payments based upon the three-month LIBOR are made quarterly.

Since pricing and duration vector formulas exist for fixed- and floating-coupon bonds, these formulas can be used to obtain the price and duration vector formulas for swaps. The price of a pay fixed/receive floating swap before its maturity can be given as follows:

$$SWAP(t) = P_{floating}(t) - P_{fixed}(t) \tag{8.2}$$

where $P_{fixed}(t)$ = Price of a fixed-coupon bond with coupon rate equal to the swap rate that is used for obtaining the fixed leg of the swap

$P_{floating}(t)$ = Price of a floating rate bond with coupon rate equal to the floating rate that is used for obtaining the floating leg of the swap

F = Face value of the fixed-coupon bond and the floating rate bond, set equal to the notional principal of the swap

At the time of initiating a swap contract, the price of the swap, $SWAP(t)$, is set to zero, by choosing an appropriate swap rate for obtaining the fixed cash flows corresponding to the fixed leg of the swap. As interest rates change, the swap dealer will change the swap rate in order to initiate new swap transactions at a zero swap price. However, from the perspective of the swap holder, the swap rate remains fixed over the life of the swap contract, and so can be assumed to be a constant equal to R. Given the constant R, the price $SWAP(t)$ in equation 8.2 will change and become nonzero as soon as interest rates change after entering into the swap transaction. The price $SWAP(t)$ determines the present value of the gain or loss to the holder of pay fixed/receive floating side of the swap, if the swapholder decides to unwind the original swap by taking a new and opposite swap position in the pay floating/receive fixed side of the swap.

Now, consider the floating leg of a swap which gives the floating rate payments at dates T_i, $i = 1, 2, \ldots, n$, where the length of the tenor is given as $\tau = T_i - T_{i-1}$. Given the notional principal of F, and the default-free money market rate $L(T_{i-1}, T_i)$ observed at time T_{i-1}, the payment from the floating leg of the swap at time T_i is given as $F \times \tau \times L(T_{i-1}, T_i)$. The payments from the floating leg are identical to the coupons paid by a default-free floating rate bond which pays $F \times \tau \times L(T_{i-1}, T_i)$ at times T_i, $i = 1, 2, \ldots, n$. Of course, the floating leg and fixed leg do not actually make notional principal payments of F at time T_n (as these would simply cancel out) but by expressing the swap price $SWAP(t)$ as a difference between $P_{fixed}(t)$ and $P_{floating}(t)$, we can compute the price of $P_{floating}(t)$ as if the swap required exchange of F between the fixed leg and the floating leg at time T_n.

To obtain the price of the floating rate bond, $P_{floating}(t)$, note that the cash flows from this bond are identical to the cash flows from investing $\$F$ into a short-term default-free time-deposit account that pays a periodic interest of $F \times \tau \times L(T_{i-1}, T_i)$, at times T_i, for $i = 1, 2, \ldots, n$, and returns the account balance F at time T_n. By definition the value of this account at the initial time $t = T_0$, equals F. At time T_1, the account pays an interest equal to $F \times \tau \times L(T_0, T_1)$, while the account's balance equals F. Similarly, at time T_2, the account pays an interest equal to $F \times \tau \times L(T_1, T_2)$, while the account balance still equals F. Hence, the account value at all reset dates must equal F, since the original investment F can be cashed out from the deposit account at any reset date.

However, between the reset dates the value of the time-deposit account behaves like a default-free zero-coupon bond maturing at the next reset date. This is because at the next reset date, the account will be worth its face value F plus an interest amount that is known today. Since this account is equivalent to the floating rate bond, the price $P_{floating}(t)$ can be given as:

$$P_{floating}(t) = \left[F + F \times \tau \times L(T_0, T_1)\right] \times P(t, T_1) \tag{8.3}$$

where $P(t, T_1)$ is the time t price of \$1 face-value default-free zero-coupon bond, maturing at time T_1. Hence, the price of the floating rate bond $P_{floating}(t)$ equals the price of a zero-coupon bond with a face value given as $F(1 + \tau \times L(T_0, T_1))$, maturing at time T_1, when $T_0 < t < T_1$. Of course, at all reset dates, $t = T_i$, as the floating coupons are paid, the price of the floating bond converges to F.

Now, consider the fixed leg of a swap which gives the fixed-coupon payments at dates S_i, $i = 1, 2, \ldots, N$, where the length of the tenor is given as $s = S_i - S_{i-1}$. To keep the analysis general, we allow the payment dates from the fixed leg to be different from the payment dates of the floating leg. The total number of fixed payments N can also be different from the total number of floating payments n. For example, the Eurodollar interest rate swaps allow quarterly payments from the floating leg and semiannual payments from the fixed leg, such that $n = 2N$. However, since we treat the swap price $SWAP(t)$ as the difference between the floating rate bond and the fixed-coupon bond in equation 8.2, we require that the offsetting payments of the face value F from these two bonds occur exactly at the same date, or the last payment dates S_N and T_n, represent the same date.

Given the swap rate R, for the fixed leg, the corresponding price of fixed-coupon bond, $P_{fixed}(t)$, can be obtained as a sum of the underlying zero-coupon bonds, as:

$$P_{fixed}(t) = \sum_{i=1}^{N} s \times R \times F \times P(t, S_i) + F \times P(t, S_N) \tag{8.4}$$

where by definition $S_N = T_n$, and $P(t, S_i)$ is the price of a default-free zero-coupon bond maturing at date S_i.

Example 8.4 Firm A initiated a five-year pay fixed/receive floating swap, 3.5 years ago (at $t = 0$), with a 6 percent swap rate, based on a notional principal of \$100 million. The floating rate of the swap is the three-month LIBOR with quarterly compounding. The floating leg of the swap makes quarterly payments, while the fixed leg of the swap makes semiannual payments. In the past 3.5 years, interest rates have steadily increased, and now the six-month, one-year, and 1.5-year LIBOR rates with continuous compounding are given as 8 percent, 8.5 percent, and 9 percent, respectively. The value of $P_{fixed}(t = 3.5)$ now equals:

$$P_{fixed}(t = 3.5) = \frac{6/2}{e^{0.08\times 0.5}} + \frac{6/2}{e^{0.085}} + \frac{100 + 6/2}{e^{0.09\times 1.5}} = \$95.63 \text{ million}$$

The value of $P_{floating}(t = 3.5)$ equals the notional value of \$100 million at the reset date, or

$$P_{floating}(t = 3.5) = \$100 \text{ million}$$

Thus, the price of the pay fixed/receive floating swap equals:

$$SWAP(t = 3.5) = 100 - 95.63 = \$4.37 \text{ million}$$

Duration Vector of an Interest Rate Swap

This section derives the duration vector of the pay fixed/receive floating swap. The duration vector of the pay floating/receive fixed swap has identical magnitudes but opposite signs of the duration vector of the pay fixed/receive floating swap. Unlike duration vector of a cash bond portfolio, which measures a change in the portfolio value as a percentage of the portfolio value, the duration vector of a swap is defined to measure a change in the swap price, not as a percentage of the swap price, but as a percentage of the swap's notional principal. This switch from swap price to the swap's notional principal is necessary for the definition of the duration vector for swaps, since swap price is always zero at the initiation of the swap. This definition of the duration vector of the swap implies that the change in swap price for hedging purposes is estimated by using the *notional value* of the swap, and not the swap price.

As mentioned earlier, we consider the floating leg of a swap with floating rate payments at dates T_i, $i = 1, 2, \ldots, n$, and fixed leg of the swap with fixed-coupon payments at dates S_i, $i = 1, 2, \ldots, N$, where $T_n = S_N$. We assume that the current date t is less than both T_1 and S_1. Using this framework, the price of a pay fixed/receive floating swap is defined in equation 8.2 as $SWAP(t) = P_{floating}(t) - P_{fixed}(t)$, where $P_{floating}(t)$ is defined in equation 8.3, and $P_{fixed}(t)$ is defined in equation 8.4. Typically, the coupon rate of the fixed leg, or the swap rate, is chosen such that the swap price at inception of the swap is zero. To avoid a potential division by zero, the weights of the portfolio in equation 8.2 are defined with respect to the swap's notional principal and not the swap price. Hence, the weights are given as:

$$w_{1swap} = \frac{P_{floating}(t)}{F} \tag{8.5}$$

and

$$w_{2swap} = -\frac{P_{fixed}(t)}{F} \tag{8.6}$$

Thus, the duration vector of a swap is a weighted average of the duration vectors of the floating rate bond and the fixed-coupon bond, or:

$$D^{swap}(m) = w_{1swap} D^{floating}(m) + w_{2swap} D^{fixed}(m), \text{ for all } m = 1, 2, \ldots, M \tag{8.7}$$

As shown in equation 8.3, the floating rate bond behaves like a zero-coupon bond maturing at the next reset date. Hence, the duration vector of the floating rate bond at time $t < T_1$, is given as follows:

$$D^{floating}(m) = (T_1 - t)^m, \text{ for all } m = 1, 2, \ldots, M \tag{8.8}$$

Using equation 8.4, the duration vector of the fixed-coupon bond is obtained as follows (see Chapter 5 for more details):

$$D^{fixed}(m) = \frac{\sum_{i=1}^{N} s \times R \times F \times P(t, S_i) \times (S_i - t)^m}{P_{fixed}(t)} + \frac{F \times P(t, S_N) \times (S_N - t)^m}{P_{fixed}(t)} \tag{8.9}$$

$$\text{for all } m = 1, 2, \ldots, M$$

Substituting the duration vectors of the floating rate bond and the fixed-coupon bond from equations 8.8 and 8.9, into equation 8.7, the duration vector of the swap can be obtained. The change in the swap price given as a percentage of the notional principal of the swap is given using a relationship similar to equation 5.10, as follows:

$$\begin{aligned} \frac{\Delta SWAP(t)}{F} = & -D^{swap}(1)\Delta A_0 \\ & -D^{swap}(2)\left[\Delta A_1 - (\Delta A_0)^2 / 2!\right] \\ & -D^{swap}(3)\left[\Delta A_2 - \Delta A_0 \Delta A_1 + (\Delta A_0)^3 / 3!\right] \\ & \vdots \\ & -D^{swap}(M)\left[\Delta A_{M-1} + \cdots + \frac{(\Delta A_0)^M}{M!}\right] \end{aligned} \tag{8.10}$$

The percentage change in the swap price defined relative to the notional principal in equation 8.10 is independent of the scale of the notional principal. In other words, the duration vector elements of the swap do not change as the notional principal increases or decreases.

Recall from Chapter 5 that ΔA_0, ΔA_1, ΔA_2, are given as the changes in the height, slope, curvature, and higher order shifts in the term structure of default-free zero-coupon yields. For hedging applications, consider a cash bond portfolio $P(t)$ with duration vector elements given as $D(1)$, $D(2)$, . . . , $D(M)$. Suppose the portfolio manager desires to change the duration vector profile of the cash portfolio to a target duration vector profile given as $D^T(1)$, $D^T(2)$, . . . , $D^T(M)$. Since this requires M duration constraints, the manager will need to use M swaps of different maturities. Consider the duration vector elements of the jth pay fixed/receive floating swap ($j = 1, 2, \ldots, M$) as follows:

$$D_j^{swap}(m), \text{ for } m = 1, 2, \ldots, M \tag{8.11}$$

where the duration vector of the swap is defined in equation 8.7. It can be shown that the notional principals for the M pay fixed/receive floating swaps can be given by the following solution:

$$\begin{bmatrix} F_1 \\ F_2 \\ \vdots \\ F_M \end{bmatrix} = P(t) \times \begin{bmatrix} D_1^{swap}(1) & D_2^{swap}(1) & \ldots & D_M^{swap}(1) \\ D_1^{swap}(2) & D_2^{swap}(2) & \ldots & D_M^{swap}(2) \\ \vdots & & & \\ D_1^{swap}(M) & D_2^{swap}(M) & \ldots & D_M^{swap}(M) \end{bmatrix}^{-1} \begin{bmatrix} D^T(1) - D(1) \\ D^T(2) - D(2) \\ \\ D^T(M) - D(M) \end{bmatrix} \quad (8.12)$$

If the notional principal F_j is positive for some j, then the manager must initiate a pay fixed/receive floating swap with that amount of notional principal. However if the notional principal F_j is negative for some j, then the manager must initiate a pay floating/receive fixed swap with the amount of notional principal given as $-F_j$. In general, the duration vector elements of pay fixed/receive floating swaps are negative as these swaps incur gains (losses) when interest rates go up (down). In contrast, the duration vector elements of pay floating/receive fixed swaps are positive as these swaps incur losses (gains) when interest rates go up (down).

Equation 8.12 is very general and allows a variety of applications for hedging interest rate risk under nonparallel term structure shifts. For most applications $M = 1$, 2, or 3, should be enough to capture the effects of nonparallel shifts on the cash portfolio. Hence, between one and three swaps of differing maturities may be generally needed for protection from interest rate risk under nonparallel term structure shifts.

By appropriate selection of the target duration vector values, different types of interest rate risk hedging applications such as protecting from instantaneous price changes, immunization at a planning horizon, bond index replication, duration gap management, or target duration matching can be designed for a variety of financial institutions.

For example, consider a trading institution interested in protecting itself from instantaneous price fluctuations. This institution requires the target duration vector values for the cash portfolio to be set to zero, or $D^T(1) = D^T(2) = \ldots = D^T(M) = 0$ in equation 8.12. In another example, consider a manager of guaranteed investment products (GICs) interested in immunizing her cash portfolio over a planning horizon of H years. This can be achieved by setting the target duration vector values for the cash portfolio to a horizon vector, given as, $D^T(1) = H$, $D^T(2) = H^2, \ldots,$ and $D^T(M) = H^M$. Of course, over time as durations change, the manager must devise a strategy to rebalance the swap positions at some discretely chosen points of time.

As another example, consider a financial institution interested in managing the duration gap between its assets and liabilities, by computing its equity duration vector. By considering the previous cash portfolio as the equity of the financial institution, you can select the target duration vector values for the equity, as some chosen values $D^T(1)$, $D^T(2)$, . . . , $D^T(M)$. Similarly, a portfolio manager interested in bond index replication can select the target duration vector values to equal the duration vector values of a given bond index, or $D^T(1) = D^{BI}(1)$, $D^T(2) = D^{BI}(2)$, . . . , $D^T(M) = D^{BI}(M)$, where $D^{BI}(1)$, $D^{BI}(2)$, . . . , $D^{BI}(M)$, are the duration vector values of the selected bond index.

FORWARD RATE AGREEMENTS

Unlike swaps, which are exchanges of two streams of multiple cash flows (where some of the exchanges may not even occur at the same date), a forward rate agreement (FRA) between two counterparties is an exchange of a single floating amount for a single fixed amount at a given future date. A typical FRA in the Eurodollar market requires an exchange of a LIBOR-based floating cash flow (known as the floating leg of the FRA) for a fixed cash flow (known as the fixed leg of the FRA), at a future time $T + \tau$, based upon the LIBOR rate observed at the future time T. The payoff of an FRA based on a notional principal of F, on the expiration date $T + \tau$, is given as:

$$F\tau\left[L(T,\ T+\tau)-K\right]=F\tau L\,(T,\ T+\tau)-F\tau K \tag{8.13}$$

where $L(T, T + \tau)$ is the LIBOR rate observed at time T for the term τ. The two expressions on the right side of equation 8.13 represent a long position in the floating leg and a short position in the fixed leg of the FRA, respectively.

The price of an FRA at any time t prior to T can be obtained by replicating the payoff of the floating leg of the FRA as a portfolio of two zero-coupon bonds, which expire at times T and $T + \tau$. The portfolio is given as a long position in the zero-coupon bond maturing at time T and a short position in the zero-coupon bond maturing at time $T + \tau$, where both bonds have their face values equal to the FRA's notional principal F.

The time T proceeds from the portfolio's long position are reinvested for τ periods at the prevailing LIBOR rate $L(T, T + \tau)$ at time T. The payoff from this portfolio at time $T + \tau$ is given as $F[1 + L(T, T + \tau)\tau] - F$, or:

$$\text{Portfolio payoff} = F\tau L(T, T+\tau) \tag{8.14}$$

The expression in equation 8.14 proves that the time $T + \tau$ payoff from the portfolio equals the payoff of the floating leg of the FRA given in equation 8.13. Therefore, using the law of one price, the time t value of the floating leg of the FRA equals the time t price of the replicating portfolio. The value of the bond portfolio at time t is given as:

$$F\left[P(t, T) - P(t, T+\tau)\right] \tag{8.15}$$

Hence, the time t price of the FRA payoff in equation 8.13, is given as:

$$\begin{aligned} FRA(t) &= F\left[P(t, T) - P(t, T+\tau)\right] - F\tau K P(t, T+\tau) \\ &= F \times P(t, T) - F(1+\tau K)P(t, T+\tau) \end{aligned} \tag{8.16}$$

The Duration Vector of an FRA

The duration vector of an FRA can be obtained in a manner similar to the duration vector of a swap. Similar to a swap, an FRA can have a zero price and, hence, its duration vector is defined to capture the change in FRA price as a percentage of the notional principal of the FRA. Using equation 8.16, the weights for the derivation of the duration vector of the FRA are given as follows:

$$w_{1FRA} = \frac{F \times P(t, T)}{F} = P(t, T) \tag{8.17}$$

and

$$w_{2FRA} = \frac{-F(1+\tau K)P(t, T+\tau)}{F} = -(1+\tau K)P(t, T+\tau) \tag{8.18}$$

Since the above weights are in two zero-coupon bonds maturing at time $T + \tau - t$ and $T - t$, the duration vector of the FRA is given as follows:

$$D^{FRA}(m) = w_{1FRA}(T-t)^m + w_{2FRA}(T+\tau-t)^m, \text{ for all } m = 1, 2, \ldots, M \tag{8.19}$$

The change in the FRA price given as a percentage of the notional principal of the FRA can be estimated with the duration vector of the FRA, using a relationship similar to equation 8.10 for swaps, and is given as follows:

$$\begin{aligned}\frac{\Delta FRA(t)}{F} = & -D^{FRA}(1)\Delta A_0 \\ & -D^{FRA}(2)\left[\Delta A_1 - (\Delta A_0)^2/2!\right] \\ & -D^{FRA}(3)\left[\Delta A_2 - \Delta A_0 \Delta A_1 + (\Delta A_0)^3/3!\right] \\ & \vdots \\ & -D^{FRA}(M)\left[\Delta A_{M-1} + \cdots + \frac{(\Delta A_0)^M}{M!}\right]\end{aligned} \tag{8.20}$$

The percentage change in the FRA price defined relative to the notional principal in equation 8.20 is independent of the scale of the notional principal. In other words, the duration vector elements of the FRA do not change as the notional principal increases or decreases.

Similar to swaps, FRAs can be used to hedge against nonparallel term structure shifts. Consider a cash bond portfolio $P(t)$ with duration vector elements given as $D(1), D(2), \ldots, D(M)$. Suppose the portfolio manager desires to change the duration vector profile of the cash portfolio to a target duration vector profile given as $D^T(1), D^T(2), \ldots, D^T(M)$. Since this requires M duration constraints, the manager will need to use M FRAs of different maturities. Consider the duration vector elements of the jth FRA ($j = 1, 2, \ldots, M$) as follows:

$$D_j^{FRA}(m), \text{ for all } m = 1, 2, \ldots, M \tag{8.21}$$

where the duration vector of the FRA is defined in equation 8.19. It can be shown that the notional principals for the M FRAs can be given by the following solution:

$$\begin{bmatrix} F_1 \\ F_2 \\ \vdots \\ F_M \end{bmatrix} = P(t) \times \begin{bmatrix} D_1^{FRA}(1) & D_2^{FRA}(1) & \dots & D_M^{FRA}(1) \\ D_1^{FRA}(2) & D_2^{FRA}(2) & \dots & D_M^{FRA}(2) \\ \vdots & & & \\ D_1^{FRA}(M) & D_2^{FRA}(M) & \dots & D_M^{FRA}(M) \end{bmatrix}^{-1} \begin{bmatrix} D^T(1) - D(1) \\ D^T(2) - D(2) \\ \\ D^T(M) - D(M) \end{bmatrix} \tag{8.22}$$

If the notional principal F_j is positive for some j, then the manager must be long in the floating leg and short in the fixed leg of the FRA. However, if the notional principal F_j is negative for some j, then the manager must be short in the floating leg and long in the fixed leg of the FRA with the amount of notional principal equal to $-F_j$. In general, the duration vector elements of long floating/short fixed FRAs are negative as these FRAs incur gains (losses) when interest rates go up (down). In contrast, the duration vector elements of long fixed/short floating FRAs are positive as these swaps incur losses (gains) when interest rates go up (down).

Similar to equation 8.12 for the case of swaps, equation 8.22 for FRAs is very general and allows a variety of applications for hedging interest rate risk under nonparallel term structure shifts. By appropriate selection of the target duration vector values, different types of interest rate risk hedging applications such as protecting from instantaneous price changes, immunization at a planning horizon, bond index replication, duration gap management, or target duration matching can be designed for a variety of financial institutions using FRAs. Discussion on how to select the target duration vector for these different applications was given earlier for the case of interest rate swaps.

PRICING AND HEDGING WITH CAPS, FLOORS, AND COLLARS USING THE LIBOR MARKET MODEL

The LIBOR market model is perhaps the most widely used model for pricing interest rate options, such as caps, floors, and collars in the Eurodollar interest rate derivatives market. The LIBOR market model had humble origins, as initially it was just a practically motivated application of Black's (1976) formula for pricing futures to the Eurodollar-based interest rate derivatives. By using the LIBOR rate as the underlying asset and the current forward rate as the expectation of the future LIBOR rate and assuming constant volatility, the Black formula immediately gave prices for European options written on the future LIBOR rate.

For some time, the theoretical underpinnings of this approach seemed dubious. How could LIBOR rate be considered a traded asset? How could the expectation of the LIBOR rate be the current forward rate? And, how could one assume constant volatility? All three assumptions seemed to not have much theoretical justification.

Yet, the practitioners were pleasantly surprised to find that all of the questions had good theoretical answers discovered recently by Brace, Gatarek, and Musiela (1996); Jamshidian (1997); and Musiela and Rutkowski (1997). These authors show that the LIBOR rate, which is the floating leg of the FRA, can be represented as a portfolio of two zero-coupon bonds (see previous section), and hence it is a traded asset. Since it is a traded asset, the method of arbitrage-free valuation can be used to price options based on the LIBOR rate. But the most useful theoretical result discovered is that the expectation of the LIBOR rate under the forward measure is indeed the current forward rate, and hence application of Black's model is fully justified. Finally, since volatility was assumed to be constant only for a specific maturity forward rate, one could calibrate the model to allow different forward rate volatilities for different maturities by using the observable prices of interest rate options on LIBOR rate.[4]

A major assumption of the LIBOR model is that under the physical probability measure, the forward rate for the term between T_i and T_{i+1} follows a log-normal distribution, or:

$$\frac{df(t, T_i, T_{i+1})}{f(t, T_i, T_{i+1})} = \mu_i dt + \sigma_i dZ_i(t) \tag{8.23}$$

where $dZ_i(t)$ is a Wiener process corresponding to maturity T_i, μ_i measures the drift, and σ_i measures the volatility of the forward rate process.[5] Brace, Gatarek, and Musiela (1996); Jamshidian (1997); and Musiela and Rutkowski (1997) show that under the forward measure in which traded securities are measured in the units of the zero-coupon bond price, $P(t, T_{i+1})$, the drift of this process is zero, and the forward rate process is given as:[6]

$$\frac{df(t, T_i, T_{i+1})}{f(t, T_i, T_{i+1})} = \sigma_i dZ_i^{Q_{T_i}}(t) \tag{8.24}$$

where the Wiener process in equation 8.24 is defined under the forward measure corresponding to the maturity T_{i+1}.

Since the forward rate has a zero drift in equation 8.24, it follows a martingale. Also, by definition, the forward rate at time T_i equals the observed LIBOR rate, or:

$$f(T_i, T_i, T_{i+1}) = L(T_i, T_{i+1}) \tag{8.25}$$

Since the forward rate is a traded asset, and has zero drift under the forward measure, its current value equals the expected future value of the LIBOR rate, or:

$$f(t, T_i, T_{i+1}) = E_t^{Q_{T_i}}\left[L(T_i, T_{i+1})\right] \tag{8.26}$$

Next we consider pricing of interest rate caps, floors, and collars, using the LIBOR market model. We give the basic formulas using the LIBOR market model and derive the duration vectors of caps, floors, and collars. A more complete theoretical development of the LIBOR market model is given in the second volume of this series.

Pricing and Hedging with Interest Rate Caps

The Pricing of a Caplet and a Cap The payoff from a caplet on the LIBOR rate at a future date $T_{i+1} = T_i + \tau$ (for $i = 0, 1, 2, \ldots, n-1$), is given as:

$$F \times \tau \times \max\left[L(T_i, T_{i+1}) - K_c, 0\right] \tag{8.27}$$

where the timeline is given as $t < T = T_0 < T_1 < T_2 < \ldots < T_n$, $L(T_i, T_{i+1})$ is the LIBOR rate observed at time T_i for the term $\tau = T_{i+1} - T_i$, F is the notional value of the caplet, and K_c is the cap rate. Using the LIBOR market model, the caplet price at time t is given as:

$$CAPLET_i(t) = F \times \tau \times P(t, T_{i+1})\left\{f(t, T_i, T_{i+1})N(d_{1,i}) - K_c N\left(d_{2,i}\right)\right\} \tag{8.28}$$

where

$$d_{1,i} = \frac{\ln(f(t, T_i, T_{i+1})/K_c) + \sigma_i^2\left(T_i - t\right)/2}{\sigma_i\sqrt{T_i - t}} \tag{8.29}$$

and

$$d_{2,i} = \frac{\ln(f(t, T_i, T_{i+1})/K_c) - \sigma_i^2(T_i - t)/2}{\sigma_i\sqrt{T_i - t}} = d_{1,i} - \sigma_i\sqrt{T_i - t}$$

A cap is defined as a portfolio of increasing maturity caplets. The price of a cap can be given as a sum of the caplet prices from equation 8.29 and is given as:

$$\begin{aligned} CAP(t) &= \sum_{i=0}^{n-1} CAPLET_i(t) \\ &= F \times \tau \sum_{i=0}^{n-1} P(t, T_{i+1})\{f(t, T_i, T_{i+1})N(d_{1,i}) - K_c N(d_{2,i})\} \end{aligned} \quad (8.30)$$

Example 8.5 Firm A has a three-year, \$100 million loan with a floating interest rate of LIBOR + 0.2 percent paid semiannually. The firm wants to hedge the risk of upward movements in the interest rates, and so it buys an interest rate cap with a cap rate of 7 percent with semiannual compounding, effective one year from now, immediately after the LIBOR reset. The 1-year, 1.5-year, 2-year, 2.5-year, and 3-year zero-coupon yields are given as 6.85 percent, 6.90 percent, 7.00 percent, 7.05 percent, and 7.05 percent. The zero-coupon bond prices corresponding to these yields are given as follows:

$$\begin{aligned} P(0, 1) &= e^{-0.0685\times 1} = 0.9338 \\ P(0, 1.5) &= e^{-0.0690\times 1.5} = 0.9017 \\ P(0, 2) &= e^{-0.07\times 2} = 0.8694 \\ P(0, 2.5) &= e^{-0.0705\times 2.5} = 0.8384 \\ P(0, 3) &= e^{-0.0705\times 3} = 0.8094 \end{aligned}$$

Using the relationship between zero-coupon bond prices and forward rates, we can compute the six-month forward rates starting 1 year, 1.5 years, 2 years, and 2.5 years from today, as follows:

$$f(t, T_i, T_{i+1}) = \frac{P(t, T_i)/P(t, T_{i+1}) - 1}{\tau} \quad (8.31)$$

And therefore,

$$f(0,\ 1,\ 1.5) = \frac{0.9338 / 0.9017 - 1}{0.5} = 7.12\%$$

$$f(0,\ 1.5,\ 2) = \frac{0.9017 / 0.8694 - 1}{0.5} = 7.43\%$$

$$f(0,\ 2,\ 2.5) = \frac{0.8694 / 0.8384 - 1}{0.5} = 7.38\%$$

$$f(0,\ 2.5,\ 3) = \frac{0.8384 / 0.8094 - 1}{0.5} = 7.18\%$$

We assume that the volatilities of the six-month forward rates mentioned previously are flat at 20 percent per year. Using the notation $t = 0$, $T_0 = 1$ year, $T_1 = 1.5$ years, $T_2 = 2$ years, $T_3 = 2.5$ years, and $T_4 = 3$ years, the current values of the caplets comprising the cap can be computed as follows.

First caplet (makes payment at 1½ years at time T_1):

$$\begin{aligned} d_{1,0} &= \frac{\ln(f(t,\ T_0,\ T_1) / K_c) + \sigma_0^2\, T_0 / 2}{\sigma_0 \sqrt{T_0}} \\ &= \frac{\ln(f(0,\ 1,\ 1.5) / K_c) + \sigma_0^2\ / 2}{\sigma_0} \\ &= \frac{\ln(0.0712 / 0.07) + 0.2^2\ / 2}{0.2} = 0.1878 \end{aligned}$$

and

$$d_{2,0} = d_{1,0} - \sigma_0 \sqrt{T_0} = 0.1878 - 0.2 = -0.0122$$

Hence, $N(d_{1,0}) = 0.5745$ and $N(d_{2,0}) = 0.4951$.

The first caplet price equals:

$$\begin{aligned} CAPLET_0(0) &= F \times \tau \times P(0,\ 1.5)\left\{f(0,\ 1,\ 1.5)N(d_{1,0}) - K_c N(d_{2,0})\right\} \\ &= 100{,}000{,}000 \times 0.5 \times 0.9017\left(0.0712 \times 0.5745 - 0.07 \times 0.4951\right) \\ &= \$282{,}520 \end{aligned}$$

TABLE 8.6 Prices of Caplets and Cap

Year	Time T_i	$P(0,T_i)$	$f(0,T_i,T_{i+1})$ (%)	$d_{1,i}$	$d_{2,i}$	$N(d_{1,i})$	$N(d_{2,i})$	Caplet Price ($)
1	0	0.9338	7.12	0.1878	−0.0122	0.5745	0.4951	282,520
1.5	1	0.9017	7.43	0.3685	0.1236	0.6438	0.5492	409,484
2	2	0.8694	7.38	0.3298	0.0469	0.6292	0.5187	425,276
2.5	3	0.8384	7.18	0.2365	−0.0797	0.5935	0.4682	397,015
3	4	0.8094						
							Cap Price:	1,514,295

Similar calculations apply to $CAPLET_1(0)$, $CAPLET_2(0)$, and $CAPLET_3(0)$. The detailed results are reported in Table 8.6.

Duration Vector of a Caplet The duration vector of the caplet can be derived using its pricing formula given in equation 8.28. However, a further simplification to the pricing formula in (8.28) is needed before we can derive the duration vector of the caplet. By substituting the forward rate from equation 8.31 into equation 8.28, the caplet can be expressed as a portfolio of two zero-coupon bonds, one maturing at time T_i and the other one at time T_{i+1}, as follows:

$$CAPLET_i(t) = F \times N(d_{1,i}) \times P(t,\ T_i) - F\left[N(d_{1,i}) + \tau K_c N(d_{2,i})\right] P(t,\ T_{i+1}) \quad (8.32)$$

where, $d_{1,i}$ and $d_{2,i}$ are defined in equation 8.29. The caplet represents a long position of $FN(d_{1,i})\ P(t, T_i)$ in the bond maturing at date T_i, and a short position of $-F\ [N(d_{1,i}) + K_c \tau\ N(d_{2,i})] P(t, T_{i+1})$ in the bond maturing on date T_{i+1}. To obtain the duration vector of the caplet, the portfolio weights can be given as follows:

$$w_{1,i} = \frac{F \times N(d_{1,i}) \times P(t,\ T_i)}{CAPLET_i(t)} \quad (8.33)$$

and

$$w_{2,i} = -\frac{F\left[N(d_{1,i}) + \tau K_c N(d_{2,i})\right]P(t,\ T_{i+1})}{CAPLET_i(t)} \tag{8.34}$$

Using the above weights, the duration vector of the caplet is given as follows:

$$D_i^{caplet}(m) = w_{1,i}(T_i - t)^m + w_{2,i}(T_{i+1} - t)^m \tag{8.35}$$

for all $m = 1, 2, \ldots, M$.

The percentage change in the caplet price can be estimated with its duration vector using a relationship similar to equation 5.10, as follows:

$$\begin{aligned}\frac{\Delta CAPLET_i(t)}{CAPLET_i(t)} &= -D_i^{caplet}(1)\Delta A_0 \\ &\quad -D_i^{caplet}(2)\left[\Delta A_1 - (\Delta A_0)^2/2!\right] \\ &\quad -D_i^{caplet}(3)\left[\Delta A_2 - \Delta A_0 \Delta A_1 + (\Delta A_0)^3/3!\right] \\ &\quad \vdots \\ &\quad -D_i^{caplet}(M)\left[\Delta A_{M-1} + \cdots + \frac{(\Delta A_0)^M}{M!}\right]\end{aligned} \tag{8.36}$$

Duration Vector of a Cap As shown in equation 8.30, a cap is defined as a portfolio of caplets. The price of a cap with payoffs beginning at time T_1 equals:

$$CAP(t) = \sum_{i=0}^{n-1} CAPLET_i(t) \tag{8.37}$$

Substituting the values of caplets from equation 8.32 into equation 8.37, the cap can be given as a portfolio of zero-coupon bonds, with its price given as follows:

$$CAP(t) = F\sum_{i=0}^{n-1}\left\{N(d_{1,i})P(t,\ T_i) - \left[N(d_{1,i}) + \tau K_c N(d_{2,i})\right]P(t,\ T_{i+1})\right\} \tag{8.38}$$

Rearranging terms in equation 8.38, we obtain:

$$CAP(t) = F\left\{\begin{array}{l} N(d_{1,0})P(t,\ T_0) + \left[\sum_{i=1}^{n-1}\left(N(d_{1,i}) - N(d_{1,i-1}) - \tau K_c N(d_{2,i-1})\right)P(t,\ T_i)\right] \\ -\left[N(d_{1,n-1}) + \tau K_c N(d_{2,n-1})\right]P(t,\ T_n) \end{array}\right\} \quad (8.39)$$

Equation 8.39 demonstrates that a cap with n reset dates is a portfolio of $n + 1$ zero-coupon bonds expiring at time T_i, for $i = 0, 1, 2, 3, \ldots, n$. The weights in each of the $n + 1$ zero-coupon bonds are given as follows:

$$w_{i,CAP} = \begin{cases} \dfrac{F \times N(d_{1,0})P(t,\ T_0)}{CAP(t)}, & \text{for } i = 0 \\ \dfrac{F\left(N(d_{1,i}) - N(d_{1,i-1}) - \tau K_c N(d_{2,i-1})\right)P(t,\ T_i)}{CAP(t)}, & \text{for } i = 1,\ 2,\ \ldots,\ n-1 \\ -\dfrac{F\left[N(d_{1,n-1}) + \tau K_c N(d_{2,n-1})\right]P(t, T_n)}{CAP(t)}, & \text{for } i = n \end{cases} \quad (8.40)$$

Using these weights, the duration vector of the cap is given as:

$$D^{cap}(m) = \sum_{i=0}^{n} w_{i,CAP}(T_i - t)^m \quad (8.41)$$

for all $m = 1, 2, \ldots, M$.

Similar to equation 8.36, the percentage change in the cap price can be estimated with its duration vector, as follows:

$$\begin{aligned} \frac{\Delta CAP(t)}{CAP(t)} &= -D^{cap}(1)\Delta A_0 \\ &\quad -D^{cap}(2)\left[\Delta A_1 - (\Delta A_0)^2 / 2!\right] \\ &\quad -D^{cap}(3)\left[\Delta A_2 - \Delta A_0 \Delta A_1 + (\Delta A_0)^3 / 3!\right] \\ &\quad \vdots \\ &\quad -D^{cap}(M)\left[\Delta A_{M-1} + \cdots + \frac{(\Delta A_0)^M}{M!}\right] \end{aligned} \quad (8.42)$$

Pricing and Hedging with Interest Rate Floors

The Pricing of a Floorlet and a Floor The payoff from a floorlet on the LIBOR rate at a future date $T_{i+1} = T_i + \tau$ (for $i = 0, 1, 2, \ldots, n-1$), is given as follows:

$$F \times \tau \times \max\left[K_f - L(T_i,\ T_{i+1}),\ 0\right] \tag{8.43}$$

where $L(T_i, T_{i+1})$ is the LIBOR rate observed at time T_i for the term $\tau = T_{i+1} - T_i$, F is the notional value of the floorlet, and K_f is the floor rate. Using the LIBOR market model, the floorlet price at time t is given as follows:

$$FLOORLET_i(t) = F \times \tau \times P(t,\ T_{i+1})\left\{K_f N(-d_{2,i}) - f(t,T_i,\ T_{i+1})N(-d_{1,i})\right\} \tag{8.44}$$

where $d_{1,i}$ and $d_{2,i}$ are as given in equation 8.29 with K_c replaced by K_f. A floor is defined as a portfolio of increasing maturity floorlets. The price of a floor can be given as a sum of the floorlet prices from equation 8.44 and is given as:

$$\begin{aligned} FLOOR(t) &= \sum_{i=0}^{n-1} FLOORLET_i(t) \\ &= F \times \tau \times \sum_{i=0}^{n-1} P(t,\ T_{i+1})\left[K_f N(-d_{2,i}) - f(t,T_i,\ T_{i+1})N(-d_{1,i})\right] \end{aligned} \tag{8.45}$$

Duration Vector of a Floorlet The duration vector of the floorlet can be derived using its pricing formula given in equation 8.44. However, a further simplification to the pricing formula in (8.44) is needed before we can derive the duration vector of the floorlet. By substituting the forward rate from equation 8.31 into equation 8.44, the floorlet can be expressed as a portfolio of two zero-coupon bonds, one maturing at time T_i and the other one at time T_{i+1}, as follows:

$$\begin{aligned} FLOORLET_i(t) = F\left[N(-d_{1,i}) + \tau K_f N(-d_{2,i})\right]P(t,\ T_{i+1}) - F \\ \times N(-d_{1,i}) \times P(t,\ T_i) \end{aligned} \tag{8.46}$$

where, $d_{1,i}$ and $d_{2,i}$ are given in equation 8.29 with K_c replaced by K_f.

A floorlet represents a long position of $F\,[N(-d_{1,i}) + K_f\,\tau\,N(-d_{2,i})]P(t, T_{i+1})$ in the bond maturing at T_{i+1}, and a short position of $-F\,N(-d_{1,i})\,P(t, T_i)$ in the bond maturing at date T_i. To obtain the duration vector of the floorlet, the portfolio weights can be given as follows:

$$w_{1,i} = -\frac{F \times N(-d_{1,i}) \times P(t,\ T_i)}{FLOORLET_i(t)} \tag{8.47}$$

and

$$w_{2,i} = \frac{F\left[N(-d_{1,i}) + \tau K_f\,N(-d_{2,i})\right]P(t, T_{i+1})}{FLOORLET_i(t)}$$

Using these weights, the duration vector of the floorlet is given as:

$$D_i^{floorlet}(m) = w_{1,i}(T_i - t)^m + w_{2,i}(T_{i+1} - t)^m \tag{8.49}$$

for all $m = 1, 2, \ldots, M$.

The percentage change in the floorlet price can be estimated with its duration vector using a relationship similar to that given in equation 8.36 for a caplet.

Duration Vector of a Floor As shown in equation 8.45, a floor is defined as a portfolio of floorlets. The price of a floor with payoffs beginning at time T_1 equals:

$$FLOOR(t) = \sum_{i=0}^{n-1} FLOORLET_i(t) \tag{8.50}$$

Substituting the values of floorlets from equation 8.46 into equation 8.50, the floor can be given as a portfolio of zero-coupon bonds, with its price given as follows:

$$FLOOR(t) = F\sum_{i=0}^{n-1}\left\{\left[N(-d_{1,i}) + \tau K_f\,N(-d_{2,i})\right]P(t,\ T_{i+1}) - N(-d_{1,i})P(t,\ T_i)\right\} \tag{8.51}$$

where $d_{1,i}$ and $d_{2,i}$ are as defined in equation 8.29 with K_c replaced by K_f.

Rearranging terms in equation 8.51, we obtain:

$$FLOOR(t) =$$

$$F\left\{\begin{array}{l} -N(-d_{1,0})P(t,\ T_0)+\left[\sum_{i=1}^{n-1}\left(N(-d_{1,i-1})+\tau K_f N(-d_{2,i-1})-N(-d_{1,i})\right)P(t,\ T_i)\right] \\ +\left[N(-d_{1,n-1})+\tau K_f N(-d_{2,n-1})\right]P(t,\ T_n) \end{array}\right\} \quad (8.52)$$

Equation 8.52 demonstrates that a floor with n reset dates is a portfolio of $n+1$ zero-coupon bonds expiring at time T_i, for $i = 0, 1, 2, 3, \ldots, n$. The weights in each of the $n + 1$ zero-coupon bonds are given as follows:

$$w_{i,FLOOR} = \begin{cases} -\dfrac{F\times N(-d_{1,0})P(t,\ T_0)}{FLOOR(t)}, & \text{if } i=0 \\ \dfrac{F\left(N(-d_{1,i-1})+\tau K_f N(-d_{2,i-1})-N(-d_{1,i})\right)P(t,\ T_i)}{FLOOR(t)}, & \text{if } i=1,\ 2,\ \ldots,\ n-1 \\ \dfrac{F\left[N(-d_{1,n-1})+\tau K_f N(-d_{2,n-1})\right]P(t,T_n)}{FLOOR(t)}, & \text{if } i=n \end{cases} \quad (8.53)$$

Using these weights, the duration vector of the floor is given as:

$$D^{floor}(m) = \sum_{i=0}^{n} w_{i,FLOOR}(T_i - t)^m \quad (8.54)$$

for all $m = 1, 2, \ldots, M$.

The percentage change in the floor price can be estimated with its duration vector using a relationship similar to that given in equation 8.42 for a cap.

Pricing and Hedging with Interest Rate Collars

A combination of a long position in a cap and a short position in a floor is known as a *collar.* If the cap and floor have the same strike price, maturity, and frequency of payments, then a long position in the cap and a short position in the floor provides the same cash flows as a swap with the fixed rate equal to the strike price of the floor and cap. Assuming that under the swap there is no exchange of payments on the first reset date, the relationship between the cap price, floor price, and swap price, also known as the put-call parity relationship between caps and floors, is given as follows:

$$CAP(t) - FLOOR(t) = SWAP(t) \tag{8.55}$$

The Pricing of a Collar A *collar* represents a portfolio with a long position in a cap and a short position in a floor, and its construction is intended to limit the losses due to sharp increases in the interest rates. A collar allows partially or fully funding the purchase of a cap using the premium obtained from writing the floor. The price of a collar is, thus, the price of a cap net of a floor, or:

$$COLLAR(t) = CAP(t) - FLOOR(t) \tag{8.56}$$

Substituting equations 8.30 and 8.45 into equation 8.56, the collar price can be obtained as a combination of zero-coupon bond prices. Only when the cap and the floor have the same strike price, maturity, and frequency of payments, a collar provides the same cash flows as a swap as shown in equation 8.55.

Duration Vector of a Collar The duration vector of a collar with a nonzero price, can be obtained by using equation 8.56. The portfolio weights for obtaining the duration vector can be defined as:

$$\begin{aligned} w_c &= \frac{CAP(t)}{COLLAR(t)} \\ w_f &= -\frac{FLOOR(t)}{COLLAR(t)} \end{aligned} \tag{8.57}$$

Using these portfolio weights, the duration vector of a collar is given as:

$$D^{collar}(m) = w_c D^{cap}(m) + w_f D^{floor}(m) \tag{8.58}$$

for M, where the duration vectors of a cap and a floor are defined in equations 8.41 and 8.54, respectively.

The percentage change in the collar price can be estimated with its duration vector using a relationship similar to that given in equation 8.42 for a cap.

Pricing of Floating-Rate Bonds with Embedded Collars

A long position in a floating rate bond gains when interest rates rise and loses when interest rates fall. These gains and losses can be capped by writing a collar while being long in the floating rate bond. Writing a collar results in a long position in the floor that ensures receiving a minimum floating interest when interest rates decrease, and a short position in the cap, which limits the gains from the floating interest when interest rates increase. The price of a floating rate bond with an embedded negative position in the collar option can be given as follows:

$$P_{\substack{floater\\-collar}}(t) = P_{floater}(t) - COLLAR(t) \tag{8.59}$$

To obtain the duration vector of the floating rate bond with an embedded collar, the portfolio weights are given as follows:

$$\begin{aligned} w_1 &= \frac{P_{floater}(t)}{P_{\substack{floater\\-collar}}(t)} \\ w_2 &= -\frac{COLLAR(t)}{P_{\substack{floater\\-collar}}(t)} \end{aligned} \tag{8.60}$$

Using these weights, the duration vector of the floating bond with embedded collar is given as:

$$D^{\substack{floater\\-collar}}(m) = w_1 D^{floater}(m) + w_2 D^{collar}(m) \tag{8.61}$$

The price and duration vectors of floating rate bonds with embedded collars given earlier can be substituted in place of the price and duration vectors of regular floating rate bonds, in the swap pricing formula and swap duration vector formulas derived earlier in this chapter. Doing this allows the floating leg of the interest rate swaps to have embedded collars.

INTEREST RATE SWAPTIONS

Interest rate swaptions give the holder the right to enter into an interest rate swap at a certain date in the future, at a particular swap rate for a specified term. A *payer swaption* gives the buyer the right to pay a fixed rate and receive a floating rate. A *receiver swaption* gives the buyer the right to pay a floating rate and receive a fixed rate. The holder of the payer swaption exercises the option only if at the swaption's expiration date, the market swap rate is higher than the strike rate. The opposite is true for the holder of a receiver swaption.

When two counterparties enter a swaption, they agree on the strike rate, length of the option period, the swap's maturity, notional amount, amortization, and frequency of the settlement. Depending on the exercise rights of the buyer, swaptions fall into three main categories:

1. *European swaptions* give the buyer the right to exercise the option only at maturity.
2. *American swaptions* give the buyer the right to exercise the option at any time during the option period.
3. *Bermudan swaptions* give the buyer the right to exercise the option on specific dates during the option period.

Example 8.6 Suppose in Example 8.5, rather than buying an interest rate cap, Firm A buys a payer swaption expiring in one year, on a two-year swap at a strike rate of 7 percent. If one year from now the two-year swap rate is above 7 percent, then firm A exercises the swaption. Then the firm will pay a fixed interest rate of 7 percent, and receive floating interest. If the two-year swap rate is lower than or equal to 7 percent, the swaption is not exercised.

The payoff from the swaption in this example consists of a series of cash flows equal to:

$$\frac{\$100 \text{ million}}{p} \max(R - 7\%,\ 0) \tag{8.62}$$

where p is the number of swap payments per year, and R is the two-year swap rate prevailing one year from now. If the swap payments are exchanged semiannually ($p = 2$) and the two-year swap rate, one year from now is 7.3 percent ($R = 7.3\%$), then the four payoffs of the swaption over the two years, are given as:

$$\frac{\$100 \text{ million}}{2} \max(7.3\% - 7\%,\ 0) = \$150{,}000$$

In general, the payoffs from a payer swaption are given as a set of cash flows equal to the following:

$$\frac{F}{p}\max(R-K,\ 0) \tag{8.63}$$

which are known at time T (such that $T < T_1$), but are paid at times T_1, $T_2, \ldots, T_{pn}$, where F is the notional principal exchanged in the swap underlying the swaption, p is the number of payments under the swap per year, n is the length of the swap in number of years, R is the n-year swap rate prevailing at the expiration date T of the swaption, and K is the swaption strike rate.

The Black Model for Pricing a Payer Swaption

Consider the time t value of a payer swaption expiring at date T, which gives pn number of payoffs (shown in equation 8.63) that are received at times T_i ($i = 1, 2, \ldots, pn$). Assuming the payoffs come at constant intervals of τ after the expiration date T, the value of τ is $1/p$.

Applying Black's model, the time t value of the payer swaption is given as follows:

$$PAYER\ SWAPTION(t) = PF\left[f_t^s N(d_1) - KN(d_2)\right] \tag{8.64}$$

where

$$P = \sum_{i=1}^{pn} \tau P(t,\ T_i)$$

$$d_1 = \frac{\ln(f_t^s / K) + \sigma^2 (T-t)/2}{\sigma\sqrt{T-t}}$$

$$d_2 = \frac{\ln(f_t^s / K) - \sigma^2 (T-t)/2}{\sigma\sqrt{T-t}} = d_1 - \sigma\sqrt{T-t}$$

and $f_t^s = E_t^Q(R)$, is the forward swap rate which is assumed to equal the expected value of the swap rate R (this is justified if expectation is taken under the forward measure with P as the numeraire) given as follows:

$$f_t^s = \sum_{i=1}^{n} x_i\ f(t,\ T,\ T_i) \tag{8.65}$$

where the weights are defined as follows:

$$x_i = \frac{\tau P(t, T_i)}{\sum_{i=1}^{n} \tau P(t, T_i)}$$

The Black model for pricing swaptions assumes that the forward swap rate f_t^s is lognormally distributed. Yet, earlier the Black model for pricing of caps assumed that the forward rates $f(t, T, T_i)$ are lognormally distributed (see equations 8.24 and 8.31). Since f_t^s is an *arithmetic* weighted average of $f(t, T, T_i)$ as shown in the above equation, the Black model for pricing swaptions is inconsistent with the Black model for pricing caps, since both f_t^s and $f(t, T, T_i)$ cannot be distributed lognormally, simultaneously. In general, since f_t^s is an *arithmetic* weighted average of $f(t, T, T_i)$, the correlations between forward rates are important for pricing swaptions. However, the market participants typically treat f_t^s as an exogenous variable that is lognormally distributed, so modeling forward rate correlations is not explicitly required unless one is comparing the prices of caps with those of swaptions.

The Black Model for Pricing a Receiver Swaption

The payoffs from a receiver swaption are given as a set of cash flows equal to the following:

$$\frac{F}{p}\max(K - R,\ 0)$$

which are known at time T, but are paid at times $T_1, T_2, \ldots, T_{pn}$, where all variables are as defined before.

The receiver swaption's price is given as:

$$RECEIVER\ SWAPTION(t) = PF\left[KN(-d_2) - f_t^s N(-d_1)\right] \qquad (8.66)$$

where all variables are as defined before.

Example 8.7 Reconsider the firm in Example 8.6, which bought a one-year payer swaption with a strike rate of 7 percent and a \$100 million notional principal. Assume a *LIBOR* rate of 6.8 percent per annum with continuous compounding and a 20 percent swap rate volatility per year.

The continuously compounded interest rate y can be converted to the semiannually compounded interest rate r as follows:

$$r = 2\left(e^{y/2} - 1\right) \tag{8.67}$$

Using this equation, the continuously compounded interest rate of 6.8 percent per year is equivalent to a 6.92 percent per year with semiannual compounding. Since we are using a flat yield curve, all forward rates are equal, and, $f_0^s = E_0^Q\ (R) = 6.92\%$. Hence, the swaption price can be now computed as follows:

$$d_1 = \frac{\ln(f_0^s / K) + \sigma^2 T/2}{\sigma\sqrt{T}} = \frac{\ln(0.0692/0.07) + 0.2^2 \times 1/2}{0.2\sqrt{1}} = 0.0425$$
$$d_2 = d_1 - \sigma\sqrt{T} = 0.0425 - 0.2\sqrt{1} = -0.1575$$

Given these values, $N(d_1) = 0.5170$, and $N(d_2) = 0.4374$.

The payer swaption's price is given by equation 8.65, and is computed as follows:

$$\begin{aligned} PAYER\ SWAPTION(0) &= PF\left[f_0^s N(d_1) - KN(d_2)\right] \\ &= \left(0.5 \times \sum_{i=1}^{4} e^{-0.068 \times T_i}\right) \times 100{,}000{,}000 \\ &\quad \times \left[0.0692 \times 0.5170 - 0.07 \times 0.4374\right] \\ &= 882{,}324 \end{aligned}$$

Duration Vectors of Payer and Receiver Swaptions

Both payer and receiver swaptions can be given as portfolios of zero-coupon bonds maturing at times T_i, $i = 1, 2, \ldots, pn$, with weights given as follows:

$$\begin{aligned} w_i^{Payer} &= \frac{P(t,\ T_i)\tau F\left[f_t^s N(d_1) - KN(d_2)\right]}{PAYER\ SWAPTION(t)} \\ w_i^{Receiver} &= \frac{P(t,\ T_i)\tau F\left[KN(-d_2) - f_t^s N(-d_1)\right]}{RECEIVER\ SWAPTION(t)} \end{aligned} \tag{8.68}$$

Using the above weights, the duration vectors of payer and receiver swaptions are given as follows:

$$D^{Payer}_{swaption}(m) = \sum_{i=1}^{pn} w_i^{Payer}(T_i - t)^m, \text{ for all } m = 1, 2, \ldots, M$$
$$D^{Receiver}_{swaption}(m) = \sum_{i=1}^{pn} w_i^{Receiver}(T_i - t)^m, \text{ for all } m = 1, 2, \ldots, M \tag{8.69}$$

NUMERICAL ANALYSIS

In this section, we perform a comparative static analysis of the durations of different derivatives considered in this chapter. The analysis focuses only on the first element of the duration vector $D(1)$. The $D(1)$ values are simulated for swaps, caps, floors, collars, floating rate bonds embedded with collars, and swaps embedded with collars, for various underlying parameter values. All of the options are priced using the LIBOR market model.

We assume that the current zero-coupon yields are given by the Nelson and Siegel (1987) exponential model as follows:

$$y(T) = \alpha_1 + (\alpha_2 + \alpha_3)\frac{\beta}{T}\left(1 - e^{-T/\beta}\right) - \alpha_3 e^{-T/\beta} \tag{8.70}$$

For the purpose of simulation, the parameter values are given as $\alpha_1 = 0.07$, $\alpha_2 = -0.02$, $\alpha_3 = 0.0009$, and $\beta = 2$. These parameters generate a smooth yield curve, with the instantaneous short rate equal to 5 percent and gradually rising yields with $y(5) = 6.29\%$.

All of the bonds, caps, floors, and swap contracts considered in this section have a face value or notional principal of \$100, and time to maturity of five years, with coupons paid or reset every six months. We also assume a flat forward rate volatility of $\sigma = 20\%$.

Using a cap rate $K_c = 9\%$, and a floor rate $K_f = 3\%$, we obtain the prices of the cap, floor, collar, and floating rate bond with a collar as: $CAP(0) =$ \$0.8337, $FLOOR(0) =$ \$0.0179, $COLLAR(0) =$ \$0.8158, $P_{floater-Collar}(0) =$ \$99.1842. The initial price of the swap is assumed to be zero. Since the price of the floating rate bond with a collar equals \$99.1842, the semiannual coupon payment is obtained by utilizing equation 8.4 and is found to equal \$3.0772. Using the benchmark parameter values, the durations of the cap, floor, collar, floater (floating rate bond with a collar), and a pay floating/

TABLE 8.7 Benchmark Values for the Parameters

Parameter	Benchmark Value (%)	Range of Change (%)
Cap rate K_c	9	6–30
Floor rate K_f	3	1–9
Forward rate volatility σ	20	10–30
Instantaneous short rate $y(0)$	5	0–8

receive fixed swap with a collar are obtained as follows: $D^{cap}(1) = -79.46$, $D^{floor}(1) = 108.96$, $D^{collar}(1) = -83.59$, $D^{floater-collar}(1) = 1.0178$ years, and $D^{swap-collar}(1) = 3.1537$ years.

After calculating these prices and durations using benchmark values, we examine how the durations of these instruments change with the cap rate, the floor rate, the forward rate volatility, and the instantaneous short rate. Each simulation lets one or two parameters vary, keeping others at their benchmark values. Table 8.7 gives the benchmark value for each parameter and the range for the sensitivity analysis.

Figure 8.3 shows how the cap duration changes with the cap rate and how the floor duration changes with floor rate. Since the cap payoff increases as interest rate increases, the cap duration is negative, and since the floor payoff decreases as interest rate increases, the floor duration is positive. It is evident that both the cap and the floor durations have large magnitudes due to the leverage implicit in these options. As noted by Nawalkha (1995) and others, out-of-the-money options have higher leverage. The cap becomes more out-of-the-money as the cap rate increases, hence, the magnitude of the cap duration increases as cap rate increases. However, floor becomes in-the-money as floor rate increases, hence, the magnitude of floor duration decreases as floor rate increases.

Figure 8.4 Panel A and Panel B on page 257 show how the collar duration changes with the cap rate and the floor rate, respectively. The complex patterns in the graphs can be explained by equations 8.56 and 8.58. A collar represents a long position in a cap and a short position in a floor. The collar duration is the weighted average of the cap duration and the floor duration, where the weights are the relative prices of the cap and floor, divided by the collar price. The collar price decreases from positive to negative as the cap rate increases, and reaches zero at some point. Since the collar price is in the denominator of equation 8.58, the weighting coefficients go to infinity in absolute value when the collar price goes to zero. As the collar price goes from positive to negative, combining with the infinite weighting

Panel A

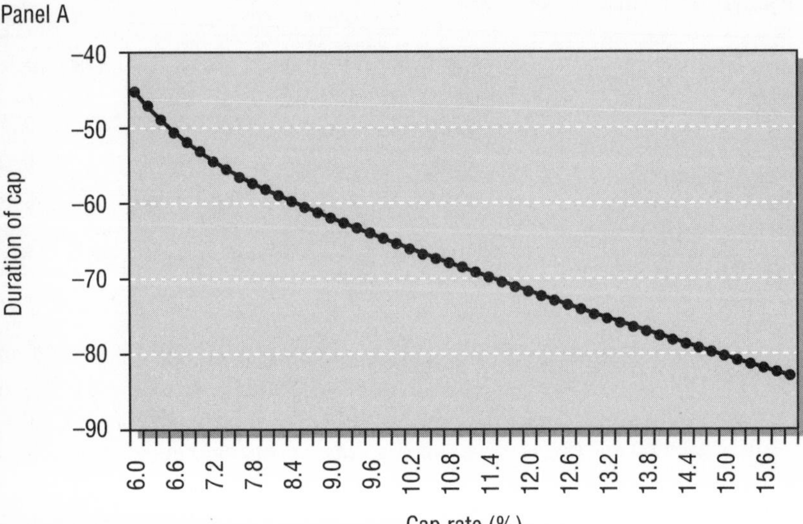

Panel B

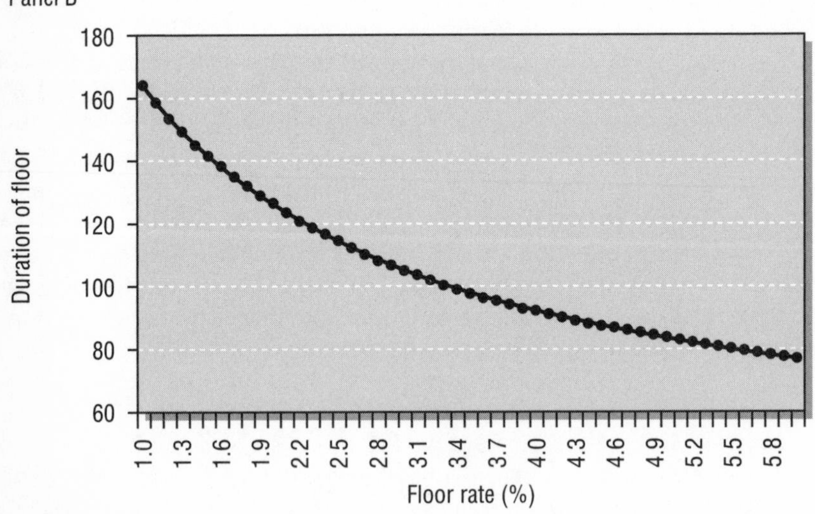

FIGURE 8.3 Panel A Plots the Duration of Cap as a Function of the Cap Rate. Panel B Plots the Duration of Floor as a Function of the Floor Rate. *Note:* The benchmark parameters are: Cap rate = 9 percent; Floor rate = 3 percent; the Instantaenous interest rate = 6 percent; the Forward rate volatility = 20 percent.

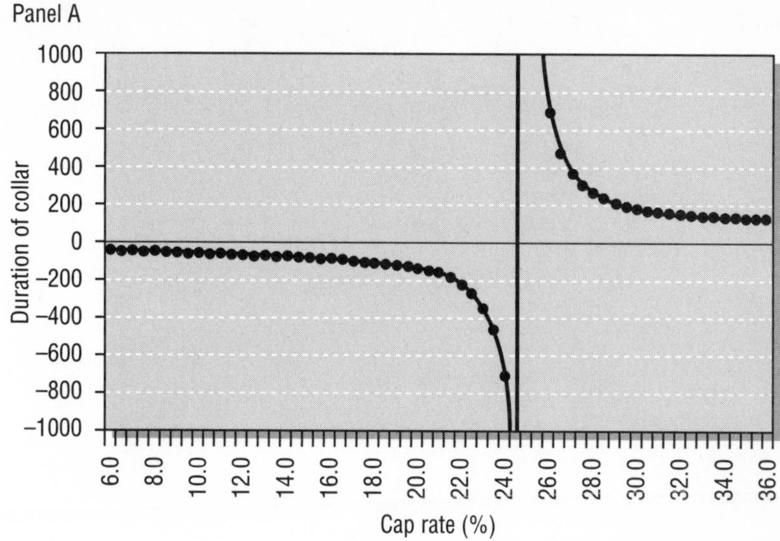

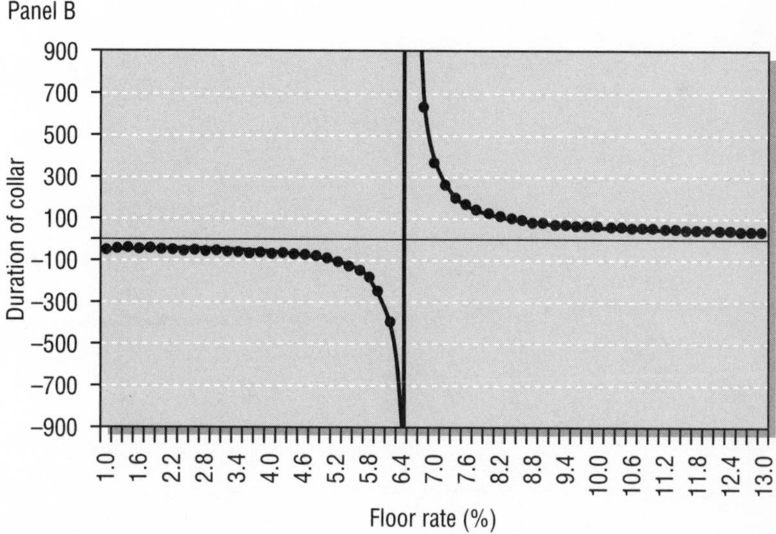

FIGURE 8.4 Panel A Plots the Duration of Collar as a Function of the Cap Rate. Panel B Plots the Duration of Collar as a Function of the Floor Rate.
Note: The benchmark parameters are: Cap rate = 9 percent; Floor rate = 3 percent; the Instantaenous interest rate = 6 percent; the Forward rate volatility = 20 percent.

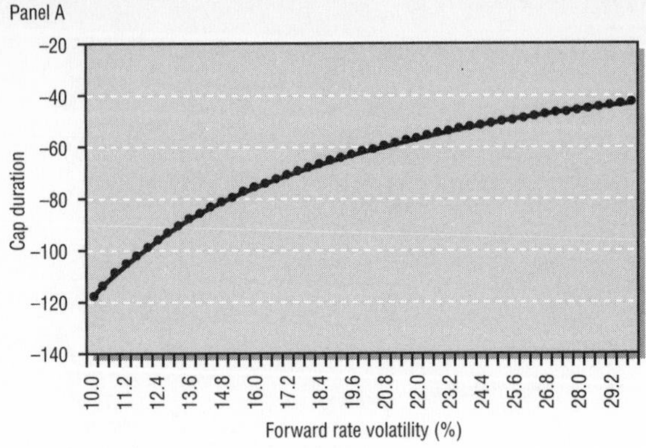

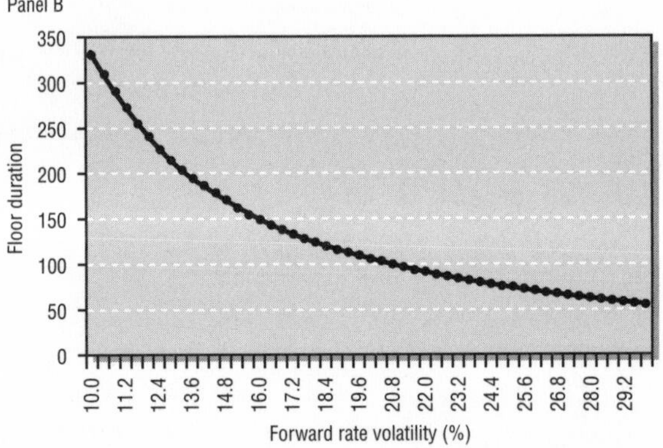

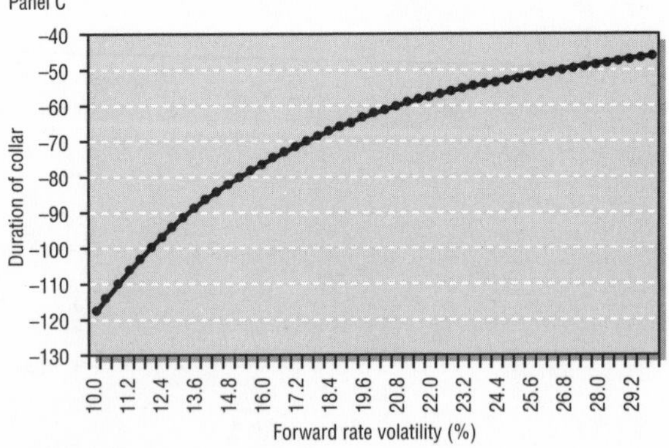

FIGURE 8.5 Panels A, B, and C Plot the Durations of Cap, Floor, and Collar, Respectively, as a Function of the Forward Rate Volatility.
Note: The benchmark parameters are: Cap rate = 9 percent; Floor rate = 3 percent; the Instantaenous interest rate = 6 percent; the Forward rate volatility = 20 percent.

coefficients, the collar duration jumps from negative infinity to positive infinity at that cap rate. Similar arguments apply to the pattern of the collar duration with respect to the floor rate.

Figure 8.5 shows that the magnitude of durations of all caps, floors, and collars decrease with forward rate volatility. This is because, as the forward rate volatility goes up, the options become less out-of-the-money (or more in-the money), and the options have less leverage.

Figure 8.6 on page 260 shows how the durations of caps, floors, and collars change with the instantaneous interest rate. As interest rate increases, the cap becomes less out-of-the-money (or more in-the-money). Again, the less leverage makes the magnitude of the cap duration decrease. For the floor, as interest rate increases, it becomes more out-of-the-money, and the high leverage increases the floor duration, initially. However, as interest rates rise, so does the interest rate volatility since volatility increases with the interest rates under the LIBOR market model. Higher volatility makes the duration of the floor decrease. Hence, even though floor duration rises initially, as interest rates increase beyond a certain level, the floor duration falls due to the high volatility effect.

As in Figure 8.4, the collar duration follows a complex pattern in Figure 8.6. At those interest rates at which the collar price reaches zero, the collar duration changes from positive infinity to negative infinity.

Figure 8.7 Panel A on page 261 shows how the duration of the floater changes with the cap rate and the floor rate. The three-dimensional surface shows that the magnitude of the floater duration decreases with the cap rate but increases with the floor rate. Under extreme values of the cap rate and the floor rate (e.g., the cap rate of 16 percent, and the floor rate of 1 percent), the floater with a collar should be similar to a regular floater. Under these extreme values, the duration of the floater with a collar equals 0.5389 years, which is close to the duration of the regular floater of 0.5 years. On the other hand, when the cap rate and the floor rate are almost equal (e.g., both the cap rate and the floor rate are 6 percent), the floater with a collar should act like a fixed rate bond. In this scenario, the duration of the floater with a collar equals 4.3963 years, which is close to the duration of the 6 percent coupon bond equal to 4.3830 years. Figure 8.7 Panel B shows that the magnitude of the duration of the floater with a collar increases as interest rate volatility increases. Figure 8.7 Panel C shows that the magnitude of the duration of the floater first decreases and then increases with the instantaneous interest rate.

Finally, Figure 8.8 on page 262 shows how the duration of the swap with a collar changes with the variation in the underlying parameter values. The swap duration is the weighted average of the fixed rate bond duration and the duration of the floater with an embedded collar. Figure 8.8 Panel A

Panel A

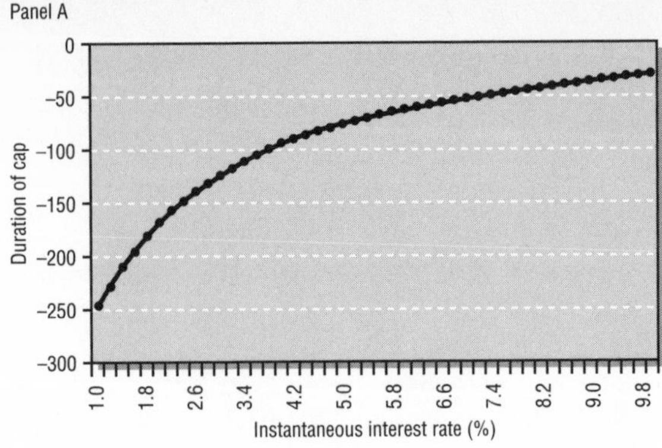

Panel B

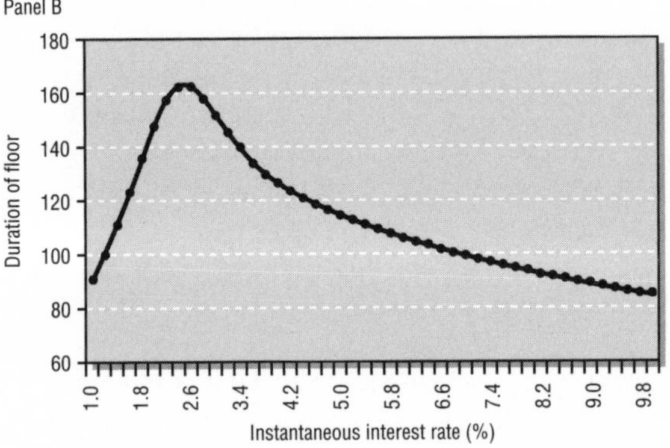

Panel C

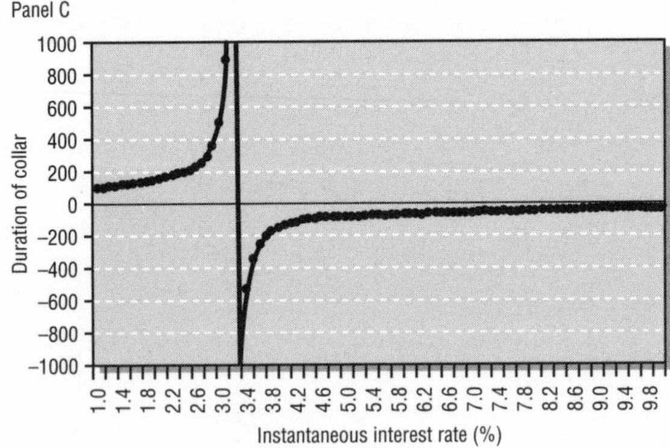

FIGURE 8.6 Panels A, B, and C Plot the Durations of Cap, Floor, and Collar, Respectively, as a Function of the Instantaneous Interest Rate.

Note: The benchmark parameters are: Cap rate = 9 percent; Floor rate = 3 percent; the Instantaenous interest rate = 6 percent; the Forward rate volatility = 20 percent.

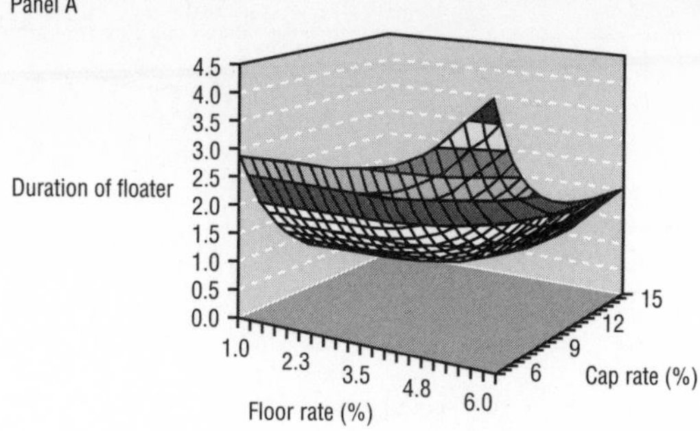

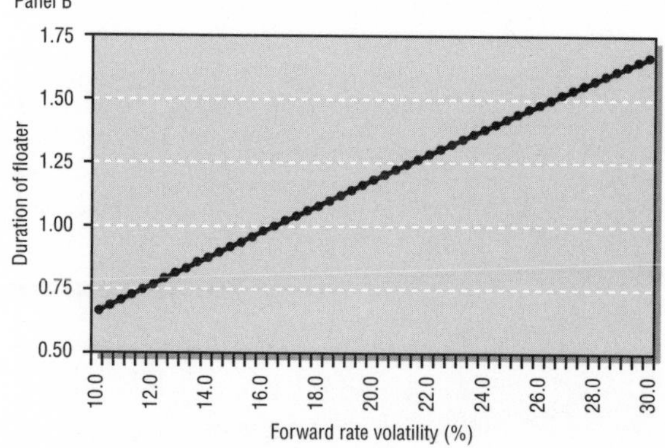

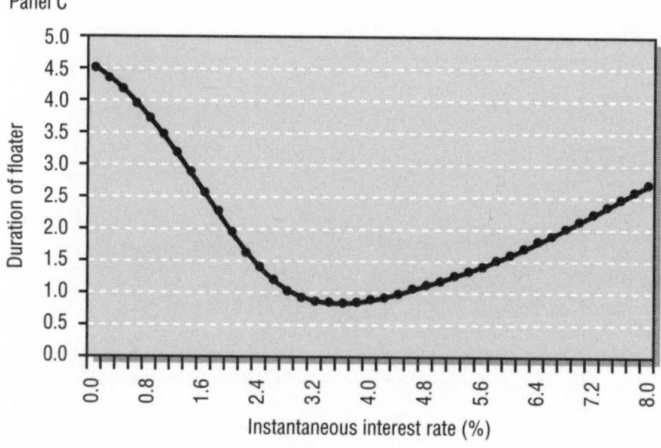

FIGURE 8.7 Panel A Plots the Duration of Floater as a Function of the Cap Rate and the Floor Rate. Panel B Plots the Duration of a Floater as a Function of the Forward Rate Volatility. Panel C Plots the Duration of a Floater as a Function of the Instantaneous Interest Rate.

Note: The benchmark parameters are: Cap rate = 9 percent; Floor rate = 3 percent; the Instantaenous interest rate = 6 percent; the Forward rate volatility = 20 percent.

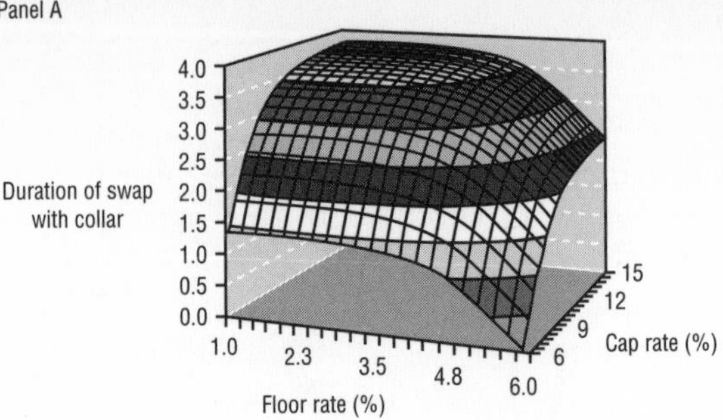

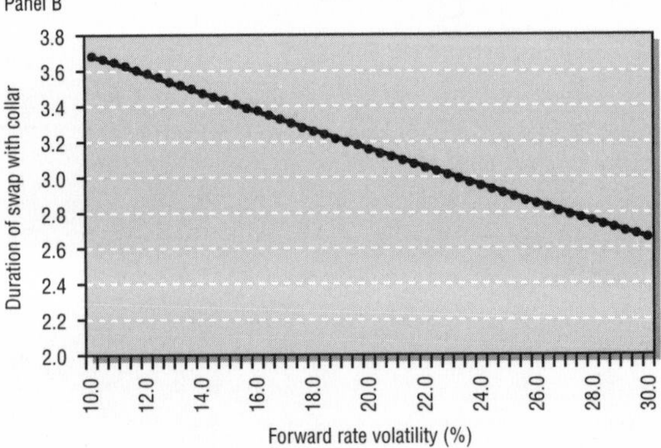

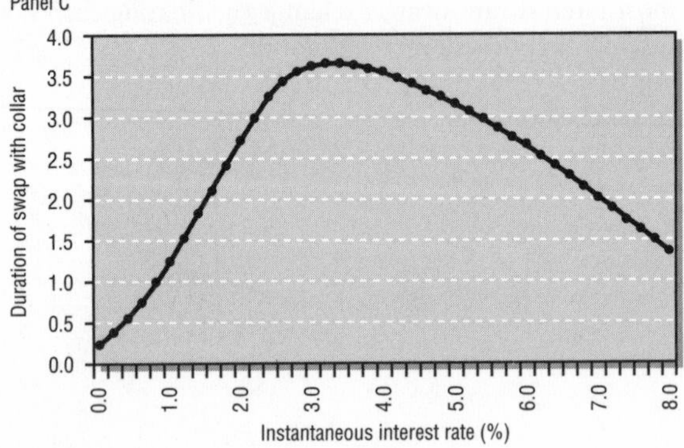

FIGURE 8.8 Panel A Plots the Duration of Swap with Collar as a Function of the Cap Rate and the Floor Rate. Panel B Plots the Duration of Swap with Collar as a Function of the Forward Rate Volatility. Panel C Plots the Duration of Swap with Collar as a Function of the Instantaneous Interest Rate.

Note: The benchmark parameters are: Cap rate = 9 percent; Floor rate = 3 percent; the Instantaenous interest rate = 6 percent; the Forward rate volatility = 20 percent.

shows that the magnitude of the swap duration increases with the cap rate, and decreases with the floor rate. Under extreme values of the cap rate and the floor rate, the swap duration is much closer to the fixed rate bond duration (in our calculation, with the cap rate at 16 percent and the floor rate at 1 percent, the swap duration is 3.8174 years while the duration of the corresponding fixed rate bond is 4.3713 years). This is because with extreme cap and floor rates, the floater with the embedded collar is close to being a regular floater whose duration is very small. When the cap rate and the floor rate are almost equal, the swap duration is close to zero since the floater with the embedded collar behaves like a fixed rate bond whose duration is almost canceled out with the duration of the other fixed rate bond (in our calculation, with both cap rate and floor rate at 6 percent, the swap duration is 0.0071 years). Figure 8.8 Panel B on page 262 shows that the magnitude of the swap duration decreases with the interest rate volatility. Figure 8.8 Panel C on page 262 shows that the magnitude of the swap duration first increases then decreases with the instantaneous short rate.

NOTES

1. See the quarterly report on http://www.bis.org/publ/otc_hy0405.pdf.
2. In reality, most interest rate swaps exchange the floating cash flows every quarter, and the fixed cash flows every six months.
3. The duration of a floating rate bond is very short and equals the date to next reset, ignoring the effects of default risk. An expression for the duration of a default-free floating rate bond is derived later in this chapter.
4. Even constant volatility for any specific forward rate is not required, as using deterministically changing volatility also results in a formula similar to that given by Black (1976).
5. The forward rate volatility can also be made deterministic. See note 4.
6. See the second volume of this series for more details on how equation 8.24 is obtained under the forward measure, and a theoretical derivation of the LIBOR market model.

CHAPTER 9

Key Rate Durations with VaR Analysis

Recently, a new class of models called the *key rate durations* have become popular among practitioners. Similar to the duration vector models given in Chapters 4 and 5, key rate durations can manage interest rate risk exposure arising from arbitrary nonparallel shifts in the term structure of interest rates. The duration vector models hedge against the shape changes in the term structure of interest rates (such as, changes in the height, slope, curvature), while the key rate durations hedge against the changes in a finite number of key interest rates that proxy for the shape changes in the entire term structure.

The key rate duration model describes the shifts in the term structure as a discrete vector representing the changes in the *key* zero-coupon rates of various maturities.[1] Interest rate changes at other maturities are derived from these values via linear interpolation. Key rate durations are then defined as the sensitivity of the portfolio value to the given key rates at different points along the term structure. These duration measures can be used in decomposing portfolio returns, identifying interest rate risk exposure, designing active trading strategies, or implementing passive portfolio strategies such as portfolio immunization and index replication.

Similar to the duration vector models, an appealing feature of the key rate model is that it does not require a *stationary* covariance structure of interest rate changes (unless performing a value at risk or VaR analysis). Hence, it doesn't matter whether the correlations between changes in the interest rates of different maturities increase or decrease or even whether these changes are positively or negatively correlated. Also, the model allows for any number of key rates, and therefore, interest rate risk can be modeled and hedged to a high degree of accuracy.

However, unlike the duration vector models, which require at most three to five duration measures, the number of key rate durations to be used and the corresponding choice of key rates remain quite arbitrary under the key rate model. For example, Ho (1992) proposes as many as 11 key rate durations to effectively hedge against interest rate risk. Further, unlike the duration vector model, where the higher order duration measures serve as linear as well as nonlinear risk measures (e.g., $D(2)$ simultaneously gives the linear exposure to slope shifts, as well as nonlinear exposure to height shifts), the key rate durations give only the linear exposures to the key rates. To measure nonlinear exposures to the key rates, key rate convexity measures are required. Hedging against a large number of key rate durations and convexities, implies large long and short positions in the portfolio, which can make this approach somewhat expensive in terms of the transaction costs associated with portfolio construction and rebalancing.

KEY RATE CHANGES

The basic idea behind the key rate model is that any smooth change in the term structure of zero-coupon yields can be represented as a vector of changes in a number of properly chosen key rates. That is:

$$TSIR\ shift = \left(\Delta y(t_1),\ \Delta y(t_2),\ \ldots,\ \Delta y(t_m)\right) \tag{9.1}$$

where $y(t_i)$ is the zero-coupon rate for term t_i and $y(t_1), y(t_2), \ldots, y(t_m)$ define the set of m key rates. The changes in all other interest rates are approximated by linear interpolation of the changes in the adjacent key rates. Thus, the shift in the term structure is approximated by a piecewise linear function of the changes in the m key rates.[2] The linear interpolation is performed in two steps:

1. Define the linear contribution $s(t, t_i)$ made by the change in the ith key rate, $\Delta y(t_i)$, to the change in a given zero-coupon rate $\Delta y(t)$, as:

$$s(t,\ t_1) = \begin{cases} \Delta y(t_1) & t < t_1 \\ \Delta y(t_1)\dfrac{t_2 - t}{t_2 - t_1} & t_1 \le t \le t_2 \\ 0 & t > t_2 \end{cases}$$

$$s(t,\ t_i) = \begin{cases} 0 & t < t_{i-1} \\ \Delta y(t_i)\dfrac{t - t_{i-1}}{t_i - t_{i-1}} & t_{i-1} \le t \le t_i \\ \Delta y(t_i)\dfrac{t_{i+1} - t}{t_{i+1} - t_i} & t_i \le t \le t_{i+1} \\ 0 & t > t_{i+1} \end{cases} \tag{9.2}$$

for $i = 2, 3, \ldots, m-1$, and

$$s(t,\ t_m) = \begin{cases} 0 & t < t_{m-1} \\ \Delta y(t_m)\dfrac{t - t_{m-1}}{t_m - t_{m-1}} & t_{m-1} \le t \le t_m \\ \Delta y(t_m) & t > t_m \end{cases}$$

2. Add up the linear contributions $s(t, t_i)$ for $i = 1, 2, \ldots, m$, to obtain the change in the given zero-coupon rate $\Delta y(t)$, as:

$$\Delta y(t) = s(t,\ t_1) + s(t,\ t_2) + \cdots + s(t,\ t_m) \tag{9.3}$$

Using the definition of $s(t, t_i)$ in equation 9.2, only two adjacent terms on the right side of the equation 9.3 can be nonzero for a given maturity t. This is because for a specific maturity t, the change in the zero-coupon rate $\Delta y(t)$ is obtained via linear interpolation of the changes in the two surrounding key rates.

Figure 9.1 shows the magnitudes of $s(t, t_i)$ under three cases, when $i = 1$, $i = j$ (for any given value of $j = 2, 3, \ldots, m - 1$), and $i = m$, consistent with equation 9.2 given previously.

Figure 9.2 shows the magnitudes of $s(t, t_i)$ under all m cases (i.e., $i = 1, 2, \ldots, m$) consistent with equation 9.2. Figure 9.2 gives a collection of "pyramid" shifts, which peaks at the specific key rate shift and which overlaps with both the preceding and the following pyramid shifts. The overlap is necessary because the changes in zero-coupon rates that are in between

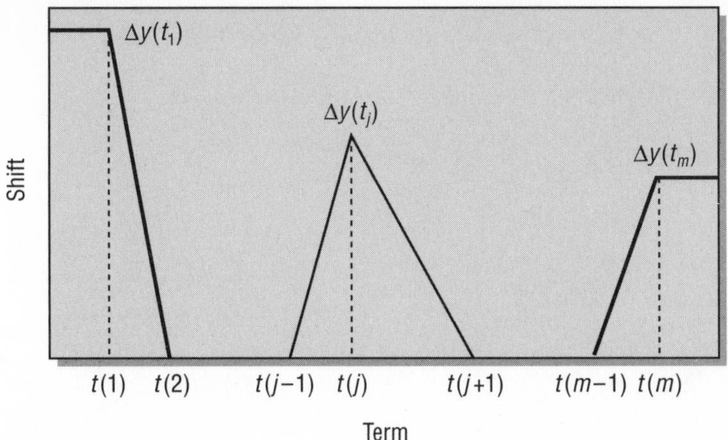

FIGURE 9.1 Linear Contributions of the Key Rate Shifts

any two key rates are obtained by a linear interpolation of the changes in those two key rates.

The sum of the key rate shifts along the maturity range leads to a piecewise linear approximation for the shift in the term structure. This approximation given by equation 9.3, together with an initial term structure gives the new term structure as shown in Figure 9.3.

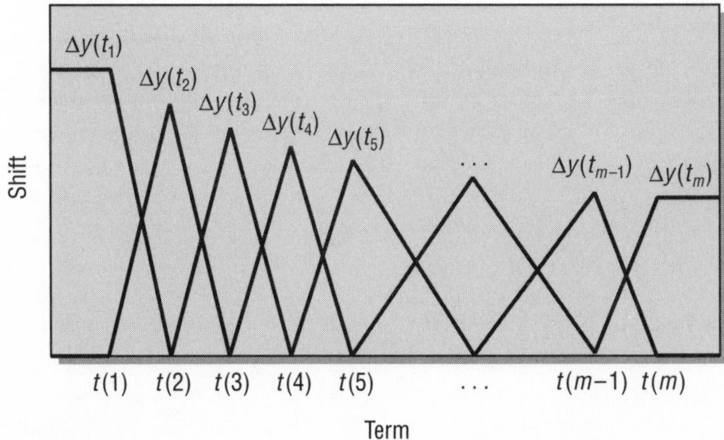

FIGURE 9.2 Collection of the Linear Contributions of the Key Rate Shifts

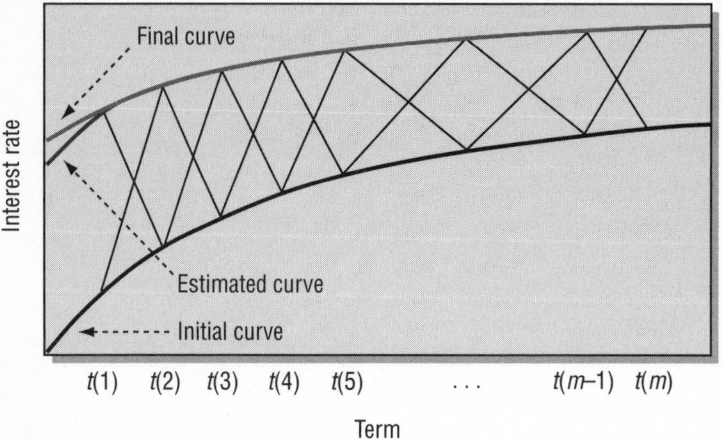

FIGURE 9.3 The Term Structure Shift

KEY RATE DURATIONS AND CONVEXITIES

This section derives key rate durations and convexities assuming that the cash flows from a bond portfolio are fixed and the maturities of the cash flows coincide with the maturities of the chosen key rates. Appendix 9.1 deals with the computation of key rate durations and convexities when cash flows are not fixed, and when the maturities of the cash flows are different from the maturities of the key rates.

Key Rate Durations

The set of key rate shifts can be used to evaluate the change in the price of any fixed-income security. In particular, an infinitesimal and instantaneous shift in a specific key rate, $\Delta y(t_i)$, results in an instantaneous price change given as:

$$\frac{\Delta P_i}{P} = -KRD(i) \times \Delta y(t_i) \tag{9.4}$$

where $KRD(i)$ is the ith key rate duration, defined as the (negative) percentage change in the price resulting from the change in the ith key rate:

$$KRD(i) = -\frac{1}{P}\frac{\partial P}{\partial y(t_i)} \tag{9.5}$$

The total price change due to all key rate changes is given as the sum of price changes resulting from individual key rate changes:

$$\Delta P = \Delta P_1 + \Delta P_2 + \cdots + \Delta P_m \tag{9.6}$$

The set of *KRD*s forms a vector of *m* risk measures, representing the first-order price sensitivities of the security to the *m* key rates:

$$KRD = \left[KRD(1) \;\; KRD(2) \ldots KRD(m)\right] \tag{9.7}$$

Since the shift in the term structure is approximated by the sum of all the key rate shifts, the total percentage change in price due to an infinitesimal shift in the term structure can be obtained as the sum of the effect of each key rate shift on the security price by substituting equation 9.4 into equation 9.6, as follows:

$$\frac{\Delta P}{P} = -\sum_{i=1}^{m} KRD(i) \times \Delta y(t_i) \tag{9.8}$$

or using matrix notation:

$$\frac{\Delta P}{P} = -KRD \times \Delta y^T \tag{9.9}$$

where $\Delta y = [\Delta y(1), \Delta y(2), \ldots, \Delta y(m)]$ is the vector of key rate changes.

Key Rate Convexities

When the shift in the term structure is noninfinitesimal, the previous framework must be extended to account for the second-order nonlinear effects of the key rate shifts. These are given as the *key rate convexities* and are defined as:

$$KRC(i, j) = KRC(j, i) = \frac{1}{P} \frac{\partial^2 P}{\partial y(t_i) \partial y(t_j)} \tag{9.10}$$

for every pair (i, j) of key rates. The set of key rate convexities can be represented by a symmetric matrix of dimension *m:*

$$KRC = \begin{bmatrix} KRC(1, 1) & KRC(1, 2) & \dots & KRC(1, m) \\ KRC(2, 1) & KRC(2, 2) & \dots & KRC(2, m) \\ \vdots & \vdots & \vdots & \vdots \\ KRC(m, 1) & KRC(m, 2) & \dots & KRC(m, m) \end{bmatrix} \tag{9.11}$$

The key rate durations and convexities of a portfolio can be obtained as the weighted average of the key rate duration and convexities of the securities in the portfolio, where the weights are defined as the proportion of each security held in the portfolio.

The percentage change in the price of a security can be approximated by a second-order Taylor series expansion using the key rate durations and convexities as follows:

$$\frac{\Delta P}{P} \approx -\sum_{i=1}^{m} KRD(i) \times \Delta y(t_i) + \frac{1}{2} \sum_{i=1}^{m} \sum_{j=1}^{m} KRC(i, j) \times \Delta y(t_i) \times \Delta y(t_j) \tag{9.12}$$

Equation 9.12 can be rewritten as:

$$\frac{\Delta P}{P} \approx -KRD \times \Delta y^T + \frac{1}{2} \Delta y \times KRC \times \Delta y^T \tag{9.13}$$

When the term structure exhibits a parallel shift, all key rates shift by the same amount and equation 9.12 can be rewritten as:

$$\frac{\Delta P}{P} \approx -D\Delta y + \frac{1}{2} CON\Delta y^2 \tag{9.14}$$

where

$$D = \sum_{i=1}^{m} KRD(i)$$

and

$$CON = \sum_{i=1}^{m} \sum_{j=1}^{m} KRC(i, j)$$

Equation 9.14 gives the familiar two-term Taylor series expansion of the bond return with continuously compounded interest rates under parallel term structure shifts (see Chapter 2). Hence, under this assumption, the key rate durations sum up to give the traditional duration, and key rate convexities sum up to give the traditional convexity.

TABLE 9.1 Description of the Bonds

Bond #	Face Value ($)	Maturity (years)	Annual Coupon Rate (%)
1	1,000	1	10
2	1,000	2	10
3	1,000	3	10
4	1,000	4	10
5	1,000	5	10

Example 9.1 Consider five bonds 1, 2, 3, 4, and 5, all of which have a $1,000 face value and a 10 percent annual coupon rate, but different maturities as shown in Table 9.1.

Also assume that the one-, two-, three-, four-, and five-year continuously compounded zero-coupon rates define the set of five key rates and are given as:

$$y(1) = 5\% \qquad y(2) = 5.5\%$$
$$y(3) = 5.75\% \qquad y(4) = 5.9\%$$
$$y(5) = 6\%$$

Consider a bond portfolio with a cash flow CF_i at time t_i (for $i = 1, 2, \ldots, N$) given as:

$$P = \sum_{i=1}^{N} \frac{CF_i}{e^{y(t_i)\times t_i}} \tag{9.15}$$

The first and second partial derivatives of the price with respect to the key rates are:

$$\begin{aligned} \frac{\partial P}{\partial y(t_i)} &= -\frac{CF_i \times t_i}{e^{t_i \times y(t_i)}} \quad \text{for all } i = 1, 2, \ldots N \\ \frac{\partial^2 P}{\partial y(t_i)\partial y(t_j)} &= 0 \quad \text{for all } i \neq j, \text{ and} \\ \frac{\partial^2 P}{\partial y(t_i)^2} &= \frac{CF_i \times t_i^2}{e^{t_i \times y(t_i)}} \quad \text{for all } i = 1, 2, \ldots N \end{aligned} \tag{9.16}$$

Key rate durations and convexities are defined as:

TABLE 9.2 Key Rate Durations and Convexities for the Five Bonds

	Bond 1	Bond 2	Bond 3	Bond 4	Bond 5
Price	\$1,046.35	\$1,080.54	\$1,110.42	\$1,137.62	\$1,162.74
KRD(1)	1.000	0.088	0.086	0.084	0.082
KRD(2)	0.000	1.824	0.161	0.157	0.154
KRD(3)	0.000	0.000	2.501	0.222	0.217
KRD(4)	0.000	0.000	0.000	3.055	0.272
KRD(5)	0.000	0.000	0.000	0.000	3.504
KRC(1,1)	1.000	0.088	0.086	0.084	0.082
KRC(2,2)	0.000	3.648	0.323	0.315	0.308
KRC(3,3)	0.000	0.000	7.503	0.666	0.651
KRC(4,4)	0.000	0.000	0.000	12.219	1.087
KRC(5,5)	0.000	0.000	0.000	0.000	17.521
D	1.000	1.912	2.748	3.518	4.229
C	1.000	3.736	7.911	13.283	19.649

$$\begin{aligned} KRD(i) &= \frac{1}{P}\frac{CF_i \times t_i}{e^{t_i \times y(t_i)}} \\ KRC(i, j) &= 0, \quad i \neq j \\ KRC(i, i) &= \frac{1}{P}\frac{CF_i \times t_i^2}{e^{t_i \times y(t_i)}} \end{aligned} \tag{9.17}$$

Using these formulas for the five bonds in Table 9.1 gives the results shown in Table 9.2. The two last rows of the table give the values of traditional duration and convexity, which correspond to the sum of the partial measures.

Now consider a \$10,000 portfolio with equal investments of \$2,000 in each of the five bonds. The proportion of investment in each bond is 0.2 and the key rate duration measures of the portfolio are computed as:

$$KRD_{PORT}(1) = 0.2 \times 1 + 0.2 \times 0.088 + 0.2 \times 0.086 + 0.2 \times 0.084 + 0.2 \times 0.082 = 0.268$$

$$KRD_{PORT}(2) = 0.2 \times 0 + 0.2 \times 1.824 + 0.2 \times 0.161 + 0.2 \times 0.157 + 0.2 \times 0.154 = 0.459$$

$$KRD_{PORT}(3) = 0.2 \times 0 + 0.2 \times 0 + 0.2 \times 2.501 + 0.2 \times 0.222 + 0.2 \times 0.217 = 0.588$$

$$KRD_{PORT}(4) = 0.2 \times 0 + 0.2 \times 0 + 0.2 \times 0 + 0.2 \times 3.055 + 0.2 \times 0.272 = 0.665$$

$$KRD_{PORT}(5) = 0.2 \times 0 + 0.2 \times 0 + 0.2 \times 0 + 0.2 \times 0 + 0.2 \times 3.504 = 0.701$$

The traditional duration of the bond portfolio given as the sum of the five key rate durations is equal to 2.681.

RISK MEASUREMENT AND MANAGEMENT

Key rate durations give the risk profile of a fixed-income security across the whole term structure. Figure 9.4 shows the typical key rate duration profile of a coupon-bearing bond. The key rate durations first increase and then decrease, except the key rate duration corresponding to the maturity term is the highest (due to the lump sum payment at bond maturity). This pattern results from two offsetting factors. The increase in the cash flow maturity increases the key rate duration, while a higher discount due to the longer maturity decreases the present value of the cash flow, which decreases the key rate duration.

Using the key rate durations, a portfolio manager can identify the interest rate risk profile of the portfolio. For example, a ladder portfolio has similar key rate durations across the maturity range and thus represents no specific bets on the shape of the term structure movements. A barbell (bullet) portfolio has high (low) key rate durations corresponding to the short and long interest rates and low (high) durations for intermediate rates, and so it is preferred if the short and the long rates fall more (less) than the intermediate rates.

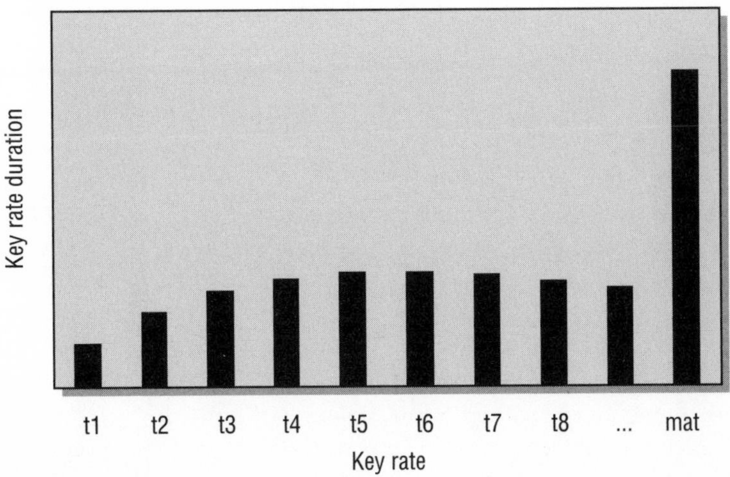

FIGURE 9.4 Key Rate Duration Profile of a Coupon-Bearing Bond

TABLE 9.3 Proportions Invested in Each Bond and Key Rate Durations of the Ladder, Barbell, and Bullet Portfolios

	Ladder	Barbell	Bullet
Bond 1	0.2	0.479	0.000
Bond 2	0.2	0.000	0.521
Bond 3	0.2	0.000	0.000
Bond 4	0.2	0.000	0.479
Bond 5	0.2	0.521	0.000
KRD(1)	0.268	0.522	0.086
KRD(2)	0.459	0.080	1.025
KRD(3)	0.588	0.113	0.106
KRD(4)	0.665	0.141	1.464
KRD(5)	0.701	1.825	0.000

Example 9.2 Reconsider the $10,000 initial investment equally distributed in the five bonds in Example 9.1. This is a ladder portfolio with a traditional duration equal to 2.681 years. Also consider two portfolios with the same initial market values and traditional durations, but one with a bullet structure and the other with a barbell structure. The barbell portfolio contains bonds maturing in years 1 and 5 and the bullet portfolio contains bonds maturing in years 2 and 4.

To determine the proportions invested in the bonds in each portfolio, we solve the following system of linear equations:

$$p_{short}D_{short} + p_{long}D_{long} = 2.681$$
$$p_{short} + p_{long} = 1$$

where p_{short} and p_{long} are the proportions invested in the short-term and the long-term bonds and D_{short} and D_{long} are the bonds' traditional durations. The proportions invested in each bond and the key rate durations of each portfolio are summarized in Table 9.3.

Figure 9.5 displays the key rate duration profiles of the three portfolios. Although the sums of the key rate durations for the three portfolios are identical (2.681 years), the interest rate exposures of the three portfolios are markedly different. Consequently, the portfolios will yield significantly different returns if the term structure exhibits nonparallel shifts.

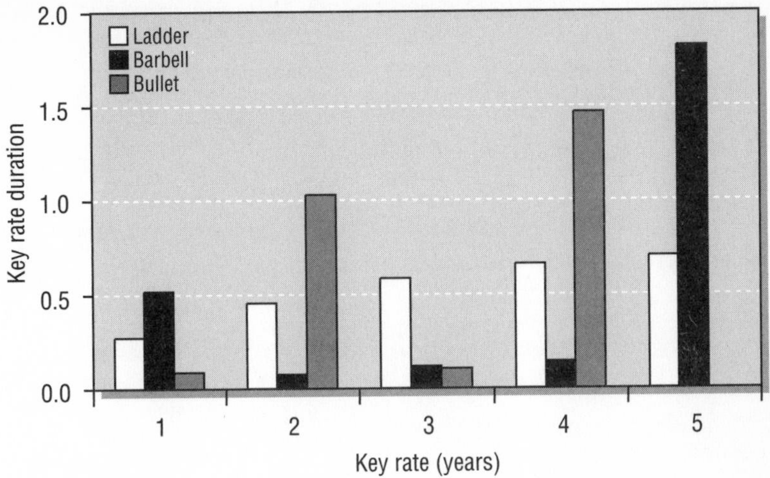

FIGURE 9.5 Key Rate Duration Profiles

Consider an instantaneous shift in the term structure given in Example 9.1 such that the one-year key rate increases 50 basis points, the two-year key rate increases 20 basis points, the four-year rate decreases 10 basis points, and the five-year rate decreases 20 basis points. This means that the term structure rotates around the three-year rate, as shown in Figure 9.6.

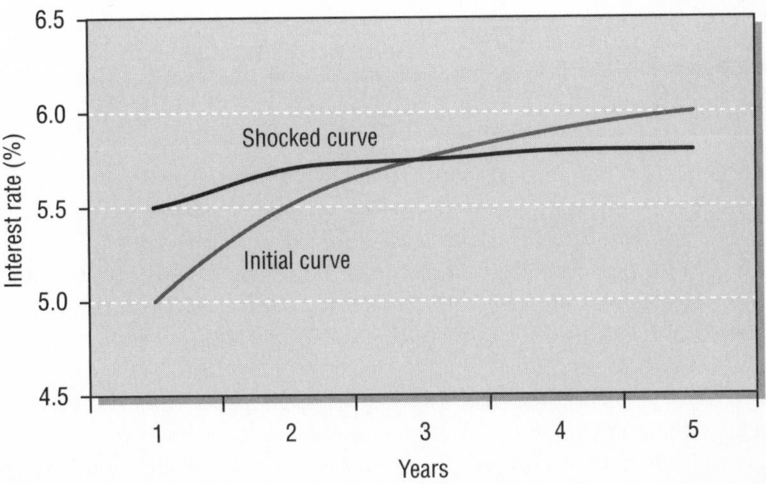

FIGURE 9.6 Instantaneous Shift in the Term Structure of Zero-Coupon Rates

Given this shift in the term structure, bonds 1 through 5 yield instantaneous returns given as:

$$R_1 = -0.499\% \quad R_2 = -0.408\% \quad R_3 = -0.075\%$$
$$R_4 = 0.233\% \quad R_5 = 0.660\%$$

Applying the weights given in Table 9.3 to the above returns, we obtain the following returns on the three portfolios:

$$\begin{aligned}
R_{Ladder} &= 0.2 \times (-0.499) + 0.2 \times (-0.408) + 0.2 \times (-0.075) + 0.2 \times 0.233 \\
&\quad + 0.2 \times 0.660 = -0.018\% \\
R_{Barbell} &= 0.479 \times (-0.499) + 0.521 \times 0.660 = 0.105\% \\
R_{Bullet} &= 0.521 \times (-0.408) + 0.479 \times 0.233 = -0.101\%
\end{aligned}$$

The returns on the portfolios can also be estimated from the Taylor series approximation given in equation 9.12 using the portfolios' key rate durations in Table 9.3. The estimated returns are computed as:

$$\begin{aligned}
R_{Ladder} &\cong -0.268 \times 0.5 - 0.459 \times 0.2 - 0.588 \times 0 - 0.665 \times (-0.1) - 0.701 \\
&\quad \times (-0.2) = -0.019\% \\
R_{Barbell} &\cong -0.522 \times 0.5 - 0.080 \times 0.2 - 0.113 \times 0 - 0.141 \times (-0.1) - 1.825 \\
&\quad \times (-0.2) = 0.102\% \\
R_{Bullet} &\cong -0.086 \times 0.5 - 1.025 \times 0.2 - 0.106 \times 0 - 1.464 \times (-0.1) - 0 \\
&\quad \times (-0.2) = -0.102\%
\end{aligned}$$

The estimated values are very close to the true instantaneous returns given before. The key rate duration profiles in Figure 9.5 explain the source of the returns. The ladder portfolio is the least affected by the shock in the term structure because the losses derived from the increase in the short-term rates are nearly cancelled out by the profits derived from the decrease in the longer-term rates. The barbell portfolio gives the highest return because of its high exposure to the five-year rate. Finally, the bullet portfolio combines gains from the decrease in the four-year rate with higher losses from the upward movement of the one- and two-year rates and thus yields a negative return.

Key rate durations and convexities can be used in a variety of portfolio strategies such as index replication, immunization, and active trading strategies. For example, to create a portfolio that replicates a given index, the manager must equate the key rate measures of the portfolio to those of the index. Having the same key rate measures, both portfolios will have the same interest rate exposure and thus will yield the same return.

To immunize the equity value of a financial institution from an arbitrary shift in the term structure, the manager can eliminate key rate duration gaps by applying the following constraints:

$$V^A KRD(i)_{ASSETS} = V^L KRD(i)_{LIABILITIES} \quad i = 1, 2, \ldots, n \tag{9.18}$$

where V^A is the present value of the assets and V^L the present value of the liabilities.

To immunize a portfolio over a given planning horizon, the portfolio's key rate durations have to be set equal to the key rate durations of a hypothetical zero-coupon bond maturing at the horizon date. Setting H as the horizon date and using the key rate, $y(H)$, for that term, the constraints on the key rate durations of the portfolio are defined as:

$$KRD(i)_{PORT} = \begin{cases} H & if\ t_i = H \\ 0 & else \end{cases} \tag{9.19}$$

Finally, managers can take active positions by determining the portfolio's key rate exposures across the term structure and choosing which interest rate changes to hedge against, and which interest rates to speculate on, based upon some interest rate forecasting model.

Example 9.3 Suppose a manager desires to create an immunized portfolio over a planning horizon of four years using the model with five key rates. Five key rates lead to five key rate durations for each bond. Hence, five immunization constraints are required to match the five key rate durations of the portfolios to the five key rate durations of a hypothetical zero-coupon bond maturing in four years. Plus, another constraint is needed to set the sum of the proportions invested in all bonds to 100 percent. This requires six bonds in order to equate the number of constraints to the number of bonds.

Consider the bonds 1, 2, 3, 4, and 5 in Example 9.1 and a new bond 6. Bond 6 is a five-year zero-coupon bond with a face value of $1,000, and a market price of \$740.82 computed using the term structure given in Example 9.1. The key rate durations of bond 6 are:

$$KRD_6(1) = KRD_6(2) = KRD_6(3) = KRD_6(4) = 0, \text{ and } KRD_6(5) = 5 \tag{9.20}$$

The six immunization constraints can be written using matrix notation as follows:

$$\begin{bmatrix} KRD_1(1) & KRD_2(1) & \dots & KRD_6(1) \\ KRD_1(2) & KRD_2(2) & \dots & KRD_6(2) \\ KRD_1(3) & KRD_2(3) & \dots & KRD_6(3) \\ KRD_1(4) & KRD_2(4) & \dots & KRD_6(4) \\ KRD_1(5) & KRD_2(5) & \dots & KRD_6(5) \\ 1 & 1 & \dots & 1 \end{bmatrix} \times \begin{bmatrix} p_1 \\ p_2 \\ p_3 \\ p_4 \\ p_5 \\ p_6 \end{bmatrix} = \begin{bmatrix} 0 \\ 0 \\ 0 \\ 4 \\ 0 \\ 1 \end{bmatrix}$$

where $p_1, \ p_2, \dots, p_6$ are the proportions of investment in each of the six bonds.

Premultiplying both sides of the above equation by the inverse of the first matrix, we obtain the proportions to be invested in the different bonds as follows:

$$\begin{bmatrix} p_1 \\ p_2 \\ p_3 \\ p_4 \\ p_5 \\ p_6 \end{bmatrix} = \begin{bmatrix} KRD_1(1) & KRD_2(1) & \dots & KRD_6(1) \\ KRD_1(2) & KRD_2(2) & \dots & KRD_6(2) \\ KRD_1(3) & KRD_2(3) & \dots & KRD_6(3) \\ KRD_1(4) & KRD_2(4) & \dots & KRD_6(4) \\ KRD_1(5) & KRD_2(5) & \dots & KRD_6(5) \\ 1 & 1 & \dots & 1 \end{bmatrix}^{-1} \times \begin{bmatrix} 0 \\ 0 \\ 0 \\ 4 \\ 0 \\ 1 \end{bmatrix}$$

Substituting the values of the key rate durations of bonds 1 through bond 5, from Example 9.1, the key rate durations of bond 6 from equation 9.20, and doing the matrix calculations, we obtain the following solution:

$$p_1 = -0.012148 \quad p_2 = -0.013799 \quad p_3 = -0.015599$$
$$p_4 = 1.422847 \quad p_5 = -1.274590 \quad p_6 = 0.893289$$

Multiplying these proportions by the portfolio value of \$10,000 gives short positions in the amounts of \$121.48, \$137.99, \$155.99, and \$12,745.90, in bonds 1, 2, 3, and 5, respectively. Adding the proceeds from the short positions to the initial portfolio value of \$10,000, the investments in bonds 4 and 6 must be \$14,228.47 and \$8,932.89, respectively. Dividing these amounts by the respective bond prices, the immunized portfolio is composed of –0.116 number of bonds 1, –0.128 number of bonds 2, –0.140 number of bonds 3, 12.507 number of bonds 4, –10.962 number of bonds 5, and 12.058 number of bonds 6.

KEY RATE DURATIONS AND VALUE AT RISK ANALYSIS

VaR analysis can also be implemented in a simple manner using key rate durations. VaR is defined as the maximum loss in the portfolio value at a given level of confidence over a given horizon. Given a multivariate normal distribution for the key rate changes, the portfolio return is distributed normally under a linear approximation, with a mean equal to:

$$\mu_R = \sum_{i=1}^{M} KRD(i) \times \mu_{\Delta y(i)} \tag{9.21}$$

and variance equal to:

$$\sigma_R^2 = \sum_{i=1}^{M} \sum_{j=1}^{M} KRD(i) \times KRD(j) \times cov\left[\Delta y(i), \Delta y(j)\right] \tag{9.22}$$

where $\mu_{\Delta y(i)}$ is the mean change in the ith key rate and $cov[\Delta y(i), \Delta y(j)]$ is the covariance between changes in the ith and the jth key rates.

Let the dollar return on the portfolio be given as $R \times V_0$, where V_0 is the initial market value of the portfolio. Then, the VaR of the portfolio at a c percent confidence level is given as:[3]

$$P\left[R \times V_0 \le -VaR\right] = 1 - c \tag{9.23}$$

Using the normal distribution:

$$P\left[R \le \mu_R + z_{1-c}\sigma_R\right] = P\left[R \le \mu_R - z_c\sigma_R\right] = 1 - c \tag{9.24}$$

where z_{1-c} is the $1 - c$ percentile of a standard normal distribution and z_c is the c percentile.

Combining equations 9.23 and 9.24, the VaR of the portfolio at a c percent confidence level is given as:

$$VaR_c = -V_0(\mu_R - z_c\sigma_R) \tag{9.25}$$

If the holding period of the VaR is very small, we may ignore the expected return and express VaR simply as:

$$VaR_c = V_0 z_c \sigma_R \tag{9.26}$$

Substituting equation 9.22 in equation 9.26, we obtain the following analytic solution to VaR:

$$VaR_c = V_0 z_c \sqrt{\sum_{i=1}^{M}\sum_{j=1}^{M} KRD(i) \times KRD(j) \times cov\left[\Delta y(i),\ \Delta y(j)\right]} \tag{9.27}$$

The VaR solution given in equation 9.27 does not apply when key rate changes are not normally distributed, or when a second-order Taylor approximation to portfolio return is considered. The VaR is then computed by first simulating changes in the key rates using a Monte Carlo simulation or other related techniques. The set of random values generated together with the key rate durations and convexities are then used to provide the entire distribution of price changes (or returns). Finally, the VaR is obtained directly from this distribution.

Example 9.4 Reconsider the three portfolios in Example 9.2 and suppose that monthly changes in the five key rates are normally distributed with covariance matrix defined as follows:

$$Var\left(\Delta y\%\right) = \begin{bmatrix} 0.076 & 0.075 & 0.068 & 0.062 & 0.057 \\ 0.075 & 0.093 & 0.092 & 0.089 & 0.083 \\ 0.068 & 0.092 & 0.097 & 0.095 & 0.091 \\ 0.062 & 0.089 & 0.095 & 0.095 & 0.092 \\ 0.057 & 0.083 & 0.091 & 0.092 & 0.090 \end{bmatrix}$$

where $\Delta y\%$ indicates that interest rate changes are expressed as percentages.

The one-month VaR at the 95 percent and 99 percent levels for each portfolio can be computed using the following formulas in the matrix form:

$$\begin{aligned} VaR_{95} &= 10{,}000 \times 1.645 \times \sqrt{KRD_{PORT} \times Var(\Delta y) \times KRD_{PORT}^{T}} \\ VaR_{99} &= 10{,}000 \times 2.326 \times \sqrt{KRD_{PORT} \times Var(\Delta y) \times KRD_{PORT}^{T}} \end{aligned} \tag{9.28}$$

where \$10,000 is the initial market value of the portfolio, 1.645 and 2.326 are the 95th and 99th percentile of a standard normal distribution, KRD_{PORT}

TABLE 9.4 Variance of Portfolio Returns and VaR Numbers

	Ladder	Barbell	Bullet
σ_R	0.788	0.756	0.806
VaR_{95}	\$129.69	\$124.42	\$132.58
VaR_{99}	\$183.42	\$175.97	\$187.51

is the portfolio's key rate duration vector and the product indicates matrix multiplication. Note that the covariance matrix that enters in equation 9.28 refers to changes in rates expressed in decimal form, not in percentages, and hence equals the matrix $Var(\Delta y\%)$ divided by 10,000 (100×100).

Table 9.4 shows the monthly standard deviation of the portfolio returns and the VaR numbers for the three portfolios. The figures reveal that the bullet portfolio is the most risky portfolio, followed by the ladder portfolio. The bullet portfolio will lose a maximum of \$132.58 with 95 percent probability over a one-month horizon. In other words, the bullet portfolio is expected to incur a loss greater than \$132.58 in only 1 out of 20 months. The VaR numbers at the 99 percent are greater because they indicate losses that are only expected to be exceeded in 1 out of 100 months.

LIMITATIONS OF THE KEY RATE MODEL

Three limitations of the key rate models can be given as follows:

1. The choice of the key rates is arbitrary,
2. The unrealistic shapes of the individual key rate shifts, and
3. Loss of efficiency caused by not modeling the history of term structure movements.

The Choice of Key Rates

The choice of the risk factors is important when dealing with multivariate models. The key rate model, however, offers no guidance about how to make this choice. Moreover, as mentioned earlier, when the model was first introduced by Ho (1992), he recommended using as many as 11 key rates.

A natural choice of the set of key rates might consist of those rates that are used often by traders and other market professionals. For example, the set of key rates identified by RiskMetrics for the U.S. money and bond markets includes 14 unevenly spaced maturities, namely, one month, three months, six months, and 1, 2, 3, 4, 5, 7, 9, 10, 15, 20, and 30 years to maturity.

Since this number of key rates is still large, the manager could still narrow her choices based upon the maturity structure of the portfolio under consideration. For example, short-term money market managers may consider a large number of key rates at the short end of the term structure, while long-term bond portfolio managers may focus on the middle and long-term rates instead of short-term rates.

The Shape of Key Rate Shifts

Although the whole set of key rate shifts taken together allows for modeling realistic movements in the term structure, each individual key rate shift has a historically implausible shape. Each key rate shock implies the kind of forward rate saw-tooth shift shown in Figure 9.7.

To address this shortcoming, a natural choice is to focus on the forward rate curve instead of the zero-coupon curve. Johnson and Meyer (1989) first proposed this methodology and called it the *partial derivative approach* or PDA. According to the PDA, the forward rate structure is split up into many linear segments and all forward rates within each segment are assumed to change in a parallel way.

Partial durations can be then defined as the minus of the partial derivatives of the portfolio's value with respect to the changes in the individual forward rates that represent these segments, divided by the portfolio's market value. As in the key rate model, the sum of partial durations is equivalent to traditional duration because if all forward rates change by the same magnitude, then the term structure of zero-coupon rates moves in a parallel fashion.

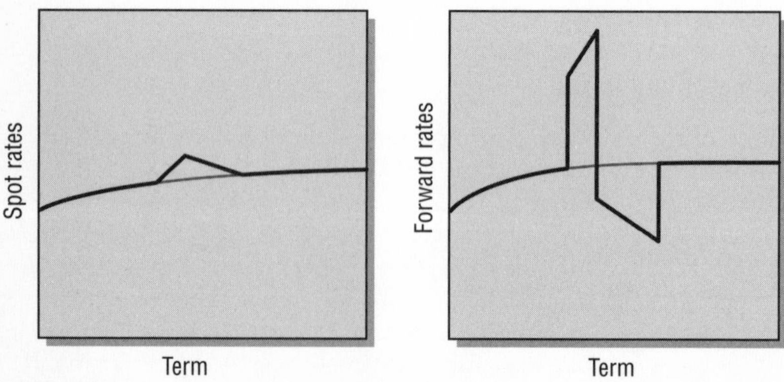

FIGURE 9.7 Key Rate Shift and Its Effect on the Forward Rate Curve

Partial durations based on forward rates can be applied in the same manner as the key rate durations for managing interest rate risk. However, the values of the partial durations are very different from those of the key rate durations. While under the key rate model each key rate only affects the present value of the cash flows around the term of the rate, under the partial duration approach each forward rate affects the present value of all cash flows occurring within or after the term of the forward rate.

To understand this, reconsider the relationship between the zero-coupon term structure and the forward rate term structure. As shown in Chapter 3, continuously compounded zero-coupon rates and instantaneous forward rates are related as:

$$y(t) = \frac{1}{t}\int_0^t f(s)ds \tag{9.29}$$

where $y(t)$ is the zero-coupon rate for term t, and $f(t)$ is the instantaneous forward rate for term t. Assuming that the forward rate intervals have a length of one-period, we obtain:

$$y(t) = \frac{1}{t}\sum_{i=1}^{t} f(i-1, i) \tag{9.30}$$

where $f(i-1, i)$ is the one-period forward rate from time $i - 1$ to i.

Equation 9.30 indicates that zero-coupon rates are simple averages of the corresponding forward rates and imply that the present value of a cash flow CF due at time t is:

$$P = \frac{CF_t}{e^{\sum_{i=1}^{t} f(i-1,i)}} \tag{9.31}$$

According to equation 9.31, the market price of the cash flow is affected by all forward rates preceding the maturity date.

Example 9.5 Reconsider the five-year, \$1,000 face value, 10 percent annual coupon bond and the one-, two-, three-, four-, and five-year continuously compounded zero-coupon rates given in Example 9.1. Setting the length of the forward period to one year, we obtain the following forward rates:

$$f(0, 1) = y(1) = 5\% \quad f(1, 2) = 6\% \quad f(2, 3) = 6.25\%$$
$$f(3, 4) = 6.35\% \quad f(4, 5) = 6.4\%$$

The present value of the bond can be calculated as follows:

$$
\begin{aligned}
P &= \frac{100}{e^{f(0,1)}} + \frac{100}{e^{f(0,1)+f(1,2)}} + \frac{100}{e^{f(0,1)+f(1,2)+f(2,3)}} + \frac{100}{e^{f(0,1)+f(1,2)+f(2,3)+f(3,4)}} + \frac{1100}{e^{f(0,1)+f(1,2)+f(2,3)+f(3,4)+f(4,5)}} \\
&= \frac{100}{e^{0.05}} + \frac{100}{e^{0.11}} + \frac{100}{e^{0.1725}} + \frac{100}{e^{0.236}} + \frac{1100}{e^{0.3}} \\
&= \$1,162.74
\end{aligned}
$$

The bond price is the same as Example 9.1. Partial durations with respect to the five forward rates are computed as follows:

$$
\begin{aligned}
PD(1) &= -\frac{1}{P}\frac{\partial P}{\partial f(0,\ 1)} \\
&= \frac{1}{P}\left[\frac{100}{e^{f(0,1)}} + \frac{100}{e^{f(0,1)+f(1,2)}} + \frac{100}{e^{f(0,1)+f(1,2)+f(2,3)}} + \frac{100}{e^{f(0,1)+f(1,2)+f(2,3)+f(3,4)}} + \frac{1100}{e^{f(0,1)+f(1,2)+f(2,3)+f(3,4)+f(4,5)}}\right] \\
&= 1
\end{aligned}
$$

$$
\begin{aligned}
PD(2) &= -\frac{1}{P}\frac{\partial P}{\partial f(1,\ 2)} \\
&= \frac{1}{P}\left[\frac{100}{e^{f(0,1)+f(1,2)}} + \frac{100}{e^{f(0,1)+f(1,2)+f(2,3)}} + \frac{100}{e^{f(0,1)+f(1,2)+f(2,3)+f(3,4)}} + \frac{1100}{e^{f(0,1)+f(1,2)+f(2,3)+f(3,4)+f(4,5)}}\right] \\
&= 0.918
\end{aligned}
$$

$$
\begin{aligned}
PD(3) &= -\frac{1}{P}\frac{\partial P}{\partial f(2,\ 3)} \\
&= \frac{1}{P}\left[\frac{100}{e^{f(0,1)+f(1,2)+f(2,3)}} + \frac{100}{e^{f(0,1)+f(1,2)+f(2,3)+f(3,4)}} + \frac{1100}{e^{f(0,1)+f(1,2)+f(2,3)+f(3,4)+f(4,5)}}\right] \\
&= 0.841
\end{aligned}
$$

$$
\begin{aligned}
PD(4) &= -\frac{1}{P}\frac{\partial P}{\partial f(3,\ 4)} \\
&= \frac{1}{P}\left[\frac{100}{e^{f(0,1)+f(1,2)+f(2,3)+f(3,4)}} + \frac{1100}{e^{f(0,1)+f(1,2)+f(2,3)+f(3,4)+f(4,5)}}\right] \\
&= 0.769
\end{aligned}
$$

$$
\begin{aligned}
PD(5) &= -\frac{1}{P}\frac{\partial P}{\partial f(4,5)} \\
&= \frac{1}{P}\times\frac{1100}{e^{f(0,1)+f(1,2)+f(2,3)+f(3,4)+f(4,5)}} \\
&= 0.701
\end{aligned}
$$

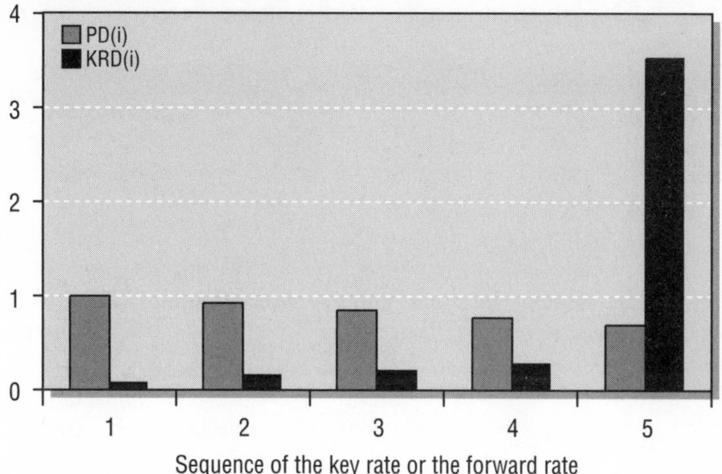

FIGURE 9.8 Partial Durations versus Key Rate Durations of a Coupon-Bearing Bond

The sum of the partial duration measures is 4.229, the traditional duration of the bond. Figure 9.8 shows these partial duration measures and the key rate durations of the bond obtained in Example 9.1. The differences between the two duration profiles are remarkable. Partial durations are decreasing in the maturity of the forward rates, accounting for the fact that changes in short-maturity forward rates have a greater impact in bond returns than changes in long-maturity forward rates.

Loss of Efficiency

Some authors assert that the key rate model is not an efficient model in describing the dynamic of the term structure because historical volatilities of interest rates provide useful information about the behavior of the different segments of the term structure and the key model disregards this information.[4]

Since each key rate change is assumed to be independent of the changes in the rest of key rates, the model deals with movements in the term structure whose probabilities may be too small to worry about. For example, a change in the term structure where the 8- and 10-year rates move in one direction and the 9-year rate moves in the opposite direction is fairly unlikely in the real world but is as likely as other kind of shocks under the key rate model.

As a result, the use of the key rate model for interest rate risk management imposes too severe restrictions on portfolio construction that leads to increased costs and a loss of degrees of freedom that might be used to satisfy other objectives and constraints. In fact, in the most general case in which all zero-coupon rates are assumed to move independently, immunization, hedging, or other passive strategies with the key rate model lead to a cash flow matching along the yield curve.[5]

A number of variations of the key rate model that try to deal with this undesirable consequence have gone through the inclusion of the covariance of interest rate changes into the analysis. For example, Falkenstein and Hanweck (1996) offer an alternative to the traditional key rate hedging called *covariance-consistent key rate hedging* that consists of finding the portfolio that minimizes the variance of portfolio returns. Reitano (1996) introduces the concept of *stochastic immunization* as a strategy that instead of seeking immunization in the traditional sense, searches for the portfolio that minimizes a risk measure defined as a weighted average of the portfolio's return variance and the worst case risk.

APPENDIX 9.1: COMPUTING KEY RATE RISK MEASURES FOR COMPLEX SECURITIES AND UNDER MATURITY MISMATCHES

Real-world fixed-income portfolios rarely fit the simple examples described in this chapter. Complex interest rate-contingent claims such as bonds with embedded options, naked bond options, interest rate options, such as caps, floors, and so forth, generally do not allow the use of simple formulas for key rate durations and convexities. Further, cash flows might occur at periods different from the maturity terms of the key rates considered in the model. This appendix deals with these issues.

Effective Key Rate Risk Measures for Complex Securities: Using Finite Difference Approximations

The derivative-based formulas for the key rate durations and convexities cannot be used directly for securities with variable cash flows that move with interest rates, such that the security's price is obtained using option-pricing-based or other theoretical models. In this case, finite difference approximations to the relevant derivatives can be used to obtain "effective" key rate durations.

The central finite difference approximation to the first-order derivative of price, *P*, with respect to the shift in the *i*th key rate, $y(t_i)$, is given as:

$$\frac{\partial P}{\partial y(t_i)} \approx \frac{P_{i(+\varepsilon)} - P_{i(-\varepsilon)}}{2\varepsilon} \tag{9.32}$$

where $P_{i(+\varepsilon)}$ and $P_{i(-\varepsilon)}$ are the prices of the security computed by the valuation model after shifting the term structure positively and negatively by an infinitesimally small magnitude ε in the *i*th key rate.

The finite difference approximation of the second-order derivative with respect to the shift in the *i*th key rate, and the cross-partial derivative with respect to the shifts in the *i*th and *j*th key rates are given as:

$$\begin{aligned} \frac{\partial^2 P}{\partial y(t_i)^2} &\approx \frac{P_{i(+\varepsilon_i)} - 2P + P_{i(-\varepsilon_i)}}{\varepsilon_i^2} \\ \frac{\partial^2 P}{\partial y(t_i)\partial y(t_j)} &\approx \frac{P_{i(+\varepsilon_i),j(+\varepsilon_j)} - P_{i(+\varepsilon_i),j(-\varepsilon_j)} - P_{i(-\varepsilon_i),j(+\varepsilon_j)} + P_{i(-\varepsilon_i),j(-\varepsilon_j)}}{4\varepsilon_i\varepsilon_j} \end{aligned} \tag{9.33}$$

where the prices on the right side of equation 9.33 are obtained after shifting the term structure by a combination of moves in the *i*th and *j*th key rates given by ε_i and ε_j.

Using the definitions given in equations 9.5 and 9.10, we obtain the effective key rate durations and convexities as:

$$\begin{aligned} KRD(i) &\approx \frac{-(P_{i(+\varepsilon)} - P_{i(-\varepsilon)})}{2P\varepsilon} \\ KRC(i,\ i) &\approx \frac{P_{i(+\varepsilon_i)} - 2P + P_{i(-\varepsilon_i)}}{P\varepsilon_i^2} \\ KRC(i,\ j) &\approx \frac{P_{i(+\varepsilon_i),j(+\varepsilon_j)} - P_{i(+\varepsilon_i),j(-\varepsilon_j)} - P_{i(-\varepsilon_i),j(+\varepsilon_j)} + P_{i(-\varepsilon_i),j(-\varepsilon_j)}}{4P\varepsilon_i\varepsilon_j} \end{aligned} \tag{9.34}$$

Maturity Mismatch: Using Interpolations and Mapping Techniques

Consider the situation in which cash flows, although deterministic, have maturities that do not match the terms of any key rates. The definition of the key rate shifts given in equation 9.2 can be used to obtain a generic expression for the change in the interest rate for any given term *t:*

$$\Delta y(t) = \begin{cases} \Delta y(t_{first}) & t \le t_{first} \\ \Delta y(t_{last}) & t \ge t_{last} \\ \alpha \times \Delta y(t_{left}) + (1-\alpha) \times \Delta y(t_{right}) & else \end{cases} \tag{9.35}$$

where $y(t_{first})$ and $y(t_{last})$ are the first and last key rates, $y(t_{left})$ and $y(t_{right})$, with $t_{left} \le t \le t_{right}$, refers to the key rate adjacent (to the left and the right) to term t, and α and $(1 - \alpha)$ are the coefficients of the linear interpolation, defined as:

$$\begin{aligned} \alpha &= \frac{t_{right} - t}{t_{right} - t_{left}} \\ 1-\alpha &= \frac{t - t_{left}}{t_{right} - t_{left}} \end{aligned} \tag{9.36}$$

Since the price of a cash flow maturing at time t is given as:

$$P = \frac{CF_t}{e^{y(t)\times t}} \tag{9.37}$$

the first and second partial derivatives of this value with respect to the ith key rate and the pair (i, j) of key rates are:

$$\begin{aligned} \frac{\partial P}{\partial y(t_i)} &= \frac{\partial P}{\partial y(t)} \frac{\partial y(t)}{\partial y(t_i)} = -\frac{CF_t \times t}{e^{y(t)\times t}} \frac{\partial y(t)}{\partial y(t_i)} \\ \frac{\partial^2 P}{\partial y(t_i)\partial y(t_j)} &= \frac{\partial^2 P}{\partial y(t)^2} \frac{\partial y(t)}{\partial y(t_i)} \frac{\partial y(t)}{\partial y(t_j)} = \frac{CF_t \times t^2}{e^{y(t)\times t}} \frac{\partial y(t)}{\partial y(t_i)} \frac{\partial y(t)}{\partial y(t_j)} \end{aligned} \tag{9.38}$$

where the partial derivatives of $y(t)$ with respect to a given key rate are obtained from equation 9.35.

Example 9.6 Consider a portfolio composed of equal investments in three zero-coupon bonds maturing in 0.5, 4, and 12 years with prices $P_{0.5}$, P_4 and P_{12}. Also assume that the set of key rates includes only three maturities, namely, 1, 5, and 10 years.

The three key rate durations of the bond portfolio can be computed as follows:

$$
\begin{aligned}
KRD(1) &= \underbrace{\frac{1}{3}\left(-\frac{1}{P_{0.5}}\frac{\partial P_{0.5}}{\partial y(1)}\right)}_{KRD_{0.5}(1)} + \underbrace{\frac{1}{3}\left(-\frac{1}{P_4}\frac{\partial P_4}{\partial y(1)}\right)}_{KRD_4(1)} + \underbrace{\frac{1}{3}\left(-\frac{1}{P_{12}}\frac{\partial P_{12}}{\partial y(1)}\right)}_{KRD_{12}(1)} \\
&= \frac{1}{3}\times 0.5\times\frac{\partial y(0.5)}{\partial y(1)} + \frac{1}{3}\times 4\times\frac{\partial y(4)}{\partial y(1)} + \frac{1}{3}\times 12\times\frac{\partial y(12)}{\partial y(1)} \\
&= \frac{1}{3}\times 0.5\times 1 + \frac{1}{3}\times 4\times\frac{5-4}{5-1} + \frac{1}{3}\times 12\times 0 = 0.5
\end{aligned}
$$

$$
\begin{aligned}
KRD(5) &= \underbrace{\frac{1}{3}\left(-\frac{1}{P_{0.5}}\frac{\partial P_{0.5}}{\partial y(5)}\right)}_{KRD_{0.5}(5)} + \underbrace{\frac{1}{3}\left(-\frac{1}{P_4}\frac{\partial P_4}{\partial y(5)}\right)}_{KRD_4(5)} + \underbrace{\frac{1}{3}\left(-\frac{1}{P_{12}}\frac{\partial P_{12}}{\partial y(5)}\right)}_{KRD_{12}(5)} \\
&= \frac{1}{3}\times 0.5\times\frac{\partial y(0.5)}{\partial y(5)} + \frac{1}{3}\times 4\times\frac{\partial y(4)}{\partial y(5)} + \frac{1}{3}\times 12\times\frac{\partial y(12)}{\partial y(5)} \\
&= \frac{1}{3}\times 0.5\times 0 + \frac{1}{3}\times 4\times\frac{4-1}{5-1} + \frac{1}{3}\times 12\times 0 = 1
\end{aligned}
$$

$$
\begin{aligned}
KRD(10) &= \underbrace{\frac{1}{3}\left(-\frac{1}{P_{0.5}}\frac{\partial P_{0.5}}{\partial y(10)}\right)}_{KRD_{0.5}(5)} + \underbrace{\frac{1}{3}\left(-\frac{1}{P_4}\frac{\partial P_4}{\partial y(10)}\right)}_{KRD_4(5)} + \underbrace{\frac{1}{3}\left(-\frac{1}{P_{12}}\frac{\partial P_{12}}{\partial y(10)}\right)}_{KRD_{12}(5)} \\
&= \frac{1}{3}\times 0.5\times\frac{\partial y(0.5)}{\partial y(10)} + \frac{1}{3}\times 4\times\frac{\partial y(4)}{\partial y(10)} + \frac{1}{3}\times 12\times\frac{\partial y(12)}{\partial y(10)} \\
&= \frac{1}{3}\times 0.5\times 0 + \frac{1}{3}\times 4\times 0 + \frac{1}{3}\times 12\times 1 = 4
\end{aligned}
$$

The key rate convexities are computed similarly:

$$KRC(1,\ 1) = \underbrace{\frac{1}{3}\left(\frac{1}{P_{0.5}}\frac{\partial^2 P_{0.5}}{\partial y(1)^2}\right)}_{KRC_{0.5}(1,1)} + \underbrace{\frac{1}{3}\left(\frac{1}{P_4}\frac{\partial^2 P_4}{\partial y(1)^2}\right)}_{KRC_4(1,1)} + \underbrace{\frac{1}{3}\left(\frac{1}{P_{12}}\frac{\partial^2 P_{12}}{\partial y(1)^2}\right)}_{KRC_{12}(1,1)}$$

$$= \frac{1}{3}\times 0.5^2 \times 1^2 + \frac{1}{3}\times 4^2 \times \left(\frac{5-4}{5-1}\right)^2 + \frac{1}{3}\times 12^2 \times 0 = 0.417$$

$$KRC(5,\ 5) = \underbrace{\frac{1}{3}\left(\frac{1}{P_{0.5}}\frac{\partial^2 P_{0.5}}{\partial y(5)^2}\right)}_{KRC_{0.5}(5,5)} + \underbrace{\frac{1}{3}\left(\frac{1}{P_4}\frac{\partial^2 P_4}{\partial y(5)^2}\right)}_{KRC_4(5,5)} + \underbrace{\frac{1}{3}\left(\frac{1}{P_{12}}\frac{\partial^2 P_{12}}{\partial y(5)^2}\right)}_{KRC_{12}(5,5)}$$

$$= \frac{1}{3}\times 0.5^2 \times 0 + \frac{1}{3}\times 4^2 \times \left(\frac{4-1}{5-1}\right)^2 + \frac{1}{3}\times 12^2 \times 0 = 3$$

$$KRC(10,\ 10) = \underbrace{\frac{1}{3}\left(\frac{1}{P_{0.5}}\frac{\partial^2 P_{0.5}}{\partial y(10)^2}\right)}_{KRC_{0.5}(10,10)} + \underbrace{\frac{1}{3}\left(\frac{1}{P_4}\frac{\partial^2 P_4}{\partial y(10)^2}\right)}_{KRC_4(10,10)} + \underbrace{\frac{1}{3}\left(\frac{1}{P_{12}}\frac{\partial^2 P_{12}}{\partial y(10)^2}\right)}_{KRC_{12}(10,10)}$$

$$= \frac{1}{3}\times 0.5^2 \times 0 + \frac{1}{3}\times 4^2 \times 0 + \frac{1}{3}\times 12^2 \times 1^2 = 48$$

$$KRC(1,\ 5) = KRC(5,\ 1) = \underbrace{\frac{1}{3}\left(\frac{1}{P_{0.5}}\frac{\partial^2 P_{0.5}}{\partial y(1)\partial y(5)}\right)}_{KRC_{0.5}(1,5)} + \underbrace{\frac{1}{3}\left(\frac{1}{P_4}\frac{\partial^2 P_4}{\partial y(1)\partial y(5)}\right)}_{KRC_4(1,5)} + \underbrace{\frac{1}{3}\left(\frac{1}{P_{12}}\frac{\partial^2 P_{12}}{\partial y(1)\partial y(5)}\right)}_{KRC_{12}(1,5)}$$

$$= \frac{1}{3}\times 0.5^2 \times 1 \times 0 + \frac{1}{3}\times 4^2 \times \frac{5-4}{5-1} \times \frac{4-1}{5-1} + \frac{1}{3}\times 12^2 \times 0 = 1$$

$$KRC(1,\ 10) = KRC(10,\ 1) = \underbrace{\frac{1}{3}\left(\frac{1}{P_{0.5}}\frac{\partial^2 P_{0.5}}{\partial y(1)\partial y(10)}\right)}_{KRC_{0.5}(1,10)} + \underbrace{\frac{1}{3}\left(\frac{1}{P_4}\frac{\partial^2 P_4}{\partial y(1)\partial y(10)}\right)}_{KRC_4(1,10)} + \underbrace{\frac{1}{3}\left(\frac{1}{P_{12}}\frac{\partial^2 P_{12}}{\partial y(1)\partial y(10)}\right)}_{KRC_{12}(1,10)}$$

$$= \frac{1}{3}\times 0.5^2 \times 1 \times 0 + \frac{1}{3}\times 4^2 \times \frac{5-4}{5-1} \times 0 + \frac{1}{3}\times 12^2 \times 0 \times 1 = 0$$

$$KRC(5,\ 10) = KRC(10,\ 5) = \underbrace{\frac{1}{3}\left(\frac{1}{P_{0.5}}\frac{\partial^2 P_{0.5}}{\partial y(5)\partial y(10)}\right)}_{KRC_{0.5}(5,10)} + \underbrace{\frac{1}{3}\left(\frac{1}{P_4}\frac{\partial^2 P_4}{\partial y(5)\partial y(10)}\right)}_{KRC_4(5,10)} + \underbrace{\frac{1}{3}\left(\frac{1}{P_{12}}\frac{\partial^2 P_{12}}{\partial y(5)\partial y(10)}\right)}_{KRC_{12}(5,10)}$$

$$= \frac{1}{3}\times 0.5^2 \times 0 + \frac{1}{3}\times 4^2 \times \frac{4-1}{5-1} \times 0 + \frac{1}{3}\times 12^2 \times 0 \times 1 = 0$$

The resulting vector of key rate durations and the matrix of key rate convexities are given as:

$$KRD = \begin{bmatrix} 0.5 & 1 & 4 \end{bmatrix}$$

$$KRC = \begin{bmatrix} 0.417 & 1 & 0 \\ 1 & 3 & 0 \\ 0 & 0 & 48 \end{bmatrix}$$

As might be expected, the key rate durations sum to the traditional duration value of 5.5 years and the key rate convexities sum to the traditional convexity value of 53.417.

An alternative procedure that allows constructing key rate duration measures equivalent to those obtained from the use of linear interpolations for interest rate changes is the mapping methodology proposed in RiskMetrics (2001). Mapping a cash flow consists of splitting it between two adjacent maturities (see Figure 9.9) within a set of prespecified maturities[6] and then proceeds as if the mapped cash flows were the actual cash flow.

There are a variety of ways to map cash flows. Indeed, RiskMetrics has provided at least three different mapping schemes. However, only the actual scheme allows obtaining duration measures (although not convexity measures) that match those described previously because this is, in fact, a constraint imposed by the method.

To illustrate, consider a payment of CF_t maturing at time t, where t is placed between two prespecified maturities t_{left} and t_{right}, with $t_{left} < t < t_{right}$.

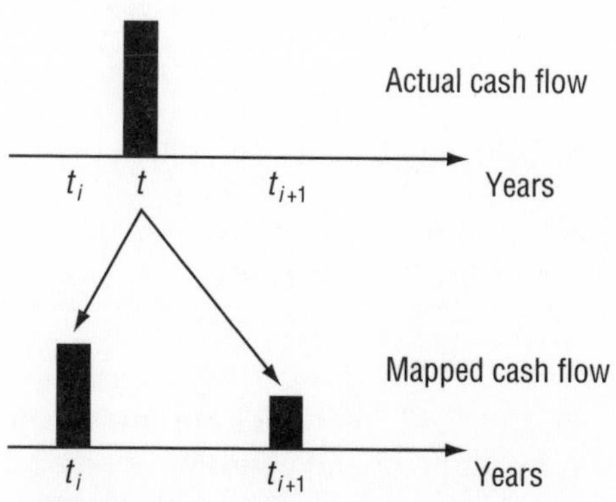

FIGURE 9.9 Riskmetrics Cash Flow Map

The payment CF_t is to be mapped into a payment of CF_{left} maturing at time t_{left}, a payment of CF_{right} at time t_{right} and a cash position of CF_0.

The mapping procedure first requires that the mapped cash flows preserve the present value P of the original cash flow:

$$P = \frac{CF_t}{e^{y(t)t}} = \frac{CF_{left}}{e^{y(t_{left})t_{left}}} + \frac{CF_{right}}{e^{y(t_{right})t_{right}}} + CF_0 \tag{9.39}$$

The sensitivity of the present value to changes in the zero-coupon rates for terms t_{left} and t_{right} must also be preserved, meaning that:

$$\begin{aligned}
\frac{\partial P}{\partial y(t_{left})} &= -\frac{CF_t \times t}{e^{y(t)t}} \frac{\partial y(t)}{\partial y(t_{left})} = -\frac{CF_{left} t_{left}}{e^{y(t_{left})t_{left}}} \\
\frac{\partial P}{\partial y(t_{right})} &= -\frac{CF_t \times t}{e^{y(t)t}} \frac{\partial y(t)}{\partial y(t_{right})} = -\frac{CF_{right} t_{right}}{e^{y(t_{right})t_{right}}}
\end{aligned} \tag{9.40}$$

If either the level (as Risk Metrics assumes) or the changes (as Ho assumes) of interest rates are given by a linear interpolation of the values for adjacent rates, the two partial derivatives of $y(t)$ are the weights α and $1 - \alpha$ defined in equation 9.36. After substitution into equation 9.40, we obtain:

$$\begin{aligned}
CF_{left} &= P \times e^{y(t_{left})t_{left}} \times \alpha \times \frac{t}{t_{left}} \\
CF_{right} &= P \times e^{y(t_{right})t_{right}} \times (1 - \alpha) \times \frac{t}{t_{right}}
\end{aligned} \tag{9.41}$$

From equations 9.39 and 9.41 we can obtain the cash position:

$$CF_0 = P \times \frac{(t - t_{left})(t - t_{right})}{t_{left} \times t_{right}} \tag{9.42}$$

Equations 9.41 and 9.42 imply that an investment of P (the present value of CF_t) in a zero-coupon bond maturing at time t can be replicated by a portfolio consisting of an investment of $P \times \alpha \times (t/t_{left})$ in a zero-coupon bond maturing at time t_{left}, an investment of $P \times (1 - \alpha) \times (t/t_{right})$ in a zero-coupon bond maturing at time t_{right} and a residual cash position. This portfolio preserves both the present value and the partial durations of the original position.

NOTES

1. See Ho (1992).
2. Ho (1992) explicitly recognizes that the linear interpolation, as opposed to other kind of interpolation, is used for reasons of simplicity.
3. The negative sign preceding VaR indicates that the value of VaR is a positive amount while losses are negative changes in market values.
4. See, for example, Hill and Vaysman (1998) and Golub and Tilman (2000).
5. This is, indeed, the case of the immunized portfolio in Example 9.3.
6. In our framework, the set of maturities must correspond to the set of key rates.

CHAPTER 10

Principal Component Model with VaR Analysis

Previous chapters derived interest rate risk hedging conditions without explicitly modeling the historical information contained in the factor structure of the interest rate changes. There were two reasons for doing so. First, many researchers have noted that the three most important principal components that drive the interest rate movements resemble the changes in the height, the slope, and the curvature of the term structure of interest rates (TSIR). Since the first three elements of the duration vector also measure the interest rate sensitivities to changes in height, slope, and curvature of the changes in the term structure, the duration vector model is not inconsistent with a principal component model for hedging. The specific term structure shifts corresponding to the first three duration vector elements capture much, if not all, of the variance captured by the first three principal components of the interest rate changes.[1]

Second, an advantage shared by the duration vector model and the key rate duration model, is that these models don't require a stationary factor structure for interest rate changes.[2] So, the hedging performance is invariant to the nonstationarities in covariance structure of rate changes. All that is required is that the shifts in the term structure remain smooth in order to be captured by a small number of risk measures.

However, there exist conditions under which a principal component model may be preferred to the duration vector model or the key rate duration model. If the covariance structure of interest rates remains stationary, then the duration vector and the key rate duration model may not be as efficient as the principal component model. Second, since the principal component model explicitly selects the factors based upon their contributions to the total variance of interest rate changes, it should lead to gains in hedging efficiency when using only a small number of risk measures. Finally, in situations where explicit or implicit short positions are not allowed, the dura-

This chapter coauthored with Cosette Chichirau.

tion vector or the key rate duration model cannot give a zero immunization risk solution, except for some trivial cases. With short positions disallowed, significant immunization risk is bound to remain in the portfolio, and this risk can be minimized with the knowledge of the factor structure of interest rate changes using a principal component model.

The principal component model assumes that the term structure movements can be summarized by a few composite variables. These new variables are constructed by applying a statistical technique called *principal component analysis* (PCA) to the past interest rate changes. Although PCA was first applied to equity markets, this technique has extended to fixed-income markets in recent years, mainly because much of the interest rate movement is *systematic.*

The use of PCA in the Treasury bond markets has revealed that three principal components (related to the height, the slope, and the curvature of the yield curve) are generally sufficient in explaining the variation in interest rate changes. The sensitivity of the portfolio value to these risk factors is measured by principal component durations and convexities. Besides the benefits of a significant reduction in dimensionality when compared with other models (such as the key rate model), the principal component model is able to produce orthogonal risk factors. This feature makes interest rate risk measurement and management a simpler task because each risk factor can be treated independently.

FROM TERM STRUCTURE MOVEMENTS TO PRINCIPAL COMPONENTS

In the previous chapter, we modeled the term structure shift as a function of a vector of key rate changes:

$$TSIR\ shift = \left(\Delta y(t_1), \Delta y(t_2), \ldots, \Delta y(t_m)\right) \tag{10.1}$$

The PCA approach provides an alternative representation of TSIR shifts by using principal components:

$$TSIR\ shift = \left(\Delta c_1, \Delta c_2, \ldots, \Delta c_m\right) \tag{10.2}$$

Using this approach, an arbitrary change in the key rates can be expressed as a unique set of realizations of principal components. Conversely, any realization of principal components implies a unique change in the key rates.

The principal components are linear combinations of interest rate changes:

$$\Delta c_j = \sum_{i=1}^{m} u_{ji}\Delta y(t_i) \quad j = 1, \ldots, m \tag{10.3}$$

where u_{ji} are called principal component coefficients.

There is no reduction in dimensionality in equation 10.2, since the number of principal components is also m, equal to the number of key rate changes. However, not all the components have equal significance. The first principal component explains the maximum percentage of the total variance of interest rate changes. The second component is linearly independent (i.e., orthogonal) of the first component and explains the maximum percentage of the remaining variance, the third component is linearly independent (i.e., orthogonal) of the first two components and explains the maximum percentage of the remaining variance, and so on. Consequently, if interest rate changes result from a few systematic factors, only a few principal components can capture TSIR movements. Moreover, since these components are constructed to be independent, they simplify the task of managing interest rate risk.

The principal components are constructed using the covariance matrix of zero-coupon rate changes. Since this matrix is symmetric by construction, it must have m normalized and linearly independent eigenvectors, $U_1, \ldots, U_m$, corresponding to m positive eigenvalues, $\lambda_1, \ldots, \lambda_m$. The coefficients of the first principal component are given as the elements of the eigenvector corresponding to the highest eigenvalue. Its variance is given by the magnitude of this eigenvalue. The coefficients of the second principal component are given as the elements of the eigenvector corresponding to the second highest eigenvalue, and so on. A discussion of eigenvalues, eigenvectors, and principal components is given in Appendix 10.1 for readers unfamiliar with this technique.

Since any TSIR shift can be described by using the m principal components and the variance of each component is given by the magnitude of its eigenvalue, the total variance of the interest rate changes is given as:

$$\sum_{j=1}^{m} \lambda_j \tag{10.4}$$

and the proportion of this variance explained by the jth principal component is:

$$\frac{\lambda_j}{\sum_{j=1}^{m} \lambda_j} \tag{10.5}$$

Since the matrix of coefficients u_{ji} given in equation 10.3 is orthogonal (a mathematical characteristic of the independent eigenvectors), the inverse of the matrix is given by its transpose. Using this relation, the changes in the m interest rates can be obtained by inverting equation 10.3 as follows:

$$\Delta y(t_i) = \sum_{j=1}^{m} u_{ji} \Delta c_j \quad i = 1, \ldots, m \tag{10.6}$$

The principal components with low eigenvalues make little contribution in explaining the interest rate changes, and hence these components can be removed without losing significant information. This not only helps in obtaining a low-dimensional parsimonious model, but also reduces the noise in the data due to unsystematic factors.

Assuming that we retain the first k components, expression (10.6) can be rewritten as:

$$\Delta y(t_i) = \sum_{j=1}^{k} u_{ji} \Delta c_j + \varepsilon_i \quad i = 1, \ldots, m \tag{10.7}$$

where ε_i is an error term that measures the changes not explained by the k principal components. Using equation 10.7, changes in the interest rates are summarized by the first k components[3] and the interest rate risk profile of a portfolio can be obtained by measuring the portfolio's sensitivity to only these components.

Table 10.1 shows the eigenvectors and eigenvalues of the covariance matrix of monthly changes in the U.S. zero-coupon rates from January 2000 through December 2002. Term structure shifts are described by

TABLE 10.1 Eigenvectors and Eigenvalues

Rates	PC(1)	PC(2)	PC(3)	PC(4)	PC(5)	PC(6)	PC(7)	PC(8)
1	0.270	−0.701	−0.565	0.292	−0.138	−0.085	0.060	−0.026
2	0.372	−0.385	0.227	−0.423	0.459	0.445	−0.240	0.132
3	0.396	−0.120	0.315	−0.328	−0.037	−0.605	0.244	−0.442
4	0.395	0.028	0.296	0.103	−0.411	−0.182	−0.054	0.735
5	0.382	0.124	0.243	0.346	−0.415	0.476	−0.166	−0.483
7	0.350	0.252	−0.031	0.344	0.444	0.149	0.682	0.102
9	0.332	0.334	−0.225	0.266	0.397	−0.348	−0.614	−0.047
10	0.312	0.393	−0.576	−0.556	−0.270	0.162	0.085	0.022
Eigenvalues	0.605	0.057	0.009	0.001	0.001	0.000	0.000	0.000

interest rate changes (in percentages) for a series of maturities including 1, 2, 3, 4, 5, 7, 9, and 10 years.

The first three principal components explain almost all of the variance of interest rate changes, a result consistent with other studies. The first factor accounts for 89.8 percent of the total variance, while the second and third factors account for 8.5 percent and 1.3 percent, respectively. In sum, the first three principal components explain 99.6 percent of the variability of the data, which indicates that these factors are sufficient for describing the changes in the term structure.

Figure 10.1 shows the shape of the eigenvectors corresponding to the first three principal components. These shapes give the impact of a unit change in each principal component on the term structure of interest rates (see equation 10.7). The change in the zero-coupon rates (on y-axis) is plotted against the maturity terms (on x-axis) with respect to each principal component.

The first principal component basically represents a parallel change in TSIR, which is why it is usually named the level or the height factor. The second principal component represents a change in the steepness, and is named the slope factor. The third principal component is called the curvature factor, as it basically affects the curvature of the TSIR by inducing a butterfly shift.

The previous visualization of the principal components is based on a characterization of approximate shapes of the eigenvectors. The

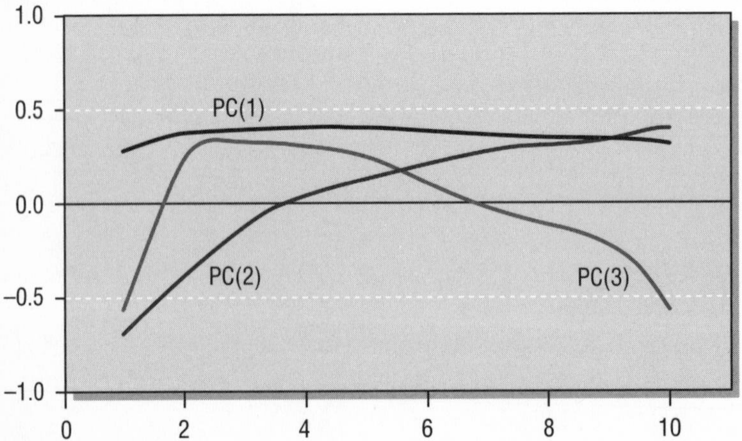

FIGURE 10.1 Impact of the First Three Principal Components on the Term Structure of Interest Rates

interpretation is not an exact representation. For example, the shape of the first principal component is never strictly parallel. If the first principal component is constrained to be parallel, it will cause other principal components to become correlated, because to obtain a parallel shape for the first principal component, it is necessary to perform a transformation on the other set of principal components.[4]

Figure 10.1 shows changes in the term structure of interest rates assuming unit shifts in the principal components. However, the eigenvalues in Table 10.1 imply very different variances for the three principal components, making unit shifts in each factor not equally likely. A better approach is to modify the model to make each factor have a unit variance. This is achieved by multiplying each eigenvector by the square root of its eigenvalue, and dividing the principal component by the square root of the eigenvalue. The model for interest rates changes then becomes:

$$\Delta y(t_i) = \sum_{j=1}^{k} \left(u_{ji} \sqrt{\lambda_j} \right) \Delta c_j^* + \varepsilon_i \quad i = 1, \ldots, m \tag{10.8}$$

where

$$\Delta c_j^* = \frac{\Delta c_j}{\sqrt{\lambda_j}}$$

The coefficients in parenthesis, which measure the impact of a one standard deviation move in each principal component on each interest rate, are called factor loadings.[5] Using simpler notation without stars, and using only three factors, equation 10.8 can be approximated as follows:

$$\Delta y(t_i) \approx l_{ih} \Delta c_h + l_{is} \Delta c_s + l_{ic} \Delta c_c \quad i = 1, \ldots, m \tag{10.9}$$

where the factors are defined as follows:

$$\Delta c_h = \Delta c_1^* = \frac{\Delta c_1}{\sqrt{\lambda_1}}, \quad \Delta c_s = \Delta c_2^* = \frac{\Delta c_2}{\sqrt{\lambda_2}} \quad \Delta c_c = \Delta c_3^* = \frac{\Delta c_3}{\sqrt{\lambda_3}}$$

and the factor loadings are defined as follows:

$$l_{ih} = u_{1i}\sqrt{\lambda_1}, \quad l_{is} = u_{2i}\sqrt{\lambda_2}, \quad l_{ic} = u_{3i}\sqrt{\lambda_3}$$

When the time interval used for zero-coupon rate changes in the PCA is different from the time interval required in a risk management model, the standard deviations obtained from the PCA must be scaled appropriately. As a rule of thumb, each eigenvalue is scaled by multiplying it by the desired horizon length. This is also the same as multiplying the standard deviation of the principal component by the square root of the desired horizon length. For example, if we use daily data for implementing the PCA, the monthly standard deviation of the principal components is assumed to be $30^{1/2}$ times the daily standard deviation.

PRINCIPAL COMPONENT DURATIONS AND CONVEXITIES

Once the principal components have been identified, principal component durations and convexities can be computed from the first and the second partial derivatives of the security with respect to the three factors as follows:

$$PCD(i) = -\frac{1}{P}\frac{\partial P}{\partial c_i} \quad i = h, s, c \tag{10.10}$$

$$PCC(i, j) = \frac{1}{P}\frac{\partial^2 P}{\partial c_i \partial c_j} \quad i, j = h, s, c \tag{10.11}$$

Using the second-order Taylor series approximation we have:

$$\frac{\Delta P}{P} = -\sum_{i=h,s,c} PCD(i) \times \Delta c_i + \frac{1}{2}\sum_{i=h,s,c}\sum_{j=h,s,c} PCC(i, j) \times \Delta c_i \times \Delta c_j \tag{10.12}$$

Since the principal components are independent, we can simplify (10.12) by disregarding the cross effects, which gives:

$$\frac{\Delta P}{P} = -\sum_{i=h,s,c} PCD(i) \times \Delta c_i + \frac{1}{2}\sum_{j=h,s,c} PCC(i, i) \times \Delta c_i^2 \tag{10.13}$$

Hence, three duration measures and three convexity measures are needed to describe the riskiness of a fixed-income security. This is true even for securities with complex cash flow characteristics as shown in Appendix 10.2.[6]

The principal component measures can also be computed directly from key rate durations and convexities. This involves substituting the expression for interest rate changes given in equation 10.9 in the Taylor series approximation for the instantaneous return based on the key rate measures in Chapter 9, and disregarding cross effects of principal component shifts:[7]

$$\frac{\Delta P}{P} = -\sum_{v=h,s,c} \Delta c_v \sum_{i=1}^{m} KRD(i) \times l_{iv} + \frac{1}{2} \sum_{v=h,s,c} \Delta c_v^2 \sum_{i=1}^{m} \sum_{j=1}^{m} KRC(i,\ j) \times l_{iv} \times l_{jv} \quad (10.14)$$

where $KRD(i)$ is the ith key rate duration, defined as the (negative) percentage change in the security price resulting from a unit shift in the ith key rate and KRC(i, j) is the (i, j)-key rate convexity, that captures the second-order effect on prices of the shifts in the pair (i, j) of key rates.

Comparing equation 10.13 with equation 10.14, the principal component durations (convexities) can be expressed as linear combinations of the key rate durations (convexities):

$$\begin{aligned} PCD(v) &= \sum_{i=1}^{m} KRD(i) \times l_{iv} \\ PCC(v) &= \sum_{i=1}^{m} \sum_{j=1}^{m} KRC(i,\ j) \times l_{iv} \times l_{jv} \quad v = h,\ s,\ c \end{aligned} \quad (10.15)$$

Though the traditional duration equals the sum of the key rate durations, the height-factor *PCD* may not always coincide with traditional duration because the first principal component does not provide an exact parallel TSIR movement. Second, even with a parallel move, normalizing the eigenvectors prevents this equivalence unless adjusted by a proportionality factor.[8]

Example 10.1 Reconsider the five bonds in Chapter 9, whose main characteristics and key rate durations with respect to the 1, 2, 3, 4, and five-year zero-coupon rates are reproduced in Table 10.2. The level of the key rates is assumed to be 5 percent, 5.5 percent, 5.75 percent, 5.9 percent and 6 percent.

Principal component durations can be computed using the vectors of key rate durations and the factor loadings of these key rates. Factor loadings shown in Table 10.3, are obtained from Table 10.1 by multiplying the eigenvector of each principal component by the squared root of the corresponding eigenvalue.

TABLE 10.2 Characteristics and Key Rate Durations for the Five Bonds

	Bond 1	Bond 2	Bond 3	Bond 4	Bond 5
Face value	$1,000	$1,000	$1,000	$1,000	$1,000
Maturity (years)	1	2	3	4	5
Annual coupon rate (%)	10	10	10	10	10
Price	$1,046.35	$1,080.54	$1,110.42	$1,137.62	$1,162.74
KRD(1)	1.000	0.088	0.086	0.084	0.082
KRD(2)	0.000	1.824	0.161	0.157	0.154
KRD(3)	0.000	0.000	2.501	0.222	0.217
KRD(4)	0.000	0.000	0.000	3.055	0.272
KRD(5)	0.000	0.000	0.000	0.000	3.504

Principal component durations for each bond are computed using equation 10.15 and are shown in Table 10.4 together with traditional duration.

The height-factor duration, $PCD(h)$, increases with the bond's maturity since the exposure to a near parallel component of the term structure shift must increase with maturity. To obtain figures comparable to those of *traditional* duration, $PCD(h)$ have to be scaled by the squared root of the number of rates included in the analysis (8 zero-coupon rates) divided by the eigenvalue of the first principal component (0.605). These scaled principal component durations are 0.765, 1.985, 3.033, 3.891, and 4.560, which are similar to the traditional durations of the bonds given in the last row of Table 10.4.

TABLE 10.3 Factor Loadings

Years	PC(1)	PC(2)	PC(3)
1	0.210	−0.168	−0.054
2	0.289	−0.092	0.022
3	0.308	−0.029	0.030
4	0.307	0.007	0.028
5	0.297	0.030	0.023

TABLE 10.4 Principal Component Durations for the Five Bonds

	Bond 1	Bond 2	Bond 3	Bond 4	Bond 5
PCD(h)	0.210	0.546	0.834	1.070	1.254
PCD(s)	−0.168	−0.183	−0.101	−0.014	0.071
PCD(c)	−0.054	0.035	0.074	0.091	0.094
D	1.000	1.912	2.748	3.518	4.229

The slope-factor duration, $PCD(s)$, benefits the first four bonds, with maturities ranging from one to four years due to an increase in the slope from falling rates at the shorter end. The five-year bond, however, is negatively affected by increases in steepness due to its high exposure to the change in the five-year rate, which rises under the shift. Similar pattern explains the reason behind the sign shifts in the curvature-factor durations, $PCD(c)$.

Principal component risk measures can be obtained similarly from the key rate measures of the portfolio or as a weighted average of the principal component measures of each security in the portfolio. To illustrate, reconsider the ladder, barbell and bullet bond portfolios in Chapter 9, whose key rate duration vectors and portfolio's composition are reproduced in Table 10.5.

TABLE 10.5 Proportions Invested in Each Bond and Key Rate Durations of the Ladder, Barbell, and Bullet Portfolios

	Ladder	Barbell	Bullet
Bond 1	0.2	0.479	0.000
Bond 2	0.2	0.000	0.521
Bond 3	0.2	0.000	0.000
Bond 4	0.2	0.000	0.479
Bond 5	0.2	0.521	0.000
KRD(1)	0.268	0.522	0.086
KRD(2)	0.459	0.080	1.025
KRD(3)	0.588	0.113	0.106
KRD(4)	0.665	0.141	1.464
KRD(5)	0.701	1.825	0.000

TABLE 10.6 Principal Component Durations of the Ladder, Barbell, and Bullet Portfolios

	Ladder	Barbell	Bullet
PCD(*h*)	0.783	0.754	0.797
PCD(*s*)	–0.079	–0.043	–0.102
PCD(*c*)	0.048	0.023	0.062

As mentioned earlier, the portfolios' key rate duration vectors together with the factor loadings in Table 10.3 allow the computation of the portfolios' principal component durations displayed in Table 10.6.

According to the absolute values of the measures, the bullet portfolio shows the highest risk exposure to the level, slope and curvature shifts in the term structure, while the barbell portfolio shows the lowest risk exposure.

RISK MEASUREMENT AND MANAGEMENT WITH THE PRINCIPAL COMPONENT MODEL

The relationship between the principal component measures and the key rate measures allows the manager to take the best of the two paradigms. Since there are no universally accepted definitions for the level, steepness, and curvature shifts, key rate durations are a valid starting point for avoiding the ambiguity inherent in principal component shifts. Managers can also benefit from the intuitive description of risk provided by the key rate durations while using principal component durations for implementing more parsimonious portfolio strategies that do not exhaust all degrees of freedom in portfolio construction.

For example, immunizing the equity value of a financial institution from arbitrary term structure shifts using principal component durations will require imposing the following three constraints:

$$V^A PCD(i)_{ASSETS} = V^L PCD(i)_{LIABILITIES} \qquad i = h,\ s,\ c \tag{10.16}$$

where V^A is the present value of the assets and V^L the present value of the liabilities.

Passive portfolio strategies, such as portfolio replication, or immunization for a given planning horizon, are constructed by matching the principal component durations of the portfolio to the principal component durations of the target portfolio.

Immunizing a portfolio for a given horizon requires choosing a portfolio composition where the three durations of the portfolio equals a zero-coupon bond's duration maturing at the end of the planning horizon, that is:

$$PCD(i)_{PORT} = PCD(i)_{zero} = H \times l_{Hi} \quad i = h,\ s,\ c \tag{10.17}$$

where H is the length of the planning horizon and l_{Hi} is the loading of principal component i on the continuously compounded zero-coupon rate for term H.

For designing active portfolio strategies, three basic term structure shifts corresponding to the three principal components can be used. Simulated effects of the resulting scenarios on portfolio returns can help managers make risk-return decisions.

Example 10.2 Chapter 9 demonstrated how a portfolio could be immunized with five key rates using six different bonds. The bond portfolio includes the five bonds given in Example 10.1 and an additional five-year zero-coupon bond 6 with a face value of \$1,000. This bond has a market price of \$740.82 and has all its key rate durations equal to zero, except the five-year key rate duration, which equals five.

The same six-bond portfolio can be immunized using the principal component model. In this case, the immunization constraints are given as follows:

$$\begin{aligned}
PCD(h) &= p_1 \times PCD_1(h) + p_2 \times PCD_2(h) + \cdots + p_6 \times PCD_6(h) = H \times l_{Hh} \\
PCD(s) &= p_1 \times PCD_1(s) + p_2 \times PCD_2(s) + \cdots + p_6 \times PCD_6(s) = H \times l_{Hs} \\
PCD(c) &= p_1 \times PCD_1(c) + p_2 \times PCD_2(c) + \cdots + p_6 \times PCD_6(c) = H \times l_{Hc} \\
& p_1 + p_2 + p_3 + p_4 + p_5 + p_6 = 1
\end{aligned}$$

Since the number of bonds exceeds the number of constraints, the system of equations has an infinite number of solutions for the bond proportions $p_1, p_2, \ldots, p_6$. To select a unique immunizing solution, we optimize by using the following quadratic function:

$$\text{Min}\left[\sum_{i=1}^{6} p_i^2\right]$$

As discussed in Chapter 5, a solution to this constrained quadratic problem can be obtained by deriving the first-order conditions using the Lagrange method. Expressing these conditions in matrix form and some matrix manipulation gives the following solution:

$$\begin{bmatrix} p_1 \\ p_2 \\ \vdots \\ p_6 \\ \lambda_1 \\ \lambda_2 \\ \lambda_3 \\ \lambda_4 \end{bmatrix} = \begin{bmatrix} 2 & 0 & \dots & 0 & PCD_1(h) & PCD_1(s) & PCD_1(c) & 1 \\ 0 & 2 & \dots & 0 & PCD_2(h) & PCD_2(s) & PCD_2(c) & 1 \\ \vdots & \vdots & \vdots & \vdots & \vdots & \vdots & \vdots & \vdots \\ 0 & 0 & \dots & 2 & PCD_6(h) & PCD_6(s) & PCD_6(c) & 1 \\ PCD_1(h) & PCD_2(h) & \dots & PCD_6(h) & 0 & 0 & 0 & 0 \\ PCD_1(s) & PCD_2(s) & \dots & PCD_6(s) & 0 & 0 & 0 & 0 \\ PCD_1(c) & PCD_2(c) & \dots & PCD_6(c) & 0 & 0 & 0 & 0 \\ 1 & 1 & \dots & 1 & 0 & 0 & 0 & 0 \end{bmatrix}^{-1} \times \begin{bmatrix} 0 \\ 0 \\ \vdots \\ 0 \\ H \times I_{Hh} \\ H \times I_{Hs} \\ H \times I_{Hc} \\ 1 \end{bmatrix}$$

The first six elements of the left column vector give the proportions to be invested in the six bonds. We obtain the following solution for the bond proportions:

$$p_1 = -0.099 \quad p_2 = -0.215 \quad p_3 = 0.525$$
$$p_4 = 0.498 \quad p_5 = 0.158 \quad p_6 = 0.133$$

The principal component solution is more diversified than the immunized portfolio obtained under the key rate model. While the latter portfolio leads to cash flow matching, the immunized portfolio under the principal component model has nonzero net cash flows every year. Hence, immunization using the key rate model resembles dedication strategies leading to near perfect hedging performance, while the principal component model's main strength is its low dimension leading to lower transaction costs and higher degrees of freedom.

VAR ANALYSIS USING THE PRINCIPAL COMPONENT MODEL

VaR analysis using the principal component model has some advantages over the key rate model. The principal components are uncorrelated by construction and the correlation matrix of principal components is the identity matrix. This simplifies the VaR analysis considerably. Further, if interest rates are assumed to follow a multivariate normal distribution, principal components are normally distributed as well. The approximation of portfolio returns based on principal component durations is then normally distributed with variance equal to:

$$\sigma_R^2 = \sum_{j=h,s,c} PCD(i)^2 \tag{10.18}$$

Each principal component contributes the square of the corresponding duration to the variance of portfolio returns. This allows a simple interpretation of the riskiness of the portfolio in terms of the three principal components.

Using equation 10.18 and the definition of VaR in Chapter 9, we obtain the VaR of a portfolio at a c percent confidence as:

$$VaR_c = V_0 z_c \sqrt{\sum_{i=h,s,c} PCD(i)^2} \tag{10.19}$$

where V_0 is the initial market value of the portfolio and z_c is the c percentile of a standard normal distribution.

Example 10.3 In Chapter 9, the one-month VaR at the 95 percent and 99 percent levels of the ladder, barbell, and bullet portfolios in Example 10.1 were obtained using the key rate model. Here we construct the same VaR measures, but using the principal component model. Since the covariance matrix used for the key rate model was based on the same data as this chapter, the two sets of VaR values can be compared directly.

The VaR values at the 95 percent and 99 percent levels for each portfolio using the principal component model are given as follows:

$$VaR_{95} = 10{,}000 \times 1.645 \times \sqrt{PCD_{PORT}(h)^2 + PCD_{PORT}(s)^2 + PCD_{PORT}(c)^2}$$

$$VaR_{99} = 10{,}000 \times 2.326 \times \sqrt{PCD_{PORT}(h)^2 + PCD_{PORT}(s)^2 + PCD_{PORT}(c)^2}$$

where, the initial market value of the portfolio equals \$10,000 and the 95th and 99th percentile of a standard normal distribution are 1.645 and 2.326, respectively. The principal component durations from Table 10.6 are divided by 100 since the rate changes are defined in percentage values when constructing the principal components.

TABLE 10.7 Variance of Portfolio Returns and VaR Numbers Using the Principal Component Model

	Ladder	Barbell	Bullet
σ_R	0.788	0.755	0.806
VaR_{95}	\$129.67	\$124.26	\$132.56
VaR_{99}	\$183.40	\$175.74	\$187.48

Table 10.7 shows the monthly standard deviation of the portfolio returns and the VaR numbers. Consistent with the levels of exposure of each portfolio revealed in Example 10.1, the bullet portfolio is the riskiest portfolio, followed by the ladder portfolio, and finally the barbell portfolio.

These figures differ only slightly from the key rate model. The maximum difference in return volatility is 0.001 percent while the maximum difference in VaR values is less than a quarter of a dollar. This demonstrates the principal component model is able to provide an accurate description of interest rate dynamics while maintaining a low number of risk factors.

LIMITATIONS OF THE PRINCIPAL COMPONENT MODEL

The principal component model has a couple of shortcomings given as follows. First, the static nature of the technique is unable to deal with the nonstationary time-series behavior of the interest rate changes. Second, principal components are purely artificial constructions that summarize information in correlated systems, but do not always lead to an economic interpretation.

Static Factors Arising from a Dynamic Volatility Structure

Application of PCA to term structure movements implies that the covariance structure of interest rate changes is constant and hence the vectors of factor loadings, which describe the shape of the principal components, are stationary as well. This is critically important because if the shapes of the principal components change frequently, then these components cannot explain the future volatility of interest rate changes.

A large number of empirical studies find evidence of a dynamic pattern in the volatility of interest rates. As shown in Bliss (1997a) or Soto (2004b), this affects the stability of the principal components. Figure 10.2 illustrates the effect of the changing volatilities of U.S. zero-coupon rates on the principal components obtained for 2000, 2001, and 2002. Though the first

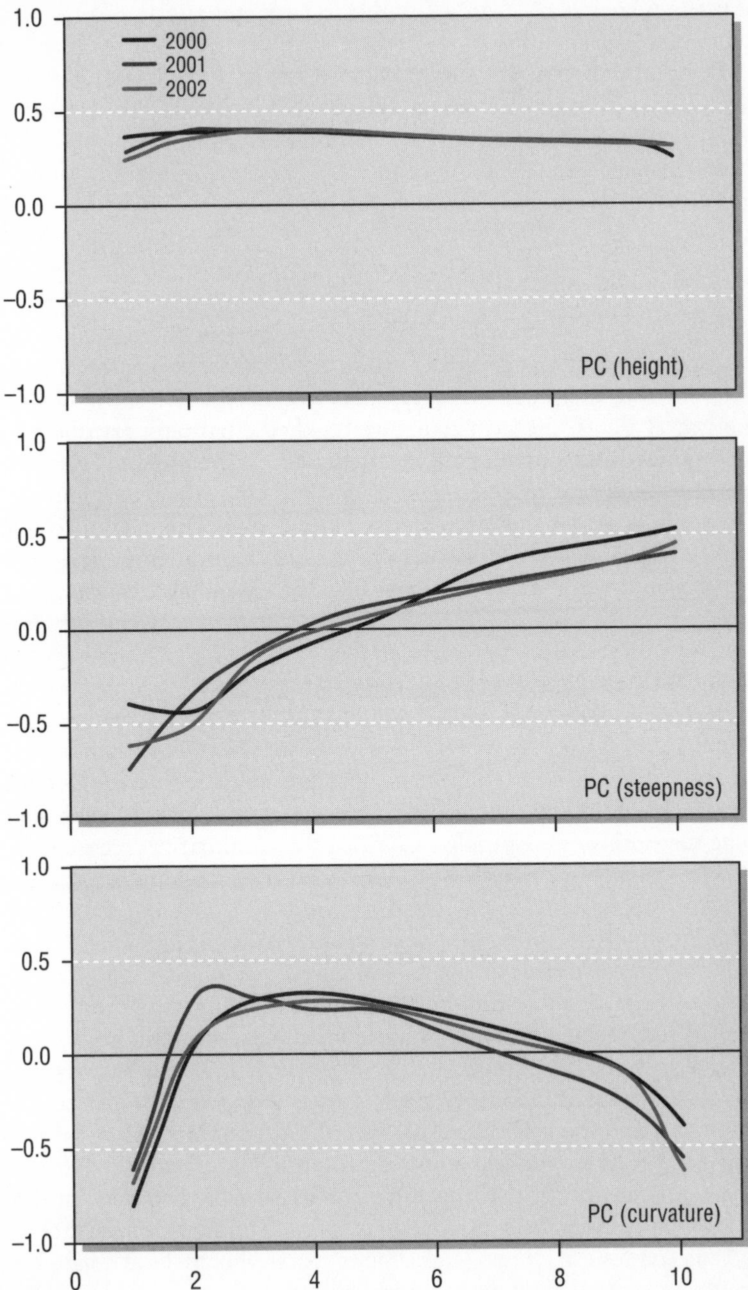

FIGURE 10.2 Principal Components for Years 2000, 2001, and 2002

principal component seems relatively stable, the second and third principal components vary significantly.

In such circumstances, the manager must estimate the model periodically and examine alternative covariance matrices to check for stationary and choose the most stable matrix. Some authors recommend that the third principal component should be disregarded because of its high instability, which hurts the performance of portfolio strategies.[9]

Principal Component Analysis: Using Zero-Coupon Rate Changes or Forward Rate Changes

In an interesting study, Lekkos (2000) questioned the economic interpretation of the three principal components as representing shifts in the height, slope, and curvature of the term structure. Lekkos attributes the shape of these three components to the aggregating process of computing zero-coupon rates from forward rates.

To illustrate, consider one-year forward rates, between 0 and 1 year, 1 and 2 years, 2 and 3 years, and so on until the last forward rate between 9 and 10 years. Assume that all forward rate changes have a unit variance, and zero correlations with each other. Under this scenario, application of PCA on the covariance matrix of forward rate changes does not allow any dimension reduction and the principal components are the 10 forward rate changes, themselves. However, application of PCA on the covariance matrix including the 1-, 2-, 3-, 4-, 5-, 6-, 7-, 9-, and 10-year zero-coupon rates reveals that the first principal component accounts for 69.7 percent of the total variance. The first and second principal components account for 87.5 percent (the second component adds 17.7 percent), and the first three principal components account for 93.9 percent (the third component adds 6.4 percent) of the total variance. Only the first three principal components are needed to explain almost the entire variance of zero-coupon rate changes even though all forward rate changes have *zero correlation* by definition. Moreover, the shape of these three principal components shown in Figure 10.3 allows us to interpret them as level, slope, and curvature factors.

In other words, the traditional interpretation of the three principal components as height, slope, and curvature factors could simply be due to the definition of zero-coupon rates as aggregates of forward rates. More importantly, in this aggregation process some information about the variability in the interest rates may be lost. Using principal component analysis on forward rate changes based upon real market data, a minimum of six factors are needed to account for 99 percent of the total variability of rate changes. The first three principal components of forward rate changes for the period January 2000 through December 2002 are shown in Figure 10.4.

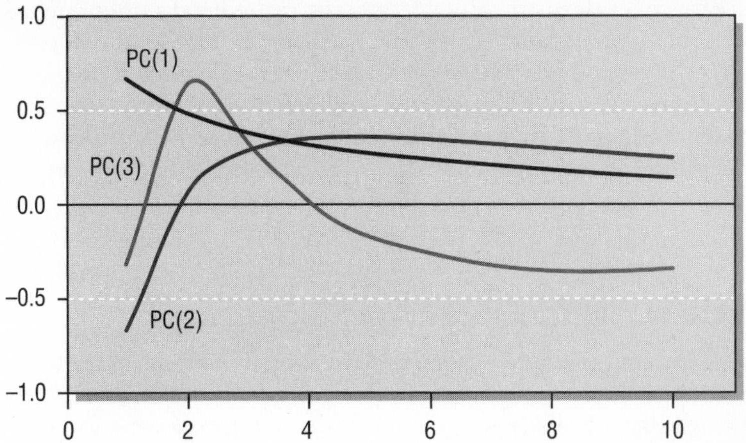

FIGURE 10.3 Eigenvectors of the First Three Principal Components of Zero-Coupon

Although the first and third forward rate-based principal components have similar shapes as the corresponding zero-coupon rate-based principal components, the second principal component does not show such similarity. Overall, the variability is spread out more evenly across the first six principal components using the forward rate changes, and the first

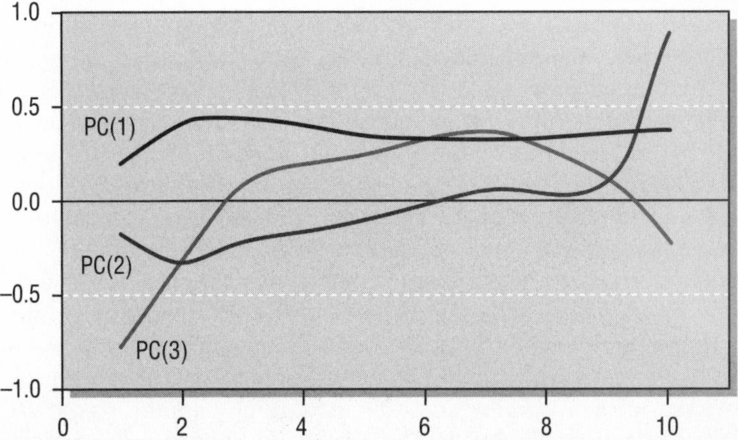

FIGURE 10.4 First Three Principal Components of the Term Structure of U.S. Forward Rates for the Period January 2000 to December 2002

principal component explains only 59 percent of the variability. In contrast, only three principal components are required using the zero-coupon rate changes. If researchers believe that important information about interest rate changes is lost in the process of aggregating forward rates into zero-coupon rates, then forward rates should be used for principal component analysis leading to a higher number of risk measures for managing interest rate risk.

APPLICATIONS TO MORTGAGE SECURITIES

So far, we presented the application of the principal component model to the U.S. Treasury market using the default-free term structure data. However, the principal components obtained from default-free term structure data can be used to compute interest rate sensitivities of securities in other markets too. In this section, we show how to apply the PCA model to compute the empirical PC durations of mortgage-backed securities (MBS). Of course, the same technique can be applied to other markets, such as corporate bonds, municipal bonds, or inflation-indexed bonds.

The U.S. mortgage securities market is the largest debt market in the world, with unprecedented growth since the 1980s, in terms of size, investors, and the number of instruments traded. The outstanding volume of agency mortgage-backed securities (MBS) is well in excess of $3 trillion and this is just the agency-securitized portion of the market. The total outstanding residential and commercial mortgage debt has jumped from about $4.5 trillion in 1995 to more than $9 trillion in 2004.[10]

The investors in mortgage-related securities include commercial banks, savings institutions, life insurance companies, agencies, trusts, and individuals. The three main products under the umbrella of MBS are mortgage pass-through securities, for which the cash flows from all the loans in the pool (principal and interest) are simply passed through to the investors on a pro rata basis; collateralized mortgage obligations (CMOs), which follow specific rules for the cash flow distributions (such as class A investors receive all monthly principal payments until they are fully paid off; then, class B investors receive all monthly principal payments until they are paid off, and so on with class C and Z); and stripped MBS—interest only/principal only (IO/PO), where the cash flows are stripped, so that IO holders receive all interest but no principal, and PO holders receive all principal payments, but no interest. In the following analysis we focus on pass-through securities, but since our analysis obtains *empirical* PC durations using daily return data on these securities, it easily generalizes to other securities in the mortgage market, and even other markets.

An important characteristic that differentiates the securities in the mortgage market from securities in other fixed-income markets is the high degree of optionality present in these securities. This naturally makes them difficult to value and hedge. The investor in MBS effectively writes two options: the option to default and the option to prepay. The prepayment option is generally a lot more significant in the valuation and hedging of MBS than the default option. When interest rates decline, most homeowners prepay through refinancing, which shortens the duration of the mortgage securities. When interest rates increase, the likelihood of prepayments reduces, as homeowners hold on to their mortgage loans financed at low rates, lengthening the duration of the mortgage securities.

Due to the prepayment option, MBS have tremendous negative convexity. When the interest rates decline, the MBS prices increase, but prepayments put an upper limit on the upside movements in the prices. However, when interest rates increase, the probability of prepayment becomes lower, and hence prices fall more rapidly with lengthening duration.

Figure 10.5 shows the monthly changes in duration for the Lehman Brothers MBS Index from June 1999 to June 2004.[11] Some of the duration changes are quite dramatic, such as one over the year 2001, when the duration dropped sharply in response to the 11 interest rate cuts by the Federal Open Market Committee (FOMC) of the U.S. central bank. After that period, even as short-term rates remained steady, the long rates increased toward the end of 2001 and the beginning of 2002, as the expectations of an

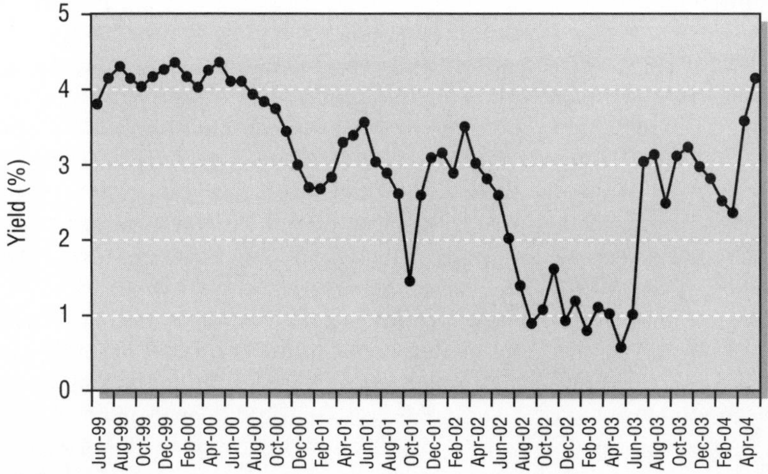

FIGURE 10.5 Monthly Duration for Lehman MBS Index

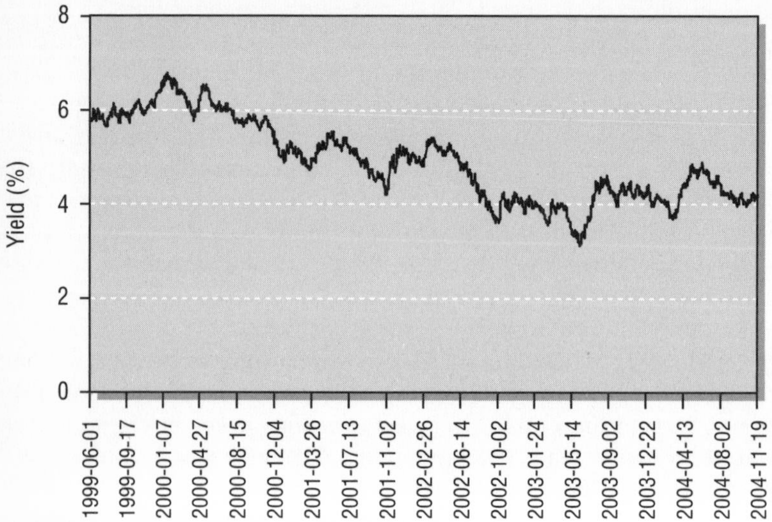

FIGURE 10.6 10-Year U.S. T-Bonds Yield

economic rebound led to an increase in longer rates as shown in Figure 10.6. The duration of the Lehman MBS index lengthened sharply over this period as can be seen from Figure 10.5. Then again, as the Iraq war talk by President George W. Bush depressed equity values and reduced long-term rates steadily through much of 2002, the duration of the Lehman MBS index shortened rapidly, followed by another rapid increase as the war in Iraq was declared "mission accomplished" in the middle of year 2003, leading to another sharp increase in the long-term rates.

The tremendous variability in the duration of the Lehman MBS index is caused by the significant influence of the prepayment option on the interest rate sensitivities of MBS. Capturing the nonstationarity in the duration of MBS is crucial in managing the interest rate risk of a mortgage portfolio. In the following discussion, we suggest an empirical PC duration approach that allows the mortgage durations to be empirically estimated using the sensitivities of the MBS to PC factors using past 30 days of return data, where the PC factors are estimated using past six months of daily changes in key U.S. Treasury rates. This allows us to capture the high nonstationarity in the MBS durations, even though the PC factors are estimated using the larger sample period of six months. The empirical estimation of PC durations is done in two stages. In the first stage, we compute the principal component factors using the methodology outlined earlier in this chapter with six months of daily rate changes in the key U.S. Treasury rates. In the second stage, we obtain the empirical PC durations of MBS by running time-series linear regressions of daily returns on the changes in the PC factors obtained in the first stage.

First Stage: Estimation of Principal Components

For expositional simplicity we pick only five key Treasury rates to do the PCA analysis with maturities given as 3 months, 1 year, 2 years, 5 years, and 10 years. Typically, the first two to three principal components explain most of the variability in interest rate changes. Our full sample includes Treasury rate changes from year 1997 to year 2004. However, at any given point of time, only six months of past daily data is used to estimate the principal components. An example of the six-month sample of daily rate changes is given in Table 10.8, which shows the first few days of daily rate changes beginning from July 18, 2003, until January 12, 2004. This period contains 120 business days for which daily changes are computed. These changes are shown in percentage form, so for example, the change in the 10-year rate on July 18, 2003, from its value on the previous day equals 2 basis points, or 0.0002 in the decimal form.

The covariance matrix of daily rate changes over this period is given in Table 10.9. These covariances use percentage rate changes as inputs, and so multiplication of 10^{-4} converts them into decimal form.

Using the procedure given in Appendix 10.1 (see example 10.4 for a demonstration) the loadings of the five PCs are obtained in Table 10.10. This matrix shows how the PCs are obtained as linear weighted averages of daily changes in rates of different maturities. For example, the first PC is obtained by giving 0.018 weight to the change in the 3-month rate, 0.286 weight to the change in 1-year rate, 0.506 weight to the change in 2-year rate, 0.607 weight to the change in 5-year rate, and 0.541 weight to the change in 10-year rate.

TABLE 10.8 Changes in Daily Interest Rates

	Change in Rate				
	3-Month	1-Year	2-Year	5-Year	10-Year
07/18/03	0.005	0.024	0.026	0.028	0.020
07/21/03	0.016	0.038	0.107	0.188	0.195
07/22/03	0.015	−0.034	−0.040	−0.022	−0.020
07/23/03	−0.010	−0.007	−0.049	−0.053	−0.048
...	...	...	...	...	...
01/12/04	0.000	0.015	0.000	−0.010	−0.004

Note: Given in percentage form. To convert to decimal form multiply by 10^{-2}.

TABLE 10.9 Covariance Matrix of Daily Rate Changes

	3m	*1y*	*2y*	*5y*	*10y*
3m	0.00016	0.00007	0.00013	0.00022	0.00023
1y	0.00007	0.00208	0.00288	0.00319	0.00277
2y	0.00013	0.00288	0.00528	0.00577	0.00499
5y	0.00022	0.00319	0.00577	0.00723	0.00630
10y	0.00023	0.00277	0.00499	0.00630	0.00595

Note: Given using percentage rate changes. To convert to decimal form multiply by 10^{-4}.

Since we have only five key rates, the five principal components explain 100 percent of the variance. Of course, most of the important information of rate changes is captured by the first two or three components, so the other components can be ignored. Over the whole sample period from 1997 to 2004, the first three PCs explain about 90 to 99 percent of the variance of rate changes.

Second Stage: Estimation of Empirical PC Durations

To obtain the empirical PC durations of any security at any given date we need to estimate the sensitivity of that security's daily return to the PCs obtained in the first stage. Though we use past six months of daily rate changes to compute the principal component loading matrix shown in Table 10.10, we only use past 30 business days of data on daily returns and the PCs to compute the empirical PC durations. For the current example, using

TABLE 10.10 Principal Component Loading Matrix

	3m	*1y*	*2y*	*5y*	*10y*
PC 1	0.018	0.286	0.506	0.607	0.541
PC 2	0.101	−0.619	−0.510	0.234	0.540
PC 3	0.072	0.721	−0.575	−0.166	0.342
PC 4	−0.056	−0.123	0.375	−0.738	0.544
PC 5	0.991	−0.001	0.106	−0.065	−0.059

TABLE 10.11 PC Estimation Using the PC Loading Matrix

	Change in Rate							
	3-Month	1-Year	2-Year	5-Year	10-Year	PC(1)	PC(2)	PC(3)
01/13/04	0.020	−0.039	−0.049	−0.070	−0.056	−0.108	0.005	−0.006
01/14/04	−0.010	0.015	0.016	−0.017	−0.044	−0.022	−0.046	−0.011
01/15/04	0.000	0.015	0.032	0.017	−0.011	0.025	−0.028	−0.014
01/16/04	0.010	0.025	0.023	0.063	0.051	0.085	0.016	0.012
...	...	...	...	...	...	...	...	...
02/25/04	−0.010	−0.019	−0.033	−0.021	−0.012	−0.042	0.016	0.004

Note: Given in percentage form. To convert to decimal form multiply by 10^{-2}.

the PC loadings obtained from 120 business days of data in Table 10.10, we compute the principal components for the following 30 business days. The PCs for the first few days of the period beginning January 13, 2004, until February 25, 2004, are shown in the last three columns of Table 10.11.

The time series of daily returns on any fixed-income security can be now regressed against the corresponding times series of daily PC values given in Table 10.11 in order to get empirical PC durations. We consider the daily returns on MBS. Most trading on mortgage pass-through securities is done on a to-be-announced (TBA) basis, under which the buyer and seller agree on general parameters, such as issuing agency (GNMA, FNMA, or FHLMC), coupon, settlement date, price, and par amount. The buyer finds out which specific pools of mortgages will be delivered only two days before the settlement. The seller can choose any pools of mortgages as long as they satisfy the Good Delivery guidelines established by the Bond Market Association. The guidelines specify the maximum number of pools per $1 million of face value, the maximum variance in the face amount from the nominal amount, and so on. Table 10.12 shows the prices of TBA FNMA pass-throughs with eight different coupons ranging from 5.5 percent to 9 percent, in increments of 0.5 percent, for a few days toward the end of period beginning January 13, 2004, until February 25, 2004. These prices are used to construct daily returns on these securities over this period.

The PC durations are computed by regressing the daily returns of these securities on the first three principal components shown in Table 10.11. For example, the daily returns on the TBA FNMA pass-through with 5.5 percent coupon, together with the three PCs are shown in Table 10.13 for the first few days of the period beginning January 13, 2004, until February 25, 2004.

TABLE 10.12 Selected Data from Price Series for Coupons Ranging from 5.5 Percent to 9 Percent

	5.5%	6%	6.5%	7%	7.5%	8%	8.5%	9%
02/13/04	102.094	103.906	105.188	106.125	107.125	108	108	108.25
02/17/04	102.063	103.906	105.188	106.125	107.125	108	108	108.25
02/18/04	102.031	103.875	105.156	106.094	107.094	108	108	108.25
02/19/04	102.094	103.906	105.156	106.125	107.125	108	108	108.25
02/20/04	101.938	103.813	105.094	106.125	107.125	108	108	108.25
02/23/04	102.063	103.875	105.094	106.125	107.125	108	108	108.25
02/24/04	102.156	103.969	105.125	106.125	107.125	108	108	108.25
02/25/04	102.219	104.000	105.125	106.125	107.125	108	108	108.25

By regressing the daily returns on the three PCs given in Table 10.13, the duration corresponding to the first PC equals 1.93 years, and the duration corresponding to the second PC equals 1.33, on February 25, 2004. The duration corresponding to the third PC is insignificant. By repeating this analysis period by period, the empirical durations corresponding to the first PC for TBA FNMA pass-through with 5.5 percent coupon and 6 percent coupon are shown in Figure 10.7. These durations have a similar pattern as was found for the duration of the Lehman MBS index in Figure 10.5. Due to higher coupon, the duration of the 6 percent pass-through is generally lower than that of the 5.5 percent pass-through.

TABLE 10.13 Daily Returns of TBA FNMA Pass-Through with 5.5 Percent Coupon

	Daily Return on 5.5% Coupon	PC(1)	PC(2)	PC(3)
01/13/04	0.154%	−0.108	0.005	−0.006
01/14/04	0.091%	−0.022	−0.046	−0.011
01/15/04	0.092%	0.025	−0.028	−0.014
01/16/04	−0.183%	0.085	0.016	0.012
...	...	...	...	...
02/25/04	0.062%	−0.042	0.016	0.004

Note: PCs are given in percentage form. The regression uses the decimal form obtained by multiplying by 10^{-2}.

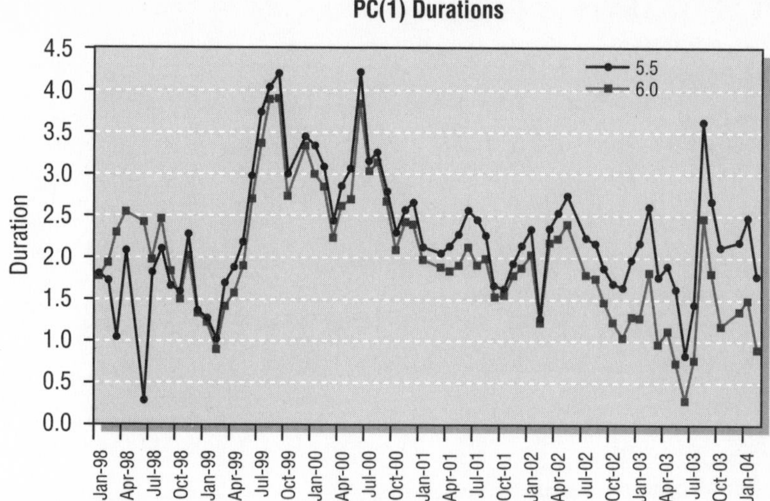

FIGURE 10.7 Empirical Durations Corresponding to the First PC for TBA FNMA Pass-Through with 5.5 Percent Coupon and 6 Percent Coupon

The empirical durations corresponding to the second PC for TBA FNMA pass-through with 5.5 percent coupon and 6 percent coupon are shown in Figure 10.8. These durations measure the sensitivity of these securities to slope shift in the Treasury yield curve. Though mostly the durations corresponding to the second PC are positive, implying a loss in value when positive slope shifts in the yield curve occur, these durations can become negative in some periods such as July through November 1998 and in April and May 2003.

APPENDIX 10.1: EIGENVECTORS, EIGENVALUES, AND PRINCIPAL COMPONENTS

This appendix describes the principal component approach and provides a step-by-step example for demonstrating its implementation. Consider a set of m variables $x_1, \ldots, x_m$ with covariance matrix Σ. Since Σ is symmetric by construction, using well-known results from matrix calculus we know that Σ has m normalized and linearly independent eigenvectors, $U_1, \ldots, U_m$, corresponding to m positive eigenvalues, $\lambda_1, \ldots, \lambda_m$. In fact, Σ can be factored as follows:

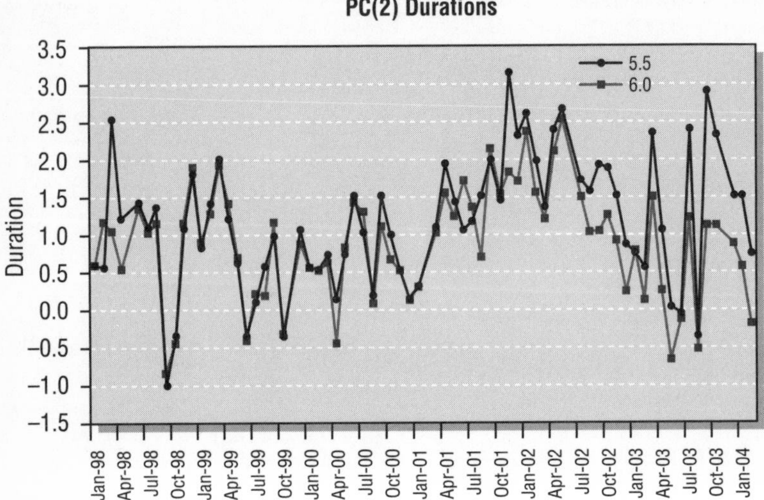

FIGURE 10.8 Empirical Durations Corresponding to the Second PC for TBA FNMA Pass-Through with 5.5 Percent Coupon and 6 Percent Coupon

$$\Sigma = U^T \Lambda U \tag{10.20}$$

where λ is a diagonal matrix with elements $\lambda_1, \ldots, \lambda_m$ along the diagonal and U is an mxm matrix whose rows correspond to the vectors $U_1, \ldots, U_m$. Since U is composed of normalized and orthogonal vectors, its inverse equals its transpose, or:

$$U^{-1} = U^T \tag{10.21}$$

The relationship between the m principal components and the m original variables is given as follows:

$$C = UX \tag{10.22}$$

where $C = [c_1 \ldots c_m]^T$ is the column vector of principal components and $X = [x_1 \ldots x_m]^T$ is the column vector of original variables. The matrix U gives the principal component coefficients. Hence, the principal components are linear combinations of the original variables and the original variables can, in turn, be expressed as linear combinations of the principal components as follows:

$$X = U^{-1}C \tag{10.23}$$

Using equation 10.21, the previous relation can be expressed as follows:

$$X = U^{T}C \tag{10.24}$$

To obtain the matrix U of principal component coefficients, we obtain the m eigenvalues of the covariance matrix Σ. The eigenvalues are obtained by solving the following equation:

$$Det\left[\Sigma - \lambda I\right] = 0 \tag{10.25}$$

where I is the identity matrix.

The eigenvectors are the nontrivial and normalized solutions to the set of equations:

$$\left(\Sigma - \lambda_j I\right)U_j = 0 \tag{10.26}$$

for $j = 1, 2, \ldots m$.

The final step in principal component analysis consists of ranking the eigenvalues by the order of their magnitudes. Since the eigenvalue of a principal component measures its variance, the principal component with the highest eigenvalue is the most important component. The eigenvector corresponding to a specific principal component gives the coefficients related to that principal component.

The dimensionality in principal component analysis is reduced by disregarding those principal components that are of minor importance in explaining the variability of the original variables (i.e., those with the lowest eigenvalues). Assuming that we retain the first k principal components, expression (10.24) can be rewritten as:

$$X = U^{T*}C^{*} + \varepsilon \tag{10.27}$$

where U^{T*} refers to the mxk matrix resulting from retaining the first k columns of the transposed matrix of ordered eigenvectors, C^* is the column vector composed of the k principal components and ε is a column vector of m error terms that contains the information not captured by the first k principal components.

Example 10.4 Consider the covariance matrix of changes (in percentages) in the U.S. one-year, three-year, and five-year zero-coupon rates over the period January 2000 through December 2002:

$$\Sigma = \begin{bmatrix} 0.0755 & 0.0679 & 0.0565 \\ 0.0679 & 0.0967 & 0.0911 \\ 0.0565 & 0.0911 & 0.0902 \end{bmatrix}$$

According to equation 10.25, the eigenvalues of this matrix are the roots of the following equation:

$$Det \begin{bmatrix} 0.0755-\lambda & 0.0679 & 0.0565 \\ 0.0679 & 0.0967-\lambda & 0.0911 \\ 0.0565 & 0.0911 & 0.0902-\lambda \end{bmatrix} = 0$$

Solving the determinant, we get the third order equation given as follows:

$$-\lambda^3 + 0.2624\lambda^2 - 0.0067\lambda + 0.00007 = 0$$

which has three different roots that are given in the ascending order as follows:

$$\lambda_1 = 0.2337 \;\; \lambda_2 = 0.0277 \;\; \lambda_3 = 0.0010$$

Substituting each of these roots in (10.26), we can obtain the corresponding eigenvectors. In particular, the eigenvector corresponding to λ_1 is composed of elements u_{11}, u_{12}, and u_{13}, and is obtained as the nontrivial solution to the following equations:

$$\begin{bmatrix} -0.1582 & 0.0679 & 0.0565 \\ 0.0679 & -0.1370 & 0.0911 \\ 0.0565 & 0.0911 & -0.1435 \end{bmatrix} \begin{bmatrix} u_{11} \\ u_{12} \\ u_{13} \end{bmatrix} = \begin{bmatrix} 0 \\ 0 \\ 0 \end{bmatrix}$$

Since the determinant of the matrix in the left side is zero, the number of independent equations is two, and hence one element must remain free at this stage. If we use u_{13} as the free variable, the solution is given as:

$$\begin{bmatrix} -0.1582 & 0.0679 & 0.0565 \\ 0.0679 & -0.1370 & 0.0911 \end{bmatrix} \begin{bmatrix} u_{11} \\ u_{12} \\ u_{13} \end{bmatrix} = \begin{bmatrix} 0 \\ 0 \end{bmatrix}$$

or

$$u_{11} = 0.8159u_{13} \quad u_{12} = 1.0692u_{13}$$

Since the eigenvector is also a normalized vector, we have:

$$u_{11}^2 + u_{12}^2 + u_{13}^2 = (0.8159u_{13})^2 + (1.0692u_{13})^2 + u_{13}^2 = 1$$

which gives two solutions as $u_{13} = -0.5967$ and $u_{13} = 0.5967$.

Substituting the two values of u_{13} in the solutions for u_{11} and u_{12}, we get the first eigenvector (corresponding to the highest eigenvalue) as one of the following two vectors:

$$U_1 = \begin{bmatrix} 0.4868 \\ 0.6380 \\ 0.5967 \end{bmatrix} \quad \text{or} \quad U_1 = \begin{bmatrix} -0.4868 \\ -0.6380 \\ -0.5967 \end{bmatrix}$$

Similarly, for the second eigenvalue, λ_2, we obtain the eigenvector as either of the following two vectors:

$$U_2 = \begin{bmatrix} 0.8513 \\ -0.1935 \\ -0.4876 \end{bmatrix} \quad \text{or} \quad U_2 = \begin{bmatrix} -0.8513 \\ 0.1935 \\ 0.4876 \end{bmatrix}$$

and similarly for the third eigenvalue λ_3, we obtain:

$$U_3 = \begin{bmatrix} 0.1956 \\ -0.7454 \\ 0.6373 \end{bmatrix} \quad \text{or} \quad U_3 = \begin{bmatrix} -0.1956 \\ 0.7454 \\ -0.6373 \end{bmatrix}$$

Taking the first solution of each eigenvector, we get the matrix of principal component loadings that gives principal components as a linear transformation of the interest rate changes as follows:

$$U = \begin{bmatrix} 0.4868 & 0.6380 & 0.5967 \\ 0.8513 & -0.1935 & -0.4876 \\ 0.1956 & -0.7454 & 0.6373 \end{bmatrix}$$

The portion of the total variance of the changes in the three interest rates explained by each principal component is given using equation 10.5 as follows:

$$\frac{\lambda_1}{\sum_{j=1}^{m} \lambda_j} = 89\%, \quad \frac{\lambda_2}{\sum_{j=1}^{m} \lambda_j} = 10.6\%, \quad \frac{\lambda_3}{\sum_{j=1}^{m} \lambda_j} = 0.4\%$$

Since the first two principal components are enough to explain the dynamics of interest rate changes, using equation 10.27, the model for interest rate changes can be expressed as:

$$\begin{bmatrix} \Delta y(1) \\ \Delta y(3) \\ \Delta y(5) \end{bmatrix} = \begin{bmatrix} 0.4868 & 0.8513 \\ 0.6380 & -0.1935 \\ 0.5967 & -0.4876 \end{bmatrix} \begin{bmatrix} c_1 \\ c_2 \end{bmatrix} + \begin{bmatrix} \varepsilon(1) \\ \varepsilon(3) \\ \varepsilon(5) \end{bmatrix}$$

and the portion of the total variance of interest rate changes captured by these two principal components equals 99.6 percent.

APPENDIX 10.2: COMPUTING PRINCIPAL COMPONENT RISK MEASURES FOR COMPLEX SECURITIES AND UNDER MATURITY MISMATCHES

Appendix 9.1 derived the key rate durations and convexities of complex securities with interest-sensitive cash flows, and for securities with mismatches between cash flows and key rate maturities. The handling of these situations under the principal component model mostly resembles the procedures described in that chapter. There are, however, some differences that are discussed next.

For complex securities, the principal component model has two special features. The orthogonality of the principal components makes it unnecessary to compute principal component convexities for the combination of shifts in two different principal components. Therefore, the finite difference method is only used to approximate the first- and second-order derivatives of price, P, with respect to the shift in each principal component, c_i, as follows:

$$\begin{aligned} \frac{\partial P}{\partial c_i} &\approx \frac{P_{i(+\varepsilon)} - P_{i(-\varepsilon)}}{2\varepsilon} \\ \frac{\partial^2 P}{\partial c_i^{\,2}} &\approx \frac{P_{i(+\varepsilon_i)} - 2P + P_{i(-\varepsilon_i)}}{\varepsilon_i^2} \end{aligned} \qquad (10.28)$$

where $P_{i(+\varepsilon)}$ and $P_{i(-\varepsilon)}$ are the prices of the security computed using a theoretical valuation model after shifting the term structure by a positive and a negative move of a very small magnitude ε in the ith principal component.

The "effective" principal component durations and convexities using finite difference approximations can be given as:

$$\begin{aligned} PCD(i) &\approx \frac{-(P_{i(+\varepsilon)} - P_{i(-\varepsilon)})}{2P\varepsilon} \\ PCC(i,\ i) &\approx \frac{P_{i(+\varepsilon_i)} - 2P + P_{i(-\varepsilon_i)}}{P\varepsilon_i^2} \end{aligned} \qquad (10.29)$$

When the cash flows and the set of zero-coupon rates have different maturities, a straightforward solution can be obtained by interpolation of the factor loadings. Using the results in Chapter 9 and substituting the changes in the key rates by their expressions in terms of factor loadings and principal components, we obtain the following expressions for the change in the interest rate for any given term t:

$$y(t) = \begin{cases} \displaystyle\sum_{i=1}^{k} l_{first,i} \times c_i & t \le t_{first} \\ \displaystyle\sum_{i=1}^{k} l_{last,i} \times c_i & t \ge t_{last} \\ \displaystyle\sum_{i=1}^{k} \left(\alpha \times l_{left,i} + (1-\alpha) \times l_{right,i}\right) \times c_i & else \end{cases} \qquad (10.30)$$

where t_{first} and t_{last} refer to the terms of the shortest and longest term zero-coupon rates in the set of initial rates, t_{left} and t_{right}, with $t_{left} \leq t \leq t_{right}$, refers to the terms of the zero-coupon rates adjacent (to the left and the right) to term t, $l_{i,j}$ is the factor loading of the jth principal component on the ith zero-coupon rate, and α and $(1 - \alpha)$ are the coefficients of the linear interpolation, defined as follows:

$$\alpha = \frac{t_{right} - t}{t_{right} - t_{left}}$$
$$1 - \alpha = \frac{t - t_{left}}{t_{right} - t_{left}} \tag{10.31}$$

NOTES

1. The empirical evidence in Soto (2004a) supports this assertion.
2. In its generality, the key rate model does not require a stationary factor structure of interest rate changes. However, for performing a VaR analysis, the covariance structure of the key rate changes must remain stationary.
3. Some researchers have applied factor analysis instead of PCA to obtain the composite variables, which are called common factors. The estimation of the common factor model can be carried out through several methods, the most common being the maximum likelihood method and the principal component method. The maximum likelihood method allows statistical tests, but requires the assumption of normally distributed variables. The principal component method does not make any data distribution assumption and focuses exclusively on the covariance or the correlation matrix. This makes it possible to incorporate other assumptions into the estimation of the matrix. For example, the structure can be obtained from GARCH models or computed using exponentially weighted observations.
4. Bliss (1997a) provides a simple method for rotating the factors.
5. This name, which is specific to factor analysis, is appropriate in this framework because equation 10.8 coincides with the final equation of a factor analysis in which the method employed to extract common factors is PCA. See note 3.
6. Appendix 10.2 deals with the computation of principal component risk measures for complex securities.
7. Direct application of equation 10.14 requires the initial vector of zero-coupon rate changes in the principal component model to include the set of key rates. Also note that slight differences might arise between the principal component durations computed directly and the key rate durations, due to convexity effects or the sensitivity of prices to nondifferentiable shifts on the forward rate curve implied by key rate shocks.

8. For the first principal component duration to match traditional duration when the first principal component reflects an exact parallel movement, Barber and Copper (1996) suggest to multiply each principal component duration by the squared root of the number, *m*, of series in the original data set.
9. For instance, see Falkenstein and Hanweck (1997).
10. *Source:* Federal Reserve Bulletin.
11. *Source:* Lehman Brothers.

CHAPTER 11

Duration Models for Default-Prone Securities

Until now virtually all chapters in the book have focused on duration models for default-free securities and their derivatives in the U.S. Treasury and the LIBOR market. Though technically mortgage-related securities are prone to default, their high loan-to-value ratios, together with the fact that mortgage loans (and mortgage-backed securities) are collateralized with the residential and commercial assets, makes the default probability quite low in this market. Hence, for most practical purposes, the mortgage securities considered in the previous chapter can be modeled as default-free securities. We now turn our attention to default-prone securities such as corporate bonds and stocks.

It is generally assumed in the fixed-income literature that corporate bonds have a lower duration, and, hence, a lower sensitivity to interest rate changes than equivalent default-free bonds. The standard reasoning given in the literature is as follows. Since the possibility of default reduces the expected maturity of the corporate bond, and since duration and expected bond maturity are directly related, the presence of default risk shortens the expected bond maturity and, hence, reduces the duration of the corporate bond. Though intuitively appealing, this reasoning is flawed.

Consider a financial institution with \$100 in assets financed by \$95 (in present value) in a zero-coupon bond maturing in one year and \$5 of equity. Let the duration of assets be equal to 10. Consider a rise of 1 percent in the default-free interest rates, such that the assets fall about \$100 × 10 × 1% = \$10 to approximately \$90. Since the assets are now only worth \$90, the market value of the bond cannot be more than \$90. Hence, the minimum loss suffered by the bondholders is (\$90 – \$95)/\$95 = –5.26% (in reality, the loss would be higher because the equity value will be slightly higher than zero, and bond value slightly lower than \$90) and, hence, the duration of the one-year corporate zero-coupon bond is at least *five* times the duration of the equivalent default-free zero-coupon bond with one-year maturity. Though the high leverage ratio assumed in the previous example may be a bit unrealistic (though not unrealistic for certain financial institutions such as Fannie Mae or commercial banks), it demonstrates that *corporate bond duration is inextricably linked with the duration of the underlying assets of the firm.*

Though the possibility of default reduces the expected maturity of the bond, we noted that the duration of the corporate bond is about five times the duration of the default-free bond in the previous example! This paradox can be resolved by making the following observation. The expected contractual maturity of a security is *not the same as the expected maturity of the cash flows of the underlying assets that can be used to replicate that security.* For example, the duration of a one-year European call option written on a five-year zero-coupon bond is at least five years, or at least five times its contractual expiration date of one year (see Table 7.1). This is because the call option can be replicated as a portfolio of a long position and a short position in two different bonds. Just because this European call option's expected contractual maturity is exactly one year, one cannot infer that its duration equals one year.

Similarly, using the option-pricing framework of Merton (1974), a corporate zero-coupon bond can be considered a replicating portfolio of an equivalent maturity default-free zero-coupon bond and the underlying assets of the firm. If the duration of assets is very high (e.g., the assets may be 30-year fixed-coupon mortgage loans), then the duration of the corporate bond can be *higher* than the duration of the equivalent default-free bond, consistent with the result shown in the previous example.

Though the duration of the corporate zero-coupon bond can be considered a weighted average of the duration of the default-free zero-coupon bond and the duration of the firm's assets, little discussion exists in the bond literature on the duration of the underlying assets of firms. The asset returns in industries tied with inflation, such as oil, gold, and so on may be positively correlated with interest rate changes, implying a negative asset duration in these industries, while asset returns in other industries, such as financial services and utilities, may be negatively correlated with interest rate changes, implying a positive asset duration.

Even though corporate bonds and stocks can be viewed as options, much of the previous work modeled the duration of corporate bonds as extensions of the simple duration model.[1] In absence of a rigorous contingent claims analysis framework, the interest rate risk characteristics of corporate bonds cannot be fully explained. For example, do increases in financial leverage and/or business risk, increase or decrease the duration of a default-prone bond? How does the interest rate sensitivity of the firm's assets affect the interest rate sensitivity of its risky debt? This chapter answers some of these questions.

Chance (1990); Shimko, Tejima, and Van Deventer (1993); Nawalkha (1996); Longstaff and Schwartz (1995); and others provide contingent claim models to answer some of the previous questions. Nawalkha generalizes Chance's model and derives new duration measures for a firm's default-prone zero-coupon bond and its non-dividend paying stock, under theoretically less restrictive conditions.[2] This extension is intuitively appealing and is consistent with the results of a number of previous empirical studies on the interest rate sensitivities of corporate stocks and bonds.

One of the main results found by Chance is that the duration of a default-prone zero-coupon bond is always positive and its magnitude is always less than its maturity. Implicitly, another important result contained in Chance's model is that the duration of the corresponding non-dividend paying stock must always be negative, *since the duration of the underlying assets of the firm is assumed to be zero.*

The duration of an asset is traditionally defined by its relative basis risk given as $-(\partial V(t)/\partial r(t))/V(t)$, where $V(t)$ is the value of the firm's assets at time t, and $dr(t)$ represents an infinitesimal change in the current level of default-free interest rate $r(t)$. The duration of a firm's assets can be given as a weighted average of the durations of its non-dividend paying stock and the zero-coupon bond, as follows:

$$D_v = \frac{S(t)}{V(t)} D_s + \frac{D(t, T)}{V(t)} D_d \tag{11.1}$$

where $S(t)$ is the market value of the stock, $D(t, T)$ is the market value of corporate zero-coupon bond or debt maturing at time T, $V(t) = S(t) + D(t, T)$, is the value of the firm's assets, and D_s, D_d, and D_v are the durations of corporate stock, bond, and the assets, respectively. Since Chance assumes a zero value for the asset duration (i.e., $D_v = 0$), equation 11.1 implies the following relationship between the stock duration and the bond duration:

$$D_s = -\left(\frac{D(t, T)}{S(t)}\right) D_d \tag{11.2}$$

Thus, not only is the stock duration always negative, but also its magnitude is relatively significant compared to the magnitude of the duration of the corporate bond, unless the debt to equity ratio is very low.

In general, the negative stock duration in equation 11.2 implies a wealth transfer from the bondholders of a firm to its stockholders due to an increase in the nominal interest rate. However, the previous wealth transfer hypothesis is inconsistent with almost all of the previous empirical findings on the interest rate sensitivity of corporate stocks. Generally, stock values fall when interest rates rise and duration values of stocks are generally *positive*. Positive durations for stocks imply that the asset durations must be positive in equation 11.1.

In this chapter, we allow positive durations values for stocks. This is done by relaxing the assumption of a zero-duration value for the assets of a firm. It is shown that if the duration of a firm's assets is positive, then the duration of the non-dividend paying stock can be negative, zero, or positive. An important consequence of a positive asset duration is that the duration of the default-prone zero-coupon bond is *higher* than when the asset duration is assumed to be zero.

PRICING AND DURATION OF A DEFAULT-FREE ZERO-COUPON BOND UNDER THE VASICEK MODEL

Vasicek (1977) assumes a mean reverting Ornstein-Uhlenbeck process for the instantaneous short rate of the form:

$$dr(t) = \alpha\left(m - r(t)\right)dt + \sigma dZ(t) \tag{11.3}$$

where $r(t)$ is the instantaneous short rate at time t, m is the long-term mean to which r reverts at a speed α, σ is the volatility coefficient and $dZ(t)$ is the standard Wiener process for the short rate (see Appendix 11.1 for an introduction to continuous-time stochastic processes).

Assuming the price of a default-free zero-coupon bond is a function of the short rate and the bond maturity, applying Ito's lemma, and using absence of arbitrage, Vasicek obtained the following equation for the bond price at time t maturing T periods hence:

$$P(t,\ T) = e^{A(t,T)-B(t,T)r(t)} \tag{11.4}$$

where

$$B(t,\ T) = \frac{1 - e^{-\alpha(T-t)}}{\alpha}$$

$$A(t,\ T) = \left(m + \frac{\sigma\gamma}{\alpha} - \frac{\sigma^2}{2\alpha^2}\right)\left[B(t,\ T) - (T-t)\right] - B(t,\ T)^2\frac{\sigma^2}{4\alpha}$$

where γ is the market price of interest rate risk. The stochastic bond price process consistent with the above equation is given as:

$$\frac{dP(t,\ T)}{P(t,T)} = \left(r(t) + \gamma\ B(t,T)\right)dt - B(t,\ T)dZ(t) \tag{11.5}$$

The relative basis risk of the default-free zero-coupon bond using equation 11.4 can be given as $-[\partial\ P(t,\ T)/\partial\ r(t)]/P(t,\ T)$, which defines the duration of the bond under the Vasicek model, given as:

$$D_p = -\left(\frac{\partial P(t,\ T)}{\partial r(t)}\right) / \ P(t,\ T) = B(t,\ T) = \frac{1 - e^{-\alpha(T-t)}}{\alpha} \tag{11.6}$$

The asymptotic value of the duration under the Vasicek model as T goes to infinity equals $1/\alpha$. The traditional Macaulay duration can be obtained as a special case of the Vasicek duration by assuming the speed of mean reversion α equals zero. This can be demonstrated by using the L'Hospital's rule to equation 11.6, which gives $D_P(\alpha = 0) = T - t$. Intuitively, the previous result obtains since a zero-mean reversion makes Vasicek's model consistent with parallel term structure shifts. In general, if the term structure is mean reverting and α is positive, the duration of a zero-coupon bond will be lower than its traditional Macaulay duration.

The Vasicek price given in equation 11.4 may not fit an existing set of default-free zero-coupon bond prices. In that case, one may wish to *calibrate* the Vasicek model by using an observable set of zero-coupon prices given at time $t = 0$ as $P(0,\ T)$. The main advantage of using an observable set of zero-coupon bond prices is that it ensures that the discrepancies between the theoretical and observable prices of default-free bonds do not lead to errors in the pricing of corporate bonds. As shown in Chapter 6 of the second course book of this trilogy, calibration to observable prices $P(0,\ T)$ can be achieved by allowing the long-term mean m of the short rate in equation 11.3 to become a time-dependent function, given as follows:

$$m(t) = \frac{1}{\alpha}\left(\frac{\partial f(0,\ t)}{\partial t} + \alpha f(0,\ t) + \frac{\sigma^2}{2\alpha}\left[1 - e^{-2\alpha t}\right] - \gamma\ \sigma\right) \tag{11.7}$$

where $f(0,\ t) = -\partial\ \ln P(0,\ t)/\partial t$
= Initially observed instantaneous forward rate at time 0 for term t

Using this deterministically changing mean, $m(t)$, instead of m in equation 11.3 ensures that the price of the zero-coupon bond in equation 11.4 exactly equals the observable price $P(0, T)$ at time $t = 0$. The changing long-term mean does not change the functional form of the bond price process in equation 11.5 or the definition of the duration measure in equation 11.6, except that evolution of $r(t)$ is different under the changing long-term mean. Using the changing long-term mean allows all of the results of this chapter to be calibrated to the initially observable default-free zero-coupon prices.

Equation 11.7 requires that the initially observable bond price function $P(0, T)$ be twice differentiable with respect to maturity. This condition is satisfied by the commonly used models for the estimation of $P(0, T)$ function (e.g., the cubic-spline model of McCulloch and Kwon, 1992, and the exponential model of Nelson and Seigel, 1987, given in Chapter 3).

THE ASSET DURATION

This section derives the duration measure of a firm's assets consistent with the contingent claims models of Shimko, Tejima, and Van Deventer (1993), Nawalkha (1996, 2004), Longstaff and Schwartz (1995), Collin-Dufresne and Goldstein (2001), and others. Since the return on the assets of a corporation and the changes in the short rate are always imperfectly correlated, the asset price cannot be given as a deterministic function of the short rate, and, hence, one cannot obtain the duration of the assets by taking the partial derivative of the asset price with respect to the short rate. For example, the asset value may increase or decrease for an increase in the short rate, and hence asset duration cannot be defined in a mathematical sense. However, the conditional *expected* change in the asset return can be measured for a given change in the short rate using a statistical regression technique. Using this insight, we define the asset duration as the sensitivity of the asset return to changes in the short rate as follows.

Assume that a firm's asset price dynamics are given by the following diffusion process:

$$\frac{dV(t)}{V(t)} = \mu\ dt + \sigma_v\ dZ_v(t) \tag{11.8}$$

Now, consider a time-series regression of the asset returns on changes in the short rate given as follows:

$$\frac{dV(t)}{V(t)} = a - D_v \ dr(t) + e_t \tag{11.9}$$

where a is the intercept and $-D_v$ is the slope coefficient of the regression, where D_v is the duration of the firm's assets. Using the definition of a regression slope coefficient, the asset duration D_v is given as follows:

$$D_v = -\frac{Cov\left(\frac{dV(t)}{V(t)}, dr(t)\right)}{Var\left(dr(t)\right)} \tag{11.10}$$

Using equations 11.3 and 11.8, the previous definition of the asset duration can be parameterized as follows:

$$D_v = -\frac{(\sigma \ \sigma_v \ \rho)dt}{\sigma^2 dt} = -\frac{\sigma_v \ \rho}{\sigma} \tag{11.11}$$

where, ρ, the correlation between the two Wiener processes $dZ(t)$ and $dZ_v(t)$ is given as:

$$E(dZ(t)dZ_v(t)) = \rho \ dt \tag{11.12}$$

The duration of the firm's assets gives the negative of the *expected* percentage change in the asset value for a given change in the short rate. It should be noted that since the short rate process and the asset price process (given by equations 11.3 and 11.8) are assumed to have constant volatility parameters, and the correlation between these two processes is also constant (defined in equation 11.12), the duration of the firm's assets is obtained as a constant.

PRICING AND DURATION OF A DEFAULT-PRONE ZERO-COUPON BOND: THE MERTON FRAMEWORK

Merton (1974) applies the Black-Scholes-Merton option-pricing model to price the debt of a firm with a simple capital structure. Merton makes standard perfect market assumptions (zero transactions costs, zero taxes, infi-

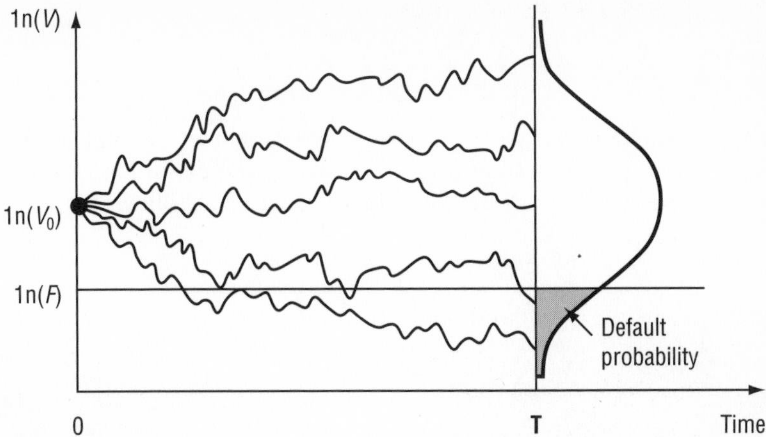

FIGURE 11.1 Firm Value Paths under Merton's Model

nite divisibility of assets, availability of costless information, no restrictions on short selling, etc.) in an economy that allows trading in continuous time. In a specific application, Merton considers a firm that has two types of claims—single homogeneous class of debt and the residual claim equity. The firm cannot issue any new claims on the firm nor can it pay cash dividends or do share repurchase prior to the maturity of debt. At the current time t, the debt has $T - t$ years remaining to maturity. Since the firm makes no coupon payments on debt, and no safety covenants exist in Merton's framework to enforce bankruptcy, the firm cannot default at any time before the bond maturity date T, even if the assets of the firm fall to only a small fraction of the face value of the bond.

Figure 11.1 illustrates different paths that the firm value process may take. If at maturity the firm value falls below the face value of debt (the shaded area), the firm cannot fully redeem the face value even by liquidating all its assets. In this case, the bondholders take over the firm and shareholders get nothing.

The payoffs to stock and zero-coupon bond at maturity are shown in Table 11.1. These payoffs are mathematically given as follows:

$$S(T) = \max\left[0,\ V(T) - F\right] \tag{11.13}$$

and

$$D(T,\ T) = \min\left[V(T),\ F\right] \tag{11.14}$$

TABLE 11.1 Payoffs to Stock and Zero-Coupon Bond at Maturity: Merton Model

	$V(T) \geq F$	$V(T) < F$
Stock value at T	$V(T) - F$	0
Bond value at T	F	$V(T)$

where the sum of stock and bond equals the firm value, or:

$$S(T) + D(T,\ T) = V(T) \tag{11.15}$$

The payoff in equation 11.13 makes the stock a call option on the firm's assets, where the exercise price of the option is equal to the face value of the bond, and option expiration is equal to the maturity of the bond. The bond payoff in equation 11.14 can be written alternatively as:

$$D(T,T) = \min\left[V(T),\ F\right] = F - \max\left[0,\ F - V(T)\right] \tag{11.16}$$

The payoff in equation 11.16 represents the default-prone zero-coupon bond as a sum of a long position in a default-free zero-coupon bond (since F is a sure payment in equation 11.16) and a short position in a put option. The put option depends on the same variables as the call option representing the firm's equity.

Nawalkha-Shimko et al. Models

Using the Merton framework given previously, Nawalkha (1996) and Shimko et al. (1993) derive the time t price of the bond in equation 11.14 by assuming that the asset return process is given by equation 11.8 and the bond return process is given by equation 11.5. Using this framework, these authors derive the price of a default-prone zero-coupon bond as follows:

$$D(t,\ T) = \left[1 - N(d_1)\right]V(t) + N(d_2)P(t,\ T)F \tag{11.17}$$

where

$$N(x) = \frac{1}{\sqrt{2\pi}} \int_{-\infty}^{x} e^{-\frac{1}{2}z^2} dz = \text{Cumulative normal distribution function at } x$$

$$d_1 = \frac{-\ln\left(L(t)\right) + \frac{1}{2}V}{\sqrt{V}}$$

$$d_2 = d_1 - \sqrt{V}$$

$$L(t) = \frac{P(t,\ T)F}{V(t)} = \text{Quasi-debt ratio}$$

and

$$V = \left(\sigma_v^2 + \frac{\sigma^2}{\alpha^2} + \frac{2\rho\sigma\sigma_v}{\alpha}\right)(T - t) - B(t,\ T)\left(\frac{2\sigma^2}{\alpha^2} + \frac{2\rho\sigma\sigma_v}{\alpha}\right) - \frac{\sigma^2}{2\alpha^3}\left(e^{-2\alpha(T-t)} - 1\right)$$

In equation 11.17 $P(t, T)$ is the Vasicek bond price of a default-free zero-coupon bond defined in equation 11.4. Also, expression $B(t, T)$ is a part of the Vasicek price defined in equation 11.4. All other variables are defined as before. Note the long-term mean of the short rate, m, does not enter anywhere in equation 11.17 except through the default-free bond price function $P(t, T)$ defined in equation 11.4. As shown in equation 11.7 when the parameter m is made a deterministic function of time, the Vasicek model can be calibrated to an initially observed set of market prices of default-free zero-coupon bonds, $P(0, T)$. By substituting $t = 0$, in equation 11.17, and using the observable market prices $P(0, T)$ (instead of Vasicek model prices with a constant m), the default-prone zero-coupon prices, $D(0, T)$, are also calibrated to $P(0, T)$. Note that to use the European formula in equation 11.7 we don't need to know the process for the long-term mean in equation 11.7, implied by the observable market prices $P(0, T)$. Of course, explicit modeling of the process for long-term mean would be essential if we were pricing securities with American-type options like callable bonds and convertible bonds.

Equation 11.17 suggests that the default-prone bond $D(t, T)$ can be considered a portfolio of the firm's assets and the \$$F$ face-value default-free zero-coupon bond maturing at time T. Specifically, $D(t, T)$ equals an investment of $N(d_2)\ P(t, T)\ F$ in the default-free zero-coupon bond (i.e., $N(d_2)$ number of \$$F$ face-value default-free zero-coupon bonds maturing at time T), and an investment of $[1 - N(d_1)]\ V(t)$ in the assets of the firm (i.e., $[1 - N(d_1)]$ number of the firm's assets).

Since the duration of a portfolio is a weighted average of the durations of the securities in the portfolio, the duration of the default-prone bond can be given as:

$$D_d = w_v D_v + w_p D_p \tag{11.18}$$

where the weights are defined as:

$$w_v = \frac{[1 - N(d_1)]V(t)}{D(t,\ T)} \tag{11.19}$$

and

$$w_p = \frac{N(d_2)P(t,\ T)F}{D(t,\ T)} \tag{11.20}$$

Since both weights are greater than zero and sum up to one, the duration of the default-prone bond lies between the duration of the assets and the duration of the default-free zero-coupon bond. If the duration of assets is greater than the duration of the default-free zero-coupon bond, then the duration of the default-prone bond is *greater* than the duration of the default-free bond. This result is in contrast with most duration models for default-prone bonds in the fixed-income literature, which claim that duration of the default-prone bond is always less than the duration of the default-free bond by implicitly or explicitly assuming that $D_v = 0$, in equation 11.18.

Using equation 11.1, the duration of the stock of the firm can be given as:

$$D_s = \frac{V(t)}{S(t)} D_v - \frac{D(t,\ T)}{S(t)} D_d \tag{11.21}$$

where, using balance sheet identity, $S(t) = V(t) - D(t,\ T)$. Hence, the duration of the stock of the firm can be computed using the asset duration of the default-prone bond duration.

Example 11.1 Consider a zero-coupon bond that promises to pay \$1 ($F = 1$) in a year ($T = 1$). Volatility of firm value is $_v = 0.2$, the risk-free rate is $r(0) =$ 6%, speed of mean reversion of the interest rate is $\alpha = 0.2$, the risk-neutral long-run mean of the interest rate is $m = 0.06$, volatility of the interest rate process is $\sigma = 0.02$, the correlation between the firm value and interest rate process is $\rho = -0.3$, and the market price of risk is $\gamma = 0$.

The value of the default-free zero-coupon bond can be computed using equation 11.4 as follows:

$$B(t,\ T) = \frac{1-e^{-\alpha(T-t)}}{\alpha} = \frac{1-e^{-0.2(1-0)}}{0.2} = 0.9063$$

$$A(t,\ T) = \left(m + \frac{\sigma\gamma}{\alpha} - \frac{\sigma^2}{2\alpha^2}\right)\left[B(t,\ T) - (T-t)\right]] - B(t,\ T)^2\frac{\sigma^2}{4\alpha}$$

$$= \left(0.06 + 0 - \frac{0.02^2}{2\times 0.2^2}\right)\times\left[0.9063 - 1\right] - 0.9063^2\frac{0.02^2}{4\times 0.2} = -0.0056$$

$$P(t,\ T) = e^{A(t,T)-B(t,T)r(t)} = e^{-0.0056-0.9063\times 0.06} = 0.9418$$

The value of the default-prone zero-coupon bond can be computed as follows. The integrated volatility V, quasi-debt ratio $L(t)$, d_1, and d_2 in equation 11.17 are given as:

$$V = \left(\sigma_v^2 + \frac{\sigma^2}{\alpha^2} + \frac{2\rho\sigma\sigma_v}{\alpha}\right)(T-t) - B(t,\ T)\left(\frac{2\sigma^2}{\alpha^2} + \frac{2\rho\sigma\sigma_v}{\alpha}\right) - \frac{\sigma^2}{2\alpha^3}\left(e^{-2\alpha(T-t)} - 1\right)$$

$$= \left(0.2^2 + \frac{0.02^2}{0.2^2} + \frac{2\times(-0.3)\times 0.02\times 0.2}{0.2}\right)\times 1$$

$$-\ 0.9063\times\left(\frac{2\times 0.02^2}{0.2^2} + \frac{2\times(-0.3)\times 0.02\times 0.2}{0.2}\right) - \frac{0.02^2}{2\times 0.2^3}\left(e^{-2\times 0.2} - 1\right) = 0.0390$$

$$L(t) = \frac{P(t,T)F}{V(t)} = \frac{0.9418\times 1}{1.2} = 0.7848$$

$$d_1 = \frac{-\ln\left(L(t)\right) + \frac{1}{2}V}{\sqrt{V}} = \frac{-\ln(0.7848) + \frac{1}{2}0.0390}{\sqrt{0.0390}} = 1.3256$$

$$d_2 = d_1 - \sqrt{V} = 1.3256 - \sqrt{0.0390} = 1.1282$$

The price of the default-prone bond can be computed using equation 11.17 as follows:

$$D(t,\ T) = \left[1 - N(d_1)\right]V(t)\ +\ N(d_2)P(t,\ T)F$$

$$= \left[1 - N(1.3256)\right]\times 0.0390 + N(1.1282)\times 0.9418\times 1 = 0.9307$$

The firm value duration can be computed using equation 11.11 as follows:

$$D_v = -\frac{\sigma_v \rho}{\sigma} = -\frac{0.2 \times (-0.3)}{0.02} = 3$$

Duration of the default-free bond can be computed using equation 11.6 as follows:

$$D_p = B(t, T) = 0.9063$$

Duration of the default-prone bond can be computed using equation 11.18 as a weighted average of the firm's asset duration and the duration of the default-free bond. The weights are given in equations 11.19 and 11.20:

$$w_v = \frac{\left[1 - N(d_1)\right]V(t)}{D(t, T)} = \frac{\left[1 - N(1.3256)\right] \times 1.2}{0.9307} = 0.1192$$
$$w_p = \frac{N(d_2)P(t, T)F}{D(t, T)} = \frac{N(1.1282) \times 0.9418 \times 1}{0.9307} = 0.8808$$

Using these weights the duration of the default-prone bond and the stock can be computed using equations 11.18 and 11.21, as follows:

$$D_d = w_v D_v + w_p D_p = 0.1192 \times 3 + 0.9908 \times 0.9063 = 1.1560$$
$$D_s = \frac{V(t)}{S(t)} D_v - \frac{D(t, T)}{S(t)} D_d = \frac{1.2}{1.2 - 0.9307} \times 3 - \frac{0.9307}{1.2 - 0.9307} \times 1.1560$$
$$= 9.3733$$

Numerical Analysis

In this section, we perform numerical analysis to see the role played by the firm's asset duration in determining the durations of the firm's default-prone bond and stock. We also investigate how the default-prone bond duration changes with respect to financial risk and business risk of the firm.

Relationship between Asset Duration, Bond Duration, and Stock Duration
Consider a firm that has both debt and equity outstanding. To keep the analysis realistic, let's assume momentarily that the interest and the dividend payments are allowed. Since the duration of a portfolio of securities can be given as the weighted average of the durations of the individual securities in the portfolio, the asset duration can be given as:

$$D_v = \left[\frac{D(t, T)}{V(t)}\right] D_d + \left[\frac{S(t)}{V(t)}\right] D_s \tag{11.22}$$

Equation 11.22 follows from balance-sheet identity and is valid even when interest and dividend payments are allowed. Based on casual empiricism, let's further assume that the duration of coupon-paying debt is greater than zero. Since $D_d > 0$, equation 11.22 implies the following result:

$$\text{If } D_v \leq 0, \text{ then } D_s < 0 \text{ and } |D_s| \geq \left| \left[\frac{D(t,T)}{S(t)}\right] D_d \right| \tag{11.23}$$

Thus, assuming that the duration of a firm's assets is less than or equal to zero implies that the duration of its stock must be significantly negative (unless the debt to equity ratio is always very low, or the magnitude of the duration of the debt is insignificant). This is counterintuitive since investors usually associate interest rate risk with bonds and not stocks. Further, many empirical studies suggest that stock returns display significantly negative sensitivities or statistically insignificant sensitivities to the changes in interest rates. In other words, the empirical evidence implies that the duration values of most stocks should be either positive or close to zero, but not significantly negative as implied by equation 11.23. Hence, under empirically realistic conditions, the duration of the assets of most firms should not be less than or equal to zero.

In this section, we offer additional insights on the signs and magnitudes of the duration of a firm's assets, the duration of its default-prone bond and the duration of its non-dividend paying stock. Since returns on the firm's assets are not directly observable, none of the empirical studies in the past have analyzed the relationship between the asset returns and the changes in the nominal interest rates. However, the sign of the duration of a firm's assets can be determined by the sign and the magnitude of the duration of its default-prone bond and the duration of its stock. Since previous empirical studies do suggest certain general results about the signs and magnitudes of the duration values of corporate bonds and corporate stocks, these results can be used to implicitly determine the sign of the duration of the firm's assets.

In the following, we obtain a stronger characterization of the relationship between the asset duration, the stock duration, and the bond duration by making certain additional assumptions. Consistent with the contingent claims valuation framework of this chapter, we now assume that a firm's outstanding liabilities are given by a single non-dividend paying stock and a single default-prone zero-coupon bond.

We analyze the relationship between the asset duration, the duration of the default-prone zero-coupon bond, and the duration of the non-dividend paying stock in more detail by considering five cases given next, which are also illustrated in Figure 11.2. These cases consider asset durations ranging from negative values (in Case 1 and Case 2), to positive values (in Case 3, Case 4, and Case 5), and show that positive duration values for assets are more consistent with empirical data on stocks and bonds. A variable that plays a key role in dividing the range of asset duration values among five cases, from the most negative to the most positive, is the quasi-debt ratio

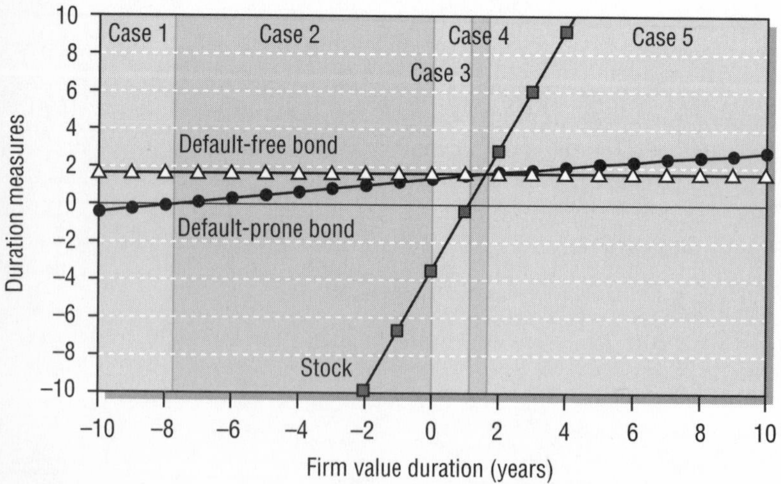

FIGURE 11.2 Relationship between Asset Duration, Bond Duration, and Stock Duration

$L(t)$, introduced in equation 11.17. To analyze these five cases, we introduce two more variables given as:

$$K_1 = \frac{N(d_2)}{N(d_1)-1}\frac{P(t,\ T)F}{V(t)} = \frac{N(d_2)}{N(d_1)-1}L(t) < 0 \tag{11.24}$$

and

$$K_2 = \frac{N(d_2)}{N(d_1)}\frac{P(t,\ T)F}{V(t)} = \frac{N(d_2)}{N(d_1)}L(t) > 0 \tag{11.25}$$

The five cases are given as:

Case 1: $D_v < K_1 D_p < 0$. Under this case:
$D_d < 0$
$D_s < 0$
$|D_s| > |D_d|$

Case 2: $K_1 D_p < D_A < 0$. Under this case:
$D_d \geq 0$
$D_s < 0$
$|D_s| \geq |D(t, T)/S(t)]D_d|$

Case 3: $0 < D_A \leq K_2 D_P$. Under this case:
$D_d > 0$
$D_s \leq 0$
$|D_s| < |[D(t, T)/S(t)]D_d|$

Case 4: $0 < K_2 D_P < D_A < D_P$. Under this case:
$D_d > 0$
$D_s > 0$
$|D_s| < |D_d|$

Case 5: $0 < D_P < D_A$. Under this case:
$D_d > 0$
$D_s > 0$
$|D_s| \geq |D_d|$

where $|x|$ defines the absolute value of x.

For the ease of exposition, these five cases are illustrated in Figure 11.2. The duration of the default-prone zero-coupon bond and the duration of the non-dividend paying stock are plotted against the duration of the firm's assets. It can be seen that Case 1 through Case 5 give successively increasing range of values for the duration of the firm's assets from highly negative to highly positive. Note that the slope of the stock duration line is greater than the slope of the bond duration line. This implies that the absolute magnitude of the stock duration is higher than that of the bond duration, both when the duration of the firm's assets is either highly negative or highly positive.

The duration of the firm's assets is less than or equal to zero both for Case 1 and Case 2. Case 1 implies that the duration of the default-prone zero-coupon bond is negative. Though this is theoretically possible if the asset duration is very highly negative, this case is generally inconsistent with the empirically observed relation between bond returns and interest rate changes.

The magnitude of the stock duration clearly dominates the magnitude of the bond duration under Case 1. Further, unless the debt to equity ratio is always low, the magnitude of the stock duration is relatively significant compared to the magnitude of the bond duration even under Case 2. Finally, the sign of the duration of the non-dividend paying stock is negative under both Case 1 and Case 2. Hence, both these cases imply *significantly negative* duration values for non-dividend paying stocks, which, as argued before, is inconsistent with the empirical evidence.

The duration of the firm's assets is greater than zero for Cases 3, 4, and 5. According to Case 3, the duration of the non-dividend paying stock must be less than or equal to zero. Comparing Case 2 and Case 3, it can be seen that even though both these cases may imply negative duration values for the stock, the magnitude of the stock duration is much closer to zero under Case 3. It can be argued that the implications of Case 3 are more consistent with the empirical results of Sweeney and Warga (1986) and Chance (1982) (since these authors find that the returns on many stocks display statistically insignificant sensitivities to interest rate changes) than those of Case 2.

Case 4 allows the stock duration to be positive. This is consistent with the observed negative correlation between the returns on stock portfolios and the changes in the nominal interest rates, demonstrated in many empirical studies. Note that under this case the magnitude of the duration of the non-dividend paying stock is less than the magnitude of the duration of the default-prone zero-coupon bond.

Case 5 may partially explain the extremely high sensitivities of the returns on some stocks to interest rate changes. Note that this case considers high positive duration values for a firm's assets. Since the slope of the stock duration line is higher than the slope of the bond duration line, the value of the stock duration can be quite high under this case. Clearly, the magnitude of stock duration dominates the magnitude of bond duration under this case.

To give an example, Sweeney and Warga (1986) find that returns on the utility industry stocks are highly sensitive to interest rate changes. The average percentage change in utility stock prices is about –70 times a given change in the annualized default-free long-term yield. Assuming parallel term structure shifts, this implies that the average duration for the utility stocks is about 70 years. It is quite probable that the duration values of the assets of the utility industry firms are highly positive, which is consistent with Case 5.

Another implication of Case 5 is that the duration of the default-prone zero-coupon bond is greater or equal to the duration of the corresponding default-free zero-coupon bond. This can be seen from equation 11.18, which implies that $D_d \geq D_p$, if $D_v \geq D_p$. Thus, unlike the duration model of Chance (1990), and others, the duration of a default-prone zero-coupon bond may be greater than the duration of a similar default-free zero-coupon bond.

From the previous discussion of the five cases, it can be inferred that the duration values of the assets of most firms, if not all, are usually positive (i.e., consistent with either of the Cases 3, 4, or 5). The condition under which the duration of a firm's asset could be less than or equal to zero (i.e., Cases 1 and 2) requires that the duration of the corresponding non-dividend paying stock must be significantly negative—a conclusion inconsistent with the interest rate risk characteristics of most stocks.

Bond and Stock Durations versus Financial and Operating Leverage The interest rate risk of bonds and stocks are related to the business risk and financial risk of a firm. This section investigates this relationship by doing a comparative static analysis of how durations of the default-prone zero-coupon bond and the non-dividend paying stock change with changes in variables that measure business risk and financial leverage.

Unlike the previous section, which investigated how the durations of the stock and the bond are related to the asset duration, this section assumes a constant asset duration, and analyzes the relationships of the default-prone bond duration and the stock duration with respect to the quasi-debt ratio $L(t)$ (i.e., to measure financial leverage) and the standard deviation of the firm's asset return σ_v (i.e., to measure business risk).

Figure 11.3 illustrates that both the default-prone bond duration and the stock duration are decreasing functions of the financial leverage, when the duration of the firm's assets is less than the duration of the default-free bond (which has the same maturity as that of the default-prone bond). In contrast, Figure 11.4 demonstrates that when the duration of the firm's assets is greater than the duration of the default-free bond, both the default-prone bond duration and the stock duration are increasing functions of the

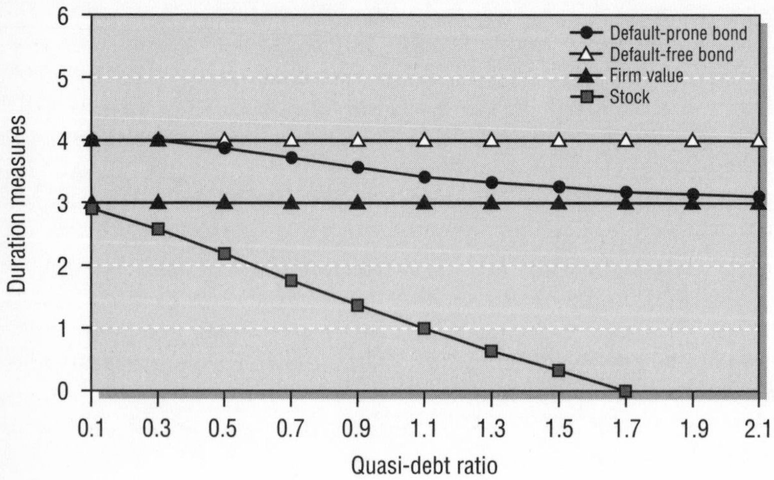

FIGURE 11.3 Bond and Stock Durations versus Financial Leverage, When the Asset Duration Is Lower Than the Default-Free Bond Duration

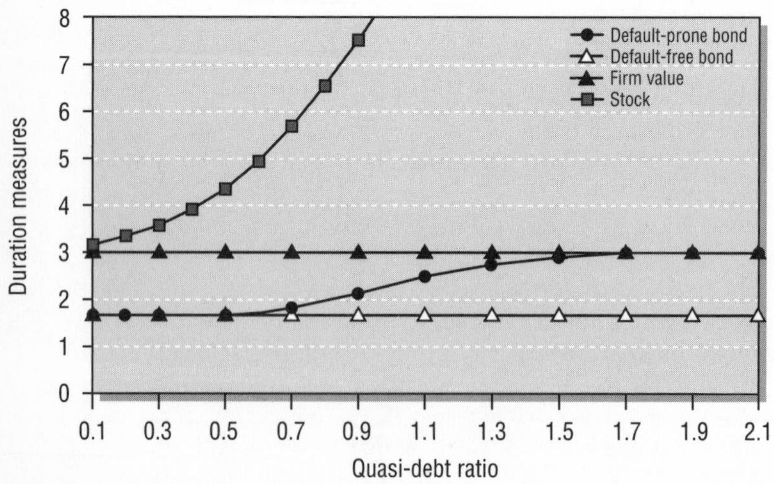

FIGURE 11.4 Bond and Stock Durations versus Financial Leverage, When the Asset Duration Is Higher Than the Default-Free Bond Duration

financial leverage. Intuitively, these findings are consistent with the fact that at extremely low levels of leverage the default-prone bond must behave like the underlying default-free bond, and at extremely high levels of leverage the default-prone bond must behave like the underlying assets of the firm in the Merton (1974) framework.

Figure 11.5 and Figure 11.6 allow the correlation coefficient between the asset return and the default-free instantaneous short rate to change, as the standard deviation of the asset return increases. This is done to keep the duration of the firm's assets constant (see equation 11.11), while investigating how the standard deviation of the firm's asset return affects the durations of the stock and the default-prone bond. Figure 11.5 demonstrates that when the asset duration is lower than the duration of the default-free bond, the default-prone bond (stock) duration is a decreasing (increasing) function of the standard deviation of the firm's asset return. However, as Figure 11.6 demonstrates, when the asset duration is higher than the duration of the default-free bond, the default-prone bond (stock) duration is an increasing (decreasing) function of the standard deviation of the firm's asset return.

These results provide new insights in relation to the well-known empirical result that interest rate risk is inversely related to default risk. The probability of default for a default-prone bond rises as both the standard deviation of the asset return and the quasi-debt ratio rise. Figures 11.3 and 11.5 are consistent with the fact that the interest rate risk of a default-prone

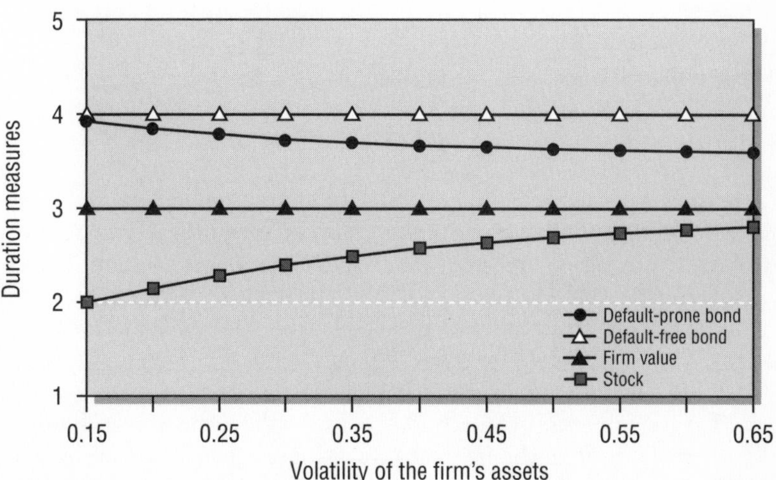

FIGURE 11.5 Bond and Stock Durations versus Business Risk, When the Asset Duration Is Lower Than the Default-Free Bond Duration

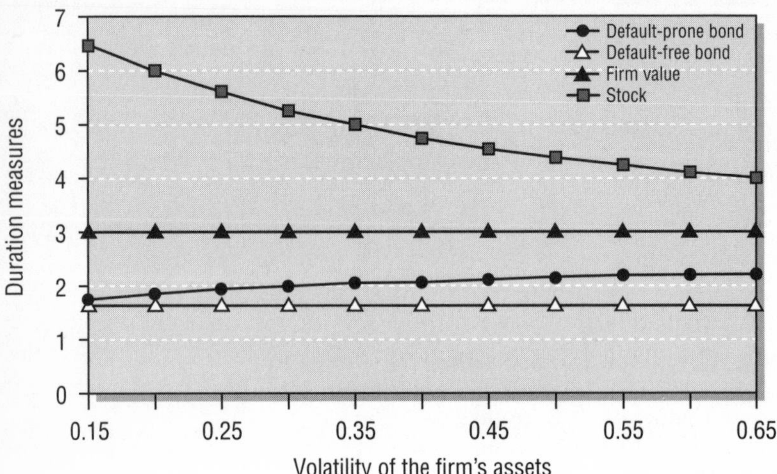

FIGURE 11.6 Bond and Stock Durations versus Business Risk, When the Asset Duration Is Higher Than the Default-Free Bond Duration

bond is inversely related to its default risk, since the duration of the default-prone bond decreases with increases in default risk. However, Figures 11.4 and 11.6 imply the opposite result. Interest rate risk of a default-prone bond is directly related to its default risk, since the duration of the default-prone bond increases with increases in default risk. Recall that both Figures 11.3 and 11.5 assume that the asset duration is lower than the duration of the underlying default-free bond (consistent with either Case 3 or Case 4 in Figure 11.2), while Figures 11.4 and 11.6 assume that the asset duration is higher than the duration of the underlying default-free bond (consistent with Case 5 in Figure 11.2).

Hence, the previous analysis questions the traditional notion that interest rate risk and default risk are inversely related. When the assets of firms are very highly sensitive to interest rate risk, such as assets of the utility industry firms (see Sweeney and Warga, 1986), or depository institutions that lend long and borrow short (such as the savings and loans associations), the interest rate risk of the default-prone bonds may actually increase as the default-risk increases (consistent with Figures 11.4, 11.6, and Case 5 in Figure 11.2). Future empirical research may confirm these theoretical findings by using the magnitude of the interest rate risk exposure of the underlying assets of firms for grouping them into different categories, and then testing the relationship between interest rate risk and default risk separately over different groups.

Relationship between Credit Spread Changes and Interest Rate Changes

A significant body of research argues that credit spreads and default-free interest rates are inversely related. In a recent study, Duffie (1998) using the Lehman brothers data of noncallable bonds finds that an increase in the three-month Treasury bill yield is accompanied by a decrease in the credit spread. He also finds that this relationship is stronger for lower rated bonds—a 10-basis points increase in the three-month yield leads to a decrease of about four basis points in the credit spread of Baa bonds. Though this relationship is consistent with previous findings, and should generally hold, more insight on this issue can be gained by studying the effects of the relationship between the asset duration and the duration of the default-free bond. For example, it can be easily demonstrated that the relationship found by Duffie may not hold if asset duration is significantly higher than the default-free bond's duration.

It was shown in the previous section that if the duration of the assets exceeds the duration of the default-free zero-coupon bond, then the duration of the default-prone bond is higher than the duration of the default-free bond. This implies that for a given increase in short rate, the default-free bond value decreases less than the default-prone bond value, leading to an increase in the credit spread. Using a similar argument, if the duration of the assets is less than the duration of the default-free zero-coupon bond, then an increase in short rate decreases the credit spread.

Hence, two important variables that determine the relationship between changes in the short rate and changes in the credit spread are:

1. The sensitivity of the underlying assets to interest rate changes, measured by the asset duration.
2. Maturity of the default-prone bond, which determines the duration of the equivalent default-free bond.

As a general result, credit spreads of shorter maturity bonds issued by corporations with highly interest rate sensitive assets will *increase,* while credit spreads of longer maturity bonds issued by corporations that have assets with low or negative interest rate sensitivity (i.e., with negative asset durations) will *decrease,* in response to an increase in the default-free short rate. Though these results are derived for zero-coupon bonds, the main implication should continue to hold even with coupon bonds under credit risk models that allow complex capital structures, as the duration risk measures can be derived to adjust for coupon effects.

The credit spread is defined as the difference between the yields-to-maturity of the default-prone zero-coupon bond and the default-free zero-coupon bond (of the same maturity):

$$s(t, T) = y_c(t, T) - y(t, T) = -\frac{1}{T-t}\ln\left(N(d_2) + \frac{(1 - N(d_1))}{L(t)}\right) \quad (11.26)$$

where $y_c(t, T)$ is the yield to maturity of the default-prone zero-coupon bond, $y(t, T)$ is the yield to maturity of the default-free zero-coupon bond ($y(t, T) = -\ln P(t, T)/(T - t)$, where $P(t, T)$ is the price of \$1 face-value, default-free zero-coupon bond defined in equation 11.4), and all other variables are as defined before.

Figure 11.7 demonstrates the relationship between the default-free short rate and the term structure of credit spreads. We choose the following base parameter values:

$$\begin{aligned} V(0) &= \$120 \\ F &= \$100 \\ r(0) &= 6\% \\ \sigma_v &= 20\% \\ \alpha &= 0.2, m = 6\% \\ \sigma &= 2\% \\ \rho &= -30\% \\ \gamma &= 0 \end{aligned}$$

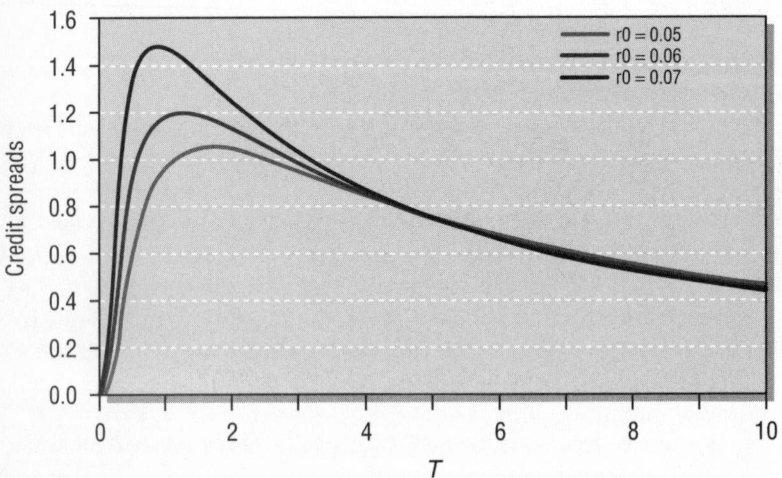

FIGURE 11.7 Effect of Change in the Level of the Default-Free Short Rate on Term Structure of Credit Spreads

Given these parameter values, the asset duration (see equation 11.11) equals:

$$D_v = -\frac{\sigma_v \rho}{\sigma} = -\frac{0.2 \times (-0.3)}{0.02} = 3 \qquad (11.27)$$

Instead of keeping the firm value constant in response to the short rate changes, we simulate credit spreads assuming that the expected change in the firm value is proportional to its asset duration. Given the asset duration equals three, when the short rate increases by 1 percent, the firm value is expected to decrease by 3 percent. Similarly, when the short rate decreases by 1 percent, the firm value is expected to increase by 3 percent. Hence, the credit spreads generated using the short rate of 7 percent assume that the firm value decreases to its conditional expected value of \$120 – \$120 × 3% = \$116.4, and the credit spreads generated using the short rate of 5 percent assume that the firm value increases to its conditional expected value of \$120 + \$120 × 3% = \$123.6.

It can be seen that when the short rate rises to 7 percent, credit spreads increase for shorter maturities, but decrease for longer maturities. Similarly, credit spreads decrease for shorter maturities, but increase for longer maturities, when the short rate falls to 5 percent. The crossover point is around 4.581 years (it is slightly away from this point due to a very small "convexity" error), the point at which the default-free bond duration equals the asset duration of three years under the Vasicek model with 0.2 speed of mean reversion. Below the crossover point, the asset duration is higher than the default-free bond duration, and above the crossover point the asset duration is lower than the default-free bond duration.

Based on this analysis, one must reconsider the previous empirical findings about the inverse relationship between credit risk and interest rate risk (e.g., Duffie, 1998). As a general result, credit spreads of shorter maturity bonds issued by corporations with highly interest rate sensitive assets *increase,* while credit spreads of longer maturity bonds issued by corporations that have assets with low or negative interest rate sensitivity (i.e., with negative asset durations) *decrease,* in response to an increase in the default-free short rate. Future research can partition the data based on the interest rate sensitivity of the assets and the maturity of the corporate bonds in order to confirm these findings.

The previous comparative static analysis is valid only for assessing *instantaneous* effects of interest rate changes on expected credit spreads. The joint evolution of the credit spreads and short rates over a long horizon is captured by the Markovian system of equations describing these processes. Since the short rate also enters the firm value process through its drift, the firm value may increase due to increases in the short rate over a long horizon, partially offsetting the effect of negative correlation between the two processes.

PRICING AND DURATION OF A DEFAULT-PRONE COUPON BOND: THE FIRST PASSAGE MODELS

The Merton (1974) framework is difficult to apply to coupon-paying bonds, since a default-prone coupon bond cannot be treated as a portfolio of default-prone zero-coupon bonds. This is because default on any given coupon-payment date implies a default on future coupon payments, too. Thus, a default-prone coupon bond is not a linear sum of the default-prone zero-coupon bonds, and compound option models such as Geske (1977), and others, must be used, since future coupons are paid *conditional* on whether the earlier coupon payments are made. Though Geske's work significantly extends the model of Merton, it has two important limitations. First, it does not allow the firm to buy back or issue more debt in order to allow a dynamic capital structure policy. Second, it assumes that assets are divided among the liability holders according to strict absolute priority rules when the firm defaults. However, a number of researchers have found that strict priority rules are rarely upheld in financially distressed organizations.[3]

In a growing stream of research, a number of authors have proposed what are known as the *first passage models* that overcome the limitations of both the Merton model and the Geske's extension of the Merton model. This stream of research began with the work of Black and Cox (1976) who proposed a new framework in which the firm defaults when the value of the firm falls enough to reach a default threshold from above for the first time. Black and Cox show that using the new framework allows the computation of the value of a coupon bond as a sum of the values of the underlying zero-coupon bonds. The probability of default under the Black and Cox model is given as the *first passage probability* of the firm value hitting the given default threshold. The Black and Cox model disallows the unintuitive feature of the Merton model that a firm's value can be virtually extinguished before the maturity of the bond, and yet it may not default if the firm value rises sufficiently at the time of maturity.

Similar to the models of Merton and Geske, Black and Cox assume constant interest rates and absolute priority rules. These two limitations of the Black and Cox model are addressed by Longstaff and Schwartz (1995) who allow stochastic interest rates as well as violations of the absolute priority rules. Collin-Dufresne and Goldstein (2001) further extend the model of Longstaff and Schwartz by correcting an error in their formula and allowing a dynamic capital structure with a stationary long-term mean. Finally, Mueller simplifies the computation of the default probability in the Collin-Dufresne and Goldstein model considerably, and allows macrovariables to affect the dynamic capital structure of the firm.

Though most of these models are covered in detail in the third volume of this series, in this section we provide an introduction to the models of Black and Cox, and Longstaff and Schwartz. Though the Black and Cox model provides much of the basic framework of the first passage models, it cannot be used for computation of durations of coupon bonds, since it assumes constant default-free rates. We apply the Longstaff and Schwartz models for computing the durations of coupon bonds. Due to the violations of absolute priority rules, and the particular specification of recovery in the event of default, the Longstaff and Schwartz model can give highly nonlinear relationships between the coupon bond duration and the underlying variables measuring business risk and financial leverage of the firm. We investigate these relationships after the introduction to the first passage models using the simple framework of Black and Cox.

Black and Cox Model

Merton assumes that the firm can default only at maturity if the asset value falls below the face value of debt. Hence, using the Merton model, the firm's assets can plummet to become a tiny fraction of the face value of the debt before the bond maturity, and yet not default if the assets recover sufficiently to become greater than the face value of debt *at maturity*. This is unrealistic and creates highly perverse, gambling incentives for stockholders, when asset value plummets. Bondholders are likely to intervene much before such gambling incentives become the choice for stockholders using some contractual agreements.

Black and Cox specify a *lower default threshold boundary,* which is the level at which the firm is forced into bankruptcy or reorganization. This level can be given exogenously as a part of indenture provisions or determined endogenously. For example, bondholders are often protected by safety covenants that give them the right to bankrupt or reorganize the firm in case the firm does not fulfill some contractual obligations, like making interest payments. In general, however, stockholders can sell the firm assets or issue more debt and use the proceeds to pay interest to the bondholders. Therefore, missing an interest payment is not a very good criterion for reorganization boundary. The specific form of the safety covenant Black and

Cox consider is that bondholders are entitled with the right to force the firm into bankruptcy if its value falls to a prespecified level, which may change over time. In this case, interest payments to the bondholders don't play a critical role.

For simplicity, we focus on the Black and Cox model to price a default-prone zero-coupon bond, even though their model can be extended to include coupon payments. Black and Cox assume that the stockholders receive a continuous dividend payment proportional to the firm value, aV. Then firm value process is given as:

$$\frac{dV(t)}{V(t)} = (\mu - a)dt + \sigma_v dZ_v(t) \tag{11.28}$$

where μ is the expected rate of return on the firm's assets.

Black and Cox suggest using a time-dependant default-threshold of an exponential form given as:

$$K(t) = Ke^{-\gamma(T-t)} \tag{11.29}$$

The terminal payoffs in the Black and Cox model are given in Table 11.2. Note that the firm value at bond maturity can never go below K. This is because the firm value $V(t)$ is always greater or equal to the default threshold $K(t)$ (defined in equation 11.29), which is an *absorbing barrier*. When the firm value $V(t)$ hits the threshold $K(t)$, the firm defaults immediately, and the bondholders receive $K(t)$ (for all $0 \le t \le T$). This translates into the following boundary conditions for the stock and the bond:

$$S(T) = \max\left[V(T) - F,\ 0\right] \tag{11.30}$$

$$D(T,\ T) = \min\left[V(T),\ F\right] \tag{11.31}$$

Since the firm may default at any time in the Black and Cox model, it is necessary to specify two more conditions describing payoffs to the stock

TABLE 11.2 Payoffs to Stock and Zero-Coupon Bond at Maturity: Black and Cox Model

	$V(T) \ge F$	$K \le V(T) < F$
Stock value at T	$V(T) - F$	0
Bond value at T	F	$V(T)$

and the bond when the firm value falls to the default threshold at any time t, before bond maturity.

$$\begin{aligned} &\text{If } V(t) = K(t), \text{ then} \\ &S(t) = 0, \text{ and} \\ &D(t, T) = K(t) = Ke^{-\gamma(T-t)} \end{aligned} \tag{11.32}$$

Using an arbitrage argument to derive a partial differential equation, subject to boundary conditions given in equations 11.30, 11.31, and 11.32, Black and Cox obtain the following solution to the zero-coupon bond price:

$$\begin{aligned} D(t, T) = {} & Fe^{-r(T-t)}\left[N(z_1) - y^{2\theta-2}N(z_2)\right] + Ve^{-a(T-t)}\left[N(z_3) + y^{2\theta}N(z_4)\right. \\ & \left. + y^{\theta+\varsigma}e^{a(T-t)}N(z_5) + y^{\theta-\varsigma}e^{a(T-t)}N(z_6) - y^{\boxed{\theta+\eta}}N(z_7) - y^{\theta-\eta}N(z_8)\right] \end{aligned} \tag{11.33}$$

where

r = the constant default-free interest rate

$$y = Ke^{-\gamma(T-t)} / V$$

$$\theta = (r - a - \gamma + \frac{1}{2}\sigma_v^2) / \sigma_v^2$$

$$\delta = (r - a - \gamma - \frac{1}{2}\sigma_v^2)^2 + 2\sigma_v^2(r - \gamma)$$

$$\varsigma = \sqrt{\delta}/\sigma_v^2$$

$$\eta = \sqrt{\delta - 2\sigma_v^2 a}/\sigma_v^2$$

$$\begin{aligned} z_1 &= \left[\ln V - \ln F + (r - a - \frac{1}{2}\sigma_v^2)(T-t)\right] \Big/ \sqrt{\sigma_v^2(T-t)} \\ z_2 &= \left[\ln V - \ln F + 2\ln y + (r - a - \frac{1}{2}\sigma_v^2)(T-t)\right] \Big/ \sqrt{\sigma_v^2(T-t)} \\ z_3 &= \left[\ln F - \ln V - (r - a + \frac{1}{2}\sigma_v^2)(T-t)\right] \Big/ \sqrt{\sigma_v^2(T-t)} \\ z_4 &= \left[\ln V - \ln F + 2\ln y + (r - a + \frac{1}{2}\sigma_v^2)(T-t)\right] \Big/ \sqrt{\sigma_v^2(T-t)} \\ z_5 &= \left[\ln y + \varsigma\sigma_v^2(T-t)\right] \Big/ \sqrt{\sigma_v^2(T-t)} \\ z_6 &= \left[\ln y - \varsigma\sigma_v^2(T-t)\right] \Big/ \sqrt{\sigma_v^2(T-t)} \\ z_7 &= \left[\ln y + \eta\sigma_v^2(T-t)\right] \Big/ \sqrt{\sigma_v^2(T-t)} \\ z_8 &= \left[\ln y - \eta\sigma_v^2(T-t)\right] \Big/ \sqrt{\sigma_v^2(T-t)} \end{aligned} \tag{11.34}$$

A small typo in the original article of Black and Cox (1976) has been corrected in equation 11.33. The terms in the box of the second to last expression on the right side of equation 11.33 are $\theta + \eta$, and not $\theta - \eta$ as in the original article. Black and Cox show how to generalize the above model for coupon bonds under absolute priority rules. Since in practice the absolute priority rules are violated almost always, we consider the generalization of Longstaff and Schwartz (1995) that allows such violations in the next section. Longstaff and Schwartz also allow stochastic interest rates, and hence we use their framework to derive the duration of default-prone coupon bonds.

Longstaff and Schwartz Model

The Longstaff and Schwartz model extends the Black and Cox model in two important ways. First, this model allows interaction between default risk and interest rate risk, by allowing for stochastic interest rates. Second, this model allows for deviations from strict absolute priority rules. The interest rate process and the asset return process are assumed to be as given in equations 11.3 and 11.8, respectively.

Longstaff and Schwartz consider a firm that issues a default-prone bond with a periodic coupon payment C, and a face value F maturing at time T. They assume that a default threshold value K exists at which financial distress occurs. The firm may have a complex capital structure with many other bond (or debt) issues, such that the value of K will be generally much higher than the face value F, of the single bond issue. The value of K is constant, but can depend upon firm-specific and industry-specific variables, and will be generally an increasing function of the total book value of the firm's bonds. As long as the firm value $V(t)$ is greater than K, the firm continues to meet its interest payments to all bondholders. If $V(t)$ reaches K, the firm defaults on all its bond obligations, simultaneously. The simultaneous default assumption is not unrealistic due to the existence of cross-default provisions and injunctions against making coupon payments on other bond issues. When financial distress is triggered, the total assets $V(t) = K$, are allocated to the various classes of bond claimants, through some form of corporate restructuring, such as Chapter 11 reorganization or liquidation, Chapter 7 liquidation, or a private debt restructuring.

Longstaff and Schwartz assume that upon reaching the default threshold K, for every \$1 of face value of a given bond, the bondholder receives $1 - w$, at maturity. An equivalent way of specifying the payoff upon default is to assume that the security holder receives $1 - w$ number of default-free zero-coupon bonds at the time of default. Since empirically the absolute priority rules are violated in most if not all corporate restructurings, the linearity of this assumption is not unrealistic. Of course, different classes of securities can be expected to have a different value of the writedown w. For example, Altman (1992) finds that the value of average writedown w, is equal to 0.40, 0.48, 0.69, 0.72, and 0.80 for secured, senior, senior subordinated, cash-pay subordinated, and noncash-pay subordinated bonds over a sample of defaulted bond issues during the 1985 to 1991 period. Franks and Torous (1994) find the value of average writedown w, is equal to 0.20, 0.53, and 0.71 for secured, senior, and junior bonds for a sample of firms that reorganized under Chapter 11 during the 1983 to 1990 period.

Though the value of the writedown w, could be different for each individual bond issued by the firm, in practice the bonds are usually grouped into a handful of categories at the time of reorganization. For example, a firm with 50 types of bonds may have three to four categories, each with a different value of w. The only constraint on w is that the total settlement of all claimants cannot exceed the lower threshold value K.

Longstaff and Schwartz also assume that the firm value is independent of its capital structure. This means that the coupon and principal payments are financed by issuing more debt thus leaving capital structure of the firm unchanged. Due to this assumption, the actual bondholders' recovery in case of default is not related to the face value of the bond. This is different from Merton's framework, which assumes that the magnitude of bondholders' loss in case of default depends on the difference between the bond's face value and the actual firm value at maturity, which makes the recovery stochastic but predictable.

The original solution for the price of default-prone bond proposed by Longstaff and Schwartz was based on the formula due to Fortet (1943). However, this formula is only valid for one-dimensional Markov processes. Therefore, the Longstaff and Schwartz solution can only be used as an approximation to the true solution. This error was recognized and corrected by Collin-Dufresne and Goldstein (2001). They proposed a solution based on a two-dimensional generalization of the Fortet's equation. Their solution involves approximating a two-dimensional integral that can be computationally costly. A much simpler solution to Longstaff and Schwartz model based on approximation of one-dimensional integral was provided by Mueller (2002) and is given as follows:

$$D(t, T) = P(t, T)F\left(1 - wQ(t, T)\right) \tag{11.35}$$

where $P(t, T)$ is the price of the default-free bond given in equation 11.4, F is the face value of the bond, and $Q(t, T)$ is the first passage probability of default given as follows:

$$
\begin{aligned}
Q(t, T) &= \sum_{i=1}^{n} q_i \\
q_1 &= \frac{N(a_1)}{N(b_{1,1})} \\
q_i &= \frac{N(a_i) - \sum_{j=1}^{i-1} N(b_{i,j}) \times q_j}{N(b_{i,i})}, \qquad i = 2, \ldots, n \\
a_i &= \frac{\ln K - M(i\Delta, T)}{\sqrt{S(i\Delta)}} \\
b_{i,j} &= \frac{\ln K - M(i\Delta, t_j, \ln K, T)}{\sqrt{S(i\Delta, t_j)}} \\
t_j &\in \left[(j-1)\Delta, j\Delta\right]
\end{aligned}
\tag{11.36}
$$

It can be shown that $(x_u | x_t, r_t, t) \sim N(M(u, T), S(u))$, where $M(u, T)$ and $S(u)$ are conditional mean and variance of x_u which can be computed as follows:

$$
\begin{aligned}
M(u, T) &= E\left[x_u \mid x_t, r_t, t\right] \\
&= x_t \\
&\quad + \left(-\frac{\sigma^2}{\alpha^2} + \frac{\alpha m - \rho\sigma_v\sigma}{\alpha} - 0.5\sigma_v^2\right) \times u \\
&\quad + \frac{1}{\alpha} \times \left(\frac{\rho\sigma_v\sigma}{\alpha} + \frac{\sigma^2}{2\alpha^2}\right) \times \left(e^{-\alpha(T-u)} - e^{-\alpha T}\right) \\
&\quad - \frac{1}{\alpha} \times \left(r_t - m + \frac{\sigma^2}{\alpha^2}\left(1 - \frac{e^{-\alpha T}}{2}\right)\right) \times \left(e^{-\alpha u} - 1\right)
\end{aligned}
\tag{11.37}
$$

$$\begin{aligned} S(u) &= Var\left[x_u \mid x_t, r_t, t\right] \\ &= \left(\sigma_v^2 + \frac{\sigma^2}{\alpha^2} + \frac{2\rho\sigma_v\sigma}{\alpha}\right) \times u \\ &- \left(\frac{2\sigma^2}{\alpha^3} + \frac{2\rho\sigma_v\sigma}{\alpha^2}\right) \times \left(1 - e^{-\alpha u}\right) \\ &+ \frac{\sigma^2}{2\alpha^3} \times \left(1 - e^{-2\alpha u}\right) \end{aligned} \tag{11.38}$$

Also, $(x_u | x_s, x_t, r_t, t) \sim N(M(u, s, x_s, T), S(u, s))$, and the conditional mean and variance of x_u in this case are computed as:

$$M(u, s, x_s, T) = M(u, T) + \frac{V(u, s)}{S(s)} \times \left(x_s - M(s, T)\right) \tag{11.39}$$

$$S(u, s) = S(u) \times \left(1 - \frac{V(u, s)^2}{S(u)S(s)}\right) \tag{11.40}$$

where $V(u, s)$ is the covariance of the random variables $(x_u | x_t, r_t, t)$ and $(x_s | x_t, r_t, t)$ given by:

$$\begin{aligned} V(u, s) &= Cov\left[x_u, x_s \mid x_t, r_t, t\right] \\ &= \left(\sigma_v^2 + \frac{2\rho\sigma_v\sigma}{\alpha} + \frac{\sigma^2}{\alpha^2}\right) \times s \\ &+ \left(-\frac{\rho\sigma_v\sigma}{\alpha^2} - \frac{\sigma^2}{\alpha^3}\right) \times \left(1 - e^{-\alpha s} - e^{-\alpha u} + e^{-\alpha(u-s)}\right) \\ &+ \frac{\sigma^2}{2\alpha^3} \times \left(e^{-\alpha(u-s)} - e^{-\alpha(u+s)}\right) \end{aligned} \tag{11.41}$$

The parameters for the short rate process and the firm value process are as defined in equations 11.3 and 11.8 earlier. Also, for the purpose of notational convenience, the variable that measures the log of the firm value, $x(t) = \ln(V(t))$ is defined as x_t, and the short rate $r(t)$ is defined as r_t. The variable $N(x)$ is the cumulative standard Normal distribution function evaluated at x.

Example 11.2 Consider a zero-coupon bond that promises to pay \$100 (i.e., $F = 100$) in one year (i.e., $T = 1$). The current value of the firm is \$120 (i.e., $V(0) = 120$). The threshold at which default occurs is $K = \$100$ and the writedown upon default occurrence is $w = 0.4$. The volatility of firm's asset return is $_v = 0.2$, the risk-free rate is $r_0 = 6\%$, speed of mean reversion of the interest rate is $\alpha = 0.2$, the risk-neutral long-run mean of the interest rate is $m = 0.06$, volatility of the interest rate process is $\sigma = 0.02$, and the correlation between firm value and interest rate process is $\rho = -0.3$.

The computation of the first passage probability in equation 11.36 requires dividing the maturity of T years into n small intervals of Δ each, or $\Delta = T/n$. Generally a value for n = 100 to 200 gives a highly accurate estimate for the first passage probability for most choices of parameters. In the above example, $T = 1$ year. For expositional purpose, we assume that $n = 5$, and show the detailed steps on how to compute the first passage probability. The extension to n = 100 or 200 should be straight forward, once these steps are understood. Given $n = 5$, $\Delta = T/n = 1/5 = 0.2$. The first passage probability, $Q(0, 1)$ can be approximated in 5 steps as follows.

Computation of q_i $(i = 1, 2, \ldots, 5)$ involves computing the values of a_i, and $b_{i,j}$. This can be done by using the following formulas:

$$a_i = \frac{\ln K - M(i\Delta,\ T)}{\sqrt{S(i\Delta)}}$$

$$b_{i,j} = \frac{\ln K - M(i\Delta,\ t_j,\ \ln K,\ T)}{\sqrt{S(i\Delta, t_j)}}$$

$$t_j \in \left[(j-1)\Delta,\ j\Delta\right]$$

Note, computation of the term $b_{i,j}$ involves the term $M(i\Delta, t_j, \ln K, T)$. By definition, $t_j \in [(j-1)\Delta, j\Delta]$. For example, if $j = 1$, then $t_1 \in [0, 0.2]$. Since we need a point value of t_j, we assumed that t_j is the mid-point of the interval $[(j-1)\Delta, j\Delta]$, or:

$$t_j = (j-1)\Delta + \frac{\Delta}{2}$$

The values of a_i, and $b_{i,j}$ are computed using the formulas given previously. We consider five cases corresponding to $i = 1, 2, 3, 4$, and 5.

The numbers in the first row of Table 11.3a provide the value of a_1 and $b_{1,1}$ computed using the formulas given previously. The second row of this table gives the standard Normal distribution function evaluated at a_1 and

TABLE 11.3a First Iteration, $i = 1$

	a_1	$b_{1,1}$
	−2.1362	−0.0733
N(.)	0.0163	0.4708

TABLE 11.3b Second Iteration, $i = 2$

	a_2	$b_{2,1}$	$b_{2,2}$
	−1.5793	−0.1267	−0.0729
N(.)	0.0571	0.4496	0.4710

TABLE 11.3c Third Iteration, $i = 3$

	a_3	$b_{3,1}$	$b_{3,2}$	$b_{3,3}$
	−1.3454	−0.1631	−0.1259	−0.0724
N(.)	0.0892	0.4352	0.4499	0.4711

TABLE 11.3d Fourth Iteration, $i = 4$

	a_4	$b_{4,1}$	$b_{4,2}$	$b_{4,3}$	$b_{4,4}$
	−1.2134	−0.1925	−0.1621	−0.1251	−0.0719
N(.)	0.1125	0.4237	0.4356	0.4502	0.4713

TABLE 11.3e Fifth Iteration, $i = 5$

	a_5	$b_{5,1}$	$b_{5,2}$	$b_{5,3}$	$b_{5,4}$	$b_{5,5}$
	−1.1282	−0.2177	−0.1913	−0.1610	−0.1243	−0.0715
N(.)	0.1296	0.4138	0.4242	0.4360	0.4506	0.4715

$b_{1,1}$. Given the values of $N(a_1)$ and $N(b_{1,1})$, the value of q_1 can be computed using equation 11.36, as follows:

$$q_1 = \frac{N(a_1)}{N(b_{1,1})} = \frac{0.0163}{0.4708} = 0.0347$$

Using similar computations in Tables 11.3b, 11.3c, 11.3d, and 11.3e, the values of q_2, q_3, q_4, and q_5 can be computed as follows:

$$q_2 = \frac{N(a_2) - N(b_{2,1}) \times q_1}{N(b_{2,2})} = \frac{0.0571 - 0.4496 \times 0.0347}{0.4710} = 0.0882$$

$$q_3 = \frac{N(a_3) - \left(N(b_{3,1}) \times q_1 + N(b_{3,2}) \times q_2\right)}{N(b_{3,3})}$$

$$= \frac{0.0892 - \left(0.4352 \times 0.0347 + 0.4499 \times 0.0882\right)}{0.4711} = 0.0732$$

$$q_4 = \frac{N(a_4) - \left(N(b_{4,1}) \times q_1 + N(b_{4,2}) \times q_2 + N(b_{4,3}) \times q_3\right)}{N(b_{4,4})}$$

$$= \frac{0.1125 - \left(0.4237 \times 0.0347 + 0.4356 \times 0.0882 + 0.4502 \times 0.0732\right)}{0.4713} = 0.0561$$

$$q_5 = \frac{N(a_5) - \left(N(b_{5,1}) \times q_1 + N(b_{5,2}) \times q_2 + N(b_{5,3}) \times q_3 + N(b_{5,4}) \times q_4\right)}{N(b_{5,5})}$$

$$= \frac{0.1296 - \left(0.4138 \times 0.0347 + 0.4242 \times 0.0882 + 0.4360 \times 0.0732 + 0.4506 \times 0.0561\right)}{0.4715}$$

$$= 0.0439$$

Given the values of $q_1, \ldots q_5$, we can compute the first passage probability of default, $Q(0, 1)$ as follows:

$$Q(0, 1) = \sum_{i=1}^{5} q_i = 0.0347 + 0.0882 + 0.0732 + 0.0561 + 0.0439 = 0.2960$$

The computation of the price of the default-prone bond requires the price of the default-free bond, $P(0, 1)$. Using the closed form of $P(t, T)$ in equation 11.4, we get:

$$P(0, 1) = e^{-0.0056 - 0.9063 \times 0.06} = 0.9418$$

Substituting the previous values of $Q(0, 1)$ and $P(0, 1)$ and the parameters, $F = 100$, and $w = 0.4$, in equation 11.35, the price of the default-prone bond, $D(0, 1)$, is given as follows:

$$D(0, 1) = 0.9418 \times 100 \times \left(1 - 0.4 \times 0.2960\right) = \$83.03$$

The value of $D(0, 1)$ converges to its true price as n becomes large. For $n = 200$, the value of $D(0, 1)$ equals \$83.04, which is one cent away from the solution given previously.

In the Longstaff and Schwartz model, the value of a coupon bond can be given as a portfolio of zero-coupon bonds, as all coupons default simultaneously when the firm hits the default threshold K for the first time. Hence, the value of the coupon bond with coupon payments, C, at dates t_k, $(1, N)$, where $t_N = T$, can be written as:

$$D_{coup}(t, T) = P(t, T)F\left(1 - wQ(t, T)\right) + \sum_{k=1}^{N} P(t, t_k)C\left(1 - w_{coup}Q(t, t_k)\right) \quad (11.42)$$

Though the writedown for the coupons, w_{coup}, in case of default can be any number from 0 to 1, in practice only the portion of principal payment is redeemed and coupon payments are written down completely, that is, $w_{coup} = 1$.

The yield to maturity of a corporate coupon bond, $y_c(t, T)$ can be obtained implicitly by solving the following equation:

$$D_{coup}(t, T) = Fe^{-y_c(t,T)\times T} + \sum_{k=1}^{N} Ce^{-y_c(t,T)\times t_k} \quad (11.43)$$

The yield to maturity of a default-free coupon bond, $y(t, T)$ can be obtained implicitly by solving the following equation:

$$P_{coup}(t, T) = Fe^{-y(t,T)\times T} + \sum_{k=1}^{N} Ce^{-y(t,T)\times t_k} \quad (11.44)$$

The credit spread is defined as the difference between the yields to maturity of the corporate coupon bond and the riskless coupon bond (of the same maturity):

$$s(t, T) = y_c(t, T) - y(t, T) \quad (11.45)$$

Duration of a Default-Prone Bond A widespread misunderstanding among fixed-income practitioners is that duration of a default-prone bond is *always* lower than the duration of an equivalent default-free bond. As mentioned in the introduction to this chapter, this misunderstanding results from confusing the expected contractual maturity of the bond with its duration. As shown using Merton's (1974) framework in the previous section, the duration of a default-prone zero-coupon bond can be higher than the duration of the equivalent default-free zero-coupon bond (which under parallel term structure shifts equals the contractual maturity of the bond) when the duration of the assets of the firm is higher than the duration of the equivalent default-free bond.

We show that another reason for this misunderstanding is that duration is frequently obtained using a simplistic comparative static analysis. For example, consider how comparative static analysis would be used to derive the duration of the default-prone zero-coupon bond using equation 11.35. By taking the partial derivative of equation 11.35, we get:

$$\frac{\partial D(t,T)}{\partial r(t)} = \frac{\partial P(t,T)}{\partial r(t)}\big(1 - wQ(t,T)\big) - wP(t,T)\frac{\partial Q(t,T)}{\partial r(t)} \tag{11.46}$$

Dividing both sides of equation 11.46 by $-D(t, T)$, duration would be defined as follows:

$$\begin{aligned} D_d &= -\frac{\partial D(t,T)/\partial r(t)}{D(t,T)} \\ &= -\frac{\partial P(t,T)/\partial r(t)\big(1 - wQ(t,T)\big)}{P(t,T)\big(1 - wQ(t,T)\big)} + \frac{wP(t,T)\partial Q(t,T)/\partial r(t)}{P(t,T)\big(1 - wQ(t,T)\big)} \\ &= -\frac{\partial P(t,T)/\partial r(t)}{P(t,T)} + \frac{w}{\big(1 - wQ(t,T)\big)}\partial Q(t,T)/\partial r(t) \\ & D_p + \frac{w}{\big(1 - wQ(t,T)\big)}\partial Q(t,T)/\partial r(t) \end{aligned} \tag{11.47}$$

Hence, the duration of the default-prone bond would be given as the sum of the duration of the default-free bond plus another term that is proportional to the partial derivative of $Q(t, T)$ with respect to $r(t)$. In general, $Q(t, T)$, which is the first passage probability of default, is a function of the current value of the firm's assets through $x(t) = \ln V(t)$, which is contained in $Q(t, T)$. However, using a comparative static analysis would require evaluating the partial derivative of $Q(t, T)$ with respect to $r(t)$, while keeping $x(t) =$

$\ln V(t)$ constant. Doing this implicitly assumes a *zero value for the asset duration* since the firm value is kept constant even though the instantaneous short rate changes. Thus, duration obtained with a comparative static approach using equation 11.47 will lead to a significant underestimation of true sensitivity of the default-prone bond to interest rate changes if the duration of the assets is extremely high. The inappropriate use of the comparative static approach is one of the reasons why some researchers have found that duration of the default-prone bond is *always* lower than the duration of the equivalent default-free bond under the Longstaff and Schwartz model, and other such models.

The comparative static approach also does not lead to a closed-form solution of the duration under the Longstaff-Schwartz model, since $Q(t, T)$ is defined in a nonlinear iterative fashion. Hence, in the following we suggest an alternative numerical approach to computing the duration of the default-prone bond under the Longstaff and Schwartz model.

The value of the default-prone zero-coupon bond $D(t, T)$ in equation 11.35 can be written as a function of the current firm value $V(t)$ and the current instantaneous short rate $r(t)$, as follows:

$$D(t, T) = D(V(t), r(t), t, T) \tag{11.48}$$

The values of $V(t)$ and $r(t)$ are contained in $D(t, T) = D(V(t), r(t), t, T)$, through $Q(t, T)$ in equation 11.35. Now consider a very small instantaneous change in $r(t)$ given as $\Delta r(t)$. Let the short rate after this instantaneous change be given as $r'(t) = r(t) + \Delta r(t)$. The *expected* change in the firm's asset value $V(t)$, caused by the change in the short rate is given as follows:

$$\Delta V(t) = -V(t) D_v \Delta r(t) \tag{11.49}$$

where D_v is the asset duration defined in equation 11.11. Define the new firm value as $V'(t) = V(t) + \Delta V(t)$. Using the new firm value and the new interest rate, compute the value of the default-prone zero-coupon bond again using equation 11.35, as follows:

$$D'(t, T) = D(V'(t), r'(t), t, T) \tag{11.50}$$

The duration of the default-prone zero-coupon bond now can be defined as follows:

$$D_d = -\frac{\Delta D(V(t), r(t), t, T) / D(V(t), r(t), t, T)}{\Delta r(t)} \tag{11.51}$$

where

$$\Delta D(V(t), r(t), t, T) = D(V'(t), r'(t), t, T) - D(V(t), r(t), t, T) \tag{11.52}$$

Computation of the duration of the default-prone zero-coupon bond using equations 11.48 through 11.52, requires using the formula given in equation 11.35 twice by changing the short rate by a small amount. Using any small amount such as $\Delta r(t) = 0.00001$ gives a highly accurate numerical estimate of the duration of the default-prone bond. Also, by expressing $D_{coup}(t, T) = D_{coup}(V(t), r(t), t, T)$, in equation 11.42 as a function of $V(t)$ and $r(t)$, the method demonstrated in equations 11.48 through 11.52, also gives the duration of the default-prone coupon bond. Since this approach accounts for the expected change in the value of the firm's assets caused by a change in the interest rate by explicitly using the asset duration defined in equation 11.11, it gives an accurate estimate of the default-prone bond duration.

Numerical Analysis Similar to the numerical analysis performed earlier on the Nawalkha-Shimko et al. models, this section investigates how interest rate risk of a default-prone bond is related to the firm's business risk and financial risk. However, unlike the Nawalkha-Shimko et al. models which are based upon an endogenous default framework of Merton (1974), the first passage models given by Longstaff and Schwartz, and others, assume that both the default threshold K and the writedown ratio w, are specified exogenously. The exogenous specification of default threshold and writedown ratio leads to certain unique and peculiar properties for the duration of the default-prone bond under the Longstaff and Schwartz model.

To analyze how the duration of the default-prone bond is related to business risk and financial risk, we assume a constant asset duration, and consider the relationship of the default-prone bond duration with respect to the volatility of the firm's asset return σ_v (i.e., to measure business risk), and the quasi-debt ratio $L(t)$ (i.e., to measure financial leverage). When the firm volatility increases, the duration of the assets is held constant by changing the correlation between asset returns and short rate changes.

We consider a 6 percent annual coupon bond, which either matures in two years or in 12 years. Considering two different maturities allows us to consider both cases, when the asset duration is higher than the equivalent default-free bond duration, and when the asset duration is lower than the default-free bond duration. The parameters for the asset price process, the short rate process, and exogenous default process, are given as $r(0) = 6\%$, $\alpha = 0.2$, $m = 6\%$, $\sigma = 2\%$, $V(0) = \$200$, $F = \$100$, $K = \$80$, $\sigma_v = 20\%$, $= -0.3$, $w = 0.4$, $w_c = 1$.

Figure 11.8 illustrates that the default-prone bond duration is initially a decreasing function of the financial leverage (measured by quasi-debt ratio), when the duration of the firm's assets is less than the duration of the default-free bond. However, unlike the endogenous model of Nawalkha (1996) (see Figure 11.3), the duration of the default-prone bond *increases* after the initial decline. At high leverage, default becomes more certain, and due to the exogenous default assumptions in the Longstaff and Schwartz model, the bondholders receive an almost certain payment of $F(1 - w)$ at maturity T, but zero-coupon payments until then (since we have assumed 100 percent writedown for coupon payments). Hence, an almost certain default makes the default-prone coupon bond behave more like a default-free zero-coupon bond. This explains why at a high quasi-debt ratio, the duration of the default-prone coupon bond exceeds even the duration of the default-free coupon bond in Figure 11.8. It is well known that the duration of the default-free coupon bond is always lower than the duration of the default-free zero-coupon bond, and the default-prone coupon bond behaves more like a default-free zero-coupon bond when default is very likely. Interestingly, the duration of the default-prone coupon bond is not as sensitive to financial leverage when the asset duration is higher than the duration of the

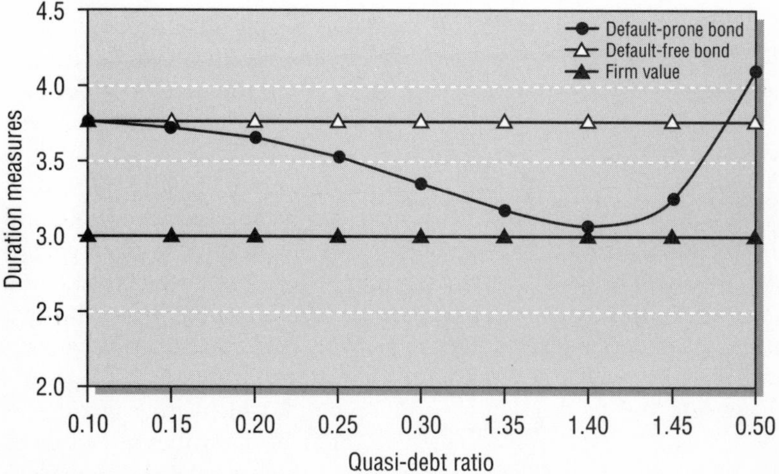

FIGURE 11.8 Default-Prone Bond Duration versus Financial Leverage, When the Asset Duration Is Lower Than the Default-Free Bond Duration

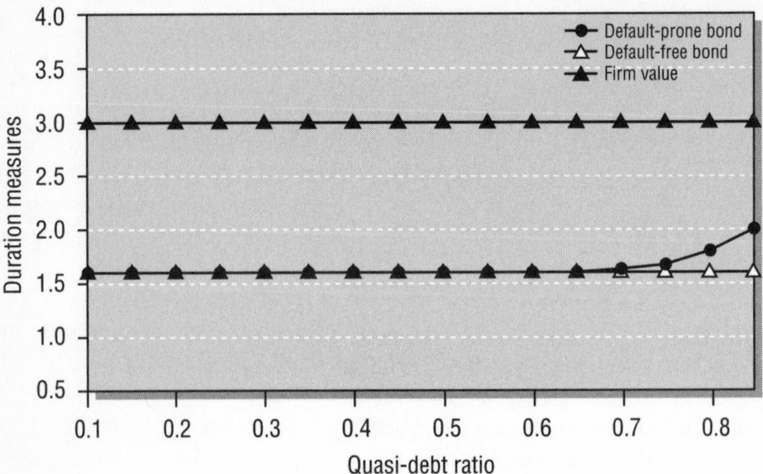

FIGURE 11.9 Default-Prone Bond Duration versus Financial Leverage, When the Asset Duration Is Higher Than the Default-Free Bond Duration

default-free coupon bond. As shown in Figure 11.9, only at extremely high financial leverage the duration of the default-prone bond starts increasing toward the asset duration value.

Figure 11.10 illustrates the relationship between the duration of the default-prone coupon bond and firm's volatility, when the asset duration is

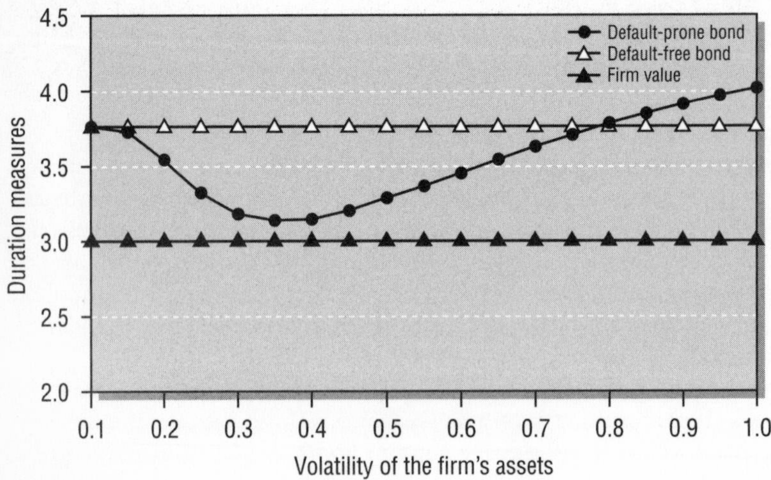

FIGURE 11.10 Default-Prone Bond Duration versus Business Risk, When the Asset Duration Is Lower Than the Default-Free Bond Duration

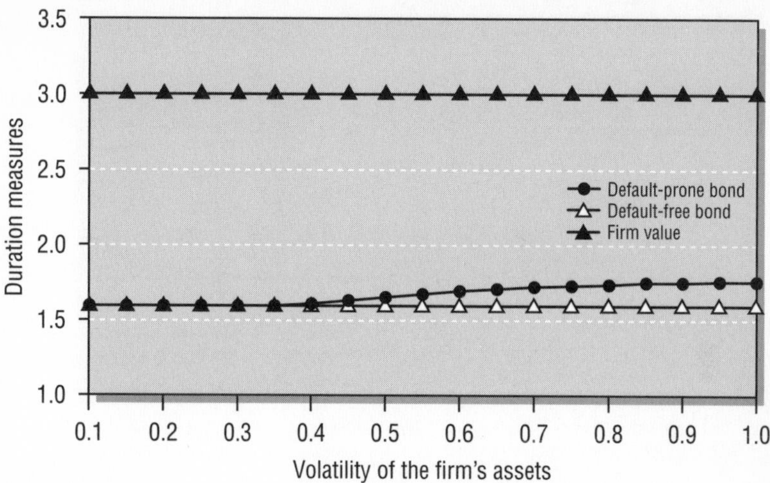

FIGURE 11.11 Default-Prone Bond Duration versus Business Risk, When the Asset Duration Is Higher Than the Default-Free Bond Duration

lower than the default-free bond duration. Higher volatility makes default more certain, and following the same reasoning as given for Figure 11.8, an almost certain default makes the default-prone coupon bond behave more like a default-free zero-coupon bond. Thus, even though the duration of the default-prone coupon bond declines initially and moves toward the asset duration, further increases in asset volatility makes it go higher, even exceeding the duration of the default-free coupon bond for very high levels of volatility.

Figure 11.11 illustrates the relationship between the duration of the default-prone coupon bond and firm's volatility, when the asset duration is higher than the default-free bond duration. Similar to Figure 11.9, the duration of the default-prone coupon bond is not as sensitive to business risk when the asset duration is higher than the duration of the default-free coupon bond. Finally, Figure 11.12 demonstrates that the duration of the default-prone coupon bond decreases with an increase in the annual coupon rate.

The exogenous default model of Longstaff and Schwartz has some unintuitive features resulting from its assumptions. In this model the duration characteristics of the default-prone coupon bond are like those of a default-free bond both when the probability of default is low and when the probability of default is high. Some of these issues have been also addressed by Acharya and Carpenter (2002) who derive durations of default-prone

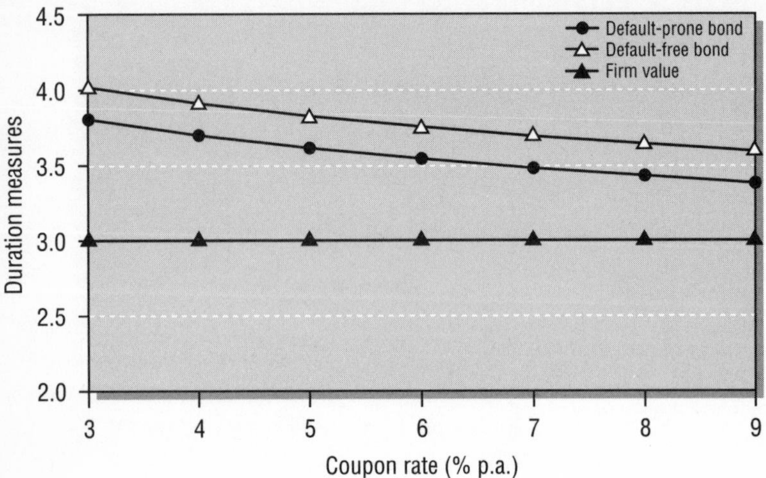

FIGURE 11.12 Default-Prone Bond Duration versus Annual Coupon Rate

coupon bonds assuming endogenous bankruptcy. Their results are closer to the results given by Nawalkha-Shimko et al. models, which also use an endogenous framework, even though the latter models apply only to zero-coupon bonds.

The appendix derives an extension of the Longstaff and Schwartz model given by Collin-Dufresne and Goldstein (2001). These authors extend the Longstaff and Schwartz model by allowing a stationary leverage ratio. In their model the default threshold itself changes as a mean reverting process, with a long-term mean for the default threshold. As firms increase the book value of the debt, the default threshold increases too, while as firms reduce the book value of debt, the default threshold falls. Since firms tend to target a long-term financial leverage ratio, the default threshold can be expected to be stationary over the long term, but nonstationary over the short term. Collin-Dufresne and Goldstein model also captures the dependence of the level of default threshold to the level of the default-free interest rate. This is very intuitive since at higher interest rates, leverage becomes more costly and default threshold may rise. Appendix 11.1 provides a full solution with an example to compute the price of the default-prone bond under the Collin-Dufresne and Goldstein model. The duration of the default-prone bond given in equation 11.51 can be easily extended to the Collin-Dufresne and Goldstein model, using the technique given in this chapter.

APPENDIX 11.1: COLLIN-DUFRESNE AND GOLDSTEIN MODEL

Collin-Dufresne and Goldstein extend the Longstaff and Schwartz model by assuming that the log of the default threshold, ln$K(t)$ follows the following process:

$$d(\ln K(t)) = k\left[\ln V(t) - v - \phi(r(t) - m) - \ln K(t)\right]dt \qquad (11.53)$$

where $K(t)$ is the time-dependet default threshold. Equation 11.53 adds three new parameters to the Longstaff and Schwartz model given as k, v, and ϕ. Collin-Dufresne and Goldstein's solution to this model involves approximation of a two dimensional integral. The solution suggested by Mueller (2002) involves an approximation of a one-dimensional integral and therefore is much simpler to compute as compared to Collin-Dufresne and Goldstein's solution. The general form of Mueller's solution for this model is the same as the solution for the Longstaff and Schwartz model presented earlier:

$$D(t, T) = P(t, T) - wP(t, T)Q(t, T) \qquad (11.54)$$

where P(t, T) is the value of a risk-free zero-coupon bond given by equation 11.4 and $Q(t, T)$ is the probability of default given by:

$$\begin{aligned}
Q(t, T) &= \sum_{i=1}^{n} q_i \\
q_1 &= \frac{N(a_1)}{N(b_{1,1})} \\
q_i &= \frac{N(a_i) - \sum_{j=1}^{i-1} N(b_{i,j}) \times q_j}{N(b_{i,i})}, \qquad i = 2, \ldots, n \qquad (11.55) \\
a_i &= \frac{\ln K - M(i\Delta, T)}{\sqrt{S(i\Delta)}} \\
b_{i,j} &= \frac{\ln K - M(i\Delta, t_j, \ln K, T)}{\sqrt{S(i\Delta, t_j)}} \\
t_j &\in \left[(j-1)\Delta, j\Delta\right]
\end{aligned}$$

$(x_u | x_t, r_t, t) \sim N(M(u, T), S(u))$, where $M(u, T)$ and $S(u)$ are conditional mean and variance of x_u,which can be computed as follows:

$$\begin{aligned} M(u, T) &= E\left[x_u \mid x_t, r_t, t\right] \\ &= x_t e^{-ku} \\ &+ \left(\nu + \frac{1}{k}\left(\frac{g_r \sigma^2}{\alpha^2} - \frac{g_r \alpha m + \rho \sigma_v \sigma}{\alpha} - 0.5\sigma_v^2\right)\right) \times \left(1 - e^{-ku}\right) \\ &+ \frac{1}{k+\alpha} \times \left(\frac{\rho \sigma_v \sigma}{\alpha} - \frac{g_r \sigma^2}{2\alpha^2}\right) \times \left(e^{-\alpha(T-u)} - e^{-ku-\alpha T}\right) \\ &- \frac{g_r}{k-\alpha} \times \left(r_t - m + \frac{\sigma^2}{\alpha^2}\left(1 - \frac{e^{-\alpha T}}{2}\right)\right) \times \left(e^{-\alpha u} - e^{-ku}\right) \end{aligned} \tag{11.56}$$

$$\begin{aligned} S(u) &= Var\left[x_u \mid x_t, r_t, t\right] \\ &= \frac{1}{2k}\left(\sigma_v^2 + \frac{g_r^2 \sigma^2}{(k-\alpha)^2} + \frac{2 g_r \rho \sigma_v \sigma}{k-\alpha}\right) \times \left(1 - e^{-2ku}\right) \\ &+ \frac{g_r^2 \sigma^2}{2\alpha_r (k-\alpha)^2} \times \left(1 - e^{-2\alpha u}\right) \\ &- \frac{1}{k+\alpha}\left(\frac{2 g_r^2 \sigma^2}{(k-\alpha)^2} + \frac{2 g_r \rho \sigma_v \sigma}{k-\alpha}\right) \times \left(1 - e^{-(k+\alpha)u}\right) \end{aligned} \tag{11.57}$$

$(x_u | x_s, x_t, r_t, t) \sim N(M(\mathrm{u, s, x_s, T}), S(u, s))$, conditional mean and variance of x_u in this case can be computed as:

$$M(u, s, x_s, T) = M(u, T) + \frac{V(u, s)}{S(s)} \times \left(x_s - M(s, T)\right) \tag{11.58}$$

$$S(u, s) = S(u) \times \left(1 - \frac{V(u, s)^2}{S(u) S(s)}\right) \tag{11.59}$$

where $V(u, s)$ is the covariance of the random variables $(x_u | x_t, r_t, t)$ and $(x_s | x_t, r_t, t)$ given by:

$$
\begin{aligned}
V(u, s) &= Cov\left[x_u, x_s | x_t, r_t, t\right] \\
&= \left(\frac{\sigma_v^2}{2k} + \frac{g_r \rho \sigma_v \sigma}{k(k-\alpha)} + \frac{g_r^2 \sigma^2}{2k(k-\alpha)^2}\right) \times \left(e^{-k(u-s)} - e^{-k(u+s)}\right) \\
&+ \left(\frac{g_r^2 \sigma^2}{2\alpha(k-\alpha)^2}\right) \times \left(e^{-\alpha(u-s)} - e^{-\alpha(u+s)}\right) \\
&- \left(\frac{g_r^2 \sigma^2}{(k+\alpha)(k-\alpha)^2} + \frac{g_r \rho \sigma_v \sigma}{(k-\alpha)(k+\alpha)}\right) \\
&\times \left(e^{-k(u-s)} - e^{-ku-\alpha s} - e^{-\alpha u - ks} + e^{-\alpha(u-s)}\right)
\end{aligned}
\tag{11.60}
$$

where $g_r = -1 - k\phi$

Example 11.3 Consider a zero-coupon bond that promises to pay \$100 (i.e., $F = 100$) in a year (i.e., $T = 1$) when the current value of the firm is \$120 (i.e., $V(0) = 120$), the initial default threshold $K(0) = \$100$, writedown is $w = 0.4$, volatility of firm's operations is $_v = 0.2$, the initial short rate is $r_0 = 6\%$, speed of mean reversion of the interest rate is $\alpha = 0.2$, the risk-neutral long-run mean of the interest rate is $m = 0.06$, volatility of the interest rate process is $\sigma = 0.02$, and the correlation between firm value and interest rate process is $\rho = -0.3$. The remaining parameters are $k = 0.18$, $\phi = 2.8$, $\nu = 0.432$. Suppose, the time interval [0, 1] is subdivided into $n = 5$ equal subintervals of length $\Delta = T/n = 1/5 = 0.2$. Then, the first passage probability, $Q(t = 0, T = 1)$, can be approximated in 5 steps as follows.

Computation of q_i ($i = 1, \ldots, 5$) involves computing the values of a_i, and $b_{i,j}$. This can be done by using the following formulas:

$$
\begin{aligned}
a_i &= \frac{\ln K - M(i\Delta, T)}{\sqrt{S(i\Delta)}} \\
b_{i,j} &= \frac{\ln K - M(i\Delta, t_j, \ln K, T)}{\sqrt{S(i\Delta, t_j)}} \\
t_j &\in \left[(j-1)\Delta, j\Delta\right]
\end{aligned}
$$

TABLE 11.4a First Iteration, $i = 1$

	a_1	$b_{1,1}$
	−2.3450	−0.2493
$N(.)$	0.0095	0.4016

TABLE 11.4b Second Iteration, $i = 2$

	a_2	$b_{2,1}$	$b_{2,2}$
	−1.8757	−0.4326	−0.2497
$N(.)$	0.0304	0.3327	0.4014

TABLE 11.4c Third Iteration, $i = 3$

	a_3	$b_{3,1}$	$b_{3,2}$	$b_{3,3}$
	−1.7095	−0.5592	−0.4331	−0.2499
$N(.)$	0.0437	0.2880	0.3325	0.4013

TABLE 11.4d Fourth Iteration, $i = 4$

	a_4	$b_{4,1}$	$b_{4,2}$	$b_{4,3}$	$b_{4,4}$
	−1.6348	−0.6624	−0.5597	−0.4333	−0.2500
$N(.)$	0.0510	0.2539	0.2878	0.3324	0.4013

TABLE 11.4e Fifth Iteration, $i = 5$

	a_5	$b_{5,1}$	$b_{5,2}$	$b_{5,3}$	$b_{5,4}$	$b_{5,5}$
	−1.6003	−0.7515	−0.6627	−0.5599	−0.4334	−0.2500
$N(.)$	0.0548	0.2262	0.2538	0.2878	0.3324	0.4013

It is assumed that t_j is equal to the mid point of the interval $[(j-1)\Delta, j\Delta]$, or:

$$t_j = (j-1)\Delta + \frac{\Delta}{2}$$

The first line of Table 11.4a provides the value of a_1 and $b_{1,1}$ computed using the formulas given earlier. The second line of the table gives the standard Normal distribution function evaluated at a_1 and $b_{1,1}$. Once we have $N(a_1)$ and $N(b_{1,1})$, we can compute q_1 as follows:

$$q_1 = \frac{N(a_1)}{N(b_{1,1})} = \frac{0.0095}{0.4016} = 0.0237$$

Using similar computations in Tables 11.4b, 11.4c, 11.4d, and 11.4e on page 374, the values of q_2, q_3, q_4, and q_5 can be computed as follows:

$$q_2 = \frac{N(a_2) - N(b_{2,1}) \times q_1}{N(b_{2,2})} = \frac{0.0304 - 0.3327 \times 0.0237}{0.4014} = 0.0560$$

$$q_3 = \frac{N(a_3) - \left(N(b_{3,1}) \times q_1 + N(b_{3,2}) \times q_2\right)}{N(b_{3,3})}$$

$$= \frac{0.0437 - \left(0.2880 \times 0.0237 + 0.3325 \times 0.0560\right)}{0.4013} = 0.0455$$

$$q_4 = \frac{N(a_4) - \left(N(b_{4,1}) \times q_1 + N(b_{4,2}) \times q_2 + N(b_{4,3}) \times q_3\right)}{N(b_{4,4})}$$

$$= \frac{0.0510 - \left(0.2539 \times 0.0237 + 0.2878 \times 0.0560 + 0.3324 \times 0.0455\right)}{0.4013}$$

$$= 0.0344$$

$$q_5 = \frac{N(a_5) - \left(N(b_{5,1}) \times q_1 + N(b_{5,2}) \times q_2 + N(b_{5,3}) \times q_3 + N(b_{5,4}) \times q_4\right)}{N(b_{5,5})}$$

$$= \frac{0.0548 - \left(0.2262 \times 0.0237 + 0.2538 \times 0.0560 + 0.2878 \times 0.0455 + 0.3324 \times 0.0344\right)}{0.4013}$$

$$= 0.0266$$

Once we have $q_1, \ldots, q_5$, we can compute the first passage probability of default, $Q(0, 1)$ as follows:

$$Q(0,1) = \sum_{i=1}^{5} q_i = 0.0237 + 0.0560 + 0.0455 + 0.0344 + 0.0266 = 0.1862$$

The computation of the price of the default-prone bond requires the price of the default-free bond, $P(0, 1)$. Using the closed-form of $P(t, T)$ in equation 11.4, we get:

$$P(0,\ 1) = e^{-0.0056-0.9063\times0.06} = 0.9418$$

Substituting the previous values of $Q(0, 1)$ and $P(0, 1)$ and the parameters, $F = 100$, and $w = 0.4$, in equation 11.55, the price of the default-prone bond, $D(0, 1)$, is given as follows:

$$D(0,\ 1) = 0.9418\times100\times(1-0.4\times0.1862) = \$87.17$$

For $n = 200$, the value of $D(0, 1)$ equals \$87.21, which is 4 cents away from the solution given previously.

NOTES

1. See Bierwag et al. (1983), Chance (1983), Jarrow (1978), Morgan (1986), and Ott (1986).
2. See Nawalkha (1996).
3. See Betker (1991, 1992), Brick and Fisher (1987), Eberhart, Moore, and Roenfeldt (1990), Fama and Miller (1972), Franks and Torous (1989, 1994), Lopucki and Whitford (1990), Smith and Warner (1979), and Weiss (1990).

References

Acharya, V. V., and J. N. Carpenter, 2002, "Corporate Bond Valuation and Hedging with Stochastic Interest Rates and Endogenous Bankruptcy," *Review of Financial Studies* 15(5), 1355–1383.

Ahn, D. H., R. F. Dittmar, and A. R. Gallant, 2002, "Quadratic Term Structure Models: Theory and Evidence," *Review of Financial Studies* 15(1), 243–288.

Alexander, G. J., 1980, "Applying the Market Model to Long-Term Corporate Bonds," *Journal of Financial and Quantitative Analysis, 15,* 1063–1080.

Altman, E. I., 1992, "Revisiting the High Yield Bond Market," *Financial Management, 21,* 78–92.

Barber, J. R., and M. L. Copper, 1996, "Immunization Using Principal Component Analysis," *Journal of Portfolio Management,* summer, 99–105.

Betker, B. L., 1991, An analysis of the returns to stockholders and bondholders in chapter 11 reorganization. *Working Paper* Ohio State University.

Bierwag, G. O., and G. G. Kaufman, 1988, "Durations of Non-Default-Free Securities," *Financial Analysts Journal,* July-August, 39–46.

Bierwag, G. O., G. G. Kaufman, and A. T. Toevs, 1983, Bond portfolio immunization and stochastic process risk. *Journal of Bank Research, 13,* 282–291.

Black, F., and J. C. Cox, 1976, "Valuing Corporate Securities: Some Effects of sBond Provisions," *Journal of Finance, 31,* 351–367.

Bliss, R. R., 1997a, "Movements in the Term Structure of Interest Rates," *Economic Review,* FRB of Atlanta, fourth quarter, 16–33.

Bliss, R. R., 1997b, "Testing Term Structure Estimation Methods," In P. Boyle, G. Pennacchi, and P. Ritchken (Eds)., *Advances in Futures and Options Research,* Vol. 9, Greenwich, CT: JAI Press.

Boquist, J. A., G. A. Racette, and G. G. Schlarbaum, 1975, "Duration and Risk Assessment for Bonds and Common Stocks: A Note," *Journal of Finance, 30,* 1360–1365.

Brace, A., D. Gatarek, and M. Musiela, 1996, "The Market Model of Interest Rate Dynamics," *Mathematical Finance,* 7, 127–154.

Brick, I. E., and L. Fisher, 1987, "Effects of Classifying Equity or Debt on the Value og the Firm under Tax Asymmetry," *Journal of Financial and Quantitative Analysis,* 22, 383–399.

Buffett, W., 2002, "Derivatives Are Financial Weapons of Mass Destruction: The Dangers Are Now Latent—But They Could Be Lethal," *Berkshire Hathaway annual report.*

Campbell, J., 1986, "A Defense of Traditional Hypotheses about the Term Structure of Interest Rates," *Journal of Finance,* 41, 183–193.

Campbell, J., and R. Shiller, 1991, "Yield Spreads and Interest Rate Movements: A Bird's Eye View," *Review of Economic Studies,* 58, 495–514.

Caprio, G., and D. Klingebiel, 1996, "Bank Insolvencies: Cross-country Experience," The World Bank Policy Research Paper.

Chacko, G., and S. Das, 2002, "Pricing Interest Rate Derivatives: A General Approach," *Review of Financial Studies* 15(1), 195–241.

Chambers, D. R., 1984, "An Immunization Strategy for Futures Contracts on Government Securities," *Journal of Futures Markets,* 4(2), 173–188.

Chambers, D. R., W. T. Carleton, and R. W. McEnally, 1988, "Immunizing Default-free Bond Portfolios with a Duration Vector," *Journal of Financial and Quantitative Analysis* 23(1), 89–104.

Chambers, D. R., W. T. Carleton, and D. W. Waldman, 1984, "A New Approach to Estimation of the Term Structure of Interest Rates," *Journal of Financial and Quantitative Analysis* 19(3), 233–252.

Chance, D. M., 1982, "Interest Sensitivity and Dividend Yields," *Journal of Portfolio Management,* winter, 69–75.

Chance, D. M., 1983, "Floating Rate Notes and Immunization," *Journal of Financial and Quantitative Analysis* 18(3), 365–380.

Chance, D. M., 1990, "Default Risk and the Duration of Zero Coupon Bonds," *Journal of Finance,* March, 265–274.

Cole, C. S., and P. J. Young, 1995, "Modified Duration and Convexity with Semiannual Compounding," *Journal of Economics and Finance* 19(1), 1–15.

Collin-Dufresne, P., and R. S. Goldstein, 2001, "Do Credit Spreads Reflect Stationary Leverage Ratios?," *Journal of Finance, 56,* 1928–1957.

Cox, J. C., J. E. Ingersoll, and S. A. Ross, 1981, "A Re-Examination of Traditional Hypotheses about the Term Structure of Interest Rates," *Journal of Finance* 36(4), 769–799.

Cox, J. J., Ingersoll, and S. A. Ross, 1985, "A Theory of the Term Structure of Interest Rates," *Econometrica, 53,* 385–408.

Culbertson, K., 1957, "The Term Structure of Interest Rates," Quarterly Journal of Economic, 71 (4), 485–517.

Dai, Q., and K. J. Singleton, 2000, "Specification Analysis of Affine Term Structure Models," *Journal of Finance* 55(5), 1943–1977.

Duffie, G. R., 1998, "The Relation between Treasury Yields and Corporate Bond Yield Spreads," *Journal of Finance, 53,* 2225–2241.

Dunetz, M. L., and J. M. Mahoney, 1988, "Using Duration and Convexity in the Analysis of Callable Bonds," *Financial Analysts Journal.* May–June, 53–73; September, 1141–1153.

Eberhart, A. C., W. T. Moore, and R. L. Rosenfeldt, 1990, "Security Pricing and Deviations from the Absolute Priority Rule in Bankruptcy Proceedings," *Journal of Finance, 45,* 1457–1469.

Fabozzi, F. J., 1996, *Bond Markets, Analysis and Strategies,* Upper Saddle River, NJ: Prentice-Hall.

Fabozzi, F. J., M. Pitts, and R. E. Dattatreya, 1995, Price Volatility Characteristics of Fixed Income Securities. In F. J. Fabozzi and T. Dessa Fabozzi (Eds.), *The Handbook of Fixed Income Securities* (pp. 83–112). New York: Irwin Professional Publishing.

Falkenstein, E., and Hanweck, J., 1996, Minimizing basis risk from non-parallel shifts in the yield curve. *Journal of Fixed Income,* 6(1), 60–68.

Falkenstein, E., and Hanweck, J., 1997, Minimizing basis risk from non-parallel shifts in the yield curve: Pt. II. Principal components. *Journal of Fixed Income* 7(1), 85–90.

Fama, E. F., 1984, Term premiums in bond returns. *Journal of Financial Economics, 13,* 529–546.

Fama, E. F., and R. Bliss, 1987, The information in long-maturity forward rates. *American Economic Review,* 77(4), 680–692.

Fama, E. F., and M. Miller, 1972, "The Theory of Finance," New York: Holt, Rinehart and Winston.

Fisher, I., 1896, "Appreciation and Interest," *Publications of the American Economic Association* XI, 23–29 and 88–92.

Fisher, L., and R. L. Weil, 1971, "Coping with the Risk of Interest Rate Fluctuations: Return to Bondholders from Naive and Optimal Strategies," *Journal of Business* 43(4), 408–431.

Fisher, M., and C. Gilles, 1998, "Around and Around: The Expectations Hypothesis," *Journal of Finance, 53,* 365–386.

Fisher, M., D. Nychka, and D. Zervos, 1995, *Fitting the Term Structure of Interest Rates with Smoothing Splines,* Working Paper 95–1, Finance and Economic Discussion Series, Federal Reserve Board.

Fong, H. G., and F. J. Fabozzi, 1985, "Appendix E: Derivation of Risk Immunization Measures," In *Fixed Income Portfolio Management,* Homewood, IL: Dow Jones-Irwin, 291–294.

Fong, H. G., and O. A. Vasicek, 1983, "The Tradeoff between Return and Risk in Immunized Portfolio," *Financial Analysts Journal,* September-October, 73–78.

Fong, H. G., and O. A. Vasicek, 1984, "A Risk Minimizing Strategy for Portfolio Immunization," *Journal of Finance* 39(5), December, 1541–1546.

Fortet, R., 1943, "Les Fonctions Aléatoires du Type de Markoff Associées a Certaines Equations Linéaires aux Dérivées Partielles du Type Parabolique," *Journal de Mathématiques Pures et Appliques, 22,* 177–243.

Franks, J., and W. Torous, 1989, "An empirical Investigation of US Firms in Reorganization," *Journal of Finance, 44,* 747–769.

Franks, J., and W. Torous, 1994, "A Comparison of Financial Recontracting in Distressed Exchanges and Chapter 11 Reorganizations," *Journal of Financial Economics,* June, 349–370.

Geske, R., 1977, "The Valuation of Corporate Liabilities as Compound Options," *Journal of Financial and Quantitative Analysis* 12(4), 541–552.

Golub, B. W., and L. M. Tilman, 2000, *Risk Management: Approaches for Fixed Income Markets,* New York: Wiley.

Grandville, O., 2001, *Bond Pricing and Portfolio Analysis,* Cambridge, MA: MIT Press.

Granito, M., 1984, *Bond Portfolio Immunization,* Greenwich, CT: JAI Press.

Heath, D., R. Jarrow, and A. Morton, 1992, "Bond Pricing and the Term Structure of Interest Rates: A New Methodology for Contingent Claims Valuation," *Econometrica,* January, 77–105.

Hicks, J. R., 1939, *Value and Capital,* New York: Clarendon Press.

Hill, C. F. H., and S. Vaysman, 1998, "An Approach to Scenario Hedging," *Journal of Portfolio Management* 24(2), 83–92.

Ho, T., 1992, "Key Rate Durations: Measures of Interest Rate Risks," *Journal of Fixed Income,* September, 29–44.

Ho, T., and S. Lee, 1986, "Term Structure Movements and Pricing Interest Rate Contingent Claims," *Journal of Finance,* December, 1011–1030.

Hull, J. C., 2001, *Options, Futures, and Other Derivatives,* 5th ed. Prentice-Hall.

Hull, J. C., and A. D. White, 1993, "One-Factor Interest Rate Models and the Valuation of Interest-Rate Derivative Securities," *Journal of Financial and Quantitative Analysis, 28,* 235–254.

Ingersoll, J. E., J. Skelton, and R. L. Weil, 1978, "Duration Forty Years Later," *Journal of Financial and Quantitative Analysis,* November, 627–650.

Jamshidian, F., 1989, "An Exact Bond Option Formula," *Journal of Finance, 44,* 205–209.

Jamshidian, F., 1997, "LIBOR and Swap Market Models and Measures," *Finance and Stochastics, 1*(4), 293–330.

Jarrow, R. A., 1978, "The Relationship between Yield, Risk and Return," *Journal of Finance, 33,* 1235–1240.

Jarrow, R. D., Ruppert, and Y. Yu, 2004, "Estimating the Term Structure of Corporate Debt with a Semiparametric Penalized Spline Model," *Journal of the American Statistical Association, 99,* 57–66.

Johnson, L. D., 1990, "Convexity for Equity Securities: Does Curvature Matter?," *Financial Analysts Journal,* September/October, 70–73.

Johnson, B. D., and K. R. Meyer, 1989, "Managing Yield Curve Risk in an Index Environment," *Financial Analysts Journal,* November/December, 51–59.

Kritzman, M., 1992, "What Practitioners Need to Know About Duration and Convexity," *Financial Analysts Journal* 48 (6), November/December, 17–21.

Lacey, N. J., and S. K. Nawalkha, 1993, "Convexity, Risk, and Returns," *Journal of Fixed Income* 3(3), 72–79.

Lekkos, I., 1999, "Distributional Properties of Spot and Forward Interest Rates: USD, DEM, GBP, and JPY," *Journal of Fixed Income* 8, March. 35–54.

Lekkos, I., 2000, "A Critique of Factor Analysis of Interest Rates," *Journal of Derivatives,* fall, 72–83.

Livingston, D. G., 1990, *Bond Risk Analysis: A Guide to Duration and Convexity,* New York: New York Institute of Finance.

Livingston, M., 1978, "Duration and Risk Assessment for Bonds and Common Stocks: A Note," *Journal of Finance, 33,* 293–295.

Longstaff, F. A., and E. S. Schwartz, 1995, "A Simple Approach to Valuing Risky Fixed and Floating Rate Debt," *Journal of Finance, 3,* 789–819.

LoPucki, L. M., and W. C. Whitford, 1990, "Bargaining over Equity's Share in the Bankruptcy Reorganization of Large, Publicly Held Companies," *University of Pennsylvania Law Review,* November, 125–196.

Macaulay, F. R., 1938, *Some Theoretical Problems Suggested by the Movements of Interest Rates, Bond Yields, and Stock Prices in the U.S. since 1856,* New York:National Bureau of Economic Research.

McCulloch, J. H., 1971, "Measuring the Term Structure of Interest Rates," *Journal of Business, 44,* 19–31.

McCulloch, J. H., 1975, "The Tax Adjusted Yield Curve," *Journal of Finance, 30,* 811–830.

McCulloch, J. H., 1993, A reexamination of traditional hypotheses about the term structure—A comment. *Journal of Finance, 2,* 779.

McCulloch, J. H., and H. C. Kwon, 1993, *U.S. Term Structure Data 1947–1991,* Ohio State University, Working Paper, 93–96.

Merton, R. C., 1973a, "An Intertemporal Capital Asset Pricing Model," *Econometrica, 41,* 867–887.

Merton, R. C., 1973b, "The Theory of Rational Option Pricing," *Bell Journal of Economics and Management Science, 4,* 141–183.

Merton, R. C., 1974, "On the Pricing of Corporate Debt: The Risk Structure of Interest Rates," *Journal of Finance, 29,* 449–470.

Modigliani, F., and R. Sutch, 1966, "Innovations in Interest Rate Policy," *American Economic Review, 2,* 178–207.

Morgan, G. E., 1986, "Floating Rate Securities and Immunization: Some Further Results," *Journal of Financial and Quantitative Analysis* 21(1), 87–94.

Mueller, C., 2000, "A Simple Multi-Factor Model of Corporate Bond Prices, Working Paper, University of Wisconsin, Madison.

Musiela, M., and M. Rutkowski, 1997, "Continuous-Time Term Structure Models: Forward-Measure Approach," *Finance and Stochastics, 1*(4), 261–292.

Nawalkha, S. K., 1995, "The Duration Vector: A Continuous-Time Extension to Default-Free Interest Rate Contingent Claims," *Journal of Banking and Finance* 19(8), 1359–1378.

Nawalkha, S. K., 1996, "A Contingent Claims Analysis of the Interest Rate Risk Characteristics of Corporate Liabilities," *Journal of Banking and Finance* 20(2), 227–245.

Nawalkha, S. K., 2004, "Another Look at the Relationship between Credit Spreads and Interest Rates, Working paper, University of Massachusetts, Amherst.

Nawalkha, S. K., and D. R. Chambers, 1996, "An Improved Immunization Strategy: The M-Absolute," *Financial Analysts Journal,* September–October, 69–76.

Nawalkha, S. K., and D. R. Chambers, 1997, "The M-Vector Model: Derivation and Testing of Extensions to the M-Square Model," *Journal of Portfolio Management* 23(2), 92–98.

Nawalkha, S. K., and D. R. Chambers, 1999, "*Interest Rate Risk Measurement and Management,* " New York: Institutional Investor.

Nawalkha, S. K., D. R. Chambers, G. M. Soto, and J. Zhang, 2004, "Hedging Nirvana using the Duration Vector," *Journal of Bond Trading and Management,* forthcoming.

Nawalkha, S. K., and N. J. Lacey, 1990, "Generalized Solutions of Higher Order Duration Measures," *Journal of Banking and Finance, 14*(6), 1143–1150.

Nawalkha, S. K., G. M. Soto, and J. Zhang, 2003, "Generalized M-Vector Models for Hedging Interest Rate Risk," *Journal of Banking and Finance,* 27(8), 1581–1604.

Nelson, C. R., and A. F. Siegel, 1987, "Parsimonious Modeling of Yield Curves," *Journal of Business* 60(4), 473–489.

Ott, R. A., Jr, 1986, "The Duration of an Adjustable-Rate Mortgage and the Impact of the Index," *Journal of Finance* 41(4), 923–934.

Prisman, E. Z., and Y. Tian, 1994, "Immunization in Markets with Tax-Clientele Effects: Evidence from the Canadian Market," *Journal of Financial and Quantitative Analysis* 29(2), 301–321.

Rebonato, R., 2002, *Modern Pricing of Interest-Rate Derivatives, The LIBOR Market Model and Beyond,* Princeton, NJ: Princeton University Press.

Redington, F. M., 1952, "Review of the Principle of Life office Valuations," *Journal of the Institute of Actuaries, 78,* 286–340.

Reitano, R. R., 1996, "Non-Parallel Yield Curve Shifts and Stochastic Immunization," *Journal of Portfolio Management,* winter, 71–78.

RiskMetrics, 2001, *Return to RiskMetrics: The Evolution of a Standard,* RiskMetrics Group, Inc.

Samuelson, P. A., 1945, "The Effect of Interest Rate Increases on the Banking System," *American Economic Review,* March, 16–27.

Sharpe, W., 1983, "Comments," In G. Kaufman, G. Bierwag, and G. Toevs (Eds.), *Innovations of Bond Portfolio Management: Duration Analysis and Immunization,* Greenwich, CT: JAI Press.

Shimko, D. C., N. Tejima, and D. R. Van Deventer, 1993, "The Pricing of Risky Debt when Interest Rates are Stochastic," *Journal of Fixed Income* 3(2), 58–65.

Smith, C., and Warner, J., 1979, On financial contracting: An analysis of bond covenants. *Journal of Financial Economics, 7,*June, 117–161.

Soto, G. M., 2001a, "Immunization derived from a Polynomial Duration Vector in the Spanish Bond Market," *Journal of Banking and Finance* 25(6), 1037–1057.

Soto, G. M., 2001b, "Modelos de Inmunización de Carteras de Renta Fija," *Revista de Economía Aplicada* IX(26), 57–93.

Soto, G. M., 2004a, "Duration Models and IRR Management: A Question of Dimensions?" *Journal of Banking and Finance* 28(5), 1089–1110.

Soto, G. M., 2004b, "Using Principal Component Analysis to Explain Term Structure Movements: Performance and Stability," In F. Tavidze (Ed.), *Progress in Economics Research* 8, New York: Nova Science Publishers, 203–226.

Steeley, J. M., 1991, "Estimating the Gilt-Edged Term Structure: Basis Splines and Confidence Intervals," *Journal of Banking, Finance and Accounting* 18(4), 513–529.

Svensson, L. E. O., 1994, *Estimating and Interpreting Forward Interest Rates: Sweden 1992–1994,* Institute for International Economic Studies.

Sweeney, R. J., and A. D. Warga, 1986, "The Pricing of Interest-Rate Risk: Evidence from the Stock Market," *Journal of Finance.* June, 393–410.

Vasicek, O., 1977, "An Equilibrium Characterization of the Term Structure," *Journal of Financial Economics, 5,* 177–188.

Vasicek, O. A., and H. G. Fong, 1982, "Term Structure Modeling Using Exponential Splines," *Journal of Finance* 37(2), 339–348.

Weiss, L. A., 1990, "Bankruptcy Resolution: Direct Costs and Violation of Priority of Claims," *Journal of Financial Economics, 27,* 285–314.

About the CD-ROM

ABOUT THE CD-ROM

This file provides you with information on the contents of the CD that accompanies this book.

SYSTEM REQUIREMENTS

- A computer with a processor running at 120 MHz or faster.
- At least 32 MB of total RAM installed on your computer. For best performance, we recommend at least 64 MB.
- A CD-ROM drive.

Note: Many popular spreadsheet programs are capable of reading Microsoft Excel files; however, Microsoft Excel is required to run this contents.

USING THE CD WITH WINDOWS

To install the items from the CD on your hard drive, follow these steps:

1. Insert the CD into your computer's CD-ROM drive.
2. The CD-ROM interface displays. The interface provides a simple point-and-click way to explore the contents of the CD.

If the opening screen of the CD-ROM does not display automatically, follow these steps to access the CD:

1. Click the Start button on the left end of the taskbar and then choose Run from the pop-up menu.
2. In the dialog box that displays, type **d:\setup.exe.** (If your CD-ROM is not drive D, fill in the appropriate letter in place of D.) This brings up the CD Interface described in the preceding set of steps.

WHAT'S ON THE CD

The following sections provide a summary of the software you'll find on the CD.

Content

Except for the introductory Chapter 1, all other chapters have at least one corresponding Excel file. Chapters 3 and 7 have two Excel files for each chapter, while other chapters have one Excel file for each chapter. These files are described as follows:

1. **Chapter 2 File name: ch02.xls** This file computes duration and convexity risk measures of coupon-paying bonds and solves for portfolio weights, using three strategies given as maturity matching, duration matching, and duration and convexity matching.
2. **Chapter 3 File name: ch03a.xls** This file gives the monthly term structures of zero-coupon yields, instantaneous forward rates, and par-bond yields, using McCulloch and Kwon (1993) data over the period from December 1946 to February 1991. Future updates with more recent data will be made available at http://www.fixedincomerisk.com.
3. **Chapter 3 File name: ch03b.xls** This file estimates the term structure of spot rates or zero-coupon yields given the input data on prices, maturities, coupons, and face values of individual bonds entered by the user. The term structures are estimated using both the McCulloch cubic-spline method and the Nelson and Siegel exponential method. Using estimated term structures, the user can price new bonds with different maturity characteristics.
4. **Chapter 4 File name: ch04.xls** This file computes duration, M-absolute, and M-square risk measures of coupon-paying bonds and solves for portfolio weights, using four strategies given as maturity matching, duration matching, minimum M-absolute, and minimum M-square.
5. **Chapter 5 File name: ch05.xls** This file computes up to six generalized duration vector risk measures for a given value of alpha, for coupon-paying bonds, and solves the portfolio weights to either immunize the portfolio at a given horizon or to match the target generalized durations.
6. **Chapter 6 File name: ch06.xls** This file computes up to three traditional duration vector risk measures of Treasury futures (on T-bills, T-notes, and T-bonds) and Eurodollar futures and solves the portfolio weights in the futures portfolio to either immunize a given cash portfolio at a given horizon or to match the target durations.

7. **Chapter 7 File name: ch07a.xls** This file computes up to three traditional duration vector risk measures of European options on zero-coupon bonds and solves the portfolio weights in the option portfolio to either immunize a given cash portfolio at a given horizon or to match the target durations.
8. **Chapter 7 File name: ch07b.xls** This file computes up to three traditional duration vector risk measures of European options on coupon bonds, using the Vasicek and the extended Vasicek models, and solves the portfolio weights in the option portfolio to either immunize a given cash portfolio at a given horizon or to match the target durations.
9. **Chapter 8 File name: ch08.xls** This file computes up to three traditional duration vector risk measures of forward rate agreements, caps, floors, collars, swaps, swaps with embedded collars, payer swaptions, and receiver swaptions, using the LIBOR market model (for interest rate options) and swap market model (for swaptions), and solves the portfolio weights in the swap derivatives portfolio to either immunize a given cash portfolio at a given horizon or to match the target durations.
10. **Chapter 9 File name: ch09.xls** This file computes between three to six key rate durations for coupon-paying bonds, and solves the portfolio weights to either immunize the portfolio at a given horizon or to match the target key rate durations. The output also gives the VaR of the hedged portfolio at 95 percent and 99 percent level of significance.
11. **Chapter 10 File name: ch10.xls** This file computes three principal component durations for coupon-paying bonds and solves the portfolio weights to either immunize the portfolio at a given horizon or to match the target principal component durations. The output also gives the VaR of the hedged portfolio at 95 percent and 99 percent level of significance.
12. **Chapter 11 File name: ch11.xls** This file computes the prices and durations of the default-prone corporate bond, corporate stock, default-free bond, and the firm's assets using the models of Nawalkha-Shimko et al., Longstaff and Schwartz, and Collin-Dufresne and Goldstein.

TROUBLESHOOTING

Your Windows Explorer may be set up so that files with .dll extensions are not displayed and some file name extensions are hidden. To change the setting of Windows Explorer proceed as follows:

1. In Windows Explorer, open the folder containing the files you want to view.
2. On the Tools menu, click Folder Options, and then click the View tab.

3. To view all hidden file types, click the "Show hidden files and folders" option. To see all file name extensions, clear the "Hide file extensions for known file types" check box. Finally, click the Apply button.

The software is optimized for a screen area of 1,024 × 768 pixels or higher and requires Windows 98 or later and Excel 1997 or later. Also, the Solver Add-in for Excel should be available for using the Excel files. If the Solver Add-in is unavailable, you will receive a message with instructions about loading the Solver; for further assistance see Help in your Excel program.

Finally, you must click Enable Macros when the Excel files are opened. Also, to allow macros to run in Excel 2000 or higher versions, the security level must be set to either Medium or Low (Medium level is recommended). To set the security level: On the Tools menu, point to Macro, and then click Security. For information on macro security, see Help in your Excel program.

Updates to the software can be downloaded from the web site at http://www.fixedincomerisk.com.

Customer Care

If you have trouble with the CD-ROM, please call the Wiley Product Technical Support phone number at (800) 762-2974. Outside the United States, call 1(317) 572-3994. You can also contact Wiley Product Technical Support at **http://www.wiley.com/techsupport.** John Wiley & Sons will provide technical support for installation and other general quality control items only. For technical support on the applications themselves, consult the author at fixedincomerisk@msn.com.

To place additional orders or to request information about other Wiley products, please call (877) 762-2974.

Index

For more information about the CD-ROM, see the About the CD-ROM section on page 383.

CUSTOMER NOTE: IF THIS BOOK IS ACCOMPANIED BY SOFTWARE, PLEASE READ THE FOLLOWING BEFORE OPENING THE PACKAGE.

This software contains files to help you utilize the models described in the accompanying book. By opening the package, you are agreeing to be bound by the following agreement: